DRESSER'S CHIEF EXECUTIVE OFFICERS AND THEIR TERMS

Solomon R. Dresser
1880–1911

Fred A. Miller
1911–1929

H. Neil Mallon
1929–1962

John Lawrence
1962–1970

John V. James
1970–Present

INITIATIVE
IN ENERGY

Dresser Industries, Inc.
1880-1978

DARWIN PAYNE

SIMON AND SCHUSTER
New York

Published by Simon & Schuster
A Division of Gulf & Western Corporation
Simon & Schuster Building
Rockefeller Center
1230 Avenue of the Americas
New York, New York 10020

Designed by Stanley S. Drate
Manufactured in the United States of America
Printed and bound by The Book Press, Inc.
1 2 3 4 5 6 7 8 9 10
Library of Congress Cataloging in Publication Data

Payne, Darwin.
  Initiative in energy.

  Bibliography: p.
  1. Dresser Industries, inc.—History.   I. Title.
HD9569.D7P39   338.7′62′1   78-12324

ISBN 0-671-24402-7

Acknowledgments

Many people, within and without Dresser Industries, assisted me in gathering the material that forms the basis for this book. I am indebted to them, many of whom I did not even have the pleasure of meeting, for the hours they spent in digging through old files and for sending me, on faith, valuable materials. Their names are too numerous for listing, and, indeed, it is impossible to know who all of them were.

Happily for me, many others who aided me in this project became what I consider to be good friends. Foremost in this regard is R. E. Reimer, longtime Dresser executive (now retired) who worked with me from the beginning. Mr. Reimer's firsthand knowledge of the company's past half century was a rich and unerring source of material, and his wide acquaintances throughout the company opened doors for interviews.

Within the Dallas corporate headquarters the list of those who rendered assistance is long. The executive with whom I worked most closely was Thomas W. Campbell, director of communications and public affairs, who did everything possible to see that I had the materials I felt I needed. He, along with other Dresser executives, displayed the attitude that I must tell the Dresser story as I found it to be and not as the company might hope it would be. The goodwill and cooperation of John V. James, chairman of the board, and Edward R. Luter, senior vice president, finance, were especially welcome. Both men displayed a keen interest in the book's progress, yet always were careful not to invade the author's prerogatives. Still other Dresser employees whose help was unfailing included Darleene White, whose endeavors are evidenced largely through the photographs she procured for this volume, and Steve Barnett, Lillian Edwards, Maria Germain, Gary Hecht, Thomas P. Hubbard, Bill Malaise, Judi Murrell, Lorraine Peterson, Herb M. Ryan, Grace Salas, and Roberta E. Swofford.

Special recognition must go to H. Neil Mallon, long-time Dresser chairman of the board, who now is retired, for consenting to several interviews and for reading the manuscript with an unusually perceptive eye. John Lawrence, another retired chairman of the board, recalled for me his days with the company, and his wife, Jan Lawrence, added unique perspectives from a wife's point of view.

One of the central areas for research into the early history of the company was Bradford, Pennsylvania, where the company was founded and remained for the first sixty-five years of its existence. All the people of this charming western Pennsylvania town displayed an eagerness to assist at every opportunity. Solomon R. Dresser's granddaughter, Mrs. Elizabeth M. Pfohl (who also happens to be the daughter of Fred A. Miller, Dresser's successor as the company's chief executive), was especially gracious in recalling her memories of the family. Without the letters, diary, photographs, and miscellaneous bits of information which she lent me, it would have been impossible to recapture the essence of the family and the company's early years. Harvey Phillips, another Bradford resident, was a kind and knowledgeable source of help. Charles Thomas, recently retired as an official of Dresser Manufacturing Division, was another who was unselfish with his time. The Bradford Public Library staff was essential to my efforts.

Many other individuals from various parts of the nation were of special assistance. Mrs. J. Martin Kelly of Milwaukee, Wisconsin, another granddaughter of Solomon R. Dresser, provided me with colorful anecdotes and trusted me with prized family photographs. William L. Graham, Sr., of Glenview, Illinois, who was 101 years of age at the time of my 1976 interview, was the only man alive who could tell me what it was like to be a Dresser employee before the turn of the century, and to him and his daughter, Mrs. Elizabeth G. Da Miano, I am grateful.

Others who helped included C. Paul Clark, Art Weis, Elmer Weis, Willard Johnson, I. W. (Ike) Hoskins, L. L. Dresser, W. H. Reeder, Beatrice Kilcoin, George Pfefferle, J. Douglas Mayson, D. B. (Bud) Harney, B. R. Stuart, Wayne Millis, Mike Davis, Ted Chrzan, Ray Benjamin, James R. Brown, Jr., Tam Mott, Howard Hinkle, R. G. Redgwell, Austin Platt, Frank Jedlikowski, Charles Maurer, J. P. Adams, Tom Falconi, Gordon Heidelberg, C. M. Winslow, Harold E. Boncutter, Neil R. Braun, G. Dean Smith, F. D. Desmone, John J. Murphy, A. G. Conway, J. K. Grigsby, Vic Samuelson, Charles T. Crawford, Griffith A. Herold, Mrs. Tom Servatious, Clarence McCormack, Eric Tanzberger, F. H. (Ted) Light, Edward H. Northrop, Frank Dunlevy, Mrs. Lillian A. Comar, Thomas W. Shea, B. A. Riley, Howard Bonsell, Francis G. Fabian, Jr., Jane Elder, Joy Mazza, G. Edward Sencabaugh, Mrs. Tom Moody, and George Bush.

Several institutions provided research facilities: the Science/ Engineering Library at Southern Methodist University, John Crerar Library in Chicago, Center for Research Libraries in Chicago, Drake Museum in Titusville, Pennsylvania, Bradford Public Library, and Dallas Public Library.

Contents

Introduction

In 1980 Dresser Industries, Inc., will celebrate one hundred years' existence as an American business institution. The company's overriding goal during this period has been constant: to provide products and services needed to develop the world's energy and natural resources. The end result of this endeavor has been the attainment of a significant contribution toward the achievement of a higher standard of living throughout the world. Dresser's long and essential role in this purpose generally has escaped public notice; its high-technology products and services are not designed for direct consumer use.

Yet, these largely unheralded products and services—those offered by Dresser as well as by other like-minded companies—have been the essential tools for finding, extracting, and using oil, natural gas, coal, iron, and other natural resources necessary for the remarkable material progress so noteworthy since the late 1800's. Even a partial list of Dresser's contributions in these fields is long. It includes geophysical services, drilling and mining equipment and services, compressors, pumps, engines, blowers, refractories, power shovels, pollution control equipment, conveyor systems, graders, cranes, hoists, gauges, valves, meters, couplings and other pipeline fittings, gasoline dispensing systems, grinding wheels, pneumatic tools, and gear motors.

The development and applications of these products and services and their inevitable impact upon daily life are an integral and compelling part of the story of mankind's material, social, cultural, and even political progress. It is a story that has been neglected by all but a few historians. This oversight soon may be remedied, for it became evident in the 1970's that the endeavor to find and use old and new energy sources was perhaps the critical factor of the future. Such an endeavor is certain to attract greater attention.

Dresser's existence for such a long period—virtually half as long as the life of the American nation itself—may surprise observers whose attention has focused on the company's recent surges in sales and profits. Its present configuration, indeed, is of modern development. But since that spring day in 1880 when Solomon R. Dresser hung up his sign in the oil boomtown of Bradford, Pennsylvania, proclaiming to drillers the superiority of his packer, the company has held true to its basic original aim. In the company's earliest days, its market was the oil fields of western Pennsylvania. Before the turn of the century, though, Dresser boldly entered the natural gas industry, and it was here that the company achieved eminence and prosperity through an original contribution of a flexible, leak-proof coupling for the transmission of natural gas through long-distance pipelines. In the last fifty years of its history, dating from its transition from a family-held firm to a publicly held corporation, Dresser broadened its aims to serve the entire spectrum of the energy and natural resources markets. It also began providing equipment and services for certain segments of general industry.

As is true for many modern corporations of substantial size, Dresser's growth has not all been internal. Acquisitions have played an important part in the company's expansions. Some of these acquisitions have longer histories than Dresser. Roots Blower Operations, an Indiana firm acquired during World War II, traces its origin as a manufacturer of blowers to 1859, and by 1880 it was one of the nation's more prosperous and better-known manufacturing firms. Ashcroft gauges, brought into the Dresser family in 1964 through the acquisition of Manning, Maxwell & Moore, have been serving industry since 1852. The history of Dresser Industries, then, is more than a history of the single firm from which the company dates its origin; it is the story of a number of American companies that made their separate contributions to the mechanical arts before uniting under the Dresser name.

As far as the parent company itself is concerned, one of the most remarkable facts about it is its stability in top management. During Dresser's ninety-eight-year history, there have been just five chief executive officers. In that period the American nation, by contrast, has experienced twenty Presidents. These Dresser executives —Solomon R. Dresser, Fred A. Miller, H. Neil Mallon, John Lawrence, and John V. James—all made separate contributions in leading the company from its humble, one-man beginning to its present situation as a multinational corporation ranking among the nation's one hundred largest.

Dresser's top management determined in 1975 that a history of the company would be an appropriate gesture toward recognizing its approaching centennial anniversary. It was hoped that such a volume would serve general readers as one part of the broader story of American technology and private enterprise as they related to the development of energy and natural resources. There also was the realization that such a book might prove beneficial for employees, stockholders, and others with special interests in Dresser who could not know of the company's intriguing background. John V. James, Dresser's chairman of the board and a man with an intense interest in history, was particularly enthusiastic about the idea, as was Edward R. Luter, senior vice president, finance. Their contributions to this project are noted elsewhere. This book, underwritten by Dresser Industries, is the culmination of their vision.

—DARWIN PAYNE

1

Some Early Beginnings

The last half of the nineteenth century in America was the heroic age of invention, the climactic period of the mechanical arts. It was a time when the veil had been lifted from the continent's great energy resources—coal, natural gas, and oil. These vital elements rested beneath the earth's surface where they had been for millions of years, largely undisturbed save for coal. Other valuable minerals —iron ore, copper, and lead—also were ripe for exploitation. The revolution in technology spawned by the steam engine remained in early bloom; now the need beckoned for additional tools and mechanical devices to move American technology to its destiny, beyond customary dependence on Europe. The age cried out for inventors, for entrepreneurs, for visionary men bold in thought and action.

Few institutions were organized in a way equal to this task. Home industry lingered; practically the only business enterprises national in scope were the railroads. Federal and state government had no mandate, no inclination, and no framework for the chore. If the job were to be accomplished, it would be done by individuals who could muster the requisite vision, nerve, and resources.

Fortunately, as we know, the American character proved equal to the task. The unsettled continent had summoned settlers who were pragmatic, adaptable, and accustomed to overcoming the problem at hand. And the problem after the Civil War was not so much that of civilizing a continent but of putting its resources to work.

It was logical that the men who emerged as larger-than-life figures of this era—save at its beginning for Lincoln—were to be entrepreneurs and inventors, not politicians. John D. Rockefeller, E. H. Harriman, James J. Hill, J. Pierpont Morgan, Andrew Carnegie, Elbert H. Gary, and others emerged to make outstanding contributions in the organization of industry. Thomas Alva Edison,

Cyrus H. McCormick, Alexander Graham Bell, George M. Pullman, George Westinghouse, and others conceived of and developed mechanical and electrical devices to transform daily life. Frequently, inventor and entrepreneur were combined in the same man, who could not only conceive of a needed product but also manufacture and market it. The successful inventor-entrepreneur could make a fortune; the pages of *Scientific American* with its lists of new inventions and descriptions of young industries gave ample testimony to that fact. And there was no lack of ambitious Americans to grasp at such an opportunity.

One such aspirant was Solomon Robert Dresser, a robust, dark-haired man who had grown up on a pioneer farm in Michigan. For nearly a dozen years Dresser had been chasing the black gold that had converted the forested Alleghenies of western Pennsylvania into a new El Dorado—or "Oildorado," as some called it. The scene rivaled in vigor, color, and character the gold rush of California. Fortunes were made and lost with scarcely a look backward; boom-towns flourished and then died overnight; gamblers, prostitutes, and thieves vied to empty the oilmen's pockets; and a successful well or merely the rumor of one was reason enough for mass migrations up and down Pennsylvania's beautiful valleys.

Unlike so many flamboyant and reckless oil seekers, Dresser was a solemn, steady man who took his family responsibilities seriously. He had a frail, artistic wife whose health was as delicate as her poetry, and his four growing children had constant needs, which he strove with difficulty to meet. Wherever Dresser went, his family went too. In eleven years they had moved nine times. In 1878 the family had lighted in the area's latest boomtown, Bradford, in the center of the most prolific oil field yet discovered in America.

Dresser, thirty-six years old and weary of the chase, knew well enough from his own experiences that the primitive art of drilling was ripe for technological advancement. After these many years of effort in the oil fields—taking two steps forward and then two backward—it occurred to him that a man, especially a family man, might do better by applying his mind and hands to the technological challenge instead of casting his fate with the luck of the drill.

He determined to analyze one mechanical problem and solve it. He turned his attention to the makeshift packers that drillers stuffed into wells to isolate oil-bearing sands from other elements—typically water. Unless the cold water and oil were separated, they created a layer of paraffin that clogged up pores and inhibited the flow of oil from the oil-bearing rock. Other men were working on

When Solomon R. Dresser posed in about 1890 for this photograph, his days in the oil fields were behind him and unusual success as a manufacturer lay just ahead.

the same problem; some "patent" packers already had appeared on the market and were beginning to replace the bags filled with flax seed that swelled upon getting wet and, with luck, prevented water from mixing with the oil-bearing strata.

Some of the most promising patent packers relied upon india rubber as a seal, but the process of lowering or raising the packer frequently pulled the rubber from its collar. This was a problem Dresser thought he could solve. And he did. He designed a unique clamping mechanism that effectively held the rubber in place, and on May 11, 1880, the U.S. Patent Office recognized his invention by issuing to him Patent No. 117,419. Dresser lost no time in capitalizing on his creation, for he had arranged for a two-column advertisement to appear on the same day in the *Bradford Era* calling oil producers' attention to the "Dresser Cap Packer," on sale at his 83

Main Street office. It offered, he claimed, a "sure pack" that producers would have no difficulty removing from the well.

So modestly did Dresser's company begin that it was hardly noticed. A sea of competitors obscured him. Yet, it was a start, and it provided a base from which a few years later another Dresser invention would be instrumental in transforming the face and life of much of the nation. This would be his flexible, leakproof coupling, a device that permitted natural gas to be delivered by pipeline from the fields to cities hundreds of miles away, and soon thereafter was applied as it is today for a myriad of industrial uses.

Meanwhile, in other parts of the nation other men whose efforts one day would be united under the company bearing Solomon Dresser's name were devising other ways to make things work better. None of them could know of that destiny. In fact, the news would have been especially astonishing to those whose enterprises had been prospering for many years before Dresser had started so modestly.

This frame structure on Patent Alley in Bradford, Pennsylvania, was one of the first sites for Solomon R. Dresser's packer works. It long since has been destroyed.

One of those men who already had achieved success was a New Englander named Edward H. Ashcroft of Lynn, Massachusetts. Ashcroft had used his fertile mind to solve problems associated with the steam engine. Despite its already profound effect upon society, the steam engine was far from perfect by mid-nineteenth century. Explosions commonly wracked locomotives, steamboats, and industrial boilers, all too frequently bringing frightful injury and loss of life. Widespread concern existed over these tragedies. How could steam power be made safer? The problem lay in the tremendous boiler pressures that built up beyond the point of containment.

Ashcroft developed in 1849 a fusible plug that melted when pressure reached the critical point, thus providing relief before an explosion could occur. This was not entirely satisfactory, but when Queen Victoria's first international industrial exposition was announced for 1851, Ashcroft arranged to display his fusible plug there. Many fabulous sights existed at this near-legendary exposition, including the glorious glass-walled Crystal Palace, but Ashcroft encountered something that fascinated him even more—a display of French inventor Eugene Bourdon's pressure gauge for steam boilers. Bourdon's gauge was ingenious in its simplicity. It consisted of a curved tube of metal that reflected the inside boiler pressure by tending to straighten. The closed outside end was attached to a pointer that moved over a graduated scale and indicated the pressure. Ashcroft saw obvious advantages in this device over his own, and he quickly obtained the American rights to Bourdon's patent, returned to Massachusetts, and established in Boston a company bearing his name for the manufacture of pressure gauges and other steam specialties. From this base, Ashcroft made improvement after improvement upon his product. By the time he was sixty-one, he had taken in his name more than sixty patents that applied primarily to steam generating equipment. The products of two companies he founded, Ashcroft Manufacturing and Consolidated Safety Valve, played a prominent role in the important railroad, steamboat, and industrial boom before and after the Civil War, just as they fulfill no less an important function throughout industry today.

At about the same time that Ashcroft founded his company, there lived in the sleepy town of Connersville, Indiana, Alanson Roots and his two sons, Philander H. and Francis Marion. Together they operated a woolen mill alongside the Whitewater Canal. The elder Roots, of New England birth, had established his first woolen

Edward H. Ashcroft, a Massachusetts man, founded the company that eventually became Manning, Maxwell, & Moore and was acquired by Dresser Industries in 1964.

When Edward H. Ashcroft visited the Crystal Palace in London, he so admired Eugene Bourdon's pressure gauge for steam boilers that he obtained American rights to it and founded a prosperous company.

Philander and Francis Roots, left and right, abandoned the woolen business to manufacture blowers after they accidentally discovered the rotary positive displacement principle.

mill in Oxford, Ohio, in 1824, when the nation's President was James Monroe. Twenty-two years later Roots transferred his mill to Connersville to take advantage of an excellent water supply and a surrounding countryside that was admirably suited for sheep raising. The business prospered—bolstered substantially by young Francis Root's successful 1849 venture into the California goldfield to find needed capital—and the father and sons constantly sought ways to make their operation more efficient.

Sometime in the 1850's the need arose for a new waterwheel.* Hoping to improve on the common overshot variety which had worn out, Philander and Francis experimented with various designs and finally devised a wheel that appeared promising. On trial, however, it proved far from satisfactory. But before placing it in the stream of water for testing, the brothers had noticed a curious thing. When the paddles, or impellers, were turned, they emitted a constant stream of air. Company legend has it that while the brothers were testing the machine this air flow blew off one of their hats, prompting the other to comment, "That's a better blower than a water motor." The idea occurred that such a device might work as a blast blower in a foundry. Indeed it did. Quite by accident, the Roots brothers had discovered the rotary positive displacement principle. In their design a pair of figure-eight impellers, machined to a close tolerance to prevent air leakage, moved in opposite directions and forced air forward by positive displacement.† In the next few years they abandoned the woolen business entirely to concentrate on the manufacture of blowers, and in future years they would win medals at the Paris Exhibition in 1867, the Vienna Exhibition in 1873, and the Philadelphia Centennial Exposition in 1876 for design, workmanship, economy, simplicity, and efficiency.

By 1880, the year that Dresser began his tiny operation in Bradford, the Roots firm was celebrated as one of the leading manufacturers in America. Pictures of its extensive plant covered the entire front of an issue that year of *Scientific American,* and the story inside celebrated the imaginative use of Roots blowers throughout the world for ventilating mines, tunnels, buildings, and steamships; for drying lumber, wool, or paper; for removing dust from grinding rooms; for pneumatic dispatch in newspaper or telegraph offices; and for many other purposes. Perhaps the most spectacular use was in a subway under Broadway in New York City. There, a blower, so huge that it had required five large platform cars to deliver it in sections, was installed in 1867 to provide power for a twenty-two-seat subway passenger car that was literally blown back

---

* The company cites 1854 as the date of its founding, and in 1954 it celebrated its centennial anniversary. However, the first patents for the blowers were not taken until March 1859 (No. 23,267), February 1860 (No. 27,239), and September 1860 (No. 30,157). Early accounts in *Scientific American* suggest 1859 as the proper date for the company's beginning. See, for example, "American Industries, No. 32," February 28, 1880, p. 127, and the obituary for Francis M. Roots, which appeared in the January 4, 1890, issue on p. 6.

† A number of Europeans already had experimented with this principle, but the Roots brothers surely could not have been aware of that. Certainly they receive credit for perfecting the design and for putting it into production on a large scale.

and forth from Murray Street to Warren Street. The name Roots and the term blowers ultimately became synonymous, and the basic principle of the Roots blower used all over the world today remains the same as it was more than a hundred years ago.

———————

As the great war between the states moved toward its climactic moment at Appomattox in the spring of 1865, a group of investors in the "Iron City" of Pittsburgh saw an opportunity. Heavy industry, especially the production of iron and steel for war use, had burgeoned in their city, and one might reasonably anticipate a postwar boom. These men planned to provide a vital though frequently overlooked requirement of industry: the firebricks necessary for lining blast furnaces and capable, if they were any good, of withstanding extremely high temperatures for long periods of time. The investors, eleven in number, capitalized their new Star Fire Brick Company at $8,000, constructed a plant at Twenty-second and Railroad Streets in the summer of 1865, and started selling firebricks in September.

In the spring of 1866 they examined their books and found that instead of making money they had lost more than $2,000. Alarmed, they hired on a half-time basis a former Pittsburgh school principal named Samuel Pollock Harbison to straighten out the accounts. The choice was a wise one. Harbison plunged into his job with an energy calculated to convert his modest five shares of stock into a fortune. He soon found that if the company was to survive he must expand his assigned duties into the field of diplomacy. The superintendent of the works, the man who had been instrumental in organizing the company, had no hesitancy in this turbulent Reconstruction period in pressing his unpopular Democratic persuasions upon his predominantly Republican customers. Harbison was equal to this delicate task. Soon he not only was keeping books but was securing orders and learning everything he could about manufacturing firebricks. At the end of 1867 the company showed a modest profit of $2,051, and before five years had passed, part-time bookkeeper Harbison found himself a principal owner in charge of the entire works. Meanwhile, he already had begun experimenting with different clays and techniques for superior bricks, and when Kloman, Carnegie & Company built its first Lucy furnace, Harbison fought for and won the order for the lining. Determined to do well on this important order—even at no profit—Harbison succeeded. He introduced what would become common practice: adding "bats," or thin slabs of fireclay, to the raw material. The result was an unusually hard friction brick that at the same time was high in refrac-

Samuel P. Harbison straightened out the tangled affairs of the Star Fire Brick Company, and the company soon bore his name as a principal owner.

tory qualities. So pleased was steel tycoon Thomas M. Carnegie with the new lining's performance that he readily testified to its fine qualities. Harbison circulated copies of Carnegie's complimentary letter to the blast-furnace trade with excellent results. "We soon began receiving orders and from that time on the manufacture of blast furnace linings was one of our leading specialties . . . I have no doubt at all [the lining] was the best that had ever been made," Harbison wrote some thirty years later.

Despite this initial achievement and the subsequent introduction of a new Benezet brick that set record after record for durability, a new crisis awaited—the financial panic of 1873. The partner Harbison had acquired, W. A. Reed, was among the many financiers who failed in this difficult time, but Harbison found a new partner with greater resources, a Scotsman named Hay Walker who already had made a fortune as a candle manufacturer. Something of Walker's character is seen in an anecdote concerning his love for reading: One evening at dinner he announced to his family that he was going to buy one of those new lamps for "rock oil" because he had heard that they gave a light far superior to the candles that he manufactured. Next day he brought home one of the new contraptions, filled it with kerosene, and lit and adjusted it as the children watched spellbound. Picking up a book, he sat down in his easy chair beside

Hay Walker, a Scotsman who earned a fortune as a candle manufacturer, became Samuel P. Harbison's partner as a refractory manufacturer in 1875.

the lamp to test it. As the splendid new light glowed steadily over the pages, he beamed happily at the prospect of so many added hours of nighttime reading, despite the obvious fact that it tolled the death knell for his candle manufacturing business. Such a man made an admirable partner. The partnership assumed the name Harbison and Walker, and to the present day its name has remained famous throughout industry for leadership in manufacturing blast furnaces and refractories.

———

When Harbison and Walker formed their partnership in 1875, the United States was burning approximately 100 million tons of coal a year and demand for it was growing. A plentiful supply was vital to the very important iron and steel industry that served as the backbone for industrial progress; coal was needed also as a fuel for factories, for locomotive boilers, and for heating homes.

Extracting this coal from beneath the earth's surface was backbreaking work. Miners struggled with picks, augers, and shovels; their daily yield was no more than two tons per worker. The difficult conditions facing the nineteenth-century coal miner are celebrated in song and legend, but the most arduous task of all was that

In the days before the invention of the automatic coal cutter, coal mining was torturous and slow work.

of undercutting the coal. To do this a miner lay on his side, with only his lamp beam illuminating the cold, dark air, and used his pick to cut a slit some three to four feet deep under the coal until the unsupported portion either fell of its own weight or was dislodged by wedging or blasting. If ever a machine were needed to ease man's burden, surely it was an automatic coal cutter.

A little-known individual named Francis M. Lechner of Waynesburg, Ohio, decided to build such a machine. He dreamed of an automatic cutter that might yield the unheard-of amount of six hundred to eight hundred tons of coal per day. In 1876 Lechner built a model for his machine and displayed it in a Columbus store front in hopes of luring a backer.

Such a man appeared in the person of a forty-year-old bank cashier named Joseph Andrew Jeffrey. Jeffrey owned some coal property himself, and the crude model he saw in the window spoke quite clearly to him if to no one else of its potential. He convinced some of his colleagues, including the president of the bank where he worked, of its promise, and in 1877 the Lechner Mining Machine Company was incorporated in Ohio with the bank president, F. C. Sessions, as president, Jeffrey as treasurer, and Lechner as general manager. Of the 480 shares authorized at $100 each, Jeffrey subscribed to 260; Lechner to 170; and three other individuals took the remaining 50.

In July 1877, Lechner's dream machine, powered by compressed air and weighing 1,350 pounds, was ready for trial. Lechner shipped it to New Straitsville, Ohio, because of the availability there of a compressor of sufficient power to activate it. A circle of men watched intently as the mine mechanic pumped the pressure to 50 pounds, then to 80, and finally to 115 pounds, at which point the machine made one revolution and jumped off its platform, landing upside down.

The Lechner Mining Machine Company was not about to give up, however, and before the year had ended, Lechner succeeded in making and offering for sale America's first automatic coal-cutting machine. A chain drive rotated a "cutter bar" that was fed into the seam of coal by a screw working through a movable nut. This cutter-bar machine was placed on the market a year ahead of the second automatic coal cutter, Harbison's "pick-machine."

In 1887 Jeffrey bought out Lechner and several minority stockholders and changed the firm's name to Jeffrey Manufacturing Company. Two years later the company substituted an electric motor for the compressor despite taunts that it could never work because of water seepage in coal mines. This application of electricity represented another first in the coal mining industry. Immediately after the electric motor was shown to be successful, interest in it developed all over the world. Its impact was to bring still other uses of

This is the original model of the Lechner cutter-bar machine patented in June 1876.

electric power into other aspects of coal mining. Today a replica of that first 1877 coal-cutting machine is at the Smithsonian Institution, and deep in mines throughout the world the machine's successor, the HELIMINER continuous miner, rips coal from seams at the rate of ten to twelve tons a minute.

In the same year that Solomon R. Dresser first offered in Pennsylvania his "cap rubber packer," two brothers named Clark who lived across the state line in New York decided to become manufacturers themselves. The fire-damaged machine shop of the Belmont Manufacturing Company in Belmont, only five miles from their home in Friendship, was for sale at a bargain price. The older brother, William P., knew the shop well, for he had been employed there since 1878. Having accumulated some money of his own and succeeding at raising more, he bought the shop. His younger brother, Charles, was completing his second year at Cornell University, but William did not have to exert much pressure to persuade him to forget college and join him in Belmont as his partner in a firm to be called Clark Bros. Company.

The old Belmont Manufacturing Company, since its inception in 1867, had looked to the area's agricultural and timber interests for its market. Its products were mowing machines, rakes, and circular saws. The energetic Clark brothers started their new business on this proved base, but they immediately began adding additional products. Charles, as vice president, engineer, and shop manager, devised an ingenious fork to ease the burden of lifting heavy bales into barn lofts. When a farmer plunged the arrowlike fork into a bale of hay, two barbs extended so that the bale—via rope and pulley—could be lifted handily into the loft. A tug on a small line released the barbs and permitted the hay to fall free. Of greater significance was Charles's invention of a device that tightened the tension in a band saw to permit a quicker, more efficient cut of timber. This new Clark band saw gained a reputation throughout the eastern timber industry as the best on the market. Eventually the firm offered an entire line of sawmill equipment. Prosperity had arrived. By 1887, with some seventy-five workers employed in five buildings, the company had begun manufacturing dynamos and the Clark-Corliss steam engine. But its most important contributions to American technology still lay ahead, and its worldwide reputation would be achieved not for its agricultural and sawmill products but for its technological breakthroughs in developing new kinds of gas-engine-

In the spring of 1888 Clark Bros. Company workers gathered in front of the plant in Belmont, New York, for this group picture.

Clark Bros. Company's earliest products, such as this huge band saw, were for the timber industry.

driven compressors that to this day are familiar sights in industry throughout the world.

In the summer of 1883 the Chicago and Atlantic Railroad was laying tracks across the state of Ohio and crews were working then near the town of Kenton. A thirty-seven-year-old Ohioan named Henry M. Barnhart, still struggling to recover from losses incurred when a fire had destroyed his sawmill in his hometown of Marion seven years earlier, was supervising the carpenters and bridge builders and overseeing operations at a gravel pit where ballast was being obtained for the roadbed. The substantial amounts of gravel needed for the roadbed required the use of a huge steam-powered shovel, which in this case was an Oswego Boom Machine, an awkward contraption mounted on rails.

The trouble was that on this particular morning the operator of the shovel was nowhere to be found. Barnhart, determined that an entire work crew not be delayed any longer because of the absence of one man, seated himself at the controls of the cantankerous machine and started to work. What Barnhart lacked in experience he more than made up for in determination, and when the man in charge of the new road, a Colonel Smith, came upon the scene he liked what he saw. He promised that if Barnhart would continue to operate the shovel he would find him an assistant to help with his other duties. It was agreed, but in the next days Barnhart's patience was sorely tried by the power shovel's frequent breakdowns. The swinging mechanism's reverse motion, handled by bevel gears and pinions, was a particular problem. Barnhart thought out a more efficient construction as he worked, and he enlisted the help of his inventive cousin, George W. King, to draw up designs and a working model to demonstrate his ideas. These they took to Marion's leading industrialist, Edward Huber, a manufacturer of threshing machines, to get his financial backing and the use of his manufacturing facilities. Huber recognized the practicality of Barnhart's idea; he knew that a market existed for efficient power shovels for they were particularly needed in this decade of rapid railroad expansion; but he was also a cautious businessman who explored all angles before committing himself to any project. They would make an investigative trip to Chicago, where an exhibition of railroad appliances included various steam shovels. These could be compared to Barnhart's model.

What they saw convinced them that Barnhart's shovel could be superior to anything on the market. A patent (No. 285,100) was obtained in the fall of 1883 in Barnhart's and Huber's names, and

Marion Steam Power Shovel Company's earliest models bore the name of inventor and company founder Henry M. Barnhart.

work began at the Huber Manufacturing Company on something affectionately labeled the "Barnhart Special" with a dipper capacity of 1.5 cubic yards.

Meanwhile, Barnhart, Huber and King incorporated their company on August 4, 1884, as the Marion Steam Shovel Company with a capital investment of $50,000. The first office was a room at Huber Manufacturing Company furnished with two plain boxes, one used as a desk and the other as a seat.

When finally completed, the Barnhart Style A, as it officially was named, boasted of several innovations that soon propelled the company to the top of the power shovel industry. Perhaps best of all was the simplification of its construction through the use of a single shaft, which made the Barnhart shovel less prone to breakdown and simpler to repair. A second distinct feature was the placement of the "swinging circle," from which the mast and boom extended, on the deck of the car rather than on the top, a circumstance that lowered the center of gravity and made the swinging circle more practical for applying the swinging power. This original Style A shovel was sold right away to the Cincinnati, Jackson & Mackinaw Railroad, which found it so satisfactory that a second one was ordered.

The Marion Steam Power Shovel Company was on its way. A manufacturing facility was obtained in Marion, twenty men were hired, and the company began full production. Innovation after innovation followed, including the introduction of the first power shovel that made a full circle in the air. After the turn of the century one of the thirty-eight Marion shovels used in excavating the Panama Canal set a world's record by handling 5,554 cubic yards of material in a single day. Marion shovels would be used effectively for quarries,

Marion power shovels played an important role in excavating the Panama Canal. One shovel set a world's record by handling 5,554 cubic yards in a single day.

irrigation work, brick and clay works, open-pit iron mining, coal stripping, copper mining, and for general contracting purposes wherever excavation was required.

Barnhart, unfortunately, died prematurely at forty-four, just six years after the company's incorporation. By then, however, the Marion Steam Power Shovel Company already was headed to the leadership of its industry.

The heavy industry that was emerging in America required the development of hoisting devices that could lift into the air extraordinary weights, such as a steam locomotive under construction or repair. It was not sufficient to anchor these cranes permanently at one spot; a degree of mobility was required when, to take another example, concrete blocks weighing fifteen tons each were being manipulated to construct a harbor. Thus, self-propelled, or "traveling," cranes of awesome dimensions were devised, the first coming in about 1850. Usually they moved on rails; occasionally models perambulated without a track. By 1880 something called the overhead traveling crane, for which an elevated runway was used, had been developed. Powered by a stationary steam engine, the crane was propelled by a system of ropes secured to the ends of the runway. The motions of the bridge, trolley, and lifting device were activated through a series of clutches. These "flying rope" cranes not only were difficult to operate but were prone to frequent breakdown.

In 1888 a flying rope crane collapsed under a ten-ton load in the Edwin P. Allis Company foundry in Milwaukee, Wisconsin, killing its operator. The accident inspired the company's master mechanic, Alton J. Shaw, to think that there must be a better way to build a traveling crane. The solution seemed to be to isolate the various functions so that they would not be so dependent upon one another. Shaw reasoned that if each basic movement of the crane's hoist, trolley, and bridge could be actuated by its own reversible electric motor rather than being linked to a single source of power, the result would be a far safer and more efficient instrument. Allis Company officials saw the possibilities in such a crane, and they authorized Shaw to build a three-motor electric crane—the first of its kind in America and probably the world—which traveled along an elevated rail in the main foundry.* So satisfactorily did this pioneer crane perform that it attracted the attention of many

---

* A single electric motor had been used for a crane in 1883 in Bourges, France.

Alton J. Shaw, founder of Shaw Electric Crane Company and inventor of the three-motor electric crane, conceived of the device as the result of a tragic accident involving a "flying rope" crane.

The thirty-ton electric traveling Shaw crane in the foreground was the first three-motor electric traveling crane ever built. It was installed in 1889 in the main foundry of the Edwin P. Allis Company in Milwaukee and is pictured here in the mid-1890's.

other companies. Shaw responded by forming a partnership with a friend named John G. Emery, Jr., and setting up operations at the Pawling and Harnischfeger Company machine shop. The second crane was built for the Beloit Wind Engine Company (later Fairbanks Morse), and the third went to the Union Pacific Railroad Shop at Cheyenne, Wyoming, where it remained in service until 1974. In 1890 civic leaders in Muskegon, Michigan, induced Shaw and Emery to move the Shaw Electric Crane Company to their city, where Shaw-Box cranes (the name was enlarged through a merger in the early 1930's with Box Crane & Hoist) continue to be manufactured to this day.

One of the new "wonder" fuels created in mid-nineteenth-century America was kerosene, the petroleum distillate whose steady glow while burning had caused candle manufacturer Hay Walker to smile. The process for making kerosene had been developed in 1854, five years before Colonel Drake at Titusville made the nation petroleum-conscious. Kerosene's acceptance as a source of illumination was slow for several reasons. It could not be burned satisfactorily in the camphene lamps available in the early days. Considerable fear of explosion, though unwarranted, also existed; and whale oil producers, seeing their fuel market facing ruin, fought against its acceptance. Nevertheless, long before the twentieth century arrived, these problems had been overcome, and kerosene and its near-cousin, "coal oil," had become common sources of fuel for light, heat, and cooking. Kerosene was dispensed to consumers in a cumbersome though logical manner: the clerk poured it from a measuring can into whatever container the customer brought with him.

In 1891 in Fort Wayne, Indiana, two mechanics named W. H. Davis and J. T. Becker found a simpler, more efficient way of distributing the liquid by devising a "measuring" pump. They formed a partnership to manufacture their product and named their company after the town: the Wayne Pump Company. When the Columbian Exposition was held in Chicago two years later, the two partners' pump won a prize in industrial competition. Their product resembled a piece of furniture. The device was enclosed in a handsome two-tiered wooden cabinet that would have been a pleasing addition to almost any Victorian parlor. Only a spout extending gracefully from the top and a pump handle at the rear hinted at its utilitarian purpose.

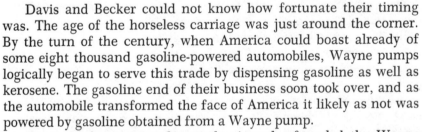

Wayne Pump Company's 1893 kerosene dispenser, predecessor to the firm's gasoline pump, won a prize at the Columbian Exposition in Chicago that year for its sleek looks.

Davis and Becker could not know how fortunate their timing was. The age of the horseless carriage was just around the corner. By the turn of the century, when America could boast already of some eight thousand gasoline-powered automobiles, Wayne pumps logically began to serve this trade by dispensing gasoline as well as kerosene. The gasoline end of their business soon took over, and as the automobile transformed the face of America it likely as not was powered by gasoline obtained from a Wayne pump.

From the beginning, the mechanics who founded the Wayne Pump Company sought accuracy of measurement. In 1904 they introduced the first full-stroke delivery pump: one stroke of the crank delivered precisely a quart or a gallon, as preferred. The attendant had merely to count the strokes and multiply that figure by the cost per quart or gallon to obtain the sum owed. Further innovations were to follow: the rotary pump, which used a meter to measure the output; the automatic dispenser, in which power replaced the crank; the large glass cylinders atop the pump, which permitted the customer to be satisfied by the color of the fuel; and many others. Little could the two Fort Wayne mechanics have known that their modest kerosene dispenser would propel them head-first into the dominant industry of the twentieth century.

Thomas Alva Edison in 1891 was working vigorously on still another of his brilliant notions. The light bulb, the phonograph, the kinetoscope, were behind him; now he was perfecting an un-usual technique for processing low-grade iron ore. At a busy, noisy site in the northwest corner of New Jersey he was mining and sending to the processing plant some two hundred tons of ore a minute. ("We are making a Yosemite of our own here; we will soon have one of the biggest artificial canyons in the world," he told a visitor.) At the processing plant the iron ore, after crushing, was separated from the sand by dropping the particles past a powerful electromagnet which attracted the ore and let the sand pass. To carry unprocessed material through the various steps, Edison had devised a lengthy series of conveyor belts. While the light canvas belts he had installed were commonly used for transporting grain and other lightweight materials, they were not designed for any-thing as bulky and heavy as ore. A belt that lasted seven or eight weeks was rare. Sturdier belts would facilitate Edison's operation, for the frequent repairs and replacements lost much valuable time. Yet, to make a sturdier belt did not seem possible because it also had to be flexible enough to ride over and around the pulleys.

In the spring of 1891 a twenty-three-year-old, twelve-dollar-a-week belt salesman named Thomas Robins, Jr., visited Edison's plant. He endured loud complaints from the superintendent about the unsatisfactory conveyor belts, and later mulled over the problem at length. Robins theorized that a belt made of compounded rubber might withstand the weight and friction of the heavy ore and yet be flexible enough to go around the pulleys. Up to this time rubber had been used to take advantage of its waterproofing characteristics (e.g., the india rubber used in Dresser's packer), excellent for boots and raincoats. Durability never had been supposed as one of its assets, and the full realization of rubber's possibilities awaited the advent of the pneumatic tire for the automobile.

Robins, though, made some simple experiments of his own with compounded rubber, and before too much time had passed, he reported back to America's most noted inventor with his unique proposal to construct a rubber-covered conveyor belt. Edison readily saw the merit of the idea, and Robins returned to his office in New York City with an order for five hundred feet of this experimental rubber belt. Robins, elated over this development, had his hopes dashed when his employer suggested that such an undertaking involved too much risk and that he should turn the order over to a willing competitor. Robins did, and when the belt was completed to his specifications it proved entirely successful at Edison's works. Encouraged by Edison, Robins quit his job to devote full time to developing a sophisticated conveyor system. Edison permitted the young salesman-turned-inventor to use his own mine as his laboratory. Soon Robins had devised an improved mechanism for carrying his new belt—a set of rollers and idlers arranged on angle brackets, which raised the sides of the belts and formed a trough for the ore to ride in. He also improved upon the rubber belt by making its face thicker at the central portions and thinner at the sides for greater flexibility along the curved sides. Robins had created the basic design for the modern belt conveyor. He looms in history as a key figure in the transition of American industry to assembly-line methods. Henry Ford later said that his reading of articles about the conveyor system used at Edison's iron ore plant inspired his own assembly-line system for the Model T Ford.

In 1896 Robins invested his life's savings of $1,000 in his own firm, the Robins Conveying Belt Company, and he promptly made several big sales which launched his important enterprise. The imaginative young salesman had founded a business that would make mining operations more efficient the world over.

All the pioneer companies described in the preceding pages and founded before 1900, as well as many others, were destined to become part of Dresser Industries, Inc., in the mid-twentieth century. All of them had historical involvement in critical aspects of American technology. Sometimes their products chanced to be working side by side. It was quite possible for a coal mine in the 1890's to be using a Jeffrey automatic cutter to obtain the coal, a Robins conveyor to move it, a Shaw crane to lift it, and a Roots blower to ventilate the mine. A Harbison-Walker refractory later might transfer its energy to make steel. By then, too, a Clark engine might power the drill in search of oil, Dresser's packer could be inside the well, and a Wayne pump might dispense the gasoline derived from petroleum. Other combinations, more elaborate, could also be constructed, and it would be difficult especially to overlook the Dresser coupling's importance to the expanding natural gas industry.

Most of the companies destined to merge with Dresser Industries had not been founded by the end of the nineteenth century, but they too would play vital roles in the nation's development of natural resources in the twentieth century. It is perhaps ironic that the one company under whose banner they all united was neither that of the oldest nor best known of them; it was the modest operation started by Solomon R. Dresser.

2

Solomon R. Dresser Founds a Company

Many years later his descendants held a vague notion that Solomon Robert Dresser ran away from home with the romantic idea of becoming a drummer boy in the Civil War. It is true that he left his parents' Michigan farm soon after the war started, but if he tried to enlist in that tragic conflict he failed. Where he ultimately landed was in the new and rowdy oil fields of western Pennsylvania. There, a new dream emerged. The realization of that dream would add another chapter to the annals of American success stories and have a substantial impact on the nation's life and industry.

The many factors that placed Dresser in Pennsylvania are duplicated in the histories of countless American families. The first American Dresser arrived on this continent in 1638 in the person of John Dresser, a passenger on the ship *John*, a vessel carrying twenty families from Rowley, Yorkshire, in search of religious freedom. They founded a settlement called Rowley, between Ipswich and Newburyport, Massachusetts, and in that community Dresser assumed a prominent role in community affairs, establishing a pattern followed by many of his descendants. His son, also named John, served six years as representative to the General Court, and in 1687 he was one of the Rowley selectmen who joined their neighbors in Ipswich in resisting the English governor's tax policies. The settlement did not escape the fury of the witch hunts that raged through New England late in the seventeenth century and ultimately touched the Dressers in a remote way. A Rowley widow named Margaret Scott, executed in 1692 at Salem for witchcraft, had a great-granddaughter named Mehitable Scott, who nearly forty years later married Aaron Dresser. Aaron Dresser continued the family custom of public service by fighting against the Indians in 1748 under Captain Wilder, and by joining in 1755 the Crown Point Expedition. One of Aaron's children, Elijah, fought in the

Battle of Bunker Hill. After the Revolutionary War Elijah's son, also named Aaron, left New England for Jefferson County in north-central New York. There he established his own business, Dresser's Tavern.

In those days a tavern served many social purposes, and Dresser's Tavern became an early center of trade, the surrounding area eventually becoming known as the town of Pamelia Four Corners. Aaron and his wife, Abigail Munroe (said to be of President James Monroe's family despite the difference in spelling), had five sons and three daughters. The fourth son, Parker, was just nineteen when he married seventeen-year-old Lydia Cronkhite in 1818. Lydia was a strong-willed girl of Dutch extraction, described years later by her granddaughter as "the driving force" of the union, being blessed with a "very determined will and a mind that ruled—kindly but firmly." Nineteen years and six children later, the cheap land available in the remaining Northwest Territory pulled Parker and Lydia Dresser westward to Michigan. Two months after that state was admitted to the Union in 1837, Parker Dresser bought 240 acres of government land at $1.25 an acre in Hillsdale County. There, near the tiny town of Litchfield, he erected a log cabin for his large family and began clearing land, breaking soil, planting crops, building fences, and doing all the backbreaking chores familiar to pioneer farmers. There, too, Lydia gave birth to the last two children of the family. The baby of the family, Solomon Robert Dresser, was born in that log cabin on February 1, 1842, at a time when Manifest Destiny was in the air and westward-bound wagons were carrying the American sphere of influence to the shores of the Pacific.

As a child Solomon Dresser encountered the typical frontier influences that shaped so many Americans of the mid-nineteenth century. With so much work to do, the large family surely had little time to spoil this youngest member; and one can imagine that as soon as he was able to toddle about, little Sollie, as he came to be known, began contributing his share of work. There was little opportunity for recreation, and the principal diversion from routine occurred when, following the neighborly customs of the day, the family took in for the night passing strangers who were headed farther west. No doubt these travelers regaled the wide-eyed boy and his four brothers and sister (two older sisters already were married) with great tales of adventure.

When Solomon was seven, the stream of travelers grew even steadier, for gold had been discovered in California! The argonauts' visions caused even Parker Dresser to succumb to the temptation. Evidently figuring that his children were big enough to take up the slack on the farm, he set aside his plow and joined the forty-niners. He eventually returned with no more than just enough gold to make two wedding rings—one for Lydia and the other for his newly married daughter, Mary Elizabeth. Solomon, of course, was too young to try his luck in California, but his older brother Hannibal, twenty-one years of age, was not. He departed in late 1849 but suffered all kinds of misfortune—dysentery, theft of his money, and hunger. Traveling on foot through Lower California, thirsty and hungry, he and his tiny band of fellow adventurers lived on rattlesnakes for eight days until they killed "an old horse some emigrant had turned out to die." These adventures he described in a letter to his brother Parker, who was tempted to join him. "You can make more money where you are than here," Hannibal warned him. As for himself, he had "seen the elephant" and wished to be back on "some farm in Michigan." Indeed, there was money to be made in farming, for the Dresser land was located in rich agricultural country, with wheat and corn as the leading crops. Chastened by his own and his son's profitless ventures for a quick fortune, Dresser settled down to his less glamorous but steadier livelihood of farming. His son Hannibal soon returned and moved to Lafayette, Indiana. By the time Solomon was eleven his father had prospered sufficiently to build a substantial stone residence.

A farm boy learned to work with his hands, and Solomon was no exception. Later he would capitalize on the lessons learned in tinkering with farm implements, but a good education was deemed important by the family too. When the residents of Hillsdale County decided to obtain their own college, Parker Dresser paid his share in the fund drive to bring Michigan Central College from Spring Arbor to Hillsdale. His contribution insured limited tuition benefits for his children. Thus, in 1856 Jasper Marion, Solomon's brother, became the 125th student to enroll at the newly located institution, which came to be called Hillsdale College. Three years later Solomon enrolled at the age of seventeen in the college's preparatory program. He studied the courses required for admittance to the regular college-level program: "mental" arithmetic, grammar, geography, Latin, Greek, algebra, natural philosophy, reading, elocution, and penmanship.

Hillsdale College was the first institution of higher learning in Michigan and the second in the nation to admit women as students on an equal basis, and one of the new students in the fall of 1860 was the precocious and frail Vesta Elizabeth Stimson, only fifteen years old. Vesta's childhood, spent on a farm between Hillsdale and Jonesville, had not been a happy one. Her mother and a younger brother had died, and despite her stepmother's best efforts, Vesta

Solomon R. Dresser posed
for this photograph when, in
1864, he married Vesta
Stimson, a young school-
teacher he had met at Hillsdale College in Michigan.
(Photo courtesy of Mrs.
Cornell Pfohl)

Vesta Stimson, at the time of her
marriage to Dresser, was a demure
teacher who spent much of her
spare time writing poetry and essays.
(Mrs. Cornell Pfohl)

grew up as a lonely, introspective child. By the time she enrolled at Hillsdale College she already had attempted to put herself "asleep forever" by eating poppy seeds. Failing, she had sought to smother herself in snow, but this had not worked either. It is possible that Vesta and Solomon Dresser, who was three years older, knew each other before entering Hillsdale College. Certainly, however, these two farmers' children became especially attracted to each other as fellow preparatory students at the small college.

Their mutual studies were brief. After two terms at the school, Solomon Dresser failed to return for the 1861 spring semester. Having completed his preparatory work, perhaps he had achieved his personal goals in education. He moved to Lafayette, Indiana, and began clerking in a dry goods store.

The Dresser family already had established ties with the town of Lafayette. Two of Solomon's older brothers, Parker and Hannibal, had married Lafayette women, and Jasper Marion had moved there in 1858. Jasper had done especially well, having read law and gained admittance to the bar. Lafayette was not too great a distance from Hillsdale County, Michigan, to prevent Dresser from continuing to court Vesta Stimson, who by 1863 had become an eighteen-year-old schoolmarm. Hardly had she begun her career than Dresser asked her to marry him. It was, in retrospect, an unlikely match. Vesta liked poetry and the arts; her suitor was gentle but rough-hewn, fascinated by objects rather than words. But she loved him, and on November 22, 1864, the Reverend Mr. E. B. Fairfield, president of Hillsdale College, married them. Back in Lafayette, where they began housekeeping, they went to D. R. Clark's Art Gallery and posed in their finest clothes for individual photographs. Dresser was robust, unsmiling, with prominent features and a full head of carefully slicked-down hair. Vesta, her hair tight in a bun, looked innocent, with tight lips and an unbeguiling stare into the camera lens. Her relatives soon were imploring her to return to Michigan. "Why don't Sollie let Vesta come home?" wailed her little cousin. Eleven months later, she did come home with her husband, but only long enough for the birth of their first child. It was a girl, Nina Vesta.

Perhaps his new responsibilities motivated him, perhaps he chose to follow his father's pioneering example; whatever the reason, Solomon Dresser determined to do something with his life other than spend it as a dry goods store clerk. His father had headed west, to the new state of Michigan, then had made a brief foray farther west to the California goldfields. Solomon Dresser went east—in search of oil, black gold. If he had any special knowledge of this risky endeavor it is difficult to imagine where or how he acquired it. No matter; the oleaginous substance was not particular about *who* found it, all that was necessary was to find it. Most of the attention was focused on the Pennsylvania fields where Colonel Drake in 1859 had triggered the founding of the modern oil industry. But there was another prominent area in West Virginia, where "Seneca Oil" had been produced in limited commercial quantities for ten years before Drake brought in his well at Titusville. In fact, this area, the Burning Springs field in Wirt County, vied with Pennsylvania for leadership in production in 1860 and 1861, and this was where Dresser went.

A hundred years earlier George Washington, visiting this place, had noted with awe the "burning springs" that "burst forth as freely as spirits and is nearly as difficult to extinguish." The natural gas that caused these "burning springs" was associated with the oil underneath, which had been discovered in 1806 by pioneers seeking salt deposits. The oil had been considered a nuisance until nearly fifty years later when commercial sales of "Seneca Oil," largely for medicinal purposes, began. The thriving industry that had developed in West Virginia was ruined in the Civil War when Confederate forces swooped down, set fire to some 300,000 barrels of oil, burned the wells, and broke up the machinery. Dresser saw an opportunity at war's end to be one of the first entrepreneurs to resume the field's development.

His activities are not known in detail, but the evidence suggests that his primary action was in arranging to take over some of the abandoned wells. Having done so, he returned to Hillsdale County to raise money among friends and relatives to form the Peninsular Petroleum Company. In a six-week period in April and May 1866, he sold 336 shares of stock at $6.25 each to forty-seven individuals. He recorded each transaction in a small, paperbound ledger book that was preserved by his descendants not because of the company records therein but because Vesta eventually took the book and used it for writing poetry and essays. The meagerness of Dresser's own personal resources was reflected in the fact that he himself had only $100 to invest, a fraction of the $2,100 raised. The company's capital almost doubled when he borrowed another $2,000.

In that first summer of operations the Peninsular Petroleum Company shipped approximately 230 barrels of oil to customers such as Wilkinson, Carter & Youmans of Boston, John W. Padden of New York City, J. Barnard of Indianapolis, and Pennsylvania Oil Company of Chicago. Unfortunately, the financial rewards were not as great as a few years earlier, for the price of oil had plummeted from a high of $10 to $12 a barrel in 1864 to an average of about $3.75 a barrel in 1866. By the fall of 1867 no more entries were made in the account book, and one can only speculate that the

A page from Dresser's 1866 ledger book shows amounts invested by his Michigan friends in his Peninsular Petroleum Company in West Virginia.

Peninsular Petroleum Company ceased to exist at about that time.

The oil boom was still in its infancy, however, and Dresser managed to stay in the business. Fortune awaited only a fortuitous twist of the drill, and who could tell when his turn would come? When word spread around 1870 of new developments near tiny White Oak, fifteen miles west of Parkersburg and just north of the Little Kanawha River, Dresser and his family went there. Overnight the community had become a boomtown of three thousand people. Its name was changed to Volcano because at night, looking down from the surrounding hills, the many flares burning off the unwanted gas from the oil wells gave the impression of a volcano's crater.

Traveling was more difficult now for the Dresser family, for it had grown with the addition of two other children at two-year intervals. A son named Parker was born on November 30, 1867, and on December 12, 1869, a daughter, Ione St. John, arrived. As the couple had done for their first child, they went back to Michigan so that the births could occur among relatives and friends. Dresser's parents by now had moved to Jonesville, not far from Litchfield. Vesta was a devoted mother to her young children. She concerned herself especially with moral and religious training, which indeed was needed in the rough-and-tumble oil-field communities.

Vesta Dresser, always at her husband's side, knew as well as anyone what an oil producer did, and the occupation was not without glamour to her. She saw in the colorful scenes about her an opportunity to launch her own avocation as a writer, and she took over the abandoned ledger book for the Peninsular Petroleum Company and began filling it with poetry, personal observations, and essays. She wrote and rewrote in her fine, delicate hand an essay entitled "A Glimpse of Oildom," apparently hoping that some eastern magazine might publish it. What she described was the basic routine not only for her husband but for the many other producers in West Virginia and Pennsylvania:

> Would you join the adventurers you must first secure as good a lease as in your judgment can be found. For this you will pay an eighth to a fourth royalty as you can agree with the land holder, and perhaps a bonus if the prospect is particularly good for a big well. . . .

> Having secured your lease you must next attend to having a rig built. There are large numbers of men who make this their special business. The rig consists of Derrick, Engine house, Boiler house, walking beam, Sampson post, bull wheel &c.

> By the time these are completed, the engine boiler and all necessary machinery should be set up and in readiness for the Contractor to take possession with his drilling tools. The drilling will occupy from three weeks to as many months or more according to luck. . . . If you meet with no bad luck, you may expect in a few weeks at least to reach the oil sand, or in other words "strike oil."

To drill a well a thousand feet deep might cost more than $3,000, and a well that was not a "duster" required additional expenditures to retrieve the oil. The amount of money to be earned varied widely with fluctuations in the price of crude oil, and the sums were not as fabulous as one might suppose since many wells produced no more than five barrels a day and a hundred-barrel-a-day producer was rare. Nevertheless, a struggling producer had hopes of wealth overnight if he brought in a prolific well. The knowledge of this caused many a man and family to undergo severe hardship in hopes that they would be next.

But the chances for this happening, as it turned out, were far less in West Virginia than in Pennsylvania. The Dressers picked up their few accumulated belongings and moved to western Pennsylvania, where oil activities seemed to grow more frenzied every year. Here they began migrating up and down the Allegheny valleys, from one oil field to another. Years later the Dresser children could not recall all the places where they had lived, but a few of the towns included Foxburg, Karns City, and Millerstown.

Dresser did not wander about willy-nilly, however; his movements indicate that he was among the many who followed the theories of Cyrus D. Angell, whose drilling successes reinforced his widely publicized belief that oil, in common with deposits of coal, occurred in nature along narrow "belt" patterns. In the year that the Dressers moved to Pennsylvania, Angell propounded a belief that a belt from three to five miles wide and thirty miles long extended from Venango County southward into Clarion, Butler, and Armstrong counties. This was in the so-called Lower Region. Angell's theories were merely intuitive and soon to be discredited, but, indeed, oil was being found where he predicted.

Butler County is where Dresser chose first to go in Pennsylvania. Numerous gushers had been recorded in which the pressure was so great that the oil spurted into the sky and fell in a black shower. Production was reaching hitherto unknown proportions. Vesta Dresser described this area as "wild and broken and beautiful from its romantic irregularity of outline." In his first summer in this fertile field, Dresser, while drilling near Petrolia, in the northeastern part of the county, brought in a well that press reporters estimated as producing one hundred barrels a day. With crude bringing $3.75 a barrel, this was a bonanza of immense dimension for the family. Yet, either the well exhausted itself prematurely or its capacity was exaggerated, for there is no evidence that the family's life-style improved dramatically.

The family soon settled, however, on nearby Millerstown (now Chicora) as a more or less permanent home. Angell himself was drilling just east of Millerstown, and operators believed the oil "belt" ran to the east of town. The Dresser family's sense of permanency was signaled by the fact that they stayed here for the birth of their fourth child, Chauncey, on November 21, 1873, rather than returning to Michigan. Vesta described Millerstown as a place of "happy homes—cheery and bright" even if the exteriors were "often rude." The family was "very comfortable," but Vesta suffered from occa-

Oil wells punctuate the landscape in Butler County, Pennsylvania, where Dresser was a producer in the 1870's. (Drake Well Museum)

sional homesickness and she had a "penchant for a home of my own for housekeeping."

Activity meant excitement and even Vesta got swept up by the drama of a busy field. Another strike by her husband along Angell's belt on the McGinley farm was a fifty-barrel producer. By this time the Pennsylvania oil regions held two thousand or so miles of two-inch pipelines to carry crude oil to storage facilities, but delivery was not so simple if no pipeline was available. In this situation the oil had to be poured into barrels and hauled by wagon to the railroad. The roads, Vesta Dresser attested, "were unusually bad, Pennsylvania mud being deep and sticky." The drama was heightened through "the shouts and imprecations of the drivers, the jolts and jars, the plunges, escapes and non-escapes as sloughs were encountered together with frequent breakages. [It] can only be imagined by

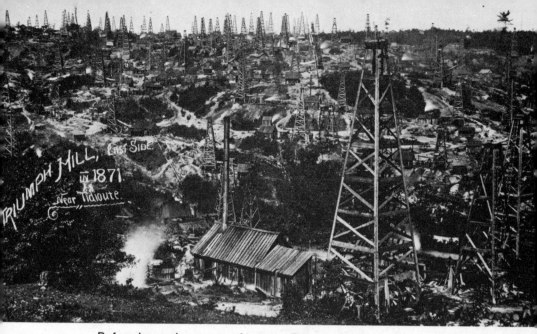

Before becoming a manufacturer, Dresser traveled from oil field to oil field, including the area around Tidioute, Pennsylvania, portrayed here as it appeared in 1871 at Triumph Hill. (Drake Well Museum)

those familiar with the scene." There were other dangers, too, for if the workers were not careful, the flow of oil and sometimes gas might ignite and consume the rig and the oil in spectacular blazes. In fact, holocausts and death were all too common experiences in the field. Huge sections of the hurriedly constructed towns sometimes were consumed by flames, and oftentimes a fire in the oil field would spread from one rig to another and over an entire network of lines and storage tanks.

Neither were the children immune from tragedy. Before 1874 had ended, the infant Chauncey, "with his sweet-face, ever bright and pleasant," died at the age of nine months. "God bless him, his sweet memory—may it be a talisman binding us ever to what is good and true, holy and pure," Vesta wrote in the old Peninsular Petroleum Company ledger book. Shortly afterward the Dressers observed their tenth wedding anniversary. Despite the sorrow, despite the harsh life that her husband's peripatetic calling had brought to her, Vesta loved him more than ever: "I spring each day to meet my Husband. If I loved then [on their wedding day], it was with a love untried. Now the jewel tested I know its worth. If then I thought and believed him good and noble, I know it now—know his gentleness, patience, honor and goodness and thank God that this I can truthfully say on this the tenth anniversary of my wedding day."

While Vesta provided the chronicle of their life through her letters and poems, her husband worked hard, not only in the oil field but in efforts to make Millerstown a more civilized place. Now grown stocky, his appearance seemed to reinforce his bulldog tenacity. He joined the local debating society and studied hard such topics as whether capital punishment should be abolished. His own position was the affirmative. By January 1876 a public school district was formed, and the record book's first entry listed Dresser as one of six board members. There was no schoolhouse, but the board paid rent to the German Lutheran Society for its building.

By this time still another baby had come—Robert Alexis, born September 9, 1875, in Millerstown. The family was complete: Nina, ten; Parker, eight; Ione, six; and now Robert. There was no permissiveness in this family; strict guidelines were set for the children's future behavior. Vesta instructed them to "solemnly pledge" themselves to "temperance in all things," and this meant abstinence from "beer, wine, all strong drinks, tobacco, tea, coffee, opium & rich stimulating food." The children were admonished to "strive always to be cheerful . . . because cheerfulness cometh always of a pure heart and contented mind." Somehow, the family had failed to affiliate with a church, but Vesta emphasized "the blessed religion of Christ Jesus" in teaching her children.

After the birth of Robert, Vesta's health—always frail—deteriorated further. Her husband shuddered to see his wife struggling daily with the wood stoves to prepare meals and to keep the rooms warm in the harsh mountain winters. He soon conceived of a plan to relieve her of this burden. In 1872 nearby Titusville had taken advantage of the presence of natural gas by laying a two-inch pipeline from the field to town, a distance of five miles, and the gas was used by 250 homes and businesses for illumination and heating. A few other towns in Ohio, Pennsylvania, and New York which were near supplies of natural gas already had made tentative efforts to pipe it into homes, and manufactured gas also was used for illumination. The presence of natural gas in conjunction with oil was a common phenomenon, but the customary practice was simply to "flare" it off as a nuisance in a continuous flame at the top of the derrick. Dresser determined to let the natural gas near Millerstown do some of Vesta's work for her, and he laid a line of gas into her kitchen, where it made a weightless and convenient fuel. Other gas outlets in the house provided illumination and heat. This experiment was entirely novel for Millerstown, but it was short-lived. Dresser's descendants later told the story that the family supply of natural gas was terminated abruptly when the Millerstown police forced him to disconnect the line and—unlikely though it may seem for a school board member—arrested him for endangering the public safety.

Vesta was suffering from what was known then as consumption and now as tuberculosis. By late 1876 she was beginning to visit sanatoriums in Dansville and Clifton Springs, New York, for prolonged periods of time, an expense that indicated a degree of financial capability. These periodic treatments and consultations with physician after physician henceforth were to be a constant fact of her life. The effect of her illness chilled the entire household, for Vesta developed a premonition of dying: "Sometimes when I am sick so much the death Angel seems to come so near I can almost feel the swoop of his wings."

Meanwhile, the oil producers' attention had begun to focus on Bradford, in McKean County, where the most productive field yet was developing. By the end of 1877, Bradford's storage capacities were overflowing; a network of pipelines hurriedly thrown together to ship out the increasing production was not adequate to the task. In 1878 the field produced 6.5 million barrels of crude oil, which amounted to 42 percent of the entire nation's production. Yet the peak still had not been reached. Disputes reverberated over the deliberate curtailing of production to hold up prices, and a local producer named Lewis Emery, Jr., was leading the independents in a battle against Standard Oil.

Dresser, now thirty-six years of age and the head of a household that included four children and a consumptive wife, once more gathered up his family and possessions and moved eighty-five miles northward to Bradford. This former lumber town was now populated by "lively delegates from every nook and cranny of Oildom [who] crowded the streets, over-ran the hotels and taxed the commissary . . . to the utmost." One year earlier Bradford had been a village of five hundred inhabitants in the pleasant Tunungwant Valley; by the summer of 1878 its population had soared to ten thousand.

The character of many of these opportunistic migrants was illustrated by an incident that spring. The flimsy frame structures that had been thrown up overnight to accommodate them were ravaged frequently by fire, and when the substantial Bradford House burned in May, approximately a thousand scavengers began stealing what goods had been salvaged while honest souls fought the fire. Not until the city police formed a vigilante squad could the devilish work of these "very bold and boisterous" thieves be stopped.

A lapse of time inevitably occurred between the overnight growth of Bradford and the institution of adequate public services. A local newspaper, *The Daily Era*, decried stagnant pools of water

When Dresser moved to Bradford, Pennsylvania, in 1878 the town already was in the midst of a furious oil boom.

standing on city streets. Already, though, a gang of laborers was installing an eight-inch natural gas pipeline along Main Street to illuminate and heat the city's homes and businesses. Another sign of civilization—or at least an attempt to create order in the numerous oil transactions that were occurring—was the presence of twenty-nine lawyers, which, the newspaper disparagingly commented, gave Bradford "more lawyers to the square inch than any town in America." There was no lack of diversion for the town's citizens. In February the "Red Stocking Minstrels" were featured at the opera house; in March Buffalo Bill's Wild West Show held forth at the same place. The first circus ever to visit pulled into town in April, and when one of the wagons became mired in a three-foot mudhole on Main Street, hundreds of spectators gathered to watch it being pulled out. That same month a wrestling match in the opera house was billed as determining the championship of the oil fields, and two celebrated billiards players from Rochester and Chicago faced each other. The streets seemed overrun with gamblers and prostitutes, but in February the righteous elements of Bradford won a victory by forcing out of town the infamous Ben Hogan and "Jennie the Notorious," operators of the most widely known brothel. All this was "Bad Bradford," the town that was to become home at last for the Dressers and a permanent center of the petroleum industry.

The family found rooms in a large, two-story frame house at 61 Congress Street,* just a few blocks from the center of town, and

* Years later Bradford's street numbers were changed. References are to the previous numbering system.

Dresser immediately began developing some oil interests. He entered into a partnership with a man named Thomas Conners and obtained a lease for a producing well with all its fittings and fixtures. He next obtained numerous other lease agreements on his own, and in May the *Era,* under the headline "Oil Matters," announced that "S. R. Dresser, on lot 7, of Babcock & Hulings, has commenced to build the rig for N[o] 2. No. 1 is doing 10 barrels." Whether he had hired out as a rig builder for the moment or whether the wells were his own is uncertain. But the ten barrels of oil a day did not represent a fortune for anyone: the area's abundant supply had helped drop the price of crude oil to less than a dollar a barrel.

The family's circumstances were less flush these days, the more prosperous times of Millerstown having vanished. Dresser's grandchildren remembered years later the story of how shortly before Christmas in 1878 or 1879 his partner became angry at him for some reason and burned down the rig on their one producing well. Never had Christmas looked more bleak. Somehow, though, Dresser and Vesta pooled their thoughts and resources to provide small gifts for the children. Years later Ione could remember receiving a muffler as her one present.

Surely Dresser had doubts about having devoted all these years to oil. Jasper, his brother in Lafayette, had gone into insurance and, as a relative wrote, was "having honors heaped upon him." He was president of the Underwriters' Association, three of his calves had brought premiums at the county fair, and he was considering the offer of a job that paid $8,000 a year. Perhaps a more prudent man would have followed Jasper's example and sought a steadier and less speculative career.

Such thoughts indeed occurred and gained dominance, for Dresser began now to turn his energies to a new challenge. Perhaps, he obviously calculated, there was more money to be made in supplying the oil industry than in finding oil itself. If the years in the oil regions had done little else for Dresser, they had made him capable of improvisation: of building a wooden derrick in a hurry, of overcoming the inevitable breakdowns involved in sending a drill a thousand feet beneath the ground, and of keeping a pump going with baling wire or whatever might be handy when it was set-up miles away from supply stores. He began spending hours now trying to solve a problem faced by all drillers: the difficulty in finding an effective packer to seal off crude oil below the surface from other elements, usually water. How long he worked at devising a packer is unknown, but he soon designed a cylindrical packer containing india rubber that expanded when the weight of the pipe was on it and contracted when the weight was withdrawn. The use of rubber for this purpose was not novel, but Dresser's manner of clamping the rubber so that it would not slip out of the packer was new. On March 24, 1880, he sent his application for a patent to Washington; in less than two months the patent was granted.*

In a remarkable example of planning, Dresser had anticipated the patent approval by renting shop space in the center of town and opening his doors for business on the exact day the patent was granted, May 11, 1880. The birth of what ultimately would become the hub of a worldwide corporation, Dresser Industries, Inc., was announced that same day in a two-column advertisement in the *Era*:

> Producers! Your attention is called to the DRESSER CAP PACKER! Patented May 11, 1880. A sure pack and no difficulty in removing from well. This is accomplished by capping both ends of the rubber and the introduction of material in upper end of rubber, so that it CANNOT EXPAND, thus necessitating the expansion from centre of rubber.

The advertisement was signed "S. R. Dresser." Both the office and the workshop of this new business were located at 83 Main Street, only a few blocks from his home on Congress Street. Precise details

PRODUCERS !

Your attention is called to

THE DRESSER CAP PACKER!

Patented May 11, 1880.

A sure pack and no difficulty in removing from well. Impossible to leave rubber in the well. This is accomplished by packing both ends of rubber and the introduction of material in upper end of rubber, so that it CANNOT EXPAND, thus necessitating the expansion from centre of rubber.

— OFFICE —

No. 83 Main Street,   -   -   -   Bradford, Pa.

P. O. Box 1,867.

S. R. DRESSER, Agent.

On May 11, 1880, the same day on which a patent was granted for his packer, Dresser placed this advertisement in the *Bradford Era*. This dates the founding of what would become Dresser Industries.

* See Chapter 1, pp. 14–16.

on how Dresser assembled his patent packer are missing, but evidently he arranged to have the basic unit made of malleable iron to his specifications at a foundry. The rubber insert came from a rubber manufacturer. He used his shop as a place for assembling and selling the finished product.

If an oil producer's life was highly competitive, being a manufacturer of oil-well products could hardly have been less so. The race for the packer business was fierce. One important supplier was the Consolidated Oil Well Packer Company, Ltd., with stores located in "all principal places in the oil regions." Another was Jarecki Manufacturing Company of Erie, Pennsylvania, which had a branch store in Bradford. All these businesses carried daily advertisements in the local newspapers. That Dresser was operating single-handedly and with meager resources against these bigger, older, and better-organized competitors was testimony not only to his packer's merits but to his courage and tenacity. His business was far from being an overnight success, but the mere fact that it survived these early days was no small accomplishment. When the federal census taker visited the Dressers that summer, he listed the head of the household as a "manufacturer of oil well packers." Here was respectability; here was a business that relied on hard work, ingenuity, and service rather than on guess and luck; here was the fulfillment of a genuine need for the growing and increasingly important oil industry.

That competition was fierce there could be no doubt. Before the year ended, war had erupted among the three principal packer producers. The issue concerned the validity of their respective patents. Consolidated Oil Well Packer Company claimed that Jarecki Manufacturing Company's product was in violation of its patent. Jarecki guaranteed customers that its packers were "absolutely free from any right of action at law or in equity" and contended that Consolidated Oil Well Packer Company's products were "made and sold in violation of . . . exclusive license made to us." The third major firm, Oil Well Supply Company, guaranteed its customers full protection from legal recourse if its products were challenged.

It is not difficult to imagine that the many claims and counterclaims resulting from this lengthy and well-publicized feud had a salutary effect on Dresser's new business, for he avoided entanglement. Fifteen months after opening his doors he was able to expand his modest enterprise to include used packers of many types and a supply of rubber "of any quality or kind for other packers." If an oilman wanted to sell his own used packers, Dresser announced his eagerness to buy them. His daily newspaper advertisement now listed two addresses, 81 Main Street (one door from the previous address) and Newell Place, the latter being an alley extending from Main to the street behind Boylston.* The alley location evidently served as Dresser's shop, while his sales office was on Main Street.

By the summer of 1882 Consolidated Oil Well Packer Company had filed lawsuits claiming patent infringements by several firms, and Dresser continued to solidify his own position by stressing his detachment from the packer dispute and by obtaining another patent for an improved version of his product. The principle on which the new packer operated, he pointed out, was "precisely similar" to that of his original one. The improvement was an ingenious one, however. The new packer was designed to permit previously wasted natural gas to be drawn off and used to operate the pump above ground. The captured gas could be burned beneath a boiler to generate steam for an engine that in turn operated the pump. The rubber used in this new packer was reinforced by inserting into it strips of canvas duck. Similarly, a metal ring was embedded in the "shoulder" of the rubber before vulcanization. Hence, it was called "armor rubber." Mindful of the unsettled disputes over other packers, Dresser carefully noted in his application the distinctions between his packer and similar ones on the market. As an additional enlargement of his business he had been able to purchase by 1882 "the oldest and only legal" patents for making corrugated rubber and he held a half interest in the patent for the Ajax packer sold by J. F. Hubbard at the Iron Tank.

Dresser's advertisements contrasted sharply with the shrill tones of the feuding manufacturers. A personal statement accompanied his daily advertisements in the summer of 1882: "Producers, I court your friendship, not your animosity. Call and examine my stock before buying elsewhere and I shall treat you fairly and generously; also, the goods shall be just as recommended." He had successfully formed a network for distribution, for the notice proclaimed that his packers could be ordered through any hardware store in the oil region.

The family's economic status brightened considerably. One of Vesta's relatives was moved to express his happiness that despite previous reverses the family was now "in prosperous circumstances," and he congratulated Solomon for having "got the better of poverty." Another sign of good times was the family's move from Congress Street, where they had shared the large frame house with a rig builder and his wife and son, to a house at 54 South Mechanic Avenue (now South Avenue), two blocks from the town square.

* Newell Place evidently was an early name for what soon came to be known as Patent Alley.

If relative prosperity had arrived, there also had been great sadness. Dresser's firstborn child, Nina, who was popular, smart and a great help and companion to her mother, had been stricken at the age of fifteen with spinal meningitis. After a prolonged illness she died on the evening of April 5, 1881. Services were held at the Dresser home and her body was carried to Jonesville, Michigan, for burial next to her brother Chauncey. As Nina's Sunday school class at the First Presbyterian Church observed in a resolution, she had been "thoughtful and attentive, and careful to improve her opportunities, commending herself to her teacher, and endearing herself to her class companions."

Nina's death had been a heavy jolt to Vesta, and in the prolonged grief that followed, her own precarious health worsened. She consulted specialists in Cincinnati and Philadelphia, experimenting in the latter city with Starkey and Palin's new "compound oxygen" treatment. Nothing seemed to help, though, and her longtime premonition of impending death returned. She announced in letters to relatives that her life was approaching its end. She wrote notes to her children directing them always to be good and honest Christians. Vesta still had not formalized a church relationship, but the need now took on greater urgency, and on January 18, 1883, she was baptized at the First Presbyterian Church. This done, her last wish was for her children to be baptized. Six weeks later, on March 4, 1883, this was accomplished. On the next day Vesta Dresser died. Funeral services once more were held at the Dresser home and Vesta's body was carried afterward to Michigan for burial beside the two children who had preceded her in death.

Sol Dresser was at the age of forty-one a widower with three children. Parker was fifteen and Ione thirteen, old enough really to take care of their own needs as well as those of seven-year-old Robert. Dresser could do nothing but seek to relieve his grief through work, which he did.

He soon saw a new opportunity to serve the oil industry: selling and detonating explosives. The use of explosives to increase oil-well production had been made popular in the 1860's by Civil War veteran E. A. L. Roberts. The company he established to "torpedo" the wells with nitroglycerine had proved highly successful. Roberts had won a patent for his torpedo despite the fact that the practice was not original with him. So broad and so unlikely did the patent seem that dozens of competitors felt safe in rushing into the field; Roberts initiated a massive series of lawsuits to protect his position, and when he died, in 1881, he held the reputation for being responsible for more litigation than any other man in the United States. Roberts' death seemed to open opportunity for new competitors, and by 1883 the

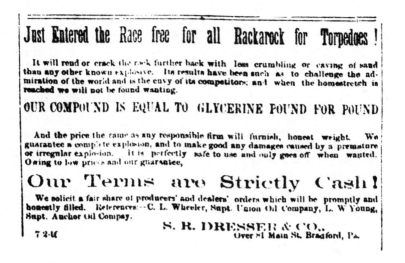

Just Entered the Race free for all Rackarock for Torpedoes !

It will rend or crack the rock further back with less crumbling or caving of sand than any other known explosive. Its results have been such as to challenge the admiration of the world and is the envy of its competitors; and when the homestretch is reached we will not be found wanting.

OUR COMPOUND IS EQUAL TO GLYCERINE POUND FOR POUND

And the price the same as any responsible firm will furnish, honest weight. We guarantee a complete explosion, and to make good any damages caused by a premature or irregular explosion. It is perfectly safe to use and only goes off when wanted. Owing to low prices and our guarantee,

Our Terms are Strictly Cash !

We solicit a fair share of producers' and dealers' orders which will be promptly and honestly filled. References:—C. L. Wheeler, Supt. Union Oil Company, L. W Young, Supt. Anchor Oil Compay.

S. R. DRESSER & CO.,
Over 81 Main St, Bradford, Pa.
7 2-tf

For a brief period Dresser de-emphasized his packer to try to sell an explosive called Rackarock, used to create an underground reservoir for collecting oil.

Era's advertising columns revealed fierce rivalry among suppliers of nitroglycerine. The torpedo business was more lucrative that year than ever before. Contemporary accounts estimated that 100,000 pounds of nitroglycerine were being detonated every month in the Pennsylvania oil regions.

The battle for this market was well under way when Dresser decided to offer a new kind of explosive for which he had acquired the rights, Rackarock. He announced his intention in a two-column newspaper advertisement on July 2, 1883, proclaiming in bold letters that he had "just entered the race" for selling torpedoes.

> We guarantee a complete explosion, and to make good any damages caused by a premature or irregular explosion. It is perfectly safe to use and only goes off when wanted. Owing to low prices and our guarantees, Our Terms Are Strictly Cash.

He listed as references the superintendents of the Union and Anchor oil companies, and again he appealed to customers on the basis of honest treatment: "We solicit a fair share of producers' and dealers' orders which will be promptly and honestly filled." While Rackarock was new to the Bradford region, Dresser's advertisement claimed that its performance had won the admiration of the world and was the "envy of its competitors." He asserted that "when the home-stretch is reached we will not be found wanting." In that same issue of the *Era* four other torpedo manufacturers boasted of their own products. One might hope that this intense rivalry was friendly be-cause at least three of the competitors were neighbors on Main Street—Dresser at 81, C. E. Tucker at 60, and Spence & Dennis at 57. To introduce Rackarock, Dresser gave a demonstration explo-sion several miles outside town. Interested producers rode the Brad-ford, Bordell & Kinzua Railroad to get there.

It was at this time that Dresser, always watchful for a competi-tive edge, acquired a novel gadget in 1883 to make his company even more accessible—a telephone. His number, 246, was noted in his advertisement. Only one other business in all of Bradford, a general merchandiser, had been alert enough to see the benefit of advertising his telephone number.

Dresser and all the other torpedo agents sold their explosives at two prices, one of which included its detonation. Rackarock cost the customer thirty-five cents a pound in the office, but for fifty cents a pound, Dresser would deliver it to the well and explode it. Many chose to have the torpedoes exploded for them, for the procedure was risky and sometimes the "shooter" as well as the rig was ripped asunder in horrible accidents. Local newspapers were replete with stories of accidental explosions, a favorite comment being that there were not enough remains of the victim to fill a quart jar. Dresser's Rackarock, which he claimed could be used with "perfect safety," was taken to the well in a "shell" already loaded and ready to be lowered and detonated. This, he claimed, dispensed with the "usual delay and danger of thawing Nitroglycerine."

At the end of 1883 Dresser, inspired perhaps by his own close brush with death, decided to quit the torpedo business. In dropping a torpedo into John P. Zane's well, it prematurely exploded and blew up $600 worth of well tools. Dresser escaped injury. True to his word, he agreed to repay Zane in full at a rate of $100 a month by supplying him additional torpedoes in that amount. How-ever, after gaining credit for $457.56, a dispute arose and payments ceased. The matter dragged on for six years until it was taken to the County Court of Common Pleas, where Dresser paid the remain-der of the debt and court costs.

So intent had been Dresser in developing his torpedo business that he had ceased all mention of packers in his 1883 advertise-ments. The 1883–84 Bradford city directory identified Dresser & Company's business only as "torpedoes." The packer business had prospered anyway. By 1884 Dresser, in addition to his Bradford operation, had "branch offices" in Allentown and Bolivar, New York,

and Clarendon, Pennsylvania. His "cap packer," he claimed, still
held the "front rank for the best malleable castings, superior quality
of rubber, the easiest removed from the well and the most durable
to resist a heavy pressure of water." Moreover, he claimed it to be
the "cheapest packer in the market."

The Dresser family had experienced far more than its share of
tragedy. Yet, still another loss came in 1885. Seventeen-year-old
Parker, to whom the mantle of eldest child had been passed upon
Nina's death, began showing symptoms of catarrh and lung trouble
in the winter of 1883–84. His problems seemed alarmingly similar to
those of his late mother. A summer spent with relatives in Michigan
—customary for the children—provided temporary relief, but in the
following winter it became clear that Parker suffered from tuberculosis. On the morning of March 24, 1885, he died. For the third time
in four years funeral services were held in the Dresser home. Afterward, the body was shipped to Michigan to be placed alongside what
now constituted the majority of the Dresser family.

There is no evidence to indicate what effect these losses had
upon Solomon Dresser. A lesser man might have lost all ambition.
Dresser pushed himself harder than ever. Parker's death occurred
while Dresser was working on a totally new product that was to
become by far his greatest success and the foundation for his
future prosperity: a flexible, leakproof coupling for uniting pipes.
By midsummer of 1885, confident that he had achieved his goal, he
sent his patent application to Washington, D.C.

Dresser had been interested in natural gas ever since he had
piped it into the house in Millerstown. Pipelines for transmitting oil,
water, and, to a more limited extent, manufactured and natural gas
were common, but a leakproof joint had not been invented. The
wrought-iron pipes customarily used were screw-threaded, but joining the pipes by this method did not hold the gas satisfactorily. An
amazing variety of substances was applied to the threads in hopes
of preventing leaks: molasses, honey, glue, mucilage, glycerine, and
the like. The wrought-iron pipe itself ultimately corroded as well,
despite an equally amazing variety of coating treatments. While oil
was commonly pumped through pipelines for distances of more
than a hundred miles—the stickiness of the substance clogging up
small leaks—natural gas could not be. Only those cities fortunate
enough to be near natural gas fields, such as Pittsburgh, Rochester,
Titusville, and Cincinnati, were able to use this energy resource
because it simply could not be contained in a pipeline at adequate
pressure to be sent over long distances.

Dresser figured correctly that if he could use rubber in his
packer to seal off water from the crude oil, he could achieve with the

same principle a perfectly tight seal in a pipeline. The "self-packing" coupling he designed was adaptable for a plain-end pipe or a threaded pipe. Inside the sleevelike iron device that covered the pipe joint, Dresser arranged for a ring to receive the force of the liquid, gas, or steam and transmit its pressure to a rubber packing. Thus, the greater the pressure, the greater the seal. It was not necessary for the pipe ends to abut; indeed, a separation was beneficial because expansion or contraction due to changing temperatures could be accommodated without problems.

This invention, a rough precursor to what ultimately would be so important to Dresser, to Bradford, to the natural gas industry, and even to the nation, almost escaped notice. The *Era* wrote simply: "Sol R. Dresser, of Bradford, has been granted a patent for a pipe coupling." His patented coupling was not the first one, for a coupling advertised daily at this time by the National Tube Works Company of Boston, Massachusetts, and McKeesport, Pennsylvania, was said to be "acknowledged by all to be the best in the market." Neither was Dresser ready to offer his coupling in competition, but having made a start, he continued to work at improving it. In fact, henceforth he would concentrate his inventive efforts on the coupling instead of the packer, even though production of the coupling was several years away.

Before 1885 had ended, Dresser took another important step. He had begun to escort a lovely young woman from Lowell, Ohio, named Caroline Kirsch. How he met her is not known, but family members later thought she had worked in Dresser's office. A smooth-skinned lady of classic features, Caroline was a more outgoing and self-assured woman than Vesta. On December 21, 1885, the two were married. Caroline sought not to replace Vesta as Ione's and Robert's mother but, as she observed a few years later, to "develop the physical rather than the emotional" sides of the children.

In the next few years Dresser began expanding even further the range of his endeavors. He served a term in 1887 as a member of Bradford's common council, and he began a long and favored association with the Masonic lodge. Ultimately he would become a 33rd-degree Mason and president of the Masonic Temple Association, initiate and lead the movement to build a new temple in downtown Bradford, which stands today, and hold the office of deputy district grand master of McKean and Potter counties. In a more profit-oriented mood he made several purchases of real estate, the largest being the acquisition of twenty-three acres of land for $3,501.

Not the least of Dresser's continuing interests was his effort to perfect the coupling. There was an obvious problem with his novel plan to let the pressure of the substance transported tighten the

Dresser's second wife, Caroline Kirsch, was an attractive woman from southern Ohio. (Mrs. Cornell Pfohl)

seal: as pressure decreased, the seal loosened. Dresser worked diligently to solve the problem, and between February and August of 1887 he applied for three separate patents. Not until the last of these did he discard his self-sealing approach. In so doing he created the basic plan that would earn him a fortune and introduce to the nation a truly leakproof coupling. The widespread adoption of this coupling was a decade away, but once accepted it would enable for the first time natural gas to be shipped for hundreds of miles in pipelines from the fields to distant cities.

He accomplished his aim by designing the coupling in two sections that were pulled together mechanically with bolts, compressing in the process an internal rubber ring. This in itself was not new, but Dresser's precision in the operation was deemed patentable. His innovation largely lay in preshaping the rubber rings so that the beveled edges conformed precisely in fitting into the space between the two pipe ends. In previous attempts the rubber was fitted simply by compression, causing it to lose requisite elasticity.

Less than a year later Dresser applied for still another patent which streamlined the coupling. This design simplified the job of connecting the pipes by adding a detachable retaining ring to hold them together until the bolts and nuts could be tightened.

Whether Dresser now tried to sell his coupling is not known, but if any sales were made they were insignificant in number. Years later, however, his son Robert told of an incident that demonstrated his father's great faith in his invention years before it was accepted. One cold winter, as the story went, Bradford's natural gas pipeline broke and all attempts to repair it failed. Dresser approached the line's owner, Lewis Emery, Jr., and bet him $100 that within twenty-four hours he could have the gas flowing. Emery, the oilman who had successfully led the area's independent producers in their battle against Standard Oil and who now was a state senator, immediately accepted the wager and jovially declared his fellow citizen to be crazy. Dresser, of course, did precisely what he promised. Citizens began to look upon his coupling with new respect.

Emery and Dresser enjoyed a great deal in common aside from being Bradford businessmen. Both men were from the same section of Michigan, with Emery having grown up in Jonesville, where Dresser's parents had moved from the farm. Emery, three years older, also had attended Hillsdale College; he also had courted his future wife there as a student; he had preceded Dresser to the oil field region by less than a year; and later Dresser, in common with Emery, would be elected to high public office by his fellow citizens.

Since Bradford already had a natural gas pipeline, installed the year Dresser had moved there, scant opportunity existed there to sell his coupling. He began looking elsewhere for a chance to see it used in quantities and to prove its effectiveness. His idea, a daring one, was to drill for his own supply of natural gas, use his own couplings to lay a pipeline into a community, and establish his own utility company to provide the service. He chose Morgan County, Ohio, as a likely place. The county was just a few miles up the Muskingum River from Caroline's hometown of Lowell, and no more than thirty miles from where natural gas had been encountered as early as 1814 at Duck Creek near Marietta. A number of Ohio towns and industries already were using natural gas, but Morgan County's attractive twin villages of Malta and McConnelsville, on opposite banks of the Muskingum, still depended on kerosene lamps and coal. Natural gas had been found two miles south of Malta in 1830 by Rufus Putnam Stone while drilling for salt, and though Stone had used this resource to evaporate the water from his salt, no one since had put it to systematic use. Thus, these two towns' residents seemed ripe for a pipeline from the field. The only thing lacking was an entrepreneur. Dresser hoped to remedy that.

Beginning in 1886, the year after he invented his first coupling, he started acquiring leases in the area. The first one he obtained was for 120 acres, but he delayed recording it in the courthouse

For many years Dresser's "cap rubber" used in his packer was protected by this trademark.

until two years later. Perhaps he postponed it until he thought his coupling was ready. In 1888 he began signing other leases, and by 1889 he had obtained rights to 224 additional acres in the hilly forests west of Malta near Wolf Creek.

All this was possible because his Bradford business was prospering and he had two steady associates who could run it in his absence. His favorite was a roughhewn former producer named George P. Boothe whose feet were planted firmly on the ground. The other was again a Bradford man, J. E. Kirk, with whom Dresser had begun still another enterprise: the manufacture of sucker rods, which tied the bottom hole pump of an oil well to the operating mechanism at the surface. Both Boothe and Kirk had served as witnesses to Dresser's recent application for a coupling patent. The packer and sucker rod operations were next door to each other at 15 and 17 Patent Alley on property bought for $600. Still another sign of prosperity was Dresser's purchase of a towering new home on South Mechanic Avenue (now South Avenue), which had a captain's walk and a second-floor porch.

Even the Dresser family was taking on new dimensions. On March 27, 1890, a son, Carl Kirsch, was born. Six months later Dresser's daughter, Ione, was married to a twenty-two-year-old Bradford man named Fred Augustus Miller. The Miller family had moved to Bradford in 1879 from Belmont, New York. Since the age of sixteen young Miller had worked with his father in the family lumberyard, A. Miller & Son. As a grand wedding gift, Dresser, flush with the accumulating proceeds from his brisk packer business, presented his daughter and new son-in-law with a three-story house just up the way from his own place and near a granite retaining wall he earlier had built on the street with the inscription "S R Dresser 1888." Young Robert Dresser was now fifteen. He had begun attending boarding school at Winter Park, Florida, being sent south apparently as a precaution against the tuberculosis that had been fatal to his brother and mother. Thus, Dresser's "first" family virtually had been reared; his business enterprises were doing well and were in capable hands; a "new" family with Caroline and young Carl had been started; and there was nothing to prevent him from striking out in his bold Ohio venture.

By 1891 Dresser had found natural gas, but before he could capitalize on it the gas ignited and destroyed his rig. He returned to Bradford for additional equipment, and the *Morgan County Democrat*, following his activities with keen anticipation, noted: "He expects to be here again in the early part of February and put down one or more wells until in his judgment the territory has been thoroughly tested."

That summer Caroline wrote to Ione: "Papa works so hard. I wish you could see him in his 'well-clothes.' They look *ill*—very." Dresser had breakfast each day by dawn, and by 7 A.M. he had left the pleasant rooms at Malta's popular Valley House for the field. It was hard and expensive work; only a vision of the future could have caused him to devote so much time and money to an enterprise that for two years did not earn him a single penny. The *Democrat* reported: "Mr. Dresser has not lost faith in the productiveness of this field and will continue operations on the lands controlled by him." Before the month of June ended he had hit a "pretty fair" gasser some five miles west of Malta. But it was not enough. He continued to drill for more, knowing that he must have a well with high pressure and good reserves to provide adequate service to the people of Malta and McConnelsville.

One evening after supper, tired from his long day, he was resting in the shade outside the Valley House when a youthful man approached and asked if his name was Dresser. Upon getting a positive response, the stranger then asked him if he formerly had lived in

The towns of McConnelsville, left, and Malta, Ohio, separated by the Muskingum River, were the markets for Dresser's natural gas company.

West Virginia, to which Dresser again answered in the affirmative. The youth then identified himself as the son of one of Dresser's friends in Volcano named Holingsworth, and they fell into a long conversation about the "old times" in that boomtown, long since destroyed by fire. "The most of them are dead broke and he thinks there is not more than 100 bbls per day production in the whole field," Dresser wrote to Ione.

By September Dresser had found enough gas to satisfy him and he was ready to pipe it to his market. He hired a crew of six men to dig the trenches and install with his couplings a 5⅝-inch line through the woods toward Malta, five miles to the northeast. There, the city council already had approved unanimously and enthusiastically an ordinance granting Dresser the right "to use and occupy and to dig and excavate in the streets, alleys and public grounds."

Progress was stalled at one point while he awaited the delivery of rubber rings for the couplings, but on good days the workers were able to tie together as many as 130 pipes. They reached Malta the last day of September. The critical question remaining was whether the line was tight and capable of holding pressure. Tests revealed one leak, but the fault proved to be a "sand hole" in the cast iron instead of a defect in the coupling. The part was replaced, and Caroline Dresser wrote to Ione proudly that the gas

shows up *strong* at this end of the line. That is the main point you know and in time I am sure it will be "a good thing." Papa does work so hard. The hot weather just tanned him til his face was blistered. But the hard work is over[,] now only to cross the river with the pipe.

The Muskingum River, as deep as thirty feet in some places, represented a barrier, but McConnelsville, the county seat and larger of the two towns, was immediately opposite and a destination greatly to be desired.

The residents of that city were just as eager as those of Malta to sample the wonders of natural gas. Winter was approaching, and the difference between handling bulky, dirty coal and having a convenient, clean natural gas outlet within the house was a revolution in daily living. Aside from gas's heating powers, its illuminating capabilities would permit the residents to throw away their kerosene lamps.

Dresser paused hardly at all at the full banks of the Muskingum. He laid his pipeline straight across the river bottom. He was, according to the *Democrat*, "sanguine of the success of his enterprise" and proclaimed an abundance of gas for "all demands likely to be made upon it."

McConnelsville's city council, not wishing to delay this happy prospect, suspended its rules and met in a special evening session to grant Dresser immediate permission to use its streets, alleys, and public grounds for laying pipe. Afterward, the entire council walked or rode across the bridge to Malta, where Dresser gave a public demonstration of this wonderful source of light and energy. It was a festive evening. Crowds chatted gaily, the local band played, and "some excellent speeches" were made. The *Democrat* proclaimed the event "a great time for Malta." Dresser announced that the main now had been laid across the river and he was returning to Bradford to order the necessary pipe to lay the full length of McConnelsville's main thoroughfare, Centre Street.

This Michigan-born one-time farm boy must have glowed with pleasure at such attention. Aside from this public demonstration of support, he had been reading favorable comments about his enterprise week after week in the *Democrat*. One of the best editorial comments came on October 30:

> Mr. Dresser has come to us differently from any other ever has in an enterprise of this kind. He has asked for no bonus from the citizens, but has born the whole cost of his enterprise and has made it as a permanent investment. His manner of doing business commends him to everybody and gives them confidence in the permanence of his enterprise.

After his many expenses it was time indeed to realize a return. To do so, Dresser opened an office just off Main Street in Malta, piped in his own natural gas to display the qualities of this invisible

During his Ohio venture Dresser often stayed at the Malta Hotel.

and weightless fuel, and began accepting orders for service at a flat monthly fee. It was not difficult to extend a line to any house in either of the two compact villages.

He named his company the Malta Natural Gas Line. Caroline Dresser was his chief bookkeeper. "This office looks like a great place to keep warm," she wrote to Ione. "There are *three* stoves and *two* gas logs all ready to light up . . . [and] to show up to possible buyers . . . I just tell you we revel in *gas*. Just imagine this office with a few big lights and half dozen fires all going. It makes one feel rich to own so much warmth ready to be distributed at so much per mo[nth]."

By October 23 the Malta Natural Gas Line was serving nearly half a hundred customers in Malta with no problems. "The gas line shows the same pressure in Malta as at the well with 45 fires on," Dresser happily reported to Ione. At the end of the month, Caroline, with one-year-old Carl a constant presence at her side, began sending out the first bills to customers. Their payments would represent the first return on Dresser's substantial investment. It was an occasion for celebration, but there was no time for that. Caroline wrote: "It seems good to have arrived at this point for dear papa has done some hard work up to this time. Everything looks favorable but there has been quite an outlay so far and it will be some time before papa takes as much money back to Bradford as he has brought here."

Dresser's son Robert posed in 1884 as a very young gentleman. (Photo courtesy of Mrs. J. Martin Kelly)

There was, of course, another new method of illumination in this era to compete with natural or manufactured gas: electricity. In January the *Democrat* dropped its advocacy of natural gas and began urging McConnelsville residents to construct their own electric-light plant. A leading local citizen, W. E. Farra, followed the suggestion by forming a corporation for that purpose, and in April the McConnelsville city council deliberated over competing bids from Dresser and Farra to light the city streets. The council chose electric lights. By June a temporary electric plant was in operation. The *Democrat* proudly commented that the light it provided was "brilliant and steady and gave universal satisfaction."

Stung by this turn of events, Dresser began drilling again in March to supplement the five-hundred-foot-deep wells he was using. "Mr. Dresser is not at all satisfied with the present service to consumers and proposes to spend more money in trying to make it satisfactory to all," the *Democrat* reported. But there was no way to forestall the electric-light plant, and his sales strategy now was to emphasize the values of *heating* with natural gas.

Still, there were problems. In the fall of 1892 some of his more unscrupulous customers found a way to increase the amount of natural gas they received. To do so they simply enlarged the hole in the "air mixer" device then used. Dresser was perturbed enough to buy space in the newspaper to issue a warning. He declared that this practice amounted to

> stealing just the same as though I should go to their money drawer and help myself to what cash there was in it. Any one who enlarges the hole in the air mixer in the future, or found using gas other than that contracted for, will be punished to the full extent of the law, and their gas will be shut off and not turned on again except by the use of meters. The following spring, when the banks of the Muskingum were filled with high waters and floating debris, the river pipeline once again broke.

Despite these adversities, life in Malta was not entirely unpleasant for the Dressers. Caroline especially was among friends, and on at least one occasion her husband surprised her in the office with a cool watermelon. Boat rides on the Muskingum added variety to the routine, and from practically any spot in town one could watch the paddle-wheelers that churned the water between Marietta and Zanesville. If the business did not reap the sums Dresser had envisioned, at least the operation was profitable. By the fall of 1892 his accounts grossed $400 monthly, and the gas pressure was holding above ten pounds.*

More to the point, there was an enormous long-term benefit. The Malta-McConnelsville pipeline demonstrated beyond a doubt (the two underwater ruptures not really reflecting on its tightness) that Dresser's coupling would carry natural gas at substantial pressure without leaking. Its tightness was to be affirmed later by an astonishing fact: as late as 1977—eighty-six years later—a portion of that original line still was used by the Columbia Gas Company, the firm that ultimately took over Dresser's operation.

By 1893 the Ohio enterprise was established to Dresser's satisfaction, and he left its operation in the hands of local employees to concentrate on his interests in Bradford. The company bearing his name now listed its products as "oil and gas well packers, couplings and regulators." The faithful George Boothe had replaced Kirk as Dresser's partner in making and selling sucker rods. This firm was identified in the city directory as Dresser & Boothe, and it would continue its separate existence until 1903. Dresser now resumed an even more active role in Bradford's community affairs. He served in 1893 on the city health board; he was a representative from 1894 to 1897 on the city's primary governing body, the select

* Dresser's property in Morgan County was valued for tax purposes in 1892 at $2,200. He paid $44.22 in taxes. (Auditor's Duplicate, 1892, pp. 43–44, Morgan County Courthouse.)

council; and he continued as president of the Masonic Temple Association.

The oil-well packer remained his staple product, but the coupling held a lock-grip on his attention. Still, he could obtain no orders for it. He submitted in 1893 two more applications to the U.S. Patent Office, one for a "detachable coupling" and the other for a repair device to stop leaky joints. The gas industry still had no effective solution to the problems of leaks, yet it was not ready to adopt the Dresser coupling. Certainly the need for it existed. One gas company, plagued by declining pressure, dug up twenty miles of pipeline and examined the more than five thousand joints for leaks. In the entire distance, officials found fewer than half a dozen that were not leaking.

Dresser's coupling, requiring only a man who could use a wrench to tighten bolts, was exceptionally simple to install. But it was more expensive than using threaded joints and "yarning," or calking, them. Moreover, few people could believe that Dresser's rubber packing would not deteriorate rapidly. They were wrong, for the enemies of rubber were heat, light, and air, and the rubber in Dresser's coupling was sealed from these agents.

Meanwhile, he stressed the packer in his advertisements, not even bothering to promote the coupling in the gas industry's authoritative and excellent publication, the *American Gas Light Journal.* He traveled extensively in the region, from Columbus, Ohio, to Malta to Pittsburgh to Sistersville, West Virginia, taking orders for packers. One of his newspaper advertisements carried his photograph and name with the identifying line "Inventor and Manufacturer." He appeared in it as a balding, heavyset, dignified man with a walrus-style mustache. Besides his newspaper advertisements, Dresser promoted his company in Bradford's annual city directories. In 1897, 1898, and 1899 his advertisements occupied the entire back cover of the directories; in following years he bought large advertisements on inside pages. His full-page advertisement for *Derrick's Hand-Book of Petroleum* in 1898 listed his company simply as "S. R. Dresser, Bradford, Pa." He described himself as "Patentee and manufacturer of specialties for oil and gas wells and lines." Those specialties included packers, wall fasteners, casing heads, rubber plugs, pipe couplings, sleeves, crosses, tees, and ells in that order. Illustrations showed his packer, coupling, and his "cap rubber" trademark. The latter consisted of a conductor's cap in the center of a circle encompassed by the words "S. R. Dresser's CAP RUBBER." This trademark, the advertisement explained, was "moulded or pasted on every genuine Dresser rubber for packers."

In 1896 he achieved at last an important breakthrough in

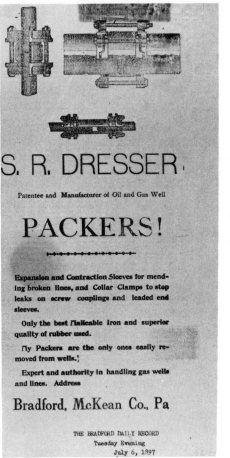

This advertisement for Dresser's packers appeared on July 6, 1897, in the *Bradford Daily Record*.

marketing his coupling. Beginning in 1888 he had made limited sales of his various products to C. P. Sloan, a superintendent for Standard Oil Company. In 1894 Sloan used nine of Dresser's sleeves, an elongated version of the coupling designed to repair breaks in lines. Sloan had been entirely satisfied, and when Standard's United Natural Gas Company decided in 1895 to construct a twelve-inch high-pressure line for the twelve miles from the Zoar gas field to Buffalo, New York, Sloan used Dresser's couplings. The completed line, with pipes made of secondhand wrought iron, carried 250 pounds of pressure. It was leakproof. Delighted with the results, Sloan proclaimed the coupling as offering "an absolutely tight joint—the only tight joint I have ever seen, or know of to-day." Five years later Sloan conducted a test to compare the Dresser-coupled line with an eight-inch screw-joint line alongside it. In the twelve-mile distance he found 257 leaks in the screw-joint line and only 7 "small leaks" in the Dresser line.

The success of the Zoar-to-Buffalo pipeline was a signal one, for Sloan then adopted the Dresser couplings for pipelines in Erie, Pennsylvania, and Canton, Massillon, and Akron, Ohio, and the sale of the coupling to other companies suddenly began in earnest.

Dresser always was seeking improvements in his coupling design, and in 1898 he applied for a patent on a variation of his basic product: an insulated coupling. This was important, for it had been learned that one of the primary reasons that pipelines under city streets rapidly disintegrated was the phenomenon of electrolytic action. Electric currents used on streetcar lines commonly strayed underground, and if they found a pipeline, they attached themselves to it and moved up and down its entire length. The result was an abnormally rapid deterioration of the entire pipe. Dresser's insulated coupling, using rubber as the key element, stopped the electric current from traveling beyond the approximately twenty-foot length of a single pipe.

Orders for this coupling came in rapid succession, for by the turn of the century a network of electric streetcar lines was customary in cities of any size, and no one before had found a solution to this difficult problem caused by them. The East Ohio Gas Company ordered the insulated Dresser couplings for every joint on three hundred miles of pipeline inside Cleveland; the Buffalo Natural Gas & Fuel Company installed insulated couplings on a hundred and fifty miles of pipeline; the Pennsylvania Natural Gas Company used insulated couplings on fifty miles of pipeline in Erie.

Success—substantial success—had arrived. The penurious circumstances of old now seemed far removed, and the Dresser family found itself prosperous indeed. The year 1898 was the best yet by far. Dresser posed that year for a photographer inside his Patent Alley shop. Clad in a vest, coat, bowler hat, and other dignified accouterments, he stood rather uncomfortably in the middle of the floor, his hands extended awkwardly along his sides, looking entirely like the classic image of the turn-of-the-century Victorian businessman. He could have gloated with justification had he chosen, for he had made a key breakthrough for the natural gas industry that would be of material significance for its rapid growth in the first third of the twentieth century. In this year of 1898 the East Ohio Gas Company used his coupling for an approximately eighty-mile-long, ten-inch pipeline carrying natural gas from fields in West Virginia to the Ohio cities of Canton, Massillon, Dennison, Canal Dover, and Akron. (Only one other natural gas line of such distance ever had been attempted, a short-lived, 120-mile pipeline from Greentown, Indiana, to Chicago, which used screwed couplings

By 1898 Dresser, standing solemnly in the foreground, had developed a modern machine shop for his packer works.

but which was soon abandoned.) A year later, in 1899, the North-western Ohio Natural Gas Company laid about one hundred miles of ten-inch high-pressure line using Dresser couplings to Toledo, and in years to follow the distances increased.

Business was so good that Dresser found himself on the verge of inundation by the paper work which he had never liked. Thus, in 1898 he hired a bright young bookkeeper-secretary from the Pittsburgh area named William L. Graham. Graham had learned of the position from a family friend who worked in Pittsburgh's Bolivar Iron and Steel Company, suppliers of the bolts and nuts for Dresser's couplings. Seventy-eight years later Graham, at the age of 101 years, retained a vivid impression of reporting to work. When he arrived he found the office in great need of organization. None of the handful of employees—Dresser, Boothe, J. W. Wick, and perhaps one or two others—had the time, talent, or inclination for such chores. They had evolved a very simple record-keeping system. Incoming orders were spiked on a hook attached to the office wall; once filled, they were recorded in a ledger book for billing purposes and transferred to a second hook an arm's reach from the first one. This had served the firm's purposes well enough previously, but now the hooks almost groaned from their growing burden and Graham saw danger in this casual approach. Within a few days he began checking to make certain that all the orders were on the proper hooks and that they had been recorded for billing. He found that an order from the East Ohio Gas Company for something more than $6,000 had not been recorded. Dresser had neglected to submit the bill for one of the biggest orders he had received. Graham checked himself two more times to make certain he was right and then informed Boothe of the omission. Boothe, shaken by the allegation, examined the evidence and exclaimed tremulously to Graham, "By God, Billy, you are right!" Graham sent the tardy bill to East Ohio with an explanatory note. Payment was promptly rendered, and Graham began developing a more sophisticated bookkeeping system.

Occasionally, the increasingly hectic routine at Patent Alley was interrupted by visits from Caroline Dresser, who invariably was accompanied by Carl and his younger brother, Solomon Richard, who had been born in 1894. (A third child, Doris Lydia, was born in 1896 but died six months later in a continuation of the tragic deaths suffered by Dresser's children.) William L. Graham believed that Mrs. Dresser appeared uncertain about the time and investment her husband spent on the couplings to the neglect of the faithful packers, and he recalled her comment to him one day: "Will, I think Sol's just throwing good money after bad and I can't understand it."

The coupling market, however, was far bigger than even the arriving orders indicated. The industry as a whole still did not realize fully that the answer to years of frustration in controlling leaks was available. In 1899 a writer for *Metal Worker*, describing problems related to city distribution systems that used totally inadequate bell and spigot joints, concluded:

> There is probably no more inviting field now open to the inventor than that which is created by the demand for better methods of joining cast iron pipe. . . . What is needed would seem to be an elastic, indestructible substance adhering strongly to iron, and flexible enough to admit of more or less disturbance without rupture or fracture. It must, of course, be tough and strong, insoluble in water, and not affected by gases . . . Whether it can be produced, who shall say?

Dresser already had found the solution to these problems with a specially designed clamp based on the same principle as his

Dresser could afford this stylish Victorian home by the 1890's, and from the back window he could almost touch the source of his initial prosperity—the oil fields.

Before the widespread adoption of Dresser's coupling, most pipelines were threaded so that the sections could be tied together with a screw collar. This practice required a tong gang to twist entire pipes for a tight fit. (Drake Well Museum)

coupling, and the industry's realization of his product's qualities was accelerating every month. The general manager of Standard Oil Company's gas department, E. Strong, attested to the worth of the Dresser coupling in 1900:

> We believe there is saving enough of leakage over other joints to pay for this joint in a very short time. . . . Our companies are using this joint in the majority of their work and I do not think for a tight and reliable joint there can be too much said in its praise.

In the next thirty years, as the industry came of age, some 90 percent of the nation's ever-lengthening natural gas lines would use the Dresser coupling.

3

Congressman
and Entrepreneur

The natural gas industry was entering a remarkable growth period at the dawn of the twentieth century. In the years 1896–1906 the output of gas more than quadrupled. This growth was confined almost entirely to the Appalachian regions of Ohio, Pennsylvania, West Virginia, New York, Kentucky, and Tennessee. Especially in Ohio, West Virginia, and western Pennsylvania an intricate network of pipelines brought the benefits of this clean, efficient, and trouble-free fuel from field to town. An integral part of this growth— whether in the pipelines that crossed mountains, streams, or other obstacles or in the service lines that tied houses to the main—was Dresser's coupling. It was effective also for pipelines that transported any gas or fluid: water, oil, compressed air, even molasses.

While the coupling had transformed significantly the size of Dresser's business and shifted its emphasis from oil to natural gas, the petroleum industry had entered a new era too. In 1901 the fabulous Spindletop in East Texas erupted in a gush of black oil that revealed a vast new source of crude deep in the earth, moved the heart of the industry to Texas, and prompted rapid technological change. Soon, with the age of the automobile, the nation's daily existence would become dependent upon oil and a distillate, gasoline.

A score of products was needed by both the oil and gas industries during these early days, and Dresser offered as many of them as he could without straying from his field of expertise. His familiar packer ($15–$75) continued to be popular for use in the well. The wall fastener ($15–$30) would hold the packer in place. If a rubber plug was needed to shut off water from an undesired strata, Dresser sold that too ($36–$38). His casing head ($4.50–$5) could be attached to the well at ground level with ease, and unlike most

The title page of Dresser's 1904 catalogue indicates that by then the coupling had become the company's primary product.

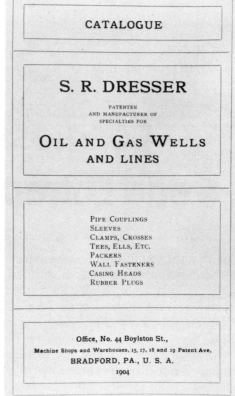

CATALOGUE

S. R. DRESSER

PATENTEE
AND MANUFACTURER OF
SPECIALTIES FOR

OIL AND GAS WELLS
AND LINES

PIPE COUPLINGS
SLEEVES
CLAMPS, CROSSES
TEES, ELLS, ETC.
PACKERS
WALL FASTENERS
CASING HEADS
RUBBER PLUGS

Office, No. 44 Boylston St.,
Machine Shops and Warehouses, 15, 17, 18 and 19 Patent Ave,
BRADFORD, PA., U. S. A.
1904

casing heads, it could be installed without sending it to a machine shop for threading. The couplings themselves, available in many styles and sizes, ranged in price from $1.35 to $7.25. The "long sleeve" ($2.85–$35.60) could repair quickly and effectively any break in a threaded pipeline, and the heavy "river sleeve" ($3.30–$31) was designed to anchor a line at the bottom of a river or stream. If a line could not be shut off during repairs, the Dresser heavy "split sleeve" attached directly over the leak; at a price of $47.80 to $111.50 this was Dresser's most expensive product. Still other related items included ells to make angles or turns in lines, tees for joining one line to another, and crosses for intersections.

These were the basic Dresser products that serviced the dramatic growth of the oil and gas industries during the first decades of the twentieth century. In the first year of this new century, Dresser resolved to make the benefits of his products more widely known by publishing his first catalogue. This pocket-size paperback booklet not only listed and illustrated the products but also told something of the history of the Dresser coupling. The catalogue was labeled simply "Illustrated Catalogue S. R. Dresser, Bradford, Pa. U.S.A." The title of the owner's opening statement summarized the catalogue's theme: "Good Goods Rather Than Low Prices."

I wish to state that I do not pretend to compete in price with others making goods used for the same purpose. My first object is to make goods that will accomplish the purpose for which they are made, to the entire satisfaction of the user. To do this it is necessary to furnish a much better quality of goods than those advertised to sell at lower prices. Therefore, I have adopted a quality of rubber much better than that used by my competitors, and I have the pleasure of knowing that the results have always been satisfactory to my patrons and myself.

My goods are specialties of my own invention. Most of them are patented and all have been experimented with, until proved to be adapted to the use for which they are made, before they are offered to the public.

Experiments are expensive, yet my prices are only what manufacturers ought to have, regardless of any patent.

Thanking my patrons for past and anticipated favors, and hoping that others will see the utility and superiority of my goods, and assuring that the high quality will be fully maintained, I remain, Yours truly, S. R. Dresser.

His first-person narrative continued throughout the sixty-eight-page catalogue. His ells, tees, and crosses were "far superior to the old method" of screw fittings because they were easier to apply and provided space to accommodate contraction and expansion. His packer was "too well known to require any comment," but he could not resist emphasizing again its virtues: "It has taken the lead from the first day it was placed on the market, and holds it now. It will continue in the lead because it is made on better principles and of better quality of material than any other packer on the market." One reason his coupling had not gained immediate acceptance in the market, Dresser acknowledged, was because of questions concerning the rubber's durability. That question had been resolved, he claimed, and "those who have used them [the couplings] are now satisfied that rubber used under these conditions will last as long as the pipe."

The catalogue was one effective way of telling the story of his products, and in 1900 another opportunity arose for Dresser to tout his company in an entirely different manner. Technological advances occurring in the last half of the nineteenth century had inspired a number of special exhibitions where manufacturers could display their achievements. The first was the 1851 international industrial exposition in London. Others followed in the United States, notably the Centennial Exposition in Philadelphia in 1876 and the Columbian Exposition in Chicago in 1893. When an exhibition was announced for Paris in 1900, Dresser saw the opportunity to introduce his coupling to Europeans and, along with a large number of American manufacturers, he reserved space. That spring he gathered several lengths of eight-inch pipe and a set of matching couplings and sailed for France.

The other six thousand or so American displays at the Champs de Mars grounds included such things as model iron bridges, drilling and riveting machines, compressed air tools, and motors. Dresser joined this vast scene, crowded with elaborate products, and set up on the last day of April his deceptively simple-looking pipeline and couplings. He united three lengths of eight-inch pipe with his insulated couplings, pumped cold water into the line at a pressure of 300 pounds, and capped it. As days passed, the line held without a leak—no surprise to him, and a fact of importance to many of the passing industrialists. But how could they know that? Amidst such competition for attention, a pipeline holding water hardly served to capture the eye. To help remedy this problem Dresser began in early July a chart on which he recorded the pressure at morning, noon, and evening for every day except Sunday—a day of rest. The pressure varied widely with changes in the water's temperature. From 300 pounds at the beginning, the pressure rose on July 20, "the hottest day Paris ever knew," to 695 pounds! On the last day, October 31, with the temperature now quite frigid, the pressure stood at 280 pounds. Through all these fluctuations, the pressure was held without reinforcement for more than six months. Dresser was so happy about the achievement that he reproduced the entire chart in his next catalogue. If the Paris exhibit opened new markets in Europe, Dresser failed to mention it in his catalogues—which would have been uncharacteristic of him—but the whole experience had been entirely satisfying.

So satisfying was it, in fact, that when the Pan-American Exposition was scheduled the next year for Buffalo, New York, he again reserved space for a display. This time he set up three lengths of four-inch pipe connected with insulated couplings and filled with gas at a pressure of 765 pounds. For more than five months— save again for the Sabbath—he charted changes in pressure as he had done in Paris. On the last day, October 31, the pressure stood at

CONGRESSMAN AND ENTREPRENEUR

755 pounds, having ranged from 865 pounds on July 1 when the thermometer stood at 85 degrees Fahrenheit to 680 pounds when the temperature had fallen to 40 degrees. This again was a remarkable record. At the height of this personal triumph an unfortunate tragedy occurred elsewhere on the exposition grounds. President William McKinley, greeting visitors on September 6, was shot by an anarchist. He died eight days later.

By this time the coupling easily had surpassed the packer as Dresser's most profitable item. The continuing expansion of natural gas pipelines from the fields in Ohio, West Virginia, and Pennsylvania to more and more cities in that region was one obvious factor; the so-called "field" coupling was appropriate for these long-distance lines across unpopulated areas. Another primary reason was more unusual. It was the realization, as mentioned before, that electrolysis from streetcar lines—not the saturation of ground from horses' urine—was the principal cause of underground pipe deterioration. With this knowledge and with the awareness that Dresser's insulated couplings solved the problem, cities and utility companies began installing the couplings in large numbers. Cleveland, Buffalo, Pittsburgh, Toledo, Erie, Wheeling, and many other cities used the insulated coupling in substantial quantities.

An electrical engineer named Brophy from Boston, Massachusetts, who examined insulated couplings in Wheeling, West Virginia, wrote that his tests "proved conclusively that . . . placing Insulated Couplings in lines of gas pipes effectually stops the destructive corrosion of such pipes due to electrolysis." Brophy sent his detailed findings to Dresser, who published them in their entirety in his catalogue. Other engineers, employed by utility companies and municipalities to make similar tests, confirmed Brophy's conclusions.

With the profits now accumulating, Dresser began adding to his property along Patent Alley. His primary acquistion was the purchase for $7,000 in 1901 of a large L-shaped lot that adjoined his Patent Alley property and fronted on Boylston Street. Eight months later he added a section that extended eastward from Patent Alley to Kennedy Street. Practically overnight he had expanded from a secluded alley location to a property that branched out to three thoroughfares and encompassed all sides of Bradford's city hall at Boylston and Kennedy.

Meanwhile, Dresser's family was growing up along with his business. Young Robert, after attending Rollins College in Winter Park, Florida, graduated from the Metropolitan Business College in Chicago. He was now dabbling in the oil business around Bradford and, having inherited his father's inventive bent of mind, was

Dresser and sons Carl and Richard pose prior to an outing in their new automobile, the first one in Bradford.

attempting to establish a business as a manufacturer of gas engines. On December 27, 1900, he had married a Bradford girl named Olive May Brady. The other two boys, Carl and Richard, still at home, enjoyed riding with their father in a curious gadget quite new to Bradford—the town's first horseless carriage. They never forgot the family's initial outing. One horse was so severely startled that it broke its leg in jumping and had to be shot.

To help Robert and his bride, Dresser bought for him a lead and zinc mine in the state of Missouri. After a wedding journey to Chicago, the couple moved to Joplin so that Robert could oversee his new property. Before many months passed, he was stricken with typhoid fever and was put to bed, presumably to die. Solomon Dresser arrived from Bradford, made preliminary arrangements with the undertaker, and consoled his pregnant daughter-in-law. Miraculously, Robert survived, and the couple's children years later were told that their mother had *refused* to let their father die by holding his hands hour after hour.

Comparing his recent success with the travail of earlier years must have filled Dresser, who became sixty in 1902, with many emotions. He had gained lasting prosperity for himself and a distinct achievement for an entire industry, and he had suffered great anguish, too, through the deaths of his first wife and four of his children. He had come to Bradford an unknown; now the town considered him to be one of its most important citizens. When the *Illustrated History of Bradford* was published in 1901, it devoted two pages and a photo to his biographical sketch. Grateful to the city that had been home for nearly a quarter of a century, Dresser was ready to repay his obligations, and the chance now arose.

When in 1902 a new congressional district was created for the counties of McKean, Clearfield, Centre, and Cameron, Republican Party leaders called upon Dresser and asked him to represent their party in the race for that office. Here was an opportunity to advance his tenets of good citizenship, hard work, and free enterprise, and to serve the region that had treated him so well. He would run for Congress.

The political campaign that followed was by present-day standards an unusually mild one. Dresser faced two opponents for the Twenty-first District congressional seat. They were the Democratic Party candidate, D. E. Hibner of Clearfield County, and a Prohibitionist named B. M. McCoy. None of the speeches of these three candidates were reported in the newspapers. Differences in their positions on issues or matters of principle were noted only through partisan newspaper editorials. The area's principal newspaper, the *Era,* supported Dresser as the "clean candidate" who stood "for Republican principles, for the perpetuation of Republic protection to American industries, [and] for endorsement of President Roosevelt." Hibner, the Democrat, was said to stand for "Democratic supremacy, free trade, free silver [and] a vote against Roosevelt and all that Roosevelt has done and is doing for the interests of all classes of citizens without regard to partisan considerations."

Dresser, the choice of the area's business interests, was not without backing from the working class. "To say that Hibner is more a friend to labor than is Dresser, is most absurd," the *Era* commented. "Mr. Dresser is an extensive employer of labor, directly and indirectly, and in no manner has he ever done aught to leave any impression but a most favorable one with reference to his feeling toward workingmen." The *Era's* position was supported by the formation of a workingman's "marching club"—the Independent Dresser Club—composed of both Democrats and Republicans in favor of Dresser's candidacy. Years later, Dresser's granddaughter Elizabeth, five years old at the time, recalled the moving sight one evening of a long torchlight parade snaking its way up Bradford's city streets to Dresser's hilltop home on South Mechanic Avenue.

For a campaign manager Dresser turned to his daughter Ione's young husband, Fred A. Miller, a former member of the city's common council who was becoming an influential man around Bradford himself. Miller now left his father's lumber business to devote full time to his father-in-law's interests.

The low-key campaign consisted mostly of speeches shouted in those preamplification days to various groups in the small towns that made up the district. There were no newspaper advertisements, no billboards, and, of course, electronic communication via radio and television was years away.

Dresser, whose life had been one of total circumspection, was not vulnerable to personal attack. As an abstainer from alcoholic beverages, he was removed even from potential jabs from the Prohibitionist. About the only "charge" that could be leveled against him was an area newspaper's comment that as a "millionaire" he could not hope to represent the average citizen's interests. (Whether or not he actually had a million dollars in assets at that date can only be guessed.) Such a comment could have little effect in a region where for many years overnight fortunes had been sought and sometimes achieved. And the individual would be rare indeed who did not know that Dresser's success was hardly of the overnight nature. Anyway, the *Era* answered the "millionaire" charge promptly and effectively.

> According to the views of demagogues a man who is shrewd in business matters and who acquires a competence through legitimate processes, immediately becomes a "millionaire." . . . Mr. Dresser is a self-made man. He commenced as a poor boy to be self-sustaining and by habits of thrift and frugality and the exercise of rare business talents he has succeeded in making his way in the world and in winning a place of prominence in business circles. By means of the industry which he has developed here hundreds of men are earning good wages, and he is regarded as one of Bradford's most useful citizens on that, as well as other, accounts. Mr. Dresser is a man of generous impulses and his deeds of charity, although not heralded to the public, are such as to demonstrate that he is a helpful man to the community. If qualities of this kind are to be urged against an upright citizen, and if the "charge" of being successful is to stand out against popular recognition, it would follow that none but the unsuccessful could obtain political preferment. The people of Bradford who are personally familiar with the admirable qualities of Mr. Dresser hold him in such esteem that regardless of partisan politics they are supporting his candidature with an enthusiasm that will certainly make a larger showing in the election returns.

As the November 4 election date grew near, Dresser emerged as the clear favorite, and the Democratic candidate redoubled his

efforts. Dresser became the subject of word-of-mouth charges—
their nature unknown—which distressed him. He considered himself to be above the rougher tactics of street politics, and in his
determination to elevate campaign standards he refused to answer
in kind. He issued, however, a statement which the *Era* reprinted
in full, the first and only time during the campaign that Dresser
was quoted directly in the newspaper.

> I have pursued a fair and honorable campaign. I have abstained,
> and have advised my friends to abstain, from what, in politics, is
> denominated "mud slinging," and, while I ask that this same honor-
> able method shall be continued, I also ask all the electors in the
> district, to be uninfluenced against me by eleventh hour slanderous
> insinuations or charges.

On the morning of the election Bradford's citizens read the
Era's hearty endorsement of Dresser. He was "a quiet, forceful,
earnest man of action . . . a plain man of the people . . . an important factor in the industrial affairs of the community." His success
in life had been achieved by "square dealing, intelligent management, and progressive methods." The *Era* thought he deserved the
voters' support.

When the ballots were counted following an uneventful election
day, Dresser was the easy 2–1 winner in every county in the
district. The final tabulation gave him 4,848 votes; Hibner, 2,526;
and the Prohibitionist, McCoy, 609. The Republican Party, including gubernatorial candidate Samuel W. Pennypacker, claimed the
entire state.

It was an exciting time to become a congressman. The nation's
eyes focused on Washington with a curiosity unmatched in years.
Theodore Roosevelt, that "damned cowboy" who had been elevated
to the Presidency upon McKinley's death, had become a forceful
figure who was in the process of transforming the once acquiescent
role of the federal government into one of action. Trust-busting,
muckracking, Senate reform, and the role of the federal government versus private enterprise were the ringing issues of the day.
It is not difficult to imagine the excitement within the Dresser
household as the family planned its move to the nation's capital.
As it turned out, there was no need for hurry, because the 58th
Congress would not hold its first session until November 9, 1903,
more than a year after the election.

Dresser did not intend to relinquish control over his company,
but he knew that when Congress convened he could not give it the
personal attention it demanded. Thus, he named Fred Miller, his

son-in-law and campaign manager, as the company's general manager. Dresser's eldest son, Robert, had no interest in joining the firm, and Carl and Richard were not old enough. Miller was very much like his father-in-law in personality, although as a tall and thin man, he was the opposite in appearance. He was quiet, courteous, and of dignified bearing. Like Dresser, he enjoyed the fellowship of other men and he was active in the Masonic lodge.

The year 1903 was significant for Dresser in still another way. Construction was completed on a magnificent new home unmatched for splendor in all of northwestern Pennsylvania. The inspiration for the house had come to Dresser at the 1901 Pan-American Exposition in Buffalo, where he had admired with many others the stately Michigan Building. He was so impressed that he hired the building's architect, Louis Kamper of Detroit, to design a house for him along the same lines. For its site Dresser selected grounds on Jackson Avenue on an elevation overlooking Bradford from the west. A local man, E. N. Unruh, supervised the construction. Dresser contracted with the William Wright Company, which had offices in both Detroit and Paris, France, to be responsible for the interior woodwork, furnishings, tapestries, and decorations.

The new house was given the name of Belleview Terrace. Its exterior was gray-white brick with trimmings of gray canyon sandstone. Its commanding view and imposing scale led to a description of it as resembling one of the "magnificent palaces of Spain." Four levels high, its gleaming presence was dominated by eight massive Greek columns supporting a front circular projection flanked by broad terraces across the entire front and sides. There were porches at all levels and a captain's walk on the very top. Porch and terrace floors were laid with terrazzo in marble. A walkway with broad terraces of steps went from the front portico to the street level below.

Inside were twenty-eight rooms, the grandest being a top-floor ballroom, 27 by 48½ feet. The ballroom included a stage and a built-in space for an organ. Among the various rooms on the second and third floors were eleven bedrooms. The first floor contained a reception hall, reception parlor, drawing room, circular den, library, kitchen, butler's pantry, servants' dining room, and laundry. On the ground floor were a coal room, vegetable room, boiler room, janitors' room, rathskeller, and cold room.

Dresser commemorated the house's completion by having printed a handsome book on slick paper with profuse illustrations entitled *The Home of Solomon R. Dresser*. The accompanying descriptions of the house were laden with adjectives, the appropriateness of which were confirmed in fact.

The interior of Dresser's home on Jackson Avenue revealed opulent decorations.

The Dresser home, completed in 1903, was said to be the finest residence in northwestern Pennsylvania.

From inception to completion nothing was left undone to make this
mansion one of the finest in the land . . . Whether viewed from
without or within, Belleview Terrace is a triumph of beauty and a
splendid creation of rare charm and rich elegance. It embodies all
that is finest and best in a modern palatial residence. Those acquainted with its interior and all the attractions of its commodious
rooms are enthusiastic over its supreme excellence as an ideal abode
and a perfect home.

Certainly the house was ostentatious; certainly it was much larger
than the Dressers needed, even with the full retinue of servants
they now had acquired; but such was the style of life at the turn of
the century for those men who had gained wealth and status.

By November of 1903 the family was in Washington for
Dresser to begin his new duties. To help with office details he
hired as his secretary his brother Jasper's son, Jasper, Jr. On the
ninth day of November, Dresser and the other members of the 58th
Congress took their oaths of office. Perhaps the best known of
the other freshman congressmen sworn in was the famous pub-
lisher who stood for everything Dresser opposed—William Ran-
dolph Hearst. The members' first vote was to choose a Speaker of
the House. Dresser supported the winner, the Republican Joseph G.
Cannon of Illinois. Surely he was pleased with the committee
assignments that followed, particularly his appointment to the
Patents Committee. His second committee was Coinage, Weights,
and Measures.

The Dresser family's imposing victoria was shipped by rail
from Bradford so that they could ride in dignified fashion through
the city's broad streets. Richard and Carl were enrolled in local
schools, where thirteen-year-old Carl came to be mistaken at times
for President Roosevelt's son Quentin. Indeed, the boys resembled
each other, attended the same public school, and both owned pinto
ponies.

One morning soon after their arrival, as a family story goes,
Caroline Dresser noticed from her front bedroom that passers-by
were looking toward her house and laughing with unusual gaiety
and interest. Upon investigating, she found that the family coach-
man, a black man named Duke Price, had deposited for the
morning all eleven of his children in the front yard. Their vigorous
antics were attracting the attention. Price had brought his children
to Washington in the same boxcar with the Dresser horses. A
handsome man, who always wore a uniform and tall silk hat when
guiding the carriage, Price had married a Caucasian. Because of
this, Bradford residents fondly labeled the couple's eleven offspring
"Duke's mixture."

Dresser's personal goal as a congressman, aside from his commitment to sound money, protective tariffs, and other basic Republican principles, was to bring honesty and integrity to the maligned endeavor of politics. In reality, scarce opportunity existed for a freshman to exert much authority regarding this intrinsically conservative goal. Bold though he had been as an entrepreneur, it was not Dresser's nature to address himself to the weaknesses that he felt existed among his colleagues. Thus, he confined himself largely to handling routine matters for his constituents.

His first public utterance in a House session came on March 21, 1904, when he asked unanimous consent to ratify and confirm a lease made by the Seneca Indian Nation of New York State to John Quilter, a man who had assigned his rights for drilling for oil and gas to one of Dresser's customers, the United Natural Gas Company. After being referred to another committee, the bill was returned the following month to be passed unanimously.

While Dresser traveled back and forth from Washington to Bradford, his business continued to flourish. In 1904, construction began in Patent Alley on a two-story red-brick warehouse containing sixteen thousand square feet of storage space. It enabled the company to stock products for direct shipment rather than to rely so heavily on the various foundries or rubber suppliers for direct shipment to work sites. More impressive in appearance was another new building that followed at 54 Boylston Street, a tasteful two-story office facility that connected the warehouse. The new offices were airy, spacious, and comfortably furnished. More than adequate space existed for future growth.

Such additions reflected the continuing acceptance of the coupling. Dresser and Miller missed few if any opportunities to follow up on their sales with inquiries to see if their customers were satisfied. They continued to reprint many of the favorable responses in the catalogues. The 1904 catalogue was enhanced by the verbatim report of a paper read by a Massachusetts gas company official, Waldo A. Learned, to the New England Association of Gas Engineers. Learned listed the Dresser coupling's advantages as:

the possibility of an absolutely gas tight line for any pressure; the making of every joint a perfect expansion joint, thus doing away with all breaks due to contraction or the settling of the pipes in the trench; the ease and facility with which pipe may be laid on top of the ground and put into the trench afterward; the saving of expense on trenches owing to the fact that a very much narrower one can be used than is possible where work must be done after the

In 1904 Dresser constructed a handsome office building on Boylston Street in Bradford.

pipe is lowered, and that by the use of the insulating style of coupling the line can be made absolutely proof against all disintegration due to electrolytic action.

A report of such nature was worth more than money could buy in advertising.

Dresser had been faithfully advertising his products on a limited basis since 1880, but not until 1903 had he begun purchasing space in the gas industry's authoritative *American Gas Light Journal.* His advertisement in that publication, printed in a single long column, promoted the insulated coupling. As was his custom, he identified his firm simply as "S. R. Dresser, Patentee and Manufacturer of Specialties for Oil and Gas Lines." Readers were asked to write for a catalogue. The same advertisement would appear in the *Journal* for three years before being replaced by a larger one. Dresser's newspaper advertising continued too, not only in the *Bradford Era* but also in the *Oil City Derrick,* where he touted the virtues of his packers. By now his packer patent had expired and many other packers were available. He made no effort to modify his packer to obtain a new patent.

Another opportunity to exhibit his couplings arose in 1904, when two more expositions were held. One was at St. Louis, Missouri, where Dresser followed the routine established at Paris and Buffalo by demonstrating the couplings' capacity to hold pressure that fluctuated with changes in temperature. And in November he and Fred Miller took the same display to the International Gas Exhibition at Earl's Court, London, attended by gasmen from throughout the world. Their intentions were to establish an agency in London, but the plan did not work out.

Before going to London, Dresser had resolved in the affirmative the question of whether he should stand for re-election. There seemed little chance that he could lose. So confident was he that he did not begin campaigning until mid-October, when he started visiting precincts throughout the district and attending occasional party rallies. The *Era* declared that his election "might as well be made unanimous" for his opponent did not have "a ghost of a chance to win."

He was joined in his speechmaking by supporters who traveled to little towns squeezed in among the district's wooded hills. As their roles ordained, his backers spared no praise in proclaiming Dresser's virtues. Typical was a speech by B. F. Jones of Bradford in Philipsburg, Centre County. As was common to the oratory of the day, the speech was overblown, but it at least portrayed the image projected for the candidate:

His life . . . is an open book, on every page of which is written honor, honesty and integrity. We all know him and to know him is to love him. The State has no more loyal subject, no truer citizen. The country has no abler representative than he who represents us in the lower house of Congress to-day. He comes before the people of this district for the second time. He comes with clean hands and a clear conscience. The embodiment of a true gentleman, a perfect man—forming his opinions boldly, expressing them gracefully; giving interest to small things whenever small things cannot be avoided and gaining elevation from great things whenever great things can be attained; holding his own esteem too highly to be guilty of dishonor and the esteem of others too considerately to be guilty of uncivility. No requirement too high to which he cannot ascend; no duty too humble to which he cannot descend. Respectful to his superiors, courteous to his equals, kind to his inferiors and wishing well to all—a man of the people, for the people and by the people.

Dresser's own casual approach to campaigning was indicated by the fact that he made no last-minute speeches. He closed his campaign several days before the election at a rally in the New Bradford Theatre, where Congressman John Dalzell of Pittsburgh spoke in his behalf.

As it turned out, there had been no need for a vigorous, stump-speaking campaign. Dresser won re-election by a 5–2 margin, with 5,129 votes as compared to his Democratic opponent, C. W. Shaffer, 1,429; the Prohibitionist, S. C. Watts, 765; and a Bradford Socialist, J. D. Blair, 282. Surely the lights in Belleview Terrace glowed in jubilation, but there were no items in the next day's newspaper to record it, for in Bradford a man's private life—even a politician's —was not subjected to intimate coverage.

The dual life in Washington and Bradford thus continued. Despite the prestige and glamour associated with any congressman's existence, for Dresser it was the Bradford life that was more satisfying. In Bradford he was in an atmosphere that he knew front to back, an atmosphere that he had mastered in establishing his business. Washington was entirely different. Here, the integrity on which Dresser had built his business seemed missing. As he saw trade-offs daily made in the inevitable give and take of political compromise, he became more and more disillusioned. Family members later recalled that he grew "beet red" in his disapproval, yet there was little to do but fidget silently in disgust.

His greatest pleasures came from business successes. A *Pittsburgh Dispatch* reporter noted one triumph when Dresser acquired a small oil-well supply manufacturer in Malta:

> Without doubt Solomon Robert Dresser was the happiest man in Congress yesterday. The Bradford man is a millionaire, therefore it ought to be something of a fairly good size that would make him happier than usual. But it was nothing more than the accomplishment of something on which he has worked for years—namely, the acquisition of a plant out at Malto [Malta], Ohio. . . . The plant competed with him in the manufacture of oil well supplies for 14 years. The competition was so keen that neither plant made money on certain lines of goods. Mr. Dresser tried to buy out this competitor several times, but always failed until last week. When he succeeded in getting the property he lost no time in going to Ohio to look it over.

Perhaps it was the purchase of this unidentified firm—the importance of which surely was exaggerated in the newspaper story since no records for it can be found—that inspired Dresser to make an important change for his company that same month. He decided to incorporate, an overdue move that would bring several legal and tax benefits. On November 17, 1905, he called together Fred Miller, his son Robert, and his associate George P. Boothe as incorporators to declare their intention to form a corporation known as the S. R. Dresser Manufacturing Company. The firm's objective was stated as the "manufacture and sale of couplings, clamps, sleeves, fittings, and appliances to be used in the construction and maintenance of pipe lines and sewers; and of packers to be used on the standpipes in deep wells . . . and the manufacture and purchase of parts of above for like use, and the assembling of the parts necessary for the same." Incorporation would be under the laws of Pennsylvania. There would be five directors—the four incorporators and Caroline Dresser. Capital stock of $500,000 would consist of 5,000 shares with a par value of $100 each. Solomon Dresser would hold 4,996 shares and the other four would own one share each. The local law firm of Tait and Jones drafted a set of bylaws, a stock certificate design, and a corporation seal.

Pennsylvania Governor Samuel W. Pennypacker signed the charter on December 13, and two weeks later the five incorporators met again in the offices on Boylston Street to complete the procedure. They unanimously elected Dresser as president, Miller as secretary-treasurer and general manager, and Boothe as superintendent. They also adopted the stock certificate design and the bylaws offered by attorney Edwin E. Tait. The eleven articles of bylaws outlined the routine duties of the officers, prescribed rules for election of company officers, set the annual stockholders' meetings for the first weekday after each New Year's Day, prescribed details for the use of the company stock certificates and seal, and listed the terms under which amendments to the bylaws could be adopted.

As president, Dresser would have "general supervision of the affairs of the Company, and attend generally to its executive business." Miller, as secretary and treasurer, would maintain records and finances, and as general manager, he would have "general charge and control of the business." Boothe, as superintendent, was charged with overseeing the manufacturing and operating departments. On January 2, 1906, the directors held their first annual meeting and voted a salary to Dresser of $1,000 a month, $500 a month for Miller, and $250 a month for Boothe.

The financial statement prepared for that initial meeting, the first one extant in the Dresser archives, showed resources of $550,000. Of this sum, the stock of coupling parts, packers, and other items stored with manufacturers in Ohio, New York, New Jersey, and Pennsylvania was valued at $134,507. (Most of these depositories were malleable iron manufacturers.) A value of

$179,992 was placed on the company's fourteen patents; accounts receivable totaled $78,860.14; cash in the bank was $22,837; machinery at Bradford and Oil City was worth $24,869; and the buildings and real estate were declared to have a value of $73,500. Aside from $50,000 in bills payable, a figure obviously representing an approximation, the company was free of debts.

Meanwhile, on the second floor of the new red-brick warehouse a second family enterprise had been founded. Ione Dresser Miller, in a half-fun, half-serious gesture, had started a business she called the William Frank Waist Company. The mother now of three children, Ione had been inspired by her first son, William Frank, to found the company. Ione, in common with other mothers, battled constantly with the buttons on her son's underwaist, a piece of underclothing to which trousers, stockings, or other items of apparel could be attached. In her frustration she devised a removable button that could be replaced, if lost, by the child without parental assistance. This was accomplished through a system of loops. Ione patented her design (No. 802,302) and began making a variety of styles of the William Frank underwaist for boys and girls. Her lighthearted approach to the business is demonstrated by this excerpt from an advertising brochure:

> *How to Minimize Button Labor for Mothers* was a question in political economy which had apparently not been thought worthwhile bringing to the attention of our august scientists and seers. No, it was reserved for the Mother of William Frank to solve this weighty problem for posterity, and as she recognized and accepted the sacredness of her mission, her heart swelled within her. No labor should be grudged, nor sacrifice bemoaned, if she might achieve the freedom of the mothers from this petty thraldom.

Ione used her children's playmates as models to illustrate the thirty-page catalogue. After some years she sold the company to the Ferris Waist Company in Binghamton, New York.

Life for the entire Dresser clan in Bradford was pleasant and comfortable in these days. Solomon Dresser, sixty-three years old in 1905, had his own children at home and grandchildren nearby to enjoy. They all were frequent guests at Belleview Terrace— Robert and his wife, Olive, and their children, Ione Helen and Virginia Louise; Ione and Fred Miller and their children, William Frank, Margaret, and Elizabeth; fifteen-year-old Carl; and eleven-year-old Richard. At frequent intervals Dresser would have Duke Price drive him in his carriage to pick up one or more of the children for lengthy rides around Bradford. The route invariably was chosen by the children. Occasionally, the automobile—the family's second car was an electric one—rather than the carriage was used. If so, Dresser himself insisted on driving.

Meals at the big house were festive events. Dresser hired a superb cook of German ancestry whose first name was Hilga. Hilga, the family was told, previously had cooked for John D. Rockefeller. She began working for Dresser so she could be near her sister, who was in a sanatorium at Mount Jewett, Pennsylvania. Each Thanksgiving two twenty-five-pound turkeys, one with oyster stuffing and the other with chestnut, would be placed at opposite ends of the long dining-room table. Dresser carved one turkey, and either Fred Miller or Robert prepared the other. Frequently, there were outside guests, and on more than one occasion Governor Pennypacker himself spent the night in the house.

The family often attended road shows that came to the Bradford opera house, sitting in their own reserved front box. Caroline, who frequently wore a grand opera cloak, always looked elegant. Vaudeville performers were warned not to tell jokes about this prominent family, for they were said to be "related to everybody."

As Dresser's second term in Congress neared an end in 1906, he drew up a bill of particular interest to his Bradford constituents. It called for the erection in his hometown of a new post office. The bill passed, but not until five years later would the cornerstone be laid for the distinctive red-brick Georgian structure that continues to function today as the post office.

Before his term ended, Dresser was stricken one day while riding in a government office building elevator. The elevator operator, seeing him collapse, thought at first that he might have been drinking. Doctors at the hospital determined the real cause of his fall—a stroke.

He was taken to Bradford to recover, but the stroke was a severe one. Dresser was unable to continue his political career, and neither was he ever able to resume anything resembling his former life. He was to be a semi-invalid for the remainder of his days, watched over by round-the-clock nurses, who by Dresser's order could not wear customary white nurses' uniforms because they reminded him of his condition. Dresser continued to enjoy certain small pleasures, especially those afforded by his children and grandchildren. He would arrange for Robert's or Ione's children to visit him one at a time in his bedroom, where they climbed up on his bed and played paper dolls or other games in which he joined. On pretty afternoons they would accompany him on leisurely carriage rides. At other times Dresser would enjoy the afternoon sun by sitting in a rocking chair on the magnificent terrace of his home.

Before his stroke Dresser had set in motion a grand scheme that would dramatically alter production techniques for the coupling. The customary practice of having various foundries manufacture the middle rings and flanges was not entirely satisfactory. Occasionally, tiny defects—sand holes or blowholes—marred these cast-iron parts. Since most of these parts were stored at the foundries, the details of shipping were too far removed from the Bradford office for efficiency. Moreover, it was impossible to schedule or to oversee production runs. Dresser decided to solve these problems by building his own manufacturing plant. He purchased a huge site on Fisher Avenue, just northwest of downtown Bradford, alongside Tuningwant Creek and the Baltimore & Ohio Railroad tracks, hired an architect to design a facility, and initiated proceedings for the development and purchase of equipment necessary to manufacture couplings.

In 1907 the new facility, a model plant containing elaborate machinery and a system of rails for "industrial cars" to haul materials, opened. Instead of being made of cast iron, the couplings now would be steel. The two principal operations were for the manufacturing of the circular flange and the middle ring. Each of these operations had its machine shops and general and special machines. Ten hydraulic presses cut out the flanges from the rectangular sheets of steel plates. The presses, from 125 to 425 tons in capacity, were powered by seven triplex high-pressure pumps driven by three Westinghouse gas engines using natural gas as fuel. The steel middle ring was cut from long lengths of skelp obtained from a rolling mill, then bent for welding by a special machine.

The conversion from cast iron to steel resulted in a marked improvement in quality. The tensile strength of steel was more than 60,000 pounds as opposed to about 32,000 pounds for malleable iron. Moreover, the steel was far more resistant to strain, its elongation factor being 25 percent as opposed to 1.5 percent for iron. Gaskets and bolts for the couplings continued to be purchased from outside suppliers.

Unfortunately and inexplicably, the minutes of Dresser's board of directors contained not a single word concerning this new manufacturing facility. Yet, the profitability of the operation was evident when the directors met on January 2, 1909, at the Boylston Street office, where the headquarters remained, and declared for the first time a quarterly dividend. It was to be 2 percent of the stated value of the capital stock.* The company's "excellent

---

* The directors followed the customary practice of the day in stating the dividend only as a percentage of the par value of the capital stock.

Dresser's new Fisher Avenue plant began operations in 1907.

financial condition" was said to warrant the payment to the stock-holders—and there were still only five of them. The same dividend was to continue each quarter until the second quarter of 1911, when it was raised to 2.5 percent, or $2.50 per share.

Meanwhile, still another favorable development had occurred. Dresser earlier had filed suit against the Worcester County Gas Company of Massachusetts, alleging an infringement of his insulated coupling patent. Worcester contended that at least two previous patents rendered Dresser's invalid, but the federal district court of original jurisdiction ruled in Dresser's favor. As the court pointed out, these earlier patents, despite their use of rubber, made no attempt at insulation. Worcester appealed the decision to the Circuit Court of Appeals, which heard the case in 1907. Dresser's attorney, Louis P. Whitaker, acknowledged, as had Dresser, that the elements in his client's patents were not entirely novel, but he contended that his client had united them in an entirely new way. The court agreed, observing that there was "uncontradicted evidence" that the earlier patents "failed of their purpose." The court acknowledged that Dresser had accomplished "for the first time . . . an underground joint so as to secure insulation and prevent electrolysis." This was a signal victory, despite the fact that Dresser was awarded only enough money to pay his legal fees. Had the decision been contrary, a host of competitors would have been free to seek to undermine his dominant position in insulated couplings. The company's continued prosperity thus was assured, for the coupling patent would not expire until 1916.

All these important developments Dresser, in his infirm condition, could only contemplate. Surely, though, on his carriage rides through town, his driver took him alongside the Fisher Avenue

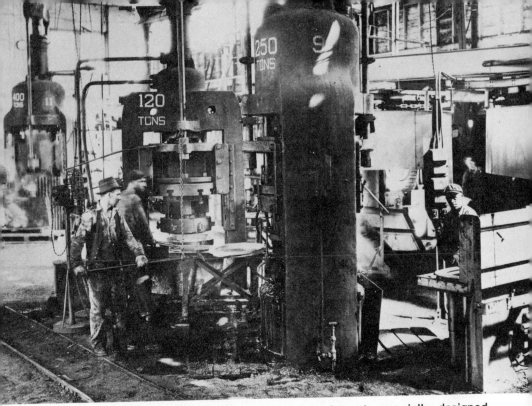

The Fisher Avenue plant contained equipment especially designed for the manufacture of couplings.

plant, and probably guided horse and buggy directly through the spacious interior, which was big enough to accommodate railroad cars for deliveries and shipments.

Dresser's health gradually worsened during these years as a result of a series of strokes. Four years after the initial collapse in Washington his condition became grave. At 8:25 A.M. on the morning of Friday, January 20, 1911, eleven days before his sixty-ninth birthday, he died.

"The announcement that the end had finally come was received with much sorrow," the page-one story in the *Era* recorded.

Mr. Dresser was personally a most congenial and friendly man. He was generous and sympathetic. No worthy cause could be allowed to pass unaided if the merits were properly brought to his attention. He was always devoted to the town's welfare—and when it would have been to his financial interest to locate elsewhere, he loyally remained in Bradford. The interest he took in the town was manifested in the immense outlay of money involved in buildings erected here by him.

Funeral services were held in the reception room at Belleview Terrace on Sunday afternoon, and an overflow crowd of some two hundred mourners spilled over into the library, drawing room, and dining room. The Reverend Mr. George M. Hickman of Homestead, Pennsylvania, former pastor at Bradford's First Presbyterian Church, delivered the eulogy. Carl, now attending Princeton University, and Richard, a student at Hill's School in Pottstown, Pennsylvania, returned for the services. Burial was at the Oak Hill Cemetery, and a tall white granite obelisk was placed at the site as a handsome monument. (Dresser's casket and the marker were moved years later to the new Willowdale Cemetery in Bradford.)

Before dying, Dresser had reduced his ownership in the company by nearly 700 shares. Miller held 500 shares; George P. Boothe, 200; Caroline and Robert, one share each; and Dresser, 4,298. Dresser's shares now were redistributed once more. His widow became the company's principal owner with 1,434 shares; the four children received 716 shares each (which Robert added to the one share he already owned, giving him 717 shares); and the number owned by Miller and Boothe remained unchanged. At Caroline's suggestion the directors purchased a single share at its book value of $141.14 from her late husband's estate and presented it to the newly elected secretary and treasurer, Clyde C. Comfort. Aside from Boothe, who seemed more like a member of the family than not, Comfort was the only nonfamily member to hold shares in the company.

Miller became president of the corporation on March 27, 1911, as well as general manager, continuing to be paid $500 a month. Boothe, as plant superintendent, still earned $250 a month, and Comfort was paid $110 monthly as secretary and treasurer. At the same meeting at which the directors set these salaries, they repeated a practice started in 1910 of authorizing bonuses of 10 percent to Miller and 2 percent to Boothe of the annual net profits. At year's end Miller's bonus totaled $3,976, a nice supplement to his $6,000 annual salary, and Boothe earned $795 to accompany his yearly pay of $3,000. The bonuses reflected the year's net profits of $39,767.

Miller indeed proved to be a capable administrator, well liked by the approximately one hundred employees, who privately referred to him as "Chief." He also proved adept at engineering, although he had no special training for it. He had begun to tinker with an improvement for the coupling, seeking to correct the occasional instance in which the rubber wedge that sealed the joint became distorted or wrinkled. This rare defect caused a deterioration of the rubber which in time could affect the joint's tightness. Miller conceived of a method to reinforce the rubber by vulcanizing and embedding into its wedge a thin piece of lead that added a degree of stiffness while remaining soft enough to adapt to the contours required for a perfectly tight joint. He applied for a patent in 1911 and it was granted on July 16, 1912. It was the only patent ever issued to Miller, and it was a singular accomplishment for an executive whose basic talents were not technical.

Miller reminded many people of an English country gentleman. His hobby was owning and working fine hunting dogs, and he showed them formally on many occasions. "No one ever thought of Dad without connecting him with his beloved dogs," his daughter, Mrs. Cornell N. Pfohl, Jr., recalled later. The care and attention he lavished on them caused his wife, Ione, to say laughingly that in the next world she wanted to be one of his dogs. In 1908 Miller and his wife had built a country home just outside Bradford which was the pastoral equal to Dresser's magnificent city house. The Millers' place, Beechwood, was surrounded by a broad expanse of handsomely landscaped grounds.

Dresser couplings undeniably stood preeminent, but the firm did not have a total monopoly. One competitor, the Dayton Pipe Coupling Company of Dayton, Ohio, initiated in 1911 an aggressive advertising campaign in the *Oil and Gas Journal*, the industry's most influential publication. Dayton's "all-steel" coupling was said to be economical and durable, and to provide tight joints permitting perfect expansion. The company also offered clamps, sleeves, split sleeves, saddles, tees, elbows, and crosses, all of which competed with Dresser products.

Until now Dresser advertising had been limited to newspapers and miscellaneous directories published in the Pennsylvania oil country. But the challenge from Dayton was not to be ignored. Two months later Dresser began its own series of advertisements in the *Oil and Gas Journal*. The first full-page advertisement—contrasting with Dayton's three-column advertisement—proclaimed that the word "Dresser" stood for "Quality, Workmanship and Finish." Not to be outdone, Dayton responded two weeks later with its own full-page advertisement. Two weeks later still another coupling manufacturer, W. W. Strickler & Bros. of Columbus, Ohio, entered the advertising war. In a full-page advertisement this company proclaimed that no bolts were required for its "fool proof" coupling. "We can save you money," the firm boasted.

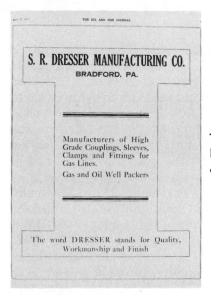

This was the first advertisement placed by Dresser in the *Oil and Gas Journal.* It appeared on April 27, 1911.

The three-way race was short-lived. Before the year ended, Strickler ceased its advertisements entirely. The Dayton Pipe Coupling Company, whose inventory was to be acquired many years later by Dresser when the firm went out of business, continued occasional advertisements until its liquidation. Dresser advertisements, though, came to be a weekly feature, appearing within the first few pages of the *Oil and Gas Journal* for many years. They have been maintained on a regular basis to the present day. The recurring message for these first years was "Dresser stands for Quality, Workmanship and Finish."

The truth of that message was borne out by the company's increasing prosperity. Quarterly dividends increased from 2 to 2½ percent to 4 percent by 1912 of the stated value of the capital stock, and extra dividends as high as 20 percent (or $20 per share) were regularly declared. In 1914 the balance sheet showed a surplus of $400,983.05, and cash on deposit was $102,398. There still were no debts.

When in 1916 secretary and treasurer Clyde C. Comfort died, he was replaced by twenty-five-year-old Carl Dresser. Carl, now graduated from Princeton and a developer of oil properties in the Bradford area, held the position in title only because of his other interests. While still a college student he had become president of his father's gas company in Malta and McConnelsville. That firm still supplied natural gas to the citizens of those two Ohio towns.

Other deaths brought more changes in the Dresser firm. Caroline Dresser died in 1917 and left her stock to Carl and Richard, who thus became the principal shareholders of the S. R. Dresser Manufacturing Company. Richard now held 1,434 shares; Carl, 1,433; Robert,* 717; Ione, 716; and Fred Miller, 500. A few months later still another change of ownership occurred when George P. Boothe died. Boothe willed his 200 shares to his wife and five other family members.

The business itself seemed never to change. Indeed, there appeared to be little need to tamper with this stable, prosperous enterprise. By the time the United States entered World War I— an event that had no noticeable impact on the company—a corps of office and supervisory personnel had developed. J. W. Wick had joined the company in 1896; Frank N. Smith and Nellie Cumiskey, 1903; Charles J. Gregg and W. F. Wolven, 1905; James P. Clark and James Meese, 1906; and James Duggan and M. A. Caverly, 1907. Dependable factory workers, most of them hired to coincide with the opening of the new manufacturing facility, included Joseph Walborn, 1904; Thomas Harlow, Albert Meese, Michael Orlin, and William Sincerney, 1906; and Thomas Hogan, Ernest Meese, Eugene Merkt, Frank and Joseph Pierotti, and Gus Rink, 1907. The closeness of these employees was strengthened by the fact that sometimes two or more members of a single family worked at the plant.

Dresser's location in Bradford was especially convenient, for the Appalachian regions, where natural gas was located most promi-

By 1914 Dresser's *Oil and Gas Journal* advertisements portrayed various styles of couplings.

---

*In 1912 Robert and his wife narrowly escaped one of the great tragedies of the century. They were booked to return from England on the ill-fated *Titanic,* but for some reason had to cancel their reservations.

nently, accounted for almost all coupling sales. However, the Southwest—on the eve of becoming the nation's foremost producer of natural gas—was waking up to its destiny, and by 1918 Dresser couplings had tied together the Lone Star Gas Company's 420-mile system to bring natural gas from West Texas and Oklahoma to Dallas and Fort Worth. Another source of sales was Canada, where nearly 550 miles of pipeline using Dresser couplings had been laid by 1918.

The installation of these increasingly long pipelines for hundreds of miles over mountains and across rivers, forests, and plains was an extraordinarily colorful sight. Brawny, tanned workers wearing overalls and floppy, wide-brimmed hats made the land echo with shouts and laughter as they cleared the right of way, dynamited rocky ledges, dug straight and narrow ditches for the pipe, and secured pipes one to another with couplings. They worked together, ate together, and slept together in makeshift work camps composed usually of canvas tents that were moved from one site to another as the work progressed. Portable wooden flooring and folding cots added a hint of luxury to the tents, which customarily measured fourteen by twenty-eight feet and slept sixteen to eighteen men. A photograph of one work camp for a pipeline from West Virginia to Cumberland, Maryland, showed half a dozen tents in one cluster and some two hundred feet away two other tents occupied by foreign workers. It was believed necessary to isolate the non-Americans. Breakfast and supper were served at camp, and the cook prepared lunches which were carried to the field by the workers. Costs for food and housing were deducted from each worker's pay. One can imagine the typical evening scene: tired, sweaty bodies relaxing with card games, impromptu singing, boisterous conversations, and occasional arguments that inevitably erupt whenever a large group of laboring men are placed in such proximity far away from other diversion.

The workers were divided into specialties: the ditchers, the grading gang, the shooters, and the tong gang. The ditchers' job was to dig a narrow trench, the dimensions varying according to the size of the pipe. A huge, automatic ditching machine was available by 1915 to do the basic trenching, but that did not dismiss the need for a great deal of shoveling by hand. When rock was encountered the shooters, or strikers, employed dynamite to clear the path. Typically, the three or so strikers were assisted by a blacksmith and helper with a portable forge. Not far behind the ditchers came the grading gang, composed of from three to ten men. Their duty was to straighten out, level, and prepare the ditch.

The job of the tong gang was to lay and connect pipe delivered

A twenty-inch Dresser-coupled pipeline is ready to be lowered into a ditch in the World War I era.

with the couplings by mule-drawn wagons and distributed along the ditch. Angle couplings, or ells, permitted the pipeline to make the necessary turns, although sometimes the pipe would be heated over a roaring fire and bent to the desired shape. One of the prime qualities of the Dresser coupling—as opposed especially to threaded pipe—was its ease of installation. A worker needed to know no more than how to tighten bolts, and the only implement needed was a wrench. "Dress 'er up with a Dresser" was a common work phrase. When ten or twelve sections of pipe were connected, they were suspended underneath wooden horses by "snubbing ropes" and lowered at a uniform rate to the bottom of the ditch. Once the line was determined to be leakproof, the ditching gang covered the pipe with the same earth that had been removed. The pipe-laying crew's work thus was completed. After the line was placed in service, however, as a safety measure, continual checks were made by men known as line-walkers who trudged fifteen to twenty miles a day. The presence of a distinctive odor or the discoloration of surrounding vegetation was an obvious sign of a leak. Another technique, effective if dangerous, was to saturate a bundle of rags with kerosene, attach the bundle to a pole, set the rags on fire, and carry this blazing torch directly over the pipeline so that any leaks would reveal themselves with flare-ups. "It is perfectly safe to the employee unless some exceptionally large leaks are met with," the author of the 1915 *Handbook of Natural Gas* wrote.

By 1918 Dresser's basic coupling, the Style 38, had been used on more than nine thousand miles of pipeline in America—a total of some 2,159,000 couplings. The largest number of these, 335,000, had been used on eight-inch lines. Comparative figures for the more expensive insulated couplings are not available, but between 1907 and 1918 a total of 135,000 were sold.

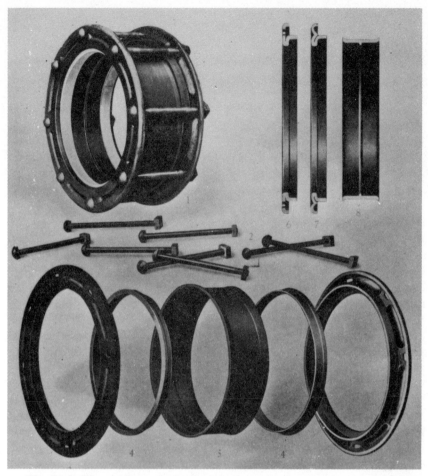

The Style 38 coupling, shown here in its component parts, was the company's best-selling coupling for many years.

In the latter year a new catalogue, illustrated with scenes of pipe laying and of Dresser products, described the company's founder as "the pioneer of the pipe coupling industry," a man who "simplified and made possible the construction of thousands upon thousands of miles of high pressure gas lines." The plant's manufacturing potential was sufficient, the catalogue pointed out, to build "all of the couplings utilized on plain end pipe in the United States and Canada." The familiar packer continued to be advertised, too, but a host of competitors now undersold it.

With such a volume of business it became clear that additional sales help was needed, and in 1919 a new executive, Merrill N. Davis, was hired from B. F. Goodrich Rubber Company to take charge of sales and promotion. A man of persuasive personality,

Davis proved to be invaluable in calling on customers throughout the land. That same year Fred and Ione's son, William Frank Miller, who as a lad had inspired the William Frank Waist Company, became the assistant secretary and treasurer of the company at a salary of $150 a month.

The advertising slogan for the 1920's was "Dresser Couplings Dominate." The claim that "more than seventy-five per cent" of all plain-end pipe was joined with Dresser couplings was modest; a few years later company statistics indicated that the claim should have been at least 90 percent. Advertisements in this decade usually showed close-up photographs of couplings, but sometimes more dramatic approaches were used. One memorable full-page advertisement showed a team of oxen under yoke hauling a load of Dresser couplings through rugged countryside with the caption: "Where the Going Is Rough." The advertising invariably stressed the high quality of the company's products, and frequently there were reminders that the coupling "revolutionized the methods of laying lines for long-distance transportation."

The company's financial statements reflected steady growth throughout the decade. Annual sales reached $1.5 million in 1923, $2.9 million in 1925, and $3.7 million in 1927. Generally from 70 to 80 percent of these sales were to natural gas companies, and almost all the rest to manufactured gas companies. The consolidated balance sheet for January 1, 1924, showed total resources for the first time of more than a million dollars. Four years later that figure had nearly doubled to $1,997,182. The Style 38 coupling, responsible for most of the profits, was being used effectively on natural gas lines, manufactured gas lines, casing head gasoline plants, by-product or coke oven gas lines, acetylene gas lines, vacuum systems, plumber service connections, meter connections, and suction dredge lines. Round-the-clock shifts with the total number of workers approaching four hundred were required at the plant to handle the volume of business.

Meanwhile, a new development in technology was posing a quiet threat to the coupling business—the practice of welding to join pipes. The first practical application of welding had come as early as 1911 when the Philadelphia & Suburban Gas Company used the oxyacetylene method on a one-mile main. In 1925 the Magnolia Gas Company, a subsidiary of the Magnolia Petroleum Company at Dallas, welded a 217-mile line from northwestern Texas and northern Louisiana to Beaumont. This was the first long-distance acetylene welded line, and it was followed by two other lines in Texas of similar length. Still, the coupling remained dominant because of lingering questions concerning the welding's

Ione Dresser Miller was the daughter of Dresser's founder and first president and the wife of the second president, Fred Miller.

durability. What might happen, for example, when hot summers expanded steel pipelines or freezing weather contracted them? Would the joints hold? And if they did, would a 200-mile line be two miles longer at the height of a heat wave? Thus, when the important 340-mile line from the Panhandle of Texas was laid in 1927 to the Denver, Colorado, area, introducing natural gas to that area, it was tied together with Dresser couplings. The line was heralded as an engineering achievement. Miller and the family owners were disquieted by the implications that welding held for their manufacturing enterprise, but as yet they could see no letup in demand for the coupling.

In 1928 Miller became sixty years old. Neither Robert, Carl, nor Richard Dresser had any inclination to take over the family business. Robert, already fifty-three himself, was involved in the manufacture of engines and compressors, and he stayed happily busy with activities as a 32nd-degree Mason and Boy Scout commissioner for Bradford. Richard, now thirty-four, and a Princeton graduate, as was his brother Carl, was an oil producer in the area. Carl, the company secretary, had moved to Tulsa, Oklahoma, where he had set up drilling for oil. He achieved some early successes, but a string of failures soon brought him a local reputation as "the world's greatest dry hole driller."

To raise new capital for further ventures Carl decided to use his stock as collateral for a loan or to sell it. In this mood he contacted in 1928 the prominent New York City investment banking firm of W. A. Harriman & Company, Inc. The Harriman firm, unfamiliar with the Dresser company, sent its own William T. Smith and an auditor from the Arthur Young and Company accounting firm to examine it. Smith, buttressed by the auditor's confirming figures, returned to New York with a glowing report. Buy Carl Dresser's shares, he urged, and if possible buy the entire company.

Carl's willingness to sell and the Harriman firm's eagerness to buy caused the other family members to reassess their situation. There was no family successor to Miller; new, vigorous leadership would be required should welding challenge coupling; the company was flourishing and was now at the peak of its market value; and there was no desire to add outsiders to what always had been a family business. Quite suddenly, the family members agreed to sell all their shares to the Harriman company.

4

New Command in a Troubled Era

W. A. Harriman & Company, Inc., had no intention of buying Dresser to keep. It planned to convert the company from the family business it had been for forty-eight years into a publicly held corporation in which management and ownership were separate. Harriman would serve as underwriter in selling shares to the public, then fade into the background.

The Harriman company had been organized in 1919 as an investment banking house by William Averell and E. Roland Harriman, sons of the famous railroad magnate E. H. Harriman. The company rapidly had become a leader in securities and underwriting. Its New York City office was in the heart of the financial district at 39 Broadway, and it had branch offices in several American cities and even in Berlin. The job of underwriting Dresser fell primarily to Roland Harriman and his former Yale classmate Prescott S. Bush, son-in-law of the firm's president, G. H. Walker.

Their task was not to be a difficult one, for the American public was in an investing mood as never before. The Great Bull Market seemed destined to convert even the lowest common stock into a pot of gold. Dresser itself, if almost entirely unknown to the general public, was a solid company with a dominant position in a growing industry with years and years of consecutive profits and no debts.

The dismantling of the old regime began in earnest on the afternoon of December 10, 1928, in a series of acts accomplished at the Boylston Street offices in Bradford. The script was written by the Harriman firm, but the primary actors had to be the legally authorized directors of Dresser. Those directors present were Fred Miller and the three Dresser sons, Robert, Richard, and Carl. Others there included William Frank Miller, corporation secretary and owner of a single share, and Charles J. Gregg, the assistant general

E. Roland Harriman of W. A. Harriman & Company was instrumental in selecting H. Neil Mallon as president of the newly organized Dresser Manufacturing Company.

manager who served as notary public. As a first step the directors increased the number of authorized shares from 5,000, the figure established in 1905, to 300,000. They similarly enacted a change in capitalization from $500,000 to $1,750,000. Of the new shares, 100,000 were designated as Class A and 200,000 as Class B. Class A shares, soon to be offered on the Curb Exchange (predecessor to the American Stock Exchange) at $48 per share, received preference for dividends.*

The next step in the afternoon script required stockholder approval of the directors' action. This was easily done since directors and stockholders were one and the same. Still another ostensibly distinct meeting was held by the election judges, Fred Miller, Richard Dresser, and Carl Dresser, to certify the validity of the stockholders' vote. At 5 P.M. another meeting of the directors was held to name the Central Union Trust Company of New York as transfer agent and the Farmers Loan and Trust Company as registrar of the newly constituted corporation. The directors also accepted the examination of the company books covering the past five years and ten months by the public accounting firm of Arthur Young and Company. With these necessary steps completed, there

* The Class B shares were held back by Harriman until the spring of 1931, when they joined the Class A shares on the curb. On October 15, 1931, both A and B stock was switched to the New York Stock Exchange.

Prescott Bush, an officer at W. A. Harriman & Company, was one of the persons responsible for transforming Dresser in 1928 from a private to a public firm. Bush then served more than two decades on the board of directors before his election as a U.S. Senator from Connecticut in 1952.

came the resignations of Carl Dresser and Ione Miller from the board and the election of their successors—Merrill N. Davis, whose knowledge and abilities were deemed necessary as a carry-over for the new regime, and Hamilton Pell, who would represent the interests of the Harriman firm.

Two days later the 100,000 shares of Class A stock were issued to a New York City broker for distribution, and on December 14, 1928, a woman from Philadelphia bought ten shares and became the company's first shareholder. She was joined that first day by twenty-six other investors, and three days later by Fred and Ione Miller, Robert Dresser, Richard and Doris Dresser, and a sizable number of other Bradford residents.

A part of the sale agreement had been that Fred Miller would remain with the reorganized company as chairman of the board. His title was to be essentially honorary, for it was understood that he would not exert his influence on a daily basis, but would be available for advice and for important customer contacts. Miller was seen as an important link between old and new. His knowledge and experience at Dresser, as well as his friendships with key customers throughout the gas industry, were assets to be treasured.

The question remained as to his successor in the pivotal position of general manager and president. This was a determination to be made by Harriman. The position required a knowledge of manu-

facturing, salesmanship, accounting, finance, and industrial relations, not to mention psychology and all the other things required
of a successful executive. To take a going concern of some four
hundred employees, to transform a family corporation to fit the very
different situation of a public corporation, and to adapt that corporation to the future without losing the momentum of the past called
for no ordinary man. The conversion of the company already had
begun, but the man who would command it was not in sight.

This was the problem being discussed one day in mid-December
by Roland Harriman, Prescott Bush, and their associate and former
Yale classmate Knight Woolley when a secretary interrupted them.
Neil Mallon, still another Yale classmate, was waiting outside to
see them. Happily surprised, they invited Mallon in at once and
learned from him that he was going home to Cincinnati after a
six-month visit in Europe. He expected to resume his former career
in can manufacturing. As Knight Woolley recalled years later, in
the midst of their lively conversation Harriman suddenly was
seized with inspiration. Pointing to Mallon without explanation, he
exclaimed, "Dresser, Dresser." Here was the president, thrown into
their laps at this crucial moment as if by fate. They must all have
lunch together to discuss the idea. They did, and afterward the still
bewildered but intrigued Mallon was ushered into the office of
Harriman's president, G. H. Walker, for an interview.

One can imagine the skepticism with which the stern Walker
must have viewed this recent European traveler who had happened
to walk into the office that day. Could this jobless, unmarried,
thirty-three-year-old man be the right person to assume the presidency of a company with resources of $2 million and whose busi-
ness he admittedly knew nothing about? Walker began asking
questions.

Henry Neil Mallon, born in Cincinnati on January 11, 1895,
was the eldest son of eight children. His father was a prominent
lawyer who earlier had served as a representative in the Ohio state
legislature and was a trustee of Ohio State University. His grandfather had been a judge in Cincinnati. The family name was a
respected one in Ohio, with a close association with the Tafts. When
Neil Mallon was a child the family had gone to Washington, D.C.,
to visit their good friends President William Howard Taft and his
family in the White House. There, young Mallon saw the first
elevator in his life, and with the other children, including the
President's son Charlie, commenced an afternoon of fun by getting
on and off the elevator, pushing button after button. The result was
a broken elevator. When he was old enough Mallon attended Horace
Taft's preparatory school in Watertown, Connecticut, then enrolled

at Yale in 1913 as his father had done before him. At Yale Mallon excelled in everything. He majored in economics and history but was fascinated even more by his study of physics; he was a star performer on the Yale basketball team and was named to the All-America intercollegiate team; his status as a student of good academic and social standing was affirmed by his selection to the prestigious secret society Skull and Bones. So revered, so secretive was Skull and Bones that no member deigned to utter its name in the presence of nonmembers. Harriman, Bush, Woolley, and Mallon had been fellow members in the society.

Mallon had intended to study law upon graduation in 1917, but World War I interrupted his plans. Instead of law, he went to officers' training school in artillery at Fort Sill, Oklahoma, and then to France with the 11th Field Artillery. He became a major at the age of twenty-three, the youngest to hold that rank in the entire U.S. Army. After the war, he worked briefly in Chicago at Continental Can for 28½ cents an hour, and then as a factory worker at U.S. Can Company in Cincinnati. He worked long hours, learned how to operate every machine in the plant, and soon advanced to department head, to factory manager, and then to general manager. When Continental Can Company bought out U.S. Can in 1928, he decided the time was appropriate to take a long-delayed vacation in Europe. The six weeks he intended to stay became six months. What delayed him were the European Alps. He became an avid alpinist and started checking off peak after peak in an effort to climb all the famous mountains before returning to America.

Some of this Walker managed to learn in his interview, but he primarily wanted to know of Mallon's experience in management. Under prompting, Mallon told how he had conceived and executed a unique policy of scattering carloads of cans on sidetracks throughout the Middle West so they could be available at the precise moment nature dictated the proper time for canning. He also explained how he had redesigned the stamping pattern for cans so that more circular end pieces could be punched from a standard tin sheet. It was a simple step but no one ever had thought of it before, and it brought great savings to U.S. Can.

The upshot of all this was that before this self-assured, soft-spoken, blue-eyed man with a tendency for understatement left the Harriman offices he had been offered the position of president and general manager of the S. R. Dresser Manufacturing Company at a salary of $25,000 a year—far more than he had ever earned. Mallon had never been to Bradford in his life. All that he knew about a coupling was what the Harriman people, who knew not that much more than he, were able to tell him. But he had proven experience as general manager of U.S. Can; his innovations there had caused others in the can business to bid for his services; and there was an air about him that inspired confidence. Thus, despite the unusual circumstances, he was not an unlikely choice. He accepted the position. It would not be official, of course, until the Dresser board of directors could act. Meanwhile, there was time to return to Cincinnati as he had planned and enjoy the Christmas holiday with his parents and brothers and sisters.

This Mallon did. But he also was thinking—inevitably—of the challenge before him. He was acutely aware that Dresser had been a family business for nearly half a century. It had prospered by virtue of superior products, and if sophisticated management skills were instituted, no one could say what heights might be reached. Mallon would need help in this enterprise, men with fresh viewpoints, to act as his lieutenants and inject new energy into the organization. He wanted young men, and to find them he turned to the one place he knew where a training program combined theory and practice, the University of Cincinnati. This institution had developed a unique cooperative program that gave engineering students both theoretical and practical knowledge by alternating classroom study with on-the-job training in industry. Mallon had used many of these "co-op" students at U.S. Can, and they invariably impressed him. He asked for the names of the program's best and most recent cooperative graduates. The most likely name to emerge was that of Rudolph E. Reimer, a spring 1928 graduate in commercial engineering, a major that combined pre-engineering courses with business administration. Reimer, too, was a Cincinnatian and Mallon called him on Christmas Eve. Would he be willing to stop by Mallon's house that evening to discuss a business opportunity?

Reimer already had a job with a local manufacturer of metal products, but he knew of Mallon by reputation, and he was certainly willing to talk. Studious, blond-haired, and a talented tenor who had considered a singing career, Reimer was the son of a German immigrant who had come to Cincinnati from the Frankfort area. The senior Reimer, eldest boy in a family of eight children, came alone to the United States. He worked diligently and saved until he had enough money to pay for the passage of his next eldest brother. Then, together in Cincinnati, the two of them worked until they accumulated enough for the next of the children to come. And so the pattern continued until all eight children were in Cincinnati. Only a brief time passed before the combined resources of the children were enough to pay for the passages of their parents to join them in the United States. When Reimer was one year old, his remarkable father died; and as soon as he was old enough, Reimer joined his two sisters and mother in working to support themselves. Now, on this Christmas Eve, he went to Mallon's home —an outsider in a house full of relatives—and listened to Mallon's suggestion that he leave his native Cincinnati and take an ill-defined job in a small town in northwestern Pennsylvania. As Reimer recalled years later, Mallon confessed to him: "I don't know what kind of place Bradford is; I don't know what a coupling is; I don't know anything about the company; but if it's the kind of company I think it is I'm going to need some help, and I would like for you to come up." Such a proposition was intriguing for an ambitious young man, and Reimer agreed to come to Bradford after the holidays to examine the situation firsthand. Meanwhile, Mallon wanted to know who had been the smartest man in Reimer's graduating class. Why, his friend and former singing partner in a college quartet, Hector P. Boncher, now at Dalton Adding Machine Company in Buffalo, Reimer replied. Reimer agreed to see if Boncher, too, would visit Bradford for an interview. When reached in Buffalo, Boncher readily agreed. He would be delighted to consider joining his friend Reimer in Bradford.

On New Year's Day, 1929, with the mountain air recording a temperature below zero and destined to stay there for another week, Mallon arrived in Bradford by train. "I thought I had landed in the North Pole," he later recalled of the snowy, Christmas-like scene that greeted him.

It had been fifty years earlier, give or take two or three months, that Solomon R. Dresser had moved his drilling rig and family to Bradford. The town now was nearing twenty thousand in population, almost twice as big as when Dresser had come, and most of the "boomtown" elements had disappeared. It was still an oil town, though, and "roughnecks" were readily identifiable up and down Main Street. The passage of time and the infusion of oil money had brought sophistication, too. European travel, the Metropolitan Opera in New York City, and the cultural activities at nearby Chautauqua Lake in New York were taken as a matter of course by the town's many prosperous families. Mallon checked into the rather decrepit Holley Hotel on Main Street, dressed himself warmly, and began walking the streets to see what kind of town this was. His steps carried him past the handsome Dresser office building on Boylston Street and through narrow Patent Alley and past the red-brick warehouse. The Boylston Street office in particular was impressive, but he wondered why the main office should be downtown when the manufacturing facility was several miles away.

Meanwhile, he still was not the president and general manager because the board of directors had not voted. He had not long to wait. On January 3—with Mallon as an invited guest—Fred Miller, Robert and Richard Dresser, and the two new board members, Merrill N. Davis and Hamilton Pell, met to complete the company's reorganization. The changes came in quick succession. Miller resigned as president and general manager and was elected chairman of the board. Mallon was elected his successor as president and general manager at the previously agreed salary of $25,000, the same amount Miller was to be paid. Robert and Richard Dresser resigned as directors, and W. Frank Miller resigned as secretary and treasurer. Five new directors were elected: Mallon and four men whose business knowledge and influence were deemed important: Floyd W. Parsons, editor of *Gas Age Record;* George L. Ohrstrom, president of G. L. Ohrstrom & Company of New York; William V. Griffin, president of Brady Security & Realty Corporation, New York; and William T. Smith, the Harriman man who had recommended Dresser so highly. An executive committee composed of Miller, Mallon, Davis, Pell, and Smith was created and authorized to act between meetings of the board of directors. Mallon had sat through the meeting as a guest; he left as Dresser's new chief executive officer.

Before he could be a capable administrator it was necessary to be a student. For the first days, Mallon spent a great deal of time walking up and down the dirt-floor aisles of the plant. Industrial cars that traveled on ground-floor rails whizzed past him with loads of steel skelp or finished products. Loud, huge machines cut out, curled, and sealed the various components of the coupling with an assortment of strange new noises. Occasionally he paused to shake hands with a worker who might be idle for a moment. It is not difficult to imagine the curious eyes that followed his every step and the attentive ears that strained to catch every casual phrase he uttered. In the first-floor office on Boylston Street, which Miller had vacated for him, there were lists of customers, inventories, incoming bills and outgoing invoices to be studied, and on a broader scale an entire industry to learn from top to bottom. He had to become acquainted with Bradford's leading citizens, frequently over lunch at the Bradford Club, which was conveniently located next door to the Boylston Street office. The club, he learned, was one good reason why the Dresser office had remained on Boylston Street, for this was where Miller and others leisurely dined each day, taking time afterward for a game of cards or pool before returning to the office. Before his first week had ended, Mallon made his first important decision: the Boylston Street-Patent Alley prop-

Merrill Davis, left, and Neil Mallon stroll down the Atlantic City board-walk during a convention of the American Gas Association.

erty must be sold. A new office would be constructed where he thought it properly belonged—next to the plant on Fisher Avenue.

When the new board of directors met for its first session at Harriman's lower Manhattan offices on February 8, Mallon won instant approval of his proposal to sell the downtown property and replace it with an office at the plant. The only stipulation was that the price obtained for the Boylston Street-Patent Alley property must be at least $20,000, and this was hardly a stipulation at all for the property was worth far more than that. Three weeks later, on the last day of February, Mallon was happy to report to the directors that a bid of $73,800 had been received. The directors, meeting again at the Harriman offices, voted to accept the offer. They also authorized Mallon to construct a new office building at an estimated cost of $42,000, and before the year was over they approved Mallon's plan to add a second floor.

Mallon noted happily that there were no shrieks of displeasure in Bradford, no complaints about useless disruption, and, as far as he could tell, no mutterings behind his back alleging foolishness on the part of this johnny-come-lately. In fact, while the news was unexpected, all parties had assumed the inevitability of change. Indeed, the only feeling Mallon could detect was a sense of relief that the new command would not be hesitant in doing what seemed right and necessary.

Meanwhile, on the day after his arrival in Bradford, Mallon had called Reimer and urged him to come immediately to look over the place. Reimer did, and at the end of the day he agreed to take the proffered job. He could report for work in two weeks. "Can't you make it in one?" Mallon asked. Reimer did, and he assumed his duties on January 15. Boncher followed, starting his job a month later. Reimer and Boncher, fast and eager learners, soon were joining Mallon in brainstorming sessions that might occur at any hour or any place—sometimes in the small bungalow Mallon had purchased some six blocks from the plant, sometimes in the room Reimer and Boncher shared in the high-school principal's home, but usually, of course, at the office.

There was an important luxury in these strategy sessions. The S. R. Dresser Manufacturing Company was in unusually sound financial condition. Orders for couplings and related products were flowing in at a record rate, and Mallon's first year as president was destined to be the company's most prosperous up to that time. The company could afford to spend money for virtually any project believed necessary. The last condensed balance sheet, dated January 1, 1928, had listed surplus funds of nearly $1.5 million, $261,847 of which was in cash at the Bradford National Bank. Gross profits for 1929 were to total $1,286,293, significantly better than the $1,014,250 of the preceding year. Moreover, the company's excellent standing in the natural gas industry remained undiminished. Its reputation for integrity and quality of products was high, and the threat of serious competition was remote when one considered the expense involved in initiating a similar manufacturing enterprise on a scale of any kind. One might think that the biggest challenge for the new management would be to safeguard this happy state through an unwillingness to tamper.

Yet—and this was a compliment to the superiority of the Dresser coupling—the family business that had developed over the years was unsophisticated in operations and organization. The bookkeeping system was primitive by any standard. There were no provisions for cost analysis. Outside auditors never had been employed until now, and the customary year-end condensed balance sheets (there were no quarterly or monthly reports) gave the barest of details. No engineering reports were developed on the products, nor were significant tests conducted to check the quality of the finished items or of incoming materials. No system of cost control or inventory control had been developed. Frequent breakdowns in the plant stopped operations for hours. There was practically no automation. The dirt floors certainly were not conducive to optimum work conditions. The company was tied closely to the coupling and

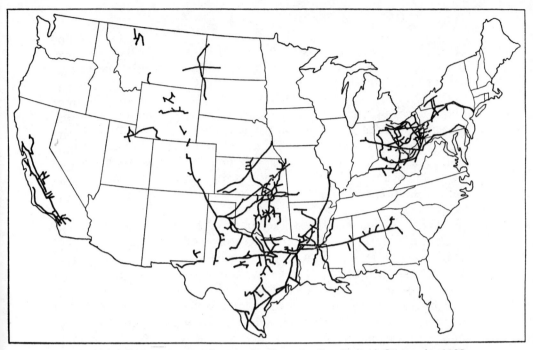

Virtually all these natural gas pipelines in the United States in 1930 were laid with Dresser couplings.

to the related tees, angles, ells, and sleeves. No ongoing research and development program existed, and no plans had been laid to broaden the product lines. Manufacturing capabilities were not sufficient to accommodate all the orders that were arriving during this peak year for construction of high-pressure natural gas pipelines. Moreover, as Mallon was beginning to realize, on the horizon was the threat of welding. There was much to be done, more than Mallon had realized at the beginning.

It was necessary to correct these deficiencies while maintaining the loyalty of the employees and the good faith of the customers, who together had brought the company to its present profitable position. Care had to be taken to alienate no one. Fred Miller was happy as chairman of the board and in his role as a fountain of knowledge who no longer was burdened with reporting to the office and fretting over routine problems. Merrill N. Davis, who had been promoted to the board of directors, continued to do what he did best: calling on customers throughout the nation and keeping the Dresser name prominent in the gas industry. William Frank Miller's resignation as secretary and treasurer had been amicable.

He had not cared to devote the time to the job that it truly demanded; he was financially able to do without the salary; and with a substantial family interest in the Forest Oil Company, he was needed there in an executive capacity. James P. Clark, the aging plant superintendent, continued in that role; Assistant General Manager Charles J. Gregg soon would become a salesman; and long-time Pattern Superintendent Frank N. Smith maintained his position. Thus, rather than displace anyone, the newcomers added a new dimension. From the beginning the citizens of Bradford welcomed them eagerly into their churches, clubs, and civic organizations.

The trio soon was to be joined in its efforts by still a fourth man from Cincinnati, a man who was to develop the engineering program: George H. Pfefferle. Mallon had asked Reimer and Boncher who was the smartest engineer they knew, and they agreed that it was Pfefferle. Pfefferle also was a graduate of the University of Cincinnati's cooperative program, and, like Boncher, he had been working at the Dalton Adding Machine Company, but in Cincinnati. As a member of the 1924 class he was a few years older than Reimer and Boncher, but Boncher especially had come to know him well at Dalton. Pfefferle, too, was agreeable to considering this opportunity, and when he arrived in Bradford for his interview, Mallon told him that Dresser would be emphasizing research and development in the future. The company needed a chief engineer who could take the lead and create new products. Pfefferle accepted this challenge, quit his job in Cincinnati, and in July brought his wife with him to Bradford to begin work.

These, then, were four young men who arrived in Bradford in 1929 to play important roles in reshaping Dresser for the future: Mallon, Reimer, Boncher, and Pfefferle. Every one of them would devote the long careers ahead of them to the company. Mallon was the strategist, the idea man, the philosopher-king who looked to the future. "Beaten paths are for beaten men" was his credo. Reimer and Boncher were the first lieutenants who joined their chief in strategy sessions and saw to it that the ideas were executed. Reimer was the controller, a man with a gift for understanding and interpreting the often cryptic message delivered by a column of figures. His work was the key, Mallon emphasized years later, for the picture it drew of the company pointed the direction for the others. Boncher was the assistant sales manager, the man who—with Merrill Davis busy in the field—handled logistics for a wide-ranging sales force and who created printed materials to tell the Dresser story. Pfefferle brought engineering skills to design new products for the industry and to perform as the laboratory scientist who could say with certainty whether a product would work, and if not, why not.

The overall goal for the company, as it is for all private enterprise, was to increase profits. Three basic plans emerged. The quickest of these was in cutting costs. This was where Reimer, as controller, played an essential role. There had been only one bookkeeper when Mallon arrived. The firm had never prepared more than one statement a year. Reimer, assisted by an Arthur Young and Company accountant for the first two months, instituted a detailed accounting system for the various departments and arranged for the preparation of monthly financial statements. This made it possible for the first time to initiate constraints on unnecessary expenditures, determine which aspects of plant operations were the costliest, develop inventory controls, and systematize purchasing. It became sheer sport to dig out in detail the costs of the various departments and then to explore ways to reduce or eliminate them.

A second way to increase profits was through higher sales. Davis, a superb salesman, was at his best on the road instead

Red-hot flanges for the Dresser couplings were placed in this huge hydraulic press to be shaped properly.

of behind a desk. Consequently, overall sales strategy had been neglected. Boncher, as assistant sales manager, energetically moved to remedy this. One of his specific goals was to find new markets for the existing products. His first area of concentration was the water industry, especially municipal waterworks. Within a few years his work here yielded dramatic results. A second of Boncher's goals pursued with equal fervor was to broaden the geographical base for all sales.

The third key lay in technological advancement, where Pfefferle was the critical man. Several things were possible. Old products could be improved, new products could be devised for diversification, and production techniques could be streamlined. Mallon's greatest hopes for the future centered in the development of innovative products that would break from traditional practices.

None of these approaches could work in isolation from the others. Typical of the cooperation required was the establishment of a new middle ring department in the first year. The need began with a Reimer cost analysis that revealed several things. The department's most substantial expense was for material—a general fact for all the manufacturing processes. This prompted the application of pressure against suppliers for discounts in return for volume. Labor constituted the second greatest expense, and the natural gas required for the hot metal process was third. If the middle rings somehow could be manufactured by a cold process, several beneficial things would happen. As Reimer explained it:

We would save all that cost of gas; we would eliminate expensive furnace repairs and maintenance; we would save the tool and die maintenance—which is also very expensive when you are working with hot metals. . . . Most of all, you were able to increase production substantially if you were working with cold metal instead of hot metal. With cold metal you could pick it up and put it in the machine and take it out by hand. But, if you were working with hot metal— and it was about 2000 degrees—you had to lift the steel with a tong about thirty-six inches long, which was very difficult and tiring. So you not only had a slow process but you had the men exposed to all that physical exertion and heat, which in turn required frequent relief periods.

Pfefferle, working in conjunction with the production department, was given the task of conceiving a way to make the middle ring without heat. Before he had been in Bradford three months, Pfefferle confirmed all that Boncher and Reimer had said of his capabilities, for he presented a plan utilizing a flash welding process that did precisely what was desired. Cost for the conversion, $57,300; savings for a year, $186,950! And this did not include additional savings on natural gas. The directors approved the plan immediately and orders were placed to buy necessary machinery for the conversion.

The board of directors already had allotted $150,000 in August for a "program of factory improvement," for it was obvious that capacity must be increased to accommodate a heavy demand for couplings coinciding with the laying of longer and longer natural gas pipelines. The proposed expenditures included not only additional machinery but also amenities for the employees such as new lockers, heaters, and toilets.

Mallon's intention to stress engineering and research, the value of which was dramatically shown in the creation of the new middle ring department, had been affirmed even before Pfefferle was hired. Another illustration of the emphasis on research was the creation of a metallurgical laboratory. Despite the fact that good steel was a basic need for every Dresser product, there was no quality control program to inspect incoming shipments of the raw product or to test the worthiness of the finished products before shipping. The one experienced engineer associated with Dresser was Plant Superintendent James P. Clark. While Clark had his name on some thirty-five Dresser patents, almost half of the seventy-three taken by the firm during its entire history, he had neither the inclination nor the talent for establishing a good quality control program. Moreover, he was past seventy and his retirement was anticipated.

A crew of pipe layers tightens Dresser couplings, probably on the natural gas line from Amarillo to Denver in the late 1920's.

The man hired for this position was a twenty-eight-year-old Ohioan named Edward P. Torgler. Torgler had learned what constituted a good metallurgical laboratory on his first job with the Youngstown Sheet and Tube Company.

Years later Torgler still vividly recalled his interview with Mallon. He listened to Mallon describe in broad strokes the future he envisioned for Dresser. "The thing that impressed me about the interview was the fact that he [Mallon] was a real young fellow, and ambitious, and he made no bones about it. He wanted to build an industrial empire—he said that." Torgler left Bradford with the distinct impression that he had seen the "opportunity of a lifetime," and to his delight, Mallon soon offered him the job. Torgler found no obstacles in establishing from scratch an excellent metallurgical laboratory, and in the months and years to come, he analyzed the quality of the raw materials shipped to Dresser, drew up rigid specifications that steel and rubber suppliers were required to meet, and introduced an area of research capability into the company.

One of the things Reimer did during the summer of 1929 was to convert a large amount of promissory notes into cash. It had been the custom of many pipeline companies to pay Dresser in notes rather than cash. "We didn't like them," Mallon recalled later, "and we got the companies to pay up. We got full value in cash for all the notes, and from that moment on we didn't take deferred notes." Neither Reimer nor Mallon had any inkling of the depression that was destined to begin within months, but several of the customers owing large sums failed. In Mallon's opinion, this innocent act of converting notes that had been accepted as a matter of course was of critical significance in surviving the troubled depression era.

The interests of the Dresser employees were not ignored during this expansive period. Working conditions improved materially. The dirt floors were filled with concrete, an assembly line was created that simplified their jobs as well as increased productivity, and other improvements were made. In November 1929, a plan was announced to permit employees to become Dresser shareholders. Those who had been at the company for at least one year could purchase Class B shares through regular payroll deductions. The price per share was from $25 to $27.50, depending on the time of purchase. As long as three years could be used to pay for them. The company set aside for this purpose a block of 4,000 shares, purchased from W. A. Harriman & Company.

In their push for reform, Mallon and his aides made occasional misjudgments. In one early endeavor they intensely pressured the

Thousands of couplings were stored outside the Dresser Fisher Avenue plant in the 1920's to be readily available for immediate shipment in case of emergency orders.

local gas company to reduce its rates because of their heavy volume of usage. The gas company resisted, Dresser would not relent, and some ill will resulted. What Mallon and his aides in their zeal did not appreciate was the fact that the gas company was a subsidiary of one of their best and biggest coupling customers. The distinct possibility emerged that this key customer, if alerted to what was happening in Bradford, might take its substantial coupling business elsewhere. Upon becoming aware of the delicate nature of the situation, Mallon hurriedly called on Fred Miller, who stepped in and soothed wounded feelings before further deterioration.

As the fall of 1929 arrived, it was obvious that the conversion of the S. R. Dresser Manufacturing Company from a family business to a publicly held corporation had been achieved without loss in sales. Indeed, the new management team had surprised everyone with its capabilities. These seemed to be glorious days for all of American business as well. On September 3, indicators of prosperity at the New York Stock Exchange reached their all-time high. Within weeks, however, came the Great Crash of '29 and the onset of the severest depression in American history. The panic erupted on Wall Street on October 23 when more than six million shares were traded at great losses and the ticker fell 104 minutes behind. The next day was even worse; blue-chip stocks like Radio Corporation of America plummeted in three hours from 68¾ to 44½ and Montgomery Ward dropped from 83 to 50. Still worse was October 29, when sixteen million shares were traded at enormous losses. In one month's time some $30 billion in capital value disappeared.

The price of Dresser Manufacturing stock on the New York Curb Exchange withstood these relentless forces at first with remarkable resistance. Offered originally at 48, the Class A shares dropped to a low of 32 by year's end. This was disconcerting, but it was not nearly as severe as what happened to so many blue-chip stocks.

Ironically, though, the immediate future for coupling sales remained promising. The year 1929 had been the most prosperous one in the firm's history, with net profits of $903,394. When the board of directors' executive committee met in Bradford on January 13, 1930, Merrill Davis called attention to the large construction programs contemplated for the coming year by the natural gas industry and expressed concern not about the possibility of lagging sales but about the firm's ability to meet demand. One of the long pipelines planned was the better-than-900-mile-long line to be laid during 1930 and 1931 from the enormous natural gas

Dresser's national advertisements in the late 1920's boasted that "Dresser Couplings Dominate."

deposits in the Texas Panhandle to Chicago, a line that would be tied with Dresser couplings. Another mammoth project for 1930 was the 526-mile pipeline that was being built with Dresser couplings alongside the Mississippi River from Louisiana to St. Louis.

Even the $150,000 factory improvement program would not be enough to provide the added manufacturing capabilities believed to be necessary. The executive committee, composed of Mallon, Miller, and Davis, agreed that an additional $100,000 must be budgeted toward factory improvements. When later that month the full board of directors met at the Harriman offices to consider this and other matters, Davis predicted that the volume of business for 1930 would exceed even that of 1929. The request for the additional $100,000 to expand capacity was approved without a dissenting vote.*

Despite the uncertainty of the nation's economic health, Dresser Manufacturing approached the future with guarded optimism. Aside from the depression, however, several obstacles would have to be overcome. For one thing, there was the growing realization that welding posed a real threat to the company's welfare. *Oil and Gas Journal* published in 1929 a 224-page supplement on pipelines, describing the virtues of welding for connecting pipes in no less than five articles. "You couldn't see the *end* of the coupling but you could see the ceiling," Neil Mallon recalled years later. The company campaigned as best it could to counter this emergent competition, speculating for instance that a welded pipeline stretching from Louisiana to St. Louis might expand so much in a summer heat wave that theoretically its end could be ten miles beyond the center of the city! Yet another development caused concern. The nation's pipe mills were beginning to manufacture pipes that were forty feet long instead of the former nineteen to twenty-one feet. This alone would cut coupling sales potential by half. Still another practice being initiated was the installation of composite lines, which alternated welded and coupled joints. The couplings represented a "hedge" of sorts against expansion and contraction problems associated with welded joints. This practice once again potentially reduced by half the market for Dresser couplings.

---

* The full amount of $250,000 included projected expenditures for the following: flash weld department, $73,200; old flange department, $56,000; new flange department, $12,300; small flange department, $15,000; small middle ring department, $21,600; machine shop, $15,900; rolling mill, $3,500; hydraulic system, $7,000; skelp storage, $20,000; arc weld department, $4,500; shipping department, $5,000; lockers, toilets, etc., $5,000.

The strategy that came to be emphasized most prominently by Dresser in facing this competition was a determined effort to expand the product line so that the company's welfare would not be tied inextricably to the coupling. The first decision was that any new product must be related to the gas and oil industries. A venture into a field in which Dresser had little knowledge or background was to be avoided. Two obvious approaches existed. New products could be conceived and developed by Dresser's own engineers or an effort could be made to acquire existing firms that already had an attractive line of products. Both possibilities were accepted as appropriate avenues.

In April, Mallon informed the board of directors that the possibility of mergers with other companies serving the oil and gas industry was being studied to see if such acts might "strengthen the position of the S. R. Dresser Manufacturing Company and be of benefit to its stockholders." Preliminary discussions already had begun with one oil-well equipment manufacturer, the Parkersburg Rig and Reel Company of Parkersburg, West Virginia. This merger did not materialize, but the idea persisted.

Before the year ended, more serious negotiations were under way with a rapidly growing manufacturer of valves for the gas, oil, and chemical industries: Merco-Nordstrom Valve Company of Oakland, California. The company's best product was a lubricated plug valve, which, like the Dresser coupling, was noted for its ease of operation and exceptional tightness. The valve was protected by patent, and the firm had resisted successfully all attempts to break it. From 1925 to 1930 Merco-Nordstrom had escalated in net worth from $548,000 to $2,300,000. Its sales offices were in fifteen major cities throughout the nation; its California plant was equipped with modern equipment; its future prospects appeared exceptionally bright; and its valve was most compatible with the Dresser line. Particularly attractive was Merco-Nordstrom's recent growth in profits. Between 1926 and 1930, net profits had increased from $144,483 to $669,784; Dresser's net profits, by contrast, had climbed less dramatically those years from $550,226 to $923,629.

Mallon and the valve company's president, C. C. Broadwater, traded visits at their plants on opposite sides of the continent, and by April 21 they had agreed to a merger based upon an exchange of shares. This presented no problems for Merco-Nordstrom, for the firm's dominant owners, the Broadwater and Merrill families, enthusiastically approved of it. Dresser's board of directors also favored the merger, and on April 21 they unanimously recommended that the stockholders approve it.

Merrill Davis was the congenial vice president in charge of sales for Dresser during the 1920's and 1930's. (Photo courtesy of Mrs. Tom Servatius)

Dresser officials would head the new company under its new name of Dresser-Nordstrom, Inc. Fred Miller was to be chairman of the board; Mallon, president; and Merrill Davis, vice president.

From all outward appearances the merger was certain to become a reality. Yet, one disconcerting element existed. Merco-Nordstrom had brought suit against another valve company, alleging violation of the patent protecting its lubricated valve. Such suits had become almost routine for Merco-Nordstrom, and under the guidance of its skillful attorney, not a case had been lost. As Dresser's board of directors began gathering in New York City in mid-May, the patent case was pending in federal court. By the time the board met in May in the offices of Brown Brothers Harriman & Company,* an unexpected tragedy had cast a cloud over what had been anticipated to be another in a string of successful patent cases. Merco-Nordstrom's chief attorney, the man who had been so successful in safeguarding the patent, had died suddenly of a heart attack.

Dresser's directors now were filled with doubt. What might happen to the patent? If the patent's validity were not upheld in the pending case, they feared that competitors would be free to enter the lubricated valve market and would destroy Merco-Nordstrom's dominant position. Mallon, still keen on the acquisi-

* W. A. Harriman & Co. merged with Brown Brothers & Co. on January 1, 1931.

tion, contended that even if the patent case were lost the company's established position in the field could not be overtaken. But the pessimistic view prevailed, and the directors voted to abandon the plan. Merco-Nordstrom eventually did lose the patent case. But the effect of the courtroom loss, just as Mallon had argued, did not deter the company from continuing to chart steady gains in profits, and many years later Mallon believed that the failure to merge with Merco-Nordstrom was one of Dresser's most significant errors of the decade.

Meanwhile, the year 1930 signaled a time for celebration. The S. R. Dresser Manufacturing Company observed its fiftieth anniversary. To commemorate the occasion Boncher prepared a sixteen-page illustrated booklet entitled "Half Century of Progress, 1880–1930." In it he gave a brief history of the company with descriptions of its present operations, key personnel, and products. Several salient facts emerged concerning the modernization of the company. Perhaps the most striking was that by August 1, 1930, the plant had nearly three times the production capacity of 1929. The work force had climbed from four hundred to five hundred, and the nearly 1,500,000 Dresser couplings manufactured in 1929 were enough to lay between seven thousand and ten thousand miles of pipe.

Another impressive publication, also prepared under Boncher's supervision, appeared in 1930. This was an attractive, lavishly illustrated 102-page catalogue. It included a succinct description of Dresser's manufacturing operations and physical facilities:

> The plants . . . cover a ground space of approximately forty acres and have a floor area in excess of 300,000 square feet. Although described as one there are, in reality, three complete plants in this ensemble. It is operated with the unit system of production, so that at one and the same time there may be long, uninterrupted runs of a number of different sizes. Several units are reserved for the production of special sizes, short runs for small orders and emergency cases, and for the production of couplings and sleeves for the maintenance of warehouse stocks of standard sizes.

> Large departments have been built up and are maintained for the production of certain specialties, such as our Welded Steel Split Sleeve Department, our Clamp Department, Packing Department, etc.

One of the catalogue's themes was the broad acceptance of the coupling by the water industry. A full-page photograph showed one of two Dresser-coupled water lines crossing Colorado's Pikes Peak.

Promotion of the Dresser packer, the product with the cap rubber trademark which had been used to found the company, was limited to two pages. The patent's expiration had made the packer vulnerable to competition, and, as the catalogue noted, competitors were "underselling our prices by running out the metal parts on a price basis and using the inferior quality of rubber." Within the next few years, production of the packer ceased altogether; it had served well, but its useful role for the company had expired for the moment.*

In December it became apparent that profits for the year, as expected, would exceed those of 1929. The board of directors voted a $7,500 bonus to Mallon and another $10,000 to be distributed as he saw fit to those in the organization who had been responsible for the favorable results. Year-end figures soon revealed that the company earned net profits of $923,629, an increase of some $20,000 over the previous year. Other figures confirmed the company's prosperity in contrast to the depressed national economy. Assets of $2,418,048 contrasted sharply with the $203,600 liabilities, providing an outstanding assets to liabilities ratio of 12–1. Sharing in this prosperity were the 1,269 individuals who constituted the ownership of the S. R. Dresser Manufacturing Company, a fourfold increase since January.

The surprise ending to the proposed merger with Merco-Nordstrom had not deterred Mallon from his goal of seeking new products. To determine the best opportunities, a survey was taken to see where the greatest amount of money was spent in pipeline construction. The pipe itself turned out to be the greatest expense; next were the compressors needed to transport the gas through pipelines; and only toward the bottom of the list did couplings appear. A pipeline that might use $1 million in couplings would use compressors valued at perhaps $20 million. Why not enter the compressor market?

In this era of transcontinental pipelines one thing was apparent to knowledgeable people: present compressor technology was outmoded. Pipelines, which had taken quantum jumps in length, logically needed more powerful compressors to push the gas farther. They had not been forthcoming. Yet, advancements in the automobile, airplane, and marine engine industries, especially in valve improvement, made it likely that certain of these concepts could be borrowed for more economical, smaller, lighter, and higher-speed compressors. Such compressors might cost no more than 60

---

* Some years later the packer once again emerged as a Dresser product when the company acquired Security Engineering Company, Inc., in November 1945.

to 70 percent of existing equipment, yet offer higher performance. The first manufacturer of such a unit could be assured a significant percentage of this lucrative market.

This was the sort of challenge Neil Mallon relished. Dresser Manufacturing had absolutely no experience in designing compressors. But its management and engineers lacked neither ambition nor the capital for such an undertaking. Early in 1931 the company quietly began to consider the possibility of designing and manufacturing a compressor that would depart radically from the models then in use.

A prominent gas engineer named Howell C. Cooper from the Hope Natural Gas Company of Pittsburgh had planted and promoted with Dresser the idea of a radical engine and compressor. Following the pattern set by airplane engines, such a machine would mount cylinders radially around a shaft instead of horizontally. A unit of this type should require less space, be lighter, less expensive, and yet be more powerful. Could it capture the lead in the market? Cooper certainly thought so, and he was the recognized leading engineer in the natural gas industry.

Mallon and Pfefferle went to Pittsburgh in May 1931 to discuss the idea with Cooper and other engineers, and a commitment was made to begin work toward what at first was called the Howell Highspeed Compressor. In the regular meetings that followed over the next months, various members of the team submitted proposals and designs for discussion and evaluation in an effort to reach a consensus.

By August some $10,000 had been spent on this "experimental account." At this point Mallon briefed the directors and gained their wholehearted support for the project. They agreed, as the minutes read, "that this work should be pushed rapidly to a point where actual construction of these machines would begin." Three weeks later Mallon presented a more detailed report and recommended that $40,000 be allocated "to complete and perfect one unit prior to the first of January, 1932." He pointed to annual profit possibilities ranging from $50,000 to $400,000 even in the face of continuing depression. His recommendation won unanimous approval. Here was a project to carry Dresser forward into the future.

Meanwhile, a serious threat to the continued sale of couplings in the Canadian market had arisen. A movement had developed to support home industry and to reduce Canada's dependency on imports. The Canadian Parliament began enacting tariff laws to protect Canada's home industries, and Dresser's Canadian customers observed that they could continue to use Dresser products only if they were manufactured in their country. Something clearly had to be done to protect this market, and the assignment was given to Boncher.

Building a new Canadian manufacturing facility was too expensive to consider, but an alternative emerged: the creation there of an assembly plant. Certain parts of the coupling and related products—bolts, rubber gaskets, and malleable iron castings— could be purchased from Canadian manufacturers according to specification. The steel middle rings and flanges, produced in Bradford by special equipment, could be shipped to Canada to be assembled with the other parts. The resulting product thus would satisfy the nationalistic movement. Boncher was given the assignment of setting up such an operation. This he did, gaining the participation of responsible Canadians to oversee operations there. As a fillip he persuaded Canadian government officials to lower the tariff on parts shipped from Bradford to Canada.

On September 24, 1931, the Dresser Manufacturing Company, Limited, located in Toronto and incorporated under the laws of the Dominion of Canada as Dresser's wholly owned subsidiary, came into existence. In the years to come, its operations, never big, proved entirely satisfactory. Dresser's next foreign venture would not materialize for many years, but the Canadian enterprise was the pioneer step in the kind of international activity that would become an integral part of the company's operations. It proved to be the type of agreement with private enterprise in other nations that would serve the company well in the years after World War II.

When 1931 ended, the much anticipated radial engine and compressor still was not completed. Nor was it anywhere near being finished. Mallon's annual message to the stockholders exuded optimism over the project. He referred to "an investment in the design of a new power unit, which will require the greater part of 1932 to perfect and, if successful, will constitute a real contribution to the transportation of gases through pipe lines."

The decline in the nation's economy by now had become evident in Dresser's earnings, which dropped from the record high in 1930 of $923,629 to $691,787 in 1931. Thus, there was a greater urgency than ever for identifying opportunities for strengthening the company.

Meanwhile, a surprise letter from an official of a French orphanage brightened one day. We have an unusually large number of children and a great need for furniture, the official said. Could you please send us any used dressers you might have? Having no used "dressers," Mallon sent a contribution and continued to do so for a number of years.

5

Preparing
for the future

By mid-1932 it was evident almost everywhere that the "great to-boggan-slide" held little hope of upturn. As many as fifteen million Americans were estimated to be out of work, and Frederick Lewis Allen reported that in New York's Park Avenue district a man might be asked for money four or five times in a ten-block walk. The *New York Times*'s Index of Business Activity had dropped to almost half its 1929 high. Many of the previous decade's most spectacularly successful corporations, such as Radio Corporation of America, whose stock had plummeted from 101 to 2½, were floundering. Public confidence in the nation's financial system and its leaders was at low ebb. More than three thousand banks already had failed. In Iowa once prosperous farmers barricaded highways and smashed windshields and punctured tires with pitchforks to keep milk from the markets and raise the prices. In the nation's capital a dour-faced Herbert Hoover struggled to balance the federal budget and to bring order out of chaos, but his basically traditional policies were as yet ineffective. As if he needed a reminder of the nation's troubles, a "Bonus Army" of jobless World War I veterans set up a shantytown near the Capitol building to demand early payment of a promised bonus. Meanwhile, the Democrats met in Chicago in June and nominated as their presidential candidate New York Governor Franklin Delano Roosevelt, described by Walter Lippmann as "a pleasant man who, without any important qualifications for the office, would very much like to be President."

In these anxious times, one of the most disturbing periods in the nation's economic history, the S. R. Dresser Manufacturing Company was reported by Neil Mallon at the end of 1931 as being in a "very strong financial position with the largest cash balance in its history." Current assets of $2.2 million were more than seventeen times the current liabilities of $129,943, and $1.2 million in cash was on hand or in the bank. Profits of $693,151 represented a 25 percent decline from the previous record year, but considering the general economy, this inspired smiles at Dresser.

Activity in the plant continued to be brisk even if it had declined from the record years of 1929 and 1930. Tonnage in recent years totaled 21,000-plus in 1927, 1928, and 1931, while tonnage in the peak years of 1929 and 1930 had been 29,138 and 27,597 respectively.

The Great Crash had not immediately affected the price of Dresser's stock, for the company's Class A shares reached in 1930 a high of 56⅞, an improvement of eight points over the boom days even of 1929. The price since had fallen by more than half, but this was not so discouraging when compared to the huge declines of so many bigger, better known, and more glamorous companies.

Despite its relative vitality, Dresser could not continue to stand alone as an island of prosperity, and the effects of the depression soon became all too evident. The inevitable decline of activity in the natural gas industry obviously was affecting sales despite encouraging efforts to broaden the market for the company's products into other fields. This became especially apparent in early 1932 when sales manager Merrill N. Davis predicted "a rather slow start" for the first quarter. The truth of his prediction was evident by spring. Mallon advised the board of directors that April sales were lower than in recent history and that fewer and fewer orders were coming in. Profits for the first four months were only $45,000. The situation called for a reduction in dividends, and the board voted to cut the Class A stock dividend from $3.50 annually to $3 and to omit entirely the dividend for Class B stock.

For the remainder of the year, business grew worse instead of better. The annual financial statement for 1932 reflected the lowest earnings on record since incorporation in 1905. The best that could be said was that the record was maintained of never having failed to make an annual profit—at least for the period in which records were available. The net profit of $11,621 was a pitiful sum, however, compared to the nearly $1 million earnings in 1930. Production for the year took a correspondingly shocking drop, the 7,491 tons of goods being one-third the total for 1931. This alarmingly low production level was destined to be repeated for the next several years. All these declining figures were reflected by a precipitous drop in the price of Dresser's Class A stock, which fell during 1932 momentarily to 5. Class B stock, which had sold in 1930 for as high as 44⅞, sold at the end of the year for 1⅝ when tax losses were being established by many shareholders. Still, the company's cash position remained strong. The bank balance at year's end was more than $1 million in excess of liabilities, and the ratio of current assets to liabilities was 66 to 1. The stock actually was selling for substantially less than the company had in cash or in the bank.

The advent of 1933—those last days of the Hoover administration when the picture darkened as never before—brought no better news for Dresser. For the first four months of operation the company lost approximately $8,000. The figures were more than mere statistics; they reflected very real and personal misfortune. For one thing, one out of every five Dresser employees was laid off, the work force being reduced by January 15, 1932, from 400 to 320 with further layoffs ahead. Jobs were eliminated across the board, not just in the factory. A high-salaried works manager, hired earlier to modernize operations, was one of the first to go. His duties were turned over to Reimer, who drew no extra compensation for the added duties. The advertising manager also was terminated. Boncher assumed his job in addition to his own, also at no extra pay. The purchasing agent also lost his job. Reimer added those duties as well to his growing list of responsibilities, and in 1932 he became treasurer as well. The practice of combining what had been several jobs into one became a common economy measure.

In retrospect it seems obvious that here was a company facing ultimate collapse. Its fine cash balance could not hold up indefinitely. To compound the trauma of depression was the fact of welding and a concomitant vanishing of the coupling market. Yet, Dresser not only was destined to survive these years, it would emerge from the depression in a stronger position than ever. How this came about represents a textbook case of farsighted management.

In the prosperous days of 1929 and 1930 the new management team had set a pattern of cost-cutting. Now made all the more imperative, the program continued with new vigor in several ways. One notable example was in the area of purchasing. Some 90 percent of the basic materials used in manufacturing consisted of steel, bolts, rubber gaskets, and malleable castings. Reimer, acting in his capacity as purchasing agent, adopted the practice of requesting bids on orders of especially large volume, then playing one bid off the other for an even lower price. This practice was successful for several years until the major suppliers worked out their own agreements about minimum prices for Dresser.

The reduction in the work force already has been cited, and

This breadline in the Bowery symbolized the profound effect of the depression on the United States and on private industry.

those employees who were fortunate enough to hold their jobs earned less money. A general pay reduction of 20 percent was enacted on May 1 for all salaried employees. The rate of pay for factory workers was maintained, but their take-home pay already was less because they were working fewer hours. Fred Miller, who had been drawing $25,000 annually, voluntarily reduced his salary by the same percentage to $20,000, and a few days later all elective officers agreed to the same reduction. This lowered Mallon's annual salary to $20,000 and Davis's to $14,400. Miller took in effect a double reduction, for his salary dropped another 20 percent to $16,000. In still another economy move the advertisements that had been appearing weekly in *Oil and Gas Journal* now were limited to every other issue.

In such hard times one bonanza for the employees was a company store that offered staple food items at discount prices. Employees, including those who had been laid off, could charge groceries to their future earnings. The amount of credit permitted was based on the size of the family—the more members, the greater the credit. Two Dresser employees had full-time assignments of managing the store. A worker could drop off a list of groceries in the morning and pick the order up at the end of the day, already sacked and ready to carry home. By 1935 a few employees with big families had run up bills as high as $5,000 or $6,000, which they were paying off at the rate of 5 percent from each paycheck. Finally, in the late 1930's, the company wrote off all such debts.

As for profit-making activities, Boncher's Canadian plant earned money in its first full year of operation, and his efforts to expand the market for Dresser products also met with marked success. Sales to the water industry increased in 1932 over the previous year by 100 percent. And if the sale of couplings declined because of the postponement of new natural gas lines and the advent of welding, the sale of repair items for older lines increased substantially. Perhaps the greatest sign of faith—as well as courage—for the future lay in the continuing enlargement of sums devoted to research and development. Funds earmarked for research and development in 1931 were $65,531, twice that of any previous year. In 1932 the amount was reduced to $33,817, but the following year it jumped again to a new high of $76,990. All this money did not go toward the new gas engine and compressor. One notable achievement was the design of a line of boltless compression fittings that was well received by industry.

Unhappily, the project on which so much hope had been placed for great new profits in the thirties, the radial engine and compressor, continued to lag. Having missed the original January 1, 1932, target date, the ensuing announcement that the unit should be ready for display by October 1 was no more accurate, for when that day arrived the engine-compressor was nowhere near completion. Mallon's letter to the stockholders in January 1933 for the first time exhibited more caution: he stated simply that the unit was "still in the process of development."

Unforeseen complications seemed to arise every day to thwart this ambitious project. Naturally, expenses also mounted. By mid-1933 authorized expenditures had reached $100,000. Mallon told the directors that despite the slow progress, natural gas engineers who were advising and cooperating on the project, such as Howell Cooper, were more enthusiastic than ever. New potential uses in the oil and gas industries for the unit seemed constantly arising.

The central problem with the radial unit was its greatest advantage—its pathbreaking nature. Orderly progression in technology generally required a series of intermediate steps before a distant goal could be reached. This unit was aiming to skip those steps. It was to generate 1,250 rpm as opposed to the conventional 250 rpm, and with this fivefold increase the machine was to be smaller

When a water line cut across a slope of Pikes Peak in Colorado in the 1930's it bore the unmistakable stamp of Dresser couplings.

and lighter than existing units. Parts customarily used on standard-model compressors were not generally adaptable for the radial unit. When a spark plug was needed, it was discovered that none existed to satisfy the new specifications. Two options existed: pay an engineering firm from $50,000 to $75,000 to develop a special spark plug or attempt to build it to specifications in the Dresser laboratory. In this instance the very difficult latter course was chosen. Another problem lay in finding a steel durable enough for the valves, which would be operated at speeds higher than ever before for a compressor. Elaborate experiments were conducted to test various kinds of steel at these speeds, and inevitably the tests took longer than anticipated. In essence, nothing could be "bought off the shelf" for the radial engine and compressor; its unique components had to be developed from scratch.

Delayed in their pursuit of the radial engine and compressor and its substantial profit potential, discouraged by a stubborn economy that had made severe inroads on the corporation's annual profits, and yet comfortably situated with large cash reserves, Dresser officials began in 1933 to think once more of a merger or acquisition. They had decided already that their expansionary activities should be designed to promote the growth of the natural gas industry. In that spirit Pfefferle had been supervising research toward the development of a gas-fired unit heater for industrial plants that could replace the dominant but expensive and cumbersome steam units. Efforts to develop such a unit had been hampered by difficulty in finding a proper material for the heat-transfer

The ambitious project on which Dresser placed great hope in the 1930's was the radial engine and compressor, a powerful unit in a relatively small package.

unit. Once again, the research department was venturing into a field in which it had no experience and could learn only from its own mistakes. Obviously, a company already involved in the heating business would be better equipped for such work, and in the spring of 1933 word was received that the well-known Bryant Heater and Manufacturing Company of Cleveland, Ohio, a pioneer in the gas heating field, was having severe financial problems. The depression and seasonal fluctuations in sales had sorely pressed its management's capabilities. Bryant was indebted for more than $257,000; it was entirely without working capital; and a receivership was imminent. The company had sustained a net loss of $183,-614 during 1932, and its losses early in 1933 continued at approximately the same disastrous rate.

Bryant's financial difficulties stemmed largely from its practice of accepting notes from dealers to pay for the heating units. The home building industry had suffered severely from the depression, heaters were not selling, and many dealers were unable to pay. The Union Trust Company of Cleveland, to whom Bryant had endorsed its dealer notes, was experiencing financial problems of its own, and it needed Bryant's money. Consequently, the company was squeezed from both sides. Unless help arrived, its assets were destined to be sold.

The company could be purchased at an obvious bargain in this distress situation, and there was much to commend that action. Bryant had been founded in 1908 by a team of engineers who developed the world's first gas-fired boiler for homes. In the intervening years it had established itself as the preeminent manufacturer and distributor of gas-heating equipment. Its well-known slogan, "Let the Pup Be Your Furnace Man," accompanied by the illustration of a friendly little Boston terrier that was a good match for the more famous RCA Victor dog, signified the carefree heating comfort made possible through the company's gas units.

The acquisition of Bryant would mean Dresser's entry into the unfamiliar arena of retail sales in which extensive mass-media advertising directed to millions of consumers was important to success. But Bryant would extend Dresser's sphere in the natural gas industry by a significant step—all the way from the pipeline to inside the home itself where the gas reached an ultimate destiny. Moreover, this business would broaden the company line beyond the coupling and related products, a very necessary step, since the days of total reliance on these seemed near an end.

Mallon briefed his directors on these facts on May 22, and they immediately agreed to pursue the matter. He was authorized to offer $65,000 to Union Trust in return for Bryant's outstanding notes in the amount of $257,000. Additionally, Bryant's stockholders could be given $110,000 of preferred stock in the newly organized company for the common stock of the old company. Dresser would own all the common stock in the new company in return for its commitment to supply the working capital to keep the company in operation.

Four days later Bryant stockholders, considering alternate offers for less money, voted their approval of the Dresser plan. On July 1, 1933, the acquisition became official. The purchase price of $65,000 was truly a bargain, for Bryant had current assets of $82,363 and total assets of $134,624.

Not being gifted with the art of prophecy, company officials could not know absolutely that this failing company could be rescued. But they felt confident that Dresser's healthy financial position would enable them to survive the temporary setbacks brought by the depression. And, indeed, in the next several years Dresser collected more than enough from the $257,000 in outstanding notes to replace the $65,000 in cash.

Meanwhile, what steps should be taken to revive this struggling company and join it to the Dresser family? Should it be dissolved and integrated into the Bradford company? Or should it be maintained as a separate but wholly owned subsidiary? The latter course was chosen. Bryant's long and favorable reputation and the goodwill of its employees and customers were deemed well worth preserving. Dresser's imprimatur would mean for Byrant a comfortable margin in financial reserves, an immediate commitment to a solid program of research and development, the transfer of power to a new Dresser-dominated board of directors, and the institution of an accounting system compatible with that of the parent company. In the last regard, Reimer began spending some three-fourths of his time at Bryant, familiarizing himself generally with Bryant operations as well as installing the new accounting system. As would become the practice in future acquisitions, Dresser installed its own controller* but otherwise generally left Bryant management alone. Lyle C. Harvey, former sales manager, became the company president shortly after the acquisition. He was to hold that position for as long as Bryant remained a part of Dresser.

The same twin goals pursued by Dresser—cost-cutting and the development of new products—were set for Bryant. Dresser's experimental work on the gas-fired heater for industrial use was transferred to Bryant, where engineers soon developed this product. With the parent company's prompting and financial backing, Bryant's engineers began creating other products to add to the line: a gas furnace, a water heater, a conversion burner, a steel furnace, and space heaters. Of special importance was the effort to design a gas-fired air-conditioning unit. No one as yet had been able to introduce one to the market despite a persistent clamor from natural gas companies. Eventually, Bryant developed a unit, but it was plagued with problems and finally was sold to Servel, where it was further developed. All the new products were envisioned as capitalizing on the recent dramatic growth of the natural gas industry and the expected resumption of that growth whenever the depression eased.

* He was Phil Scott, who had been assistant controller at Bradford and was another University of Cincinnati cooperative training graduate.

Among the novel uses of the Dresser coupling was this one: tying a fuel line in 1931 to the *Graf Zeppelin.*

Meanwhile, in Bradford the radial engine and compressor was costing more money and bringing disappointments. By early 1934 the first experimental model, two years delayed, was ready for operation; but it failed to function satisfactorily, and changes were deemed necessary in the valve construction. Dutifully, the directors authorized additional expenditures of up to $125,000. The news in March, as reflected by Merrill Davis's minutes of the directors' meeting, seemed better:

> The time has now arrived when the final completion date of the gas engine and compressor is actually in sight. Machine No. 1, which has borne the burden of testing and experimental load, is being redesigned. The result will be Machine No. 2, which will incorporate, not only the mechanical and engineering improvements indicated to be necessary by recent tests, but will take on a finished outward appearance, as well. This second machine should be ready for field trial by the end of the summer, thus putting us in a position to accept a few trial orders for additional machines before the next season of maximum gas demand.

However, the two units were not ready for operation until November 1935. The No. 1 engine was connected to an electric generator in the Dresser plant, developing more than 600 horsepower and performing satisfactorily. Better yet, the No. 2 engine was in the field at Lawrenceville, New York, pumping gas continuously into the Syracuse pipeline. These preliminary results were encouraging but not conclusive, and the directors authorized still additional expenditures to bring the total to $250,000. Part of these funds went to streamline the machine's ungainly appearance. Noted industrial designer Walter Dorwin Teague was hired for this purpose. Teague transformed the machine's external image from what one publication called a "confusion of pipes and joints" into a sleek unit encased in steel. Photographs reproduced in *Business Week* and the *New York Herald Tribune* showed before and after appearances. Meanwhile, the directors were told that the gas industry's interest continued to be aroused.

In April, Mallon told the directors of "continuing difficulties" concerning lubrication and vibration. The New York State Natural Gas Corporation, watching the machine at Lawrenceville with the idea of buying one, lost interest. Dresser's total expenses had reached $260,000, and costs were continuing at the rate of $10,000 to $12,000 a month. It was time, the directors agreed, to obtain an objective study from an outside source to see if the radial engine and compressor truly was feasible.

Mallon promptly hired the Detroit consultant and management engineering firm of A. J. Brandt, Inc., to evaluate the project. Within a month Brandt submitted a twelve-page analysis. To the relief of all, Brandt concluded that the project definitely was worthy of pursuit. "Had the Dresser company asked our opinion before starting such a development program four or five years ago," Brandt wrote, "we probably would have advised against it because the type of work is so radically different from that in which your company is regularly engaged. However, you have spent considerable time and money in bringing this development forward and we do not believe that it should be dropped." Two situations, Brandt pointed out, needed to be remedied: (1) Dresser did not have enough engineers with experience in compressors, and (2) production facilities in the Bradford plant were inadequate for the ambitious task. He suggested that Dresser resolve these problems and move ahead with all speed. "This job should be completed quickly and production started in order that you may gain two or three years' start on competition. With such a start and the right kind of organization to continue the development of better and more advanced designs there is no question in our mind but that this can be made a very profitable venture." Mallon sent copies of the report to the ten other directors, and in July they approved an additional $100,000 to construct two or three new units.

As recommended, the company began seeking a more experienced team of compressor engineers and a better facility for production work. They had not far to look. One of the nation's leading engine and compressor manufacturers was located some twenty miles away just over the mountain ridge and the state line at Olean, New York. The firm was Clark Bros. Company, the enterprise founded in the same year as Dresser by William P. and Charles Clark in Belmont, New York, and which had moved to Olean in

Clark Bros. huge manufacturing facility, shown here in midwinter prior to its acquisition by Dresser, employed more workers than any other business in the town of Olean, New York.

1912 after a fire swept through their plant.* In the years since its founding the company had converted from making sawmill and farming implements to designing and manufacturing a varied line of engines and compressors for the area's oil and gas industries. Clark Bros. and its new president, Cornell engineering graduate C. Paul Clark, son of cofounder Charles Clark, naturally had their own ideas about compressors. Presumably, Dresser's new compressor would be in competition with their own units. Nevertheless, Clark needed the business and was happy to work with Dresser on the project, though skeptical about its practicality.

Before 1936 ended, success seemed at hand. The Columbia Gas & Electric Company agreed to buy one of the radial units for its Sugar Grove, Ohio, field. The moment seemed appropriate for a serious effort to market this new product. A handsome two-color brochure entitled "Dresser Presents an Engineering Achievement!" boasted of "the beginning of a new development in the economics of gas transportation." Dresser's radial gas engine and compressor, fourteen feet long, seven feet wide, and seven feet high, was said to offer greater horsepower per unit of space and greater horsepower per unit of cost because of its innovative design. The com-

* The founding of Clark Bros. Company is described in Chapter 1, p. 26.

pany seemed on the verge of the long-awaited technological and marketing breakthrough.*

_____

While much attention was focused on the profit potential of the radial engine and compressor, Dresser was making steady if undramatic progress in its efforts to combat the depression. Production figures for the Bradford plant told the story. From a low of 6,597 tons of finished goods in 1933, production had increased steadily from 7,608 tons in 1934 to 8,732 in 1935 and to 13,568 in 1936. Yet, the 1936 figure was not even half that of the peak year of 1929. The number of employees also had begun to rise, up from 246 at the beginning of 1935 to 305 by the end of the next year. Net profits for those years climbed accordingly, totaling $45,606 in 1933, $96,308 in 1934, $140,679 in 1935, and $426,841 in 1936. Of the 1936 profits, Dresser in Bradford contributed approximately 61 percent; Bryant, 35 percent; and the Canadian operation, 4 percent.

These figures reflected remarkable strength in the face of the depression and the reduced market for couplings. The emphasis on cost-cutting and the development of new products and markets had served the company well. As an example, an important milestone occurred in 1935 when an eighty-five-mile-long oil pipeline was joined entirely by Dresser couplings. It was the first time an *oil* line of appreciable length had used Dresser couplings exclusively. Even more encouraging was the progress made in attracting the water industry. Near the end of 1936 Merrill Davis told the directors that the volume of sales in that industry would show an increase of between 200 and 250 percent. The essential product for these sales was the familiar Style 38 coupling, which accounted for more than half of Dresser Manufacturing Company's sales. Another farsighted plan for gaining new business and goodwill was the institution of a policy encouraging pipeline companies to send their field problems to the Dresser laboratory. Approximately half of Dresser's engineering personnel became involved in solving these

_____

* The unit was mounted in two self-contained sections on a common bed-plate and connected through an all-metal flexible coupling. The engine was eight-cylinder radial, two-cycle, and water-cooled with an eight-inch bore by eight-inch stroke. It generated 500 BHP at 1,000 rpm. Total piston displacement was 3,217 cubic inches. The compressor was a four- or eight-cylinder radial with an eight-inch stroke. Total piston displacement was 1,062 to 5,036 cubic inches. A copy of the descriptive brochure is preserved in George Pfefferle's files.

problems—at no cost to the customer. Expensive in the short run, this free research service was an important key for the future. It not only emphasized Dresser's capabilities as an authority on all pipeline needs, but the exposure to unusual problems inspired the company to conceive of new products and to foresee future pipeline needs and trends.

Still another encouraging note by the mid-1930's was Bryant Heater's remarkable recovery. Having been acquired in mid-summer at the seasonal peak for home construction, the monthly losses had turned to profits almost immediately. The first winter had been accompanied as expected by sluggish sales and monthly losses, yet Dresser's financial situation was adequate to accommodate them as well as to continue spending greater funds for research and development.

By the end of 1934, the first full year in which Bryant's operations were under Dresser, significant steps already had been taken to upgrade the company. Mallon told the stockholders that Bryant had "more than met the expectations of management." The line of boilers had been redesigned and given fancy colors because American families were adapting their basements to game rooms and the old boilers were unpleasant in appearance. Other new equipment was being perfected too. A year later the picture brightened even further. Bryant's gross sales for 1935 of approximately $789,000 were some 30 percent higher than those of the previous year. Greatly increased engineering and research expenses cut down the profits that normally would have accrued. These expenses were devoted to developing air-conditioning equipment, unit heaters, an improved warm-air furnace, and a new conversion burner. "While these new developments will produce little immediate increase in earnings," Mallon told the shareholders, "that introduction constitutes a forward step in the program of product diversification now under way." Before the 1930's were over, the entire Bryant line would be redesigned, broader distribution gained, and a complete line of residential, commercial, and industrial gas-fired heating and air-conditioning equipment achieved.

The pursuit of new products included an effort to develop a refrigerator powered by natural gas. The Electrolux gas refrigerator, manufactured by Servel, Inc., was attracting great attention through its novelty and efficiency. A contract signed in 1936 with Allyne Laboratories, Inc., of Cleveland, authorized Bryant to manufacture and sell the gas refrigerators being developed by that company. When Allyne failed to perfect the gas refrigerator, Bryant engineers attempted final development work themselves. However, the gas refrigerator never materialized.

Hector P. Boncher, seen here as he appeared in the mid-1930's, provided sales and promotional leadership for Dresser from 1929 until his retirement in 1969.

An attempt was made to add a gas kitchen range to the line. The best way to enter this market, it was determined, was to acquire a firm that already manufactured kitchen ranges. The experiences in developing the radial engine and compressor had taught Dresser a lesson: it was preferable to buy a company that already had the desired product rather than to attempt to design it anew. But after examining half a dozen kitchen range manufacturers and failing in an attempt to acquire the most promising one, the idea was dropped.

All this activity was not without results. In the middle of 1936 Mallon was able to report that Bryant's operations had attained profitability despite large expenditures for research and development. A surge of activity in residential construction had found Bryant ready with an enhanced line of products.

Indeed, by 1936 all of Dresser was prospering. Merrill Davis told the board of directors in April that business in every branch of operations was up some 60 percent as compared to the previous year. Coupling orders for use on water lines for the first four months of the year were at a volume nearly as great as that of any previous full year, and the eighty-five-mile oil pipeline completed in 1935 with Dresser couplings was working so well and generating such flattering testimony that further orders for the same purpose seemed assured.

At the end of the year Dresser (including Bryant) had made its highest net profits since 1931—$392,754. The directors authorized dividends of $3 per share on Class A stock and $1 per share on Class B stock, a total of $353,500. This was twice the amount paid the previous year. Prospects for 1937 appeared bright, too, as Mallon told the stockholders in his annual message.

> The foundation on which the business is building has been broadened to include more customers than ever before in our history, spread over an increasing number of industries. It seems advisable at the beginning of 1937 to prepare for a further business expansion, and both Dresser and Bryant are extending their sales activities by the addition of new men and by the adoption of more vigorous merchandising policies.

He added another optimistic note concerning the radial engine and compressor: "This new product is now approaching a stage of completion that leads us to believe it may be successfully introduced into the pipe-line industry during the coming year."

If this statement once again was unduly optimistic—as it was—one interesting and unexpected opportunity had arisen as a result of the radial engine and compressor project. It had dawned on Mallon that Clark Bros. was a promising possibility as an acquisition. The company had a long and fine reputation as a manufacturer of internal combustion engines; its products were sold the world over; and a string of annual losses during the depression had impaired seriously its financial integrity but left unharmed its engineering skills. Clark Bros. desperately needed an inflow of new capital, and capital was something that Dresser had. Mallon and C. Paul Clark began comparing balance sheets and earnings statements in early 1936, and a year later Dresser's board of directors authorized Reimer to arrange for an audit of Clark Bros. as a preliminary to an acquisition proposal.

When the board met in June 1937 at the Lunch Club on New York City's Wall Street, each member already had received Reimer's complete report on Clark Bros. Company. The firm had total assets of $2.3 million, which compared to $4 million consolidated total assets of Dresser. Preliminary terms for the acquisition already had been reached, and Reimer outlined them in his report. Clark Bros. Company's enthusiasm for the merger was shown by the fact

Charles E. Clark abandoned his studies at Cornell University in 1880 to join his brother in a manufacturing firm called Clark Bros. Company.

that the owners had optioned all their stock and deposited it in escrow. Dresser's board members, after discussing the proposed acquisition's impact on their own cash resources and working capital requirements, agreed unanimously that the deal would not impair their own ability to finance the needs of Dresser's expanding business. They voted to proceed with the takeover. The terms were simple: 20,000 shares of Dresser Class A stock for 10,000 shares of Clark Bros. stock. The market value of these shares at the time of acquisition was $980,000, but the net cost to Dresser had been only $500,000.* The acquisition, effective July 1, 1937, was perhaps the most fortuitous ever to be made by Dresser. Within three years Clark Bros. Company's sales would be greater than those of Dresser Manufacturing and Bryant combined, and within just

* The transaction occurred in two stages. Dresser first turned over 16,000 shares of its own stock purchased earlier at an average price of $19 per share. Four thousand additional shares needed to complete the transaction were bought on the market at approximately $49 per share.

William P. Clark bought a burned-out machine shop in 1880 to serve as the nucleus for Clark Bros. Company in Belmont, New York. The company moved to Olean, New York, after the new facility burned before World War I.

a few more years it would be earning greater profits annually than its total purchase price.

Clark Bros. Company's shift from an emphasis on agricultural implements to the oil and gas industries' needs had occurred soon after World War I when its engineers developed a four-cylinder, four-cycle gas engine, one of the early internal-combustion machines built specifically for oil-well drilling. This early engine, mounted high and awkwardly above four iron wheels, proved very popular in oil fields across the continent. In 1920 Clark Bros. built its first horizontal gas-engine-driven compressor, an 80-horsepower machine with one power cylinder and one compressor cylinder. This was followed shortly by twin cylinder machines. These compressors were used for gas lines, the gas lift method of oil production, and the recovery of natural gas. Other innovative products followed, and a key one developed just prior to the acquisition was the new "angle" engine and compressor, with upright power cylinders driving horizontal compressors—the "Super 2." This compact engine and compressor, whose development had been directed by

Paul Clark, held great promise for future sales, but the firm lacked financial strength to market it adequately. The merger with Dresser represented an opportunity to realize to a fuller extent the potential of this machine.

Clark Bros., being a family-controlled enterprise, was marked by many of the deficiencies of the early Dresser enterprise: less than adequate cost controls, a limited line of products, and unsophisticated management techniques. An added handicap was the fact that Clark Bros. Company's engines and compressors were capital goods items, and sales fluctuated up and down with the economy. These weaknesses, not at all obvious in prosperous times, had become painfully evident during the depression, when a steady string of losses had been incurred.

Dresser had no plans to alter the basic structure of the company, for the acquisition in itself would add two elements that Clark alone lacked: greater financial resources and a broader product line. The most important immediate change lay in establishing accounting procedures that were compatible with Dresser's. To assist in this transition, Reimer began driving some three times a week to the Clark Bros. Company's offices in Olean. And, as had been done with Bryant, Dresser's controller was transferred to Olean. At the same time that new cost controls were implemented to cut needless expenses, expenditures for research and development were increased. Clark's management team, aside from the position of controller, was left unchanged. Paul Clark remained not only as the company president but also became a director for Dresser. The Clark Bros. Company's distinctive logo was maintained without change, too, just as Bryant's had been.

One of the most important new assets of Clark Bros. was a gregarious forty-year-old salesman of Irish descent named John Brislan O'Connor. O'Connor was a native of Augusta, Georgia, who had left the University of Georgia in World War I to drive an Army ambulance in France. Ernest Hemingway and John Dos Passos, future literary greats, were fellow ambulance drivers. After the armistice O'Connor headed with a friend for the oil field excitement in Texas and Oklahoma, where he learned the basics of the business as a roustabout for a drilling crew. His next oil field jobs were with the Prairie Oil & Gas Company and the Vacuum Oil Company, and then he joined Clark Bros. as a salesman in 1927. Quickly establishing himself with his enthusiasm and affable personality, he was brought to Olean and made sales manager. In the intervening decade O'Connor had combined his wanderlust with his affection for the oil and gas industries, and the entire world had been his stage for making sales and friends. He was in appearance a taller

As this photograph from the 1920's indicates, Clark Bros. had a long record of service to the petroleum industry by the time Dresser acquired the firm in 1937. The man in white shirt and tie at left is C. Paul Clark, later to become president of Clark Bros.

version of the day's matinee idol, Clark Gable, complete with the well-trimmed mustache. With Clark Bros. employees, who numbered during the 1930's something less than four hundred, he obtained a reputation as a miracle worker. They remembered the occasion just before one Christmas when they faced the almost certain prospect of a severe round of layoffs and a gloomy holiday until O'Connor suddenly arrived from Russia waving a fistful of orders for compressors. All idled workers were called back, the plant hummed once more with activity, Christmas came with the usual festivities, and O'Connor was remembered in the prayers of more than one worker.

The year 1937 brought reasons other than Clark's acquisition for jubilance in the Bradford offices. It appeared finally that the depression had been overcome. Gross income from manufacturing in the United States had recovered to $61 billion by 1937, almost equal to the $68 billion in 1929. Unemployment nationwide was down to less than eight million. At the same meeting on June 24 at which the directors approved the acquisition of Clark, Merrill Davis reported that sales for Dresser Manufacturing at Bradford had increased some 40 percent over the same period in 1936. Mal-

Dresser and Clark Bros. officials enjoy a convivial evening business meeting in Olean, New York. Left to right: Merrill Davis, John B. O'Connor, Hector P. Boncher, and C. C. Hill.

lon echoed Davis's happy report in his analysis of Bryant Heater operations. By year's end, earnings before taxes for the company should approach $200,000, he said, indicating public acceptance of the improved appearance and efficiency in substantially all of the products. A new gas-fired warm-air furnace had been especially well received, and the Bryant plant already had started manufacturing goods for the peak sales season of late summer and early fall. Bryant also was ready in the face of an improved economy to adopt a new sales practice for consumers. Until now customers had paid cash only for their heaters. But installment buying, started the decade before by the automobile industry, now was expanding into other areas. Eager to take part in this burgeoning consumer habit of time payments, the company entered into a contract with Commercial Investment Trust, Inc., to handle the notes.

The midsummer optimism, however, soon was crushed, for in August the economy faltered and in September the stock market again plunged downward. Dresser and especially Bryant suffered along with the nation. Consolidated earnings for the last quarter dropped to $61,965, less than half the average for the first three quarters. The result was a top-heavy inventory and an improper balance between cash and accounts receivable. Cash on hand at year's end was 55 percent lower than the previous year, but earnings before taxes of $510,665 were up more than 10 percent. The directors debated whether or not the annual dividend—$3 for

Class A stock in 1936 and $1.50 in 1935—should be paid. A dividend payment might so reduce the cash position that it would risk the progress made at a time when business indices called for conservatism. On the other hand, should not every attempt be made to provide the stockholders with as substantial a return as possible? The question was complicated by a new federal law that placed a surtax on undistributed profits. If a substantial portion of the profits was undistributed, would shareholders resent the fact that a significant amount of that sum would go to the government instead of to them? One thing was clear: a repeat of the previous dividend would require a loan if the company were to maintain an adequate cash position. A compromise decision was reached to pay $1.50 a share to Class A stockholders and nothing to those owning Class B shares.

The directors also authorized Mallon to investigate the possibility of borrowing or obtaining an option to borrow up to a million dollars over a term of years. Within the month Mallon obtained options from the Marine Midland Trust Company of New York and

Dresser officials obviously enjoyed themselves at a natural gas convention in the late 1930's at Atlantic City. Left to right are C. Paul Clark, president of Clark Bros.; Merrill Davis, executive vice president, Dresser; unidentified; and William Frank Miller, former Dresser secretary, son of Fred A. Miller and grandson of Solomon R. Dresser.

the National City Bank of Cleveland to borrow that amount if necessary.

Most of the concern was directed at Bryant. The recession inopportunely had prevented the company from capitalizing on the expected fall bonanza of business. Distributors of Bryant products showed accounts receivable of $600,000, and if economic recovery did not come soon those accounts would be endangered. To assess this situation and to prevent its recurrence, the directors asked that a complete survey be made of Bryant's merchandising methods, including a recommendation for a "safer and yet effective sales policy" for the future. Fortunately, before 1938 ended, business and industrial indices turned upward, and Dresser looked forward once more with the rest of the nation to the eventual return of full economic prosperity.

The year also saw the culmination of the career of the man whose ties to Dresser had lasted longer even than those of its founder. On the day of his seventieth birthday, May 27, Fred Miller submitted his resignation as chairman of the board and director. He had been affiliated with the company since January 1, 1903, when he had become general manager upon his father-in-law's election to Congress. Now his health was failing and he wanted to sever all business connections. The directors, accepting his resignation with "sincere regret," immediately elected him honorary chairman of the board in recognition of his many years of service. Less than three months later, on August 22, Miller died. The directors summed up his contributions to Dresser in a resolution:

> In the thirty-five years in which he served the Company, Fred Miller saw it prosper greatly, and that prosperity was due in a large measure to his able management and sound business judgment. He was universally known, loved, and respected in the gas industry, which consumes the greater portion of the Company's products, and in the eyes of that industry for many years Fred Miller *was* the Dresser Company.

> His integrity of character and ability won the respect of his associates on the Board of Directors and in the Company, and his kindliness, his tolerance of their viewpoints, and his genuine liking for them won in return their affection.

To fill the vacancy on the board, the directors chose Clark Bros. vice president and sales manager John B. O'Connor, whose continued superlative salesmanship had helped Clark Bros. shine brightly during the otherwise dismal business years of late 1937 and 1938.

Clark Bros. Company's new angle engine and compressor was the firm's most promising product in the late 1930's.

Other changes occurring in 1938 involved the reincorporation and recapitalization of Dresser. Both Bryant and Clark Bros., while wholly owned and controlled, had maintained their legal status as separate corporations even though their financial statements were consolidated with Dresser's. On the last day of 1938 Dresser and Clark merged in a newly chartered corporation named simply Dresser Manufacturing Company, the cumbersome initials "S. R." being dropped. Dresser thus became both an operating company and a holding company. Clark now would be a division, but its distinctive Clark Bros. name as well as its management would be retained. As far as Clark Bros. customers were concerned, no changes could be detected. Bryant Heater continued to be separately chartered and to have a distinct board of directors controlled by Dresser officials.

The most important reason for the consolidation of Dresser and Clark was the fact that it enabled the company to eliminate the cumbersome Class A and Class B stock distinctions. This arrangement seemed to pit the interests of the two classes of owners against one another, and it was certain to present obstacles toward the expected acquisition of other companies. Now there would be just one class of common shares, 350,000 in number with no par value. This was achieved by exchanging one share of Class B for one share of the newly organized corporation's stock, and one share of Class A for two new shares.

It was at about this time that the radial engine and compressor project finally was abandoned. Developed at a cost of half a million dollars, it was quietly discontinued after the sale of just eight units. The goal of coupling power with light weight had been achieved, but the units simply had been too light to withstand continuous operation at such speeds. Disappointment was made easier by the unexpected degree of success achieved by Clark Bros. Company's new and much heavier angle compressor.

Moreover, the project in many ways had created a pattern for Dresser in the future—an indication of its unwillingness to follow the well-worn ruts of others and of its realization of the need to allot significant sums of money for research. The project also emphasized that even if a distant goal proved unattainable, the effort to get there brought unexpected benefits. In this case the acquisition of Clark Bros. had been a direct result of the radial engine and compressor project.

No one could foresee it at the end of 1938 but the real beginning of recovery lay just months away. It was impossible to measure to any accurate degree the losses suffered by Americans in the depression. Several cold statistics hinted at their magnitude. The Commissioner of Labor Statistics testified before the Temporary National Economic Committee that during nine years American workers lost $119 billion; farmers, $38.4 billion; and investors, $20.1 billion. Figures compiled by Dun & Bradstreet indicated the failure of some 185,000 businesses.

Dresser, amazingly, was a stronger company at the end of this perilous period in American history than it had been at the beginning. The company not only had endured but had built a solid base for future growth. Bryant Heater and Clark Bros. had been acquired at bargain prices that Dresser easily could afford; 128 new types of products had been added between 1936 and 1939; overall operations had shown profits even in the worst of years; the coupling business had been promoted so successfully in different markets that the introduction of welding had had scant effect; recapitalization had simplified the corporation's financial base; the emphasis on research and development had been expanded ($1,097,791 was spent on engineering between 1936 and 1939 to develop the product lines, an amount six times greater than that spent by other companies surveyed in the same field); and substantial write-offs had

A Clark Bros. Bobcat engine is shown in operation at a Continental Oil Company lease.

been made to eliminate obsolete inventories, machinery, tools, fixtures, and patterns.

Dresser officials later would summarize the period that lay immediately before them in this way:

The sales possibilities ... were explosive in character. Plans for new catalytic refineries were sweeping the oil industry making new engines, compressors and pumps by the hundreds imperative. More oil wells were going deeper, requiring immense amounts of our equipment. Liquefaction of gas was about to revolutionize the gas industry and in this we were a leading light. In short, both the oil and gas industries were on the verge of momentous changes. Low-cost homes, too, were just around the corner, with thousands and thousands of our heating units to be supplied. ... *And we were ready* —with standard products and *new* products—for this upsurge of mammoth construction and buying.

Dresser and the
Nation Go to War

The economic recovery that began in 1939 resulted from an event even more tragic than the depression. Nazi Germany's sudden invasion of Poland in September was the spark that ignited World War II and carried industry to a fever pitch. Few if any sectors of society in the civilized world could be immune to the awesome impact of war. Although the United States' own entry did not take place until after Pearl Harbor, the nation began transforming itself almost immediately into the world's "arsenal of democracy." A psychological change was evident before even the first government defense contracts were let. "It was like watching blood drain back into the blanched face of a person who had fainted," economic historian Broadus Mitchell has written. More specifically, Price Administrator Leon Henderson said that

> memories of the first World War—memories of insatiable demand, of shortages, of inflation—were rekindled and there was an immediate and sharp increase in buying. The businessman who customarily bought one carload put in an order for three. Prices rose precipitately, basic commodities and basic raw materials both jumping about 25 percent in the single month of September. The rise of prices itself evoked widespread accumulation of inventories that further fed the stream of buying. A speculative boom was on.

The dramatic change was especially evident for Dresser. The last half of 1939 was the most profitable of any comparable period in its history. Consolidated earnings for the first half of the year had been only $81,383—"an inauspicious start," as Mallon noted—but that figure increased eightfold in the second half to bring the year's total earnings to $765,611. Aside from the general economic recovery, several additional important factors were involved. Clark Bros. operations, bolstered by the success of the angle engine and compressor, were particularly profitable, and a healthy backlog of unfilled orders accumulated. The streamlining and broadening of Bryant Heater's line of products bore significant fruit too. In 1939 residential construction passed the billion-dollar mark for the first time since the start of the depression. The Bradford operation continued to show consistent strength, and significant reductions in general and administrative expenses had been made in the first part of the year.

The man who was so instrumental in introducing the angle engine and compressor to the oil and gas industries was O'Connor. His energy and daring were typified by his first airplane flight to Africa. He departed from Marseilles on a French flying boat en route to Tripoli with only two Englishmen as fellow passengers. While making a stopover on the island of Castelrosso, just off the coast of Asia Minor, the pilot accidentally rammed the wings into some chains of sailing vessels anchored in the harbor. The French pilot and copilot discovered that the damaged wing tips had been added for better stability after the flying boat had been constructed. Inspired, they pulled off the damaged sections and put them ashore, leaving the wings squared, and announced that they were ready for takeoff. The two Englishmen silently pondered the gravity of the situation, but O'Connor declared that if the Frenchmen were crazy enough to fly the boat, he was crazy enough to go with them. The Englishmen, unable to resist O'Connor's lead, joined him in boarding the aircraft. Try as hard as they would, though, the pilots were unable to lift the plane off the mirrorlike water in the bay, so they taxied out into the open sea and desperately bounced the plane off the waves, finally getting airborne. They arrived in Tripoli after dark and landed with the help of flares shot into the air from the ground.

Neil Mallon, quieter, more studious than O'Connor, was, of course, equally fervent in his belief that a successful company must *make* things happen instead of waiting for things to happen. In this spirit Mallon and O'Connor presented to the board of directors in October of 1939 a proposal to back a novel distillate recovery plant in the Agua Dulce natural gas field in Nueces County, Texas. Three Texas men were seeking financing for a plant that could recover butane and propane from the "wet gas" (that is, pressurized natural gas that contained other compounds in liquid form) in the field, then return the stripped gas to the formation from which it originally came. Dresser's involvement not only would assure the sale of some $300,000 in Clark Bros. compressors, but likely would ensure the use of Clark compressors in similar plants in the future.

The process was a logical outgrowth of the new petrochemical industry. This industry had realized that natural gas, when broken into its components, could be converted into fertilizers, antifreeze, plastics, vinyl plastics, synthetic fibers, neoprene rubber, solvents, refrigerants, and rubber compounding—products destined to usher American life into a new synthetic age. The processing plants for these operations required substantial investments, and powerful compressors constituted their most essential ingredient.

Impressed by Mallon's and O'Connor's arguments, the directors decided to invest $125,000 of Dresser money in the newly organized Gulf Plains Corporation, thus ensuring the sale of Clark Bros. compressors. As a result of the plant's immediate success, Clark Bros. gained a virtual monopoly in supplying compressors as similar plants soon were constructed throughout the world.

A year later another novel venture attracted Dresser management's attention. This was a chromium-plating process patented by a Dutch expatriate named Hendrick Van der Horst, who had fled war-torn Europe and left behind his production facilities in Holland as well as his family. Once again, it was O'Connor who had made the initial contact. Van der Horst had developed a technique that electrolytically plated cylinder walls, piston rings, and other wearing parts of engines and compressors with something similar to chromium called "Porus-Krome." No one had devised a way to lubricate chromium because of its glasslike surface, but Porus-Krome was covered with tiny pit holes that conveniently held lubricating oils. This promised to extend the life of moving parts to a significant degree, and tests indicated that Porus-Krome indeed lengthened the life span of cylinders from four to twenty times. It seemed reasonable to assume that if Clark Bros. plated their products' cylinders with this substance their life spans would be so greatly increased that a distinct advantage over competitors would accrue.

O'Connor submitted to the board for approval a plan calling for a fifty-fifty split in the Van der Horst Corporation of America to exploit the chromium-plating patents. O'Connor had bargained for more, but Van der Horst insisted on an equal partnership. The board agreed and Van der Horst was given space at the Clark Bros. plant in Olean. The war soon interrupted Dresser's plans to develop the company, but the process was used to advantage during the war. By plating the bores of 16-inch battleship cannons, the friction from shells was reduced and thus the cannon barrels' life span was lengthened significantly. The process also was used to advantage in replating cylinders of aircraft engines used in the North African deserts, where particles of sand had been causing great damage.

The Van der Horst project was promising, but Dresser officials, eyeing the continuing growth in the petroleum and petrochemical industries, knew in 1940 that a more urgent need for the company was to acquire a solid line of pumps to complement the Clark Bros. compressors and engines. These industries required pumps for the liquid phase of the substance handled and compressors for the gaseous phase. Despite its success in marketing compressors, Clark Bros. labored under a slight handicap. Competitors such as Ingersoll-Rand, Cooper, and Worthington offered a line of pumps in addition to compressors; thus, their salesmen often could outmaneuver Clark salesmen by quoting a single price for both compressors and pumps. To remedy this situation Dresser officials began scouting for a good pump manufacturer. They soon settled on Pacific Pump Works of Huntington Park, California. Pacific held a fine reputation for high-quality centrifugal pumps designed for the exacting requirements of high pressures and high temperatures associated with oil refineries. The company had been founded in 1923 by a group of hydraulic engineers to manufacture vertical turbine pumps

Pacific Pumps manufacturing plant, about 1940.

for the deep water wells needed for Southern California's irrigation projects. The development of specialized pumps for the petroleum industry had been prompted two years afterward when the Pan-American Oil Company of Wilmington, California, developed a new high-pressure gas-oil cracking process. When a full-sized production plant was undertaken, a critical problem arose in finding pumps of sufficient capacity to handle the new process. Pacific engineers answered the call and built and installed four ten-stage centrifugal pumps with capacities of 400 gallons of oil per minute at approximately 250 degrees Fahrenheit and at a pressure of 2,000 pounds.

The pumps operated successfully from the start, and Pacific's pumps thus became integral to the improved cracking processes developed in the next years. The key men in Pacific's operation had been Arthur R. Weis and George E. Bigelow, each of whom had 24½ percent ownership, and a Southern California backer whose 51 percent interest had since been assumed by the Times-Mirror Company. Weis's brother, Elmer, also had been instrumental in the company's growth, having joined it as a salesman after its founding.

Pacific Pump Works, despite its engineering successes, was ripe for a takeover. Its net worth was only $531,318, and it lacked the resources for wider distribution of its fine pumps. Bigelow was experiencing financial difficulties, and the Times-Mirror was on the verge of calling in stock he had pledged to the company. With the Times-Mirror being the principal owner of Pacific, that company's publisher, Norman Chandler, was the proper bargaining agent, but since pump manufacturing was so far removed from his company's field of endeavor, Chandler deferred to Arthur Weis. Weis, who knew O'Connor slightly, favored the advantages of merging. What especially appealed to him was Dresser's knowledge and interest in the oil and gas industries as opposed to the Times-Mirror Company's lack of familiarity with them. Dresser obviously would be willing and eager to broaden the market for Pacific's pumps, and it had the resources to do so.

The proposal as worked out was to exchange 35,000 shares of Dresser stock to Pacific owners for their 150,000 shares. Pacific also would be given representation on Dresser's board of directors. Negotiations proceeded with a minimum of difficulty; all parties agreed that the acquisition was mutually beneficial; and on October 1, 1940, the transaction was completed and Dresser had a new West Coast subsidiary. By now the procedure for integrating new companies into the corporate structure was familiar, and the basic routine established with Bryant Heater and Clark Bros. was followed. Pacific's management, with the exception of Bigelow,

Art Weis, a founder of Pacific Pumps, became president of that company and a director of Dresser when Pacific joined Dresser in 1940.

was retained. The company's established identity would be maintained, but accounting and cost control procedures were adjusted to coincide with the other companies. And, of course, larger expenditures were allotted for research and development.

Arthur Weis, Pacific's president, was named to Dresser's board before the year was over, and it was understood that Chandler would be elected a director at the next opportune moment.* Weis's addition meant that every Dresser subsidiary had representation on the board except for Bryant Heater. Thus, it seemed logical to place Bryant's president, Lyle C. Harvey, on the board, and this was done.

The election of Weis and Harvey brought board membership to eleven, two more than the nine directors elected in 1929. Of that original group, Hamilton Pell, William T. Smith, W. Frank Miller, and Fred A. Miller had been replaced by Clark, O'Connor, Weis, Harvey, and William A. McAfee, an attorney from Cleveland who served as the company counsel and who was elected in 1933. Of these board members the newcomer Weis owned more shares of Dresser stock than any other, 7,843 shares. Mallon was next with 5,050 shares. The other board members' holdings, as of March 1941, were: Clark, 3,124; Bush, 1,900; O'Connor, 1,204; Davis, 1,100; McAfee, 300; and Griffin, Harvey, and Parsons, 100 each. Ohrstrom owned no shares.

Still another acquisition occurred before Pearl Harbor day. Clark Bros. Company's continuing prosperity had taxed its production capacity to the limit, and when it became known that a Brad-

* Chandler's election came on May 20, 1943.

ford oil-well-supply manufacturing firm was available, a deal was quickly made, primarily to gain the space and equipment for government orders. The company was Bovaird & Seyfang, a firm founded in 1879 by David Bovaird, a native of Scotland, and German-born John T. Seyfang. Their original purpose had been to repair oil driller's tools, but the business soon had been expanded to manufacturing products for oil field needs. Dresser bought the company, which was located in downtown Bradford, for $592,135. Bovaird & Seyfang's facility contained 147,000 square feet, and it was equipped with heavy machine tools, a boiler shop, and a foundry. Some of Clark's production was transferred to the new location, but the Bovaird & Seyfang name was retained for the manufacture of pumping jacks, engines, and a small line of compressors.

The last full year of peace before the United States entered the war, 1940, was, as Neil Mallon reported to Dresser's 1,560 shareholders, the best in history from the standpoint of sales, earnings, and general progress. Consolidated sales of $11.8 million were nearly double those of 1939's $6.9 million. Net income of $1.1 million exceeded the former high of $923,629 earned in 1930. The $635,000 paid as dividends ($2 per share) constituted the biggest amount in the company's history. Every division in the company was operating profitably, and the total backlog of orders was the largest ever.

Until that year the company's annual reports seldom had been anything more than four-page leaflets containing Mallon's annual message, a balance sheet, profit and loss statement, and a list of the directors. The 1940 annual report represented a turning point, for shareholders received a thirty-six-page, fully illustrated booklet. Its theme was to demonstrate Dresser's involvement in providing "all along the line" service to the gas, oil, and water industries.

> Gas for cooking and for heating, oil and gasoline for your car, water in abundance at your faucet—all these are speeded on their way to you by nearly 100 different Dresser products made by 1,700 workmen. . . . "all the way along the line"—all through the long and complicated processes that these gifts of nature follow from source to you—some Dresser product plays its part in many of the various steps—production, refining, transmission, distribution, maintenance, utilization, and research.

An artist's sketch across two pages demonstrated the involvement of Dresser, Bryant, Clark, and Pacific products in bringing oil, gas, and water from their point of origin to the consumer.

Of the various divisions, Clark easily led in sales, accounting for approximately two-thirds of the consolidated total.* Clark's business had been stimulated by its contributions to such developments as "pressure maintenance," a practice that doubled or tripled ultimate recovery from oil wells. Pressure maintenance involved reinjecting the natural gas accompanying crude oil into the ground to maintain the natural pressure. The world's largest compressor installation for pressure maintenance was at Ville Platte, Louisiana, where a double row of Clark Bros. "angles" generated 8,600 horsepower. The new "recycling" process introduced on a large scale at Agua Dulce in Texas by now had spread elsewhere, and Clark Bros. compressors were utilized in some 80 percent of all such operations. Clark engines and compressors also continued to be used for more common practices associated with the oil industry from the well to the finished products. A particularly encouraging addition to the compressor line was the "big angle," introduced in 1940, which developed 1,600 horsepower. This was more than had been envisioned for the radial engine and compressor.

Dresser's original Bradford operation accounted for the second-largest percentage of sales. The concentrated effort to broaden the use of the couplings, fittings, and repair devices had been exceptionally successful. The line now contained more than one thousand different sizes of its standard items for gas, oil, water, sewage, gasoline, brine, and air; in mines, quarries, and factories; on compressors, pumps, and valves; and in the railroad, construction, and paper industries. One of the most spectacular orders had come from Rangoon, Burma, where huge couplings were needed for a fifty-eight-inch water line over a forty-two-mile length. A peculiar problem arose on this job. When the workers returned each day to the pipeline, they were puzzled to find dismantled as many as half of the couplings assembled the previous day. It finally was learned that the natives were disassembling the couplings and using the nuts from the bolts for decorating their necklaces and bracelets. This perplexing problem finally was solved by drilling a hole at the end of each bolt and inserting a steel pin to prevent the nut's removal.

Bryant Heater surely had had further to go in achieving profitability than any of the Dresser companies. But modern designs and

---

* Precise figures are not available, but Mallon estimated in September 1940 that 1940's profits would break down as Clark, $1,100,000; Dresser, $350,000; Bryant, $130,000; Dresser Ltd., $10,000. Pacific Pumps was not included.

innovative products had been achieved just in time for the housing boom beginning in 1939, and equipment introduced in the past five years now constituted some 70 percent of the sales.

All these developments would not have been possible except for Dresser's willingness and ability to spend money with long-term rather than immediate gains in mind. The company spent five times the industry on research and development. Between 1936 and 1940 the industry average was 0.9 percent of net sales; Dresser allocated 4.8 percent of net sales for that purpose in the same period.

In recognition of recent achievements and as a spur for the future, Dresser's board of directors adopted in mid-1940 a uniform incentive compensation plan for key executives to reward "extra effort, ingenuity, and effective planning." Previously, plans had varied from company to company. Net income achieved above a certain figure in the various companies would be rewarded by bonuses totaling 10 percent of the excess amount. At the end of the year $119,715 in bonuses was paid. Paul Clark and John B. O'Connor received the largest amounts—$29,430 each. Mallon received $26,460; Reimer, $6,615; and F. H. Light of Clark Bros., $6,540.

———————

Dresser's remarkable progress between 1939 and 1941 was destined to be overshadowed by the enormous impact caused by the nation's transition to a war economy. The change at first was subtle. Couplings, for example, began to be used to tie together water and gas lines hurriedly laid over the nation and world at new military posts. Pipeline and distribution companies began building up inventories of couplings and repair devices for immediate restoration of service in case of enemy air attack or sabotage, for these links would be primary targets. The Bradford plant also won a contract to manufacture 81-mm and 105-mm shell forgings and the rough machining for aircraft engine crankcase mounts. Bryant Heater's usual products at first went to new military installations; then the company converted almost entirely to making bogie-wheel units for tanks. Clark Bros. compressors were in demand for refinery expansion programs to increase the output of aviation gasoline. The company won one of the largest orders ever placed in the United States when a new defense chemical plant was constructed for the compression of gases. Clark Bros. also began manufacturing 2,600-horsepower triple-expansion steam engines for Liberty ships in a massive program to build up an emergency fleet of freighters. One of the most critical uses made of Clark

Dresser Manufacturing Company's bulletin board outside the plant at Bradford was covered with posters encouraging exceptional effort in production for the war.

Bros. compressors was in the creation of synthetic rubber to replace the interrupted supply of natural rubber. The West Coast aircraft industry, knowing of Pacific Pumps' precision engineering, turned to that company as a subcontractor for making hydraulic-actuating assemblies for landing gear, wing flaps, bomb doors, and other similar units. By July 1941, Dresser's total defense business already amounted to $4.2 million.

All parties enjoyed this burst of prosperity. The price of Dresser stock had risen from $6 a share in 1939 to a high of $23⅛ in 1941. Dresser employees rapidly increased in number to 1,670 before Pearl Harbor. In 1939 the average work week for a Dresser factory employee had been forty-three hours with average annual earnings of $1,473; for 1941 the average work week had increased to fifty-three hours and annual earnings were up to $2,046. Plant expansions were started and in some cases completed at all Dresser locations during 1941 at a cost of $763,278, and this was only a token of the additions that would continue throughout the war.

By Pearl Harbor day the Dresser companies were almost totally involved in the defense effort. After 1941 the work simply became more imperative, for the nation's very survival depended to a great degree on how well industry could provide the materials needed to fight a war extending over the entire globe. President Roosevelt's two-year war production goals staggered the imagination. He called for 185,000 airplanes, 120,000 tanks, and eight million deadweight tons of new merchant shipping. The War Production Board established quotas and priorities, but private industry was responsible for retooling and getting production going on a scale that dwarfed anything in the past. The nation's biggest manufacturers, particularly those of the automotive industry, assumed key roles, but the volume of work was so mammoth that thousands of subcontractors joined in the all-encompassing campaign to produce war goods. The war effort became the common enterprise of all Americans.

The difference in volume of business for Dresser between 1941 and the following first full year of war was enormous. Sales for 1941 totaled just under $12 million; the figure rose dramatically in 1942 to nearly $29 million. Almost half of this total came from the ninety-five entirely new products manufactured specifically for the war effort. These early defense products were of wide variety, and a short list only hints at the difficulties involved in converting plants and equipment for their manufacture. In 1942 alone they included parts for armored tanks such as wheel rims, volute-spring-suspension assemblies, fenders, water-can racks, escape door assemblies, and turret locks; parts for aircraft such as hydraulic-actuating assemblies for the wing flap, nose wheel, cowl flap, strut, and brake lockout, and seat brackets, gun supports, and fuel tank fittings; parts for antiaircraft guns; 75-mm, 81-mm, and 105-mm shell forgings; experimental rocket projectiles; panels and doors for Signal Corps trucks; half-track wheel bases; and reducing adapters for Navy torpedoes. As the war continued, this list multiplied to include such items as portable oxygen units for high-altitude flying, compressors for petroleum-jelly flame throwers, portable nose hangars for repairing aircraft, 1,000-pound semi-armor-piercing bombs, and pontoons. And, of course, products typically produced by Dresser—couplings, engines, compressors, heating units, pumps—were used almost entirely for military purposes.

One of the most important of these wartime endeavors, and the largest in volume for any Dresser company, was the manufacturing of volute-spring bogie-wheel suspension assemblies for America's medium tanks and mobile gun carriages. This was basically the wheel unit that rolled on the Caterpillar tracks. Bryant Heater Company, acting as a subcontractor to the primary tank manu-

The wheel units for LVT's, used throughout the Pacific theater, were manufactured by Bryant Heater Company, as were the wheel units for tanks. (Dallas Public Library)

facturers, assumed the lead role. Total contracts for this massive volume of work for the nine-month period preceding September 1942 alone reached $34.2 million. This work was so different from the company's usual manufacturing business that new facilities had to be located. By the end of 1942 Bryant had arranged for ninety-eight of its own subcontractors from across the continent to assist in manufacturing. The difficulty of the job was underlined by the Ordnance Department's requirement that no new buildings or machine tools could be constructed for this purpose. As a result, desperate overnight conversions of a wide variety of manufacturing facilities were made. A limestone mill in southern Indiana, for example, was rescued from closing because it contained planers that had been used on rough stone. No one knew for certain that these machines would adapt to steel castings, nor whether the stonemen there could be educated to handle that kind of work. But as a Dresser official later commented: "Here were the *types* of machines needed; it was absolutely impossible to obtain them elsewhere. It was an opportunity. We went to work." The large volume of business required the hiring of many new executives. There was a ready supply: the independent distributors

Clark Bros. Company's outstanding contribution to the war effort earned the company an "E" award from the government. A federal official is at the podium, and standing at right are John B. O'Connor and C. Paul Clark.

of Bryant products whose business had nearly vanished with the curtailment of new heating units. Many of these otherwise idle men were brought to Cleveland for this war work. So successful was Bryant's wartime conversion that the Ordnance Department in Washington, D.C., sent representatives to the company to study its subcontractor arrangement. In recognition of Bryant's achievements in this critical endeavor for the war effort, the War Department awarded the company the Army-Navy "E" flag for excellence.

Other Dresser companies achieved similar successes under severe hardships. At Dresser Manufacturing in Bradford, a delay in steel deliveries created a serious bottleneck on production of six-inch couplings urgently needed to complete an important pipeline project in the Near East. The War Department implored Dresser to overcome the lost time by speeding up the manufacturing process. When the steel at last arrived, the employees produced the entire quantity of 115,000 couplings, weighing 1,430 tons, in twenty-one days, beating the deadline by a full day and cutting thirty-nine days off the normal production time. This was the largest tonnage run on couplings in such short time in the company's history. To recognize the uniqueness of the success, War Department officials presented the company a special commendation at an employee celebration.

To achieve the rate of production required for the war effort, Dresser plants stayed busy twenty-four hours a day in three shifts, assuming an entirely different atmosphere. Armed guards stood at factory gates; employees wore identification badges. One of the company's most difficult problems at every plant was in finding enough workers. Much of the available labor pool had entered the armed services. For the first time in the firm's history women were hired for manufacturing duties. By late 1942 more than 12 percent of the overall factory employees were women, and in two plants that figure reached nearly 25 percent. The women welders at Bradford gained considerable attention as the subject of a national magazine's picture story on females assuming the jobs of the departed men. Members of minority groups also were hired in greater proportions than ever before.

The long, hard hours devoted to the common cause of winning the war created a special sense of camaraderie among workers. On one notable day the company treated the Bradford employees and the Bradford city council to a trip by special train to Cleveland, where after being greeted by Cleveland's mayor they attended an Army "war show" to see the ultimate use of war products. The employees wore armbands with the words "War Worker, Dresser Mfg. Co.," and before returning late that night to Bradford, they enjoyed a free box lunch courtesy of Dresser. For many of

The mammoth size of some of the Clark Bros. compressors is indicated here. The man is C. Paul Clark, president of Clark Bros.

the employees it was their first visit to a metropolitan city and their first train ride.

———————

Surely the most mammoth and vital project of the war was the secret undertaking to build the atomic bomb. This urgent endeavor, known as the Manhattan Project, grew out of Albert Einstein's theory that small amounts of matter might be transformed into vast amounts of energy. The basic problem was in arranging and controlling this release of energy. At least two Dresser companies, Pacific Pumps and Clark Bros., were involved in this project. Pacific's participation, the more substantial, was associated with the development of the huge facility at Oak Ridge, Tennessee, a location chosen because the area's long ridges of mountains would contain the effects of enemy bombings or of cataclysmic accident. The object at Oak Ridge was the very difficult task of converting the heavy metal uranium into a gas called uranium hexafluoride and passing that gas thousands of times through a filter, or "barrier," containing hundreds of millions of pores per square inch to separate the uranium hexafluoride into the components U-235 and U-238. The lighter U-235 was the critical element for manufacturing an atomic bomb, for scientists believed that if they could obtain a sufficient amount of the highly radioactive U-235, a chain reaction could be started and would culminate in a massive release of energy. A Texas-born engineer named Percival C. (Dobie) Keith of the M. W. Kellogg Company was placed in charge of constructing the gaseous diffusion plant that would separate the uranium hexafluoride. Keith, a good friend of O'Connor's, asked Pacific Pumps to develop a special pump for handling an extremely corrosive coolant liquid required to remove the heat of compression from the cascade.

Pacific engineers, such as D. B. Harney (who later would become Pacific's president), had no idea what use would be made of these special pumps, but the secrecy involved clearly indicated that the project had absolutely top governmental priority. To test the seals in the pump that was ultimately developed, five gallons of the coolant were flown under armed guard by an Army bomber to Huntington Park. When first tested, the pumps, despite all precautions, could not hold the volatile material. Some of the coolant came through the cast iron and vaporized. A change to steel finally solved the problem. Before returning the top-secret coolant to Oak Ridge, the Army guards weighed the material to make certain none was missing. As mentioned, some of the material had vaporized in the first tests, and Pacific's engineers were hard-pressed in accounting for the loss to the Army's satisfaction. During 1944 and 1945, as the Manhattan Project headed for its epochal climax in Japan, Pacific supplied more than six hundred of these pumps to Oak Ridge.

Pacific also manufactured two other kinds of pumps for Oak Ridge: horizontal centrifugal and "Silver Queen" pumps. The three "Silver Queen" pumps, weighing more than four tons each, went to a thermal diffusion plant critical to the gaseous diffusion cycle.

Clark Bros. involvement in the Manhattan Project came earlier, while scientists sought to determine the most likely process for obtaining U-235. The company's engineers were hired on a sub-contracting basis to design prototype models of a leakless compressor and a cooling apparatus that could be used if the centrifuge method of separation were adopted. As it turned out, of course, the decision was made to use the gaseous diffusion process, and the models were never put into production.

The impact of the war at its height throughout the Dresser companies could be seen clearly in sales figures. For fiscal 1943—the peak year in war production, when Dresser employed 3,707 persons—combined net sales were $62.5 million. This was more than five times the 1940 figure of $11.8 million, which in itself had nearly doubled the sales of the preceding year. This increase did not signify, however, a proportionate increase in profits. In 1943 the net profits compared to net sales were just 3 percent, while the same figure for 1940 was 10.1 percent. Total net profits for 1943 of $1.8 million compared to $1.1 million in 1940. A graph depicting sales and percentage of profits for that span of years would show a rapid climb in sales and an equally sharp decline in percentage of profits.

Accompanying the massive effort involved in war production were a number of other significant changes for the company. One of the most visible was the adoption of a new name. The acquisition of other companies had caused a complication for the old name. Did the word "Dresser" refer to the manufacturing plant in Bradford or collectively to the family of companies? It was often confusing. To solve this problem there gradually evolved the term "Dresser industries," a reference to the entire group of companies. The first informal recognition of this appellation came in the 1941 annual report when the term was used as the title for a section describing the activities of the subsidiaries. It was used again the

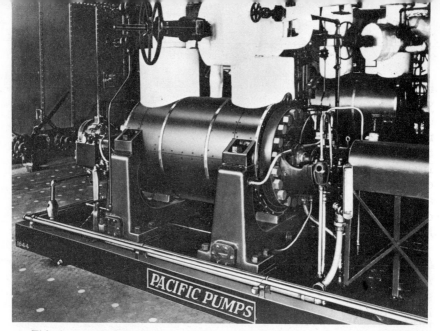

This is one of Pacific Pumps' first boiler feed pumps. It was placed in service in 1940 at Commonwealth Edison in Chicago.

next year with an explanatory note calling it the "informal name for the Dresser family." Finally, on June 23, 1944, the directors voted to formalize the name by amending the bylaws so that the company name was changed from Dresser Manufacturing Company to Dresser Industries, Inc. Mallon explained to the shareholders that "our enterprise can no longer properly go under the name of a single manufacturing company, because it has, in fact, become a group of related industries." The Bradford plant became known as the Dresser Manufacturing Division.

Two other changes occurred as the result of the deaths of two valued members of the company. Merrill N. Davis, who had been associated with the company since 1919, died in 1943. A memorial passed by the board of directors praised his "winning and expansive personality" and his remarkable sales abilities, which had been so instrumental in the company's growth. To fill Davis's seat the directors followed an earlier decision to elect Norman Chandler, president of the Times-Mirror Company and a major Dresser shareholder since the exchange of stock in the acquisition of Pacific Pump Works. The other loss was that of Floyd W. Parsons, who had served as a director of the company since 1929. Parsons died on August 7, 1941.

A new development that Dresser as well as much of the nation's industry faced during the war was an increase in activity by organized labor. The influx of additional workers during these years, the end of the depression, the long hours required for urgent rush orders, prosperity brought by war production, and new federal laws coalesced to make the period ripe for the formation of unions. Prior to 1942 the only organized unions in the Dresser plants were an independent one and a CIO affiliate, both of them quiescent, but in the immediate years that followed, labor assumed an increasingly activist stance. To handle the growing complexity of industrial relations, a specialist, Tom L. Moody, was hired to oversee negotiations with workers in all the Dresser plants.

Perhaps the most complicated labor situation was in Olean, New York, where a nonaffiliated union called the Employees' Association, Inc., represented the Clark Bros. employees. In the spring of 1943 the UAW-CIO determined to organize the workers into one of its own locals to replace the independent union. In leaflets and at organizational meetings, spokesmen for the UAW-CIO contended that workers' pay had not kept pace with the cost of living, that the independent union was really a "company" union that was not effective in representing legitimate grievances, and that seniority rights of employees were not being given adequate protection. The National Labor Relations Board set an election for August 30, 1943, and as that date neared, the campaign became increasingly bitter on both sides. The organizing committee for the UAW-CIO claimed that "company unions are like bed bugs. They come out and suck the blood of the workers to benefit the Company. . . . They never do anything for the workers except under pressure of a real union when the Company figures they had better give a little to save themselves." The Employees' Association replied that the UAW-CIO campaign was the "usual Un-American, communistic stuff . . . you know what the C.I.O. means? It means 'Crisis In Our Factory and Jobs.' It means Sit Down, Slow Down, Shut Down." When the votes were counted the Employees' Association won, but less than a year later the UAW-CIO renewed its efforts. In January 1945 still another election was held, in which the workers were offered three choices: the UAW-CIO, the Employees' Association, or neither. The Employees' Association received 448 votes; the UAW-CIO, 444; and 34 votes were cast for neither. In the runoff that followed, the Employees' Association won by a clear 585 to 394 majority, but an NLRB examiner ruled that Clark officials had "coerced and intimidated its employees" in talks over a loudspeaker system.

The NLRB ordered the firm to "cease and desist from interfering in any future collective bargaining election." Paul Clark declared that such an order was a violation of his First Amendment right of freedom of speech and that he would not abide by it, nor would he post notices of the NLRB findings as ordered. Thus, there emerged a significant test case of the right of the NLRB to order an employer to refrain from participating in such an election. The issue received widespread publicity. Still another election was ordered, and one notable event in the ensuing campaign was a debate in Olean's town hall between Walter Reuther of the UAW-CIO and George Romney of the Automobile Manufacturers Association. With the free speech issue unresolved, Clark workers in April 1946 once again affirmed their faith in the Employees' Association by a vote of 617 to 261.

The Clark situation was illustrative of the labor complications that arose during the war at all Dresser plants and throughout industry between 1941 and 1945, when union membership rose from 10.5 million to 14.75 million. At both Dresser Manufacturing and Bovaird & Seyfang, NLRB-supervised elections resulted in victories for the International Association of Machinists, the International Brotherhood of Blacksmiths, Drop Forgers and Helpers, and the International Molders and Foundry Workers of North America—all of them affiliates of the American Federation of Labor. In January 1944 a three-day unauthorized walkout by 650 out of 725 workers briefly halted war production at Dresser Manufacturing.

Dresser employees indeed worked harder during the war years, and they also earned more money. Between 1939 and 1943 the average Dresser factory employee increased his time on the job per week from forty-three to fifty hours. At the same time the average annual wage increased from $1,473 to $2,866.

Still another new aspect prompted in large part by the war was the need for borrowing money. The huge government defense contracts awarded to American manufacturers could not be met without significant investments for expansion and retooling. To assist private enterprise in financing the costs for conversion to war products and for the purchase of adequate inventories of raw materials, the federal government initiated a program of guaranteed "V" loans negotiated independently with commercial banks. Bryant Heater, for example, needed a substantial loan to achieve a manufacturing capacity of four million volute-spring assemblies a month. Clark Bros. also required a major infusion of capital for its extensive production of triple-expansion steam engines for Liberty ships. Before the war ended, Dresser had borrowed $9.5 million through the "V" program, most of it for Bryant and Clark Bros.

Yet another increasingly complicated aspect of Dresser affairs during the war resulted from the federal government's new tax requirements. As the government sought to finance this most expensive war in history, the taxes assessed corporations as well as individuals reached new levels. In 1939 less than $3 of every $100 in Dresser sales had been paid in local, state, and federal taxes. That picture took on an entirely new face with the Second Revenue Act of 1940, which raised taxes that year to $10 out of every $100 in sales. By 1943 the amount had climbed to $13.10 of every $100 in sales, or $8.1 million. Taxes now constituted the company's third-largest expenditure, following raw materials ($57.30 of every $100) and wages and salaries ($16.20 of every $100).

One wartime change not entirely unrelated to taxes was the company's adoption of a new fiscal year. Beginning in 1941 Dresser closed its fiscal year on October 31 instead of with the calendar year. Reimer recommended the change for several reasons. October 31 was a more logical time to close the company books because September and October signaled the end of the peak fall season for many Dresser products. Also, a greater opportunity existed at that time to obtain competent outside auditors prior to the increase in demand for their services at the end of every calendar year. The central reason for the change, however, was the realization that new tax laws invariably become effective January 1 in a given year, and with a fiscal year begining November 1, Dresser would have ten months' grace before being affected.

By 1944 the large volumes of war products being manufactured were being handled with considerably greater administrative skill. Having overcome initial start-up problems with signal success, Neil Mallon and his management team began looking seriously toward the postwar era. The goal of providing comprehensive service for the oil, gas, and water industries was far from being fulfilled despite progress made before the war toward that ambitious end. Having a cash position that was healthier than ever, it seemed logical to think of further acquisitions. By now Mallon had adopted an informal rule concerning acquisitions. It said, "Two and two must make five." It was not enough, he insisted, to acquire a company merely to enlarge the size of Dresser Industries. An acquisition had to offer the distinct probability that the combination would bring with it a spark that would generate an extra impetus. Moreover, it had to fall within Dresser's declared emphasis on the oil, gas, and water industries.

By the spring of 1944 a careful survey of appropriate companies indicated the availability of one large corporation—about half the size of Dresser Industries—that fulfilled all these requirements: International-Stacey Corporation of Columbus, Ohio. Reimer, who studied the company, wrote a memorandum to Mallon pointing out that its acquisition would give Dresser an established line of oil-field equipment with solid markets. Its addition would permit Dresser to reap the benefits of the anticipated postwar expansion in the petroleum industry without the time, expense, and uncertainty that would accompany an independent effort to develop its own new products.

International-Stacey was the parent company of a group of five subsidiaries. Three of these subsidiaries, identically named and generally identified as one, were called the International Derrick & Equipment Company. Their manufacturing plants were in Beaumont, Texas; Torrance, California; and Columbus, Ohio. The products of these three were sold under the "Ideco" trade name. The Texas and California factories specialized in such oil-field products as derricks, rotary drilling rigs, draw works, and masts. The Ohio unit specialized in steel buildings for oil-field use, radio towers, and airport equipment.

The second major element of International-Stacey was the Roots-Connersville Blower Corporation, the enterprise founded in 1854 by the Roots brothers in Connersville, Indiana, as a result of their accidental discovery of the rotary positive displacement principle.* The blowers manufactured by the company since that time had become standard the world over, the words "Roots" and "blower" being practically inseparable. The blower was especially important to the gas industry for moving low-pressure gas (the compressor was used for high pressures), and its almost effortless efficiency made it valuable for handling gases and fumes common to foundries, chemical and steel plants, paper and cotton mills, mines, and many other sites. Roots also produced a line of pumps, meters, exhausters, and compressors for general industrial use.

The third unit, located in Cincinnati, Ohio, was called Stacey Bros. Construction Company. This firm manufactured and installed various types of gas storage holders, high-pressure tanks, gas purifiers, condensers and scrubbers for steel and chemical plants, and storage and special tanks, vats, kettles, and vessels for process work in the oil, food, and chemical industries.

The continuing growth of natural gas at the expense of manufactured gas signaled a decline in Stacey Bros. Construction's key

* See Chapter 1, pp. 17–21, for a description of the company's origin.

This Ideco mast, produced by the company that was largely responsible for ending the day of the wooden derrick, is being lifted into position. Ideco was acquired by Dresser in 1944.

This group of sturdy-looking men constituted the work force at Roots Bros. in the 1860's. The two men in vests in the foreground are believed to be company founders Philander and Francis Roots.

product, storage holders for manufactured gas, and Dresser knew that. But the attraction of Ideco in particular and its drilling rigs more than offset that negative because of the anticipated postwar boom in exploration for oil. The foreign governments with which Dresser had been doing business before the war always wanted drilling rigs, and that demand too was certain to increase in the postwar era. Dresser's inability to supply this basic need for oil-field development had handicapped its international bids for other oil-field business. Roots-Connersville, too, had an excellent future as well as a solid past record of earnings.

International-Stacey's consolidated net worth of $4,754,243 was about half that of Dresser's $10,067,545, and its 1943 earnings of $842,333 were just under half those of Dresser's $1,851,143. The company's last fiscal year had shown a superlative earnings record: $8.17 per share for its 103,000 common shares as opposed to Dresser's $5.53 per share on its 335,000 common shares. The addition of this big, healthy company and its broad range of related products to the Dresser family was an attractive possibility.

When International-Stacey's chief executive officer, Oscar M. Havekotte, was approached, he viewed the possibility of a merger with equal favor—provided the terms were beneficial. His board of directors also saw an advantage in uniting with Dresser, and by

July 1944 terms were agreed upon. The deal involved simply a one-for-one exchange of Dresser stock for the 103,000 outstanding shares of Stacey-International. In October, Dresser stockholders signified their consent by voting to increase the company's 350,000 shares of authorized stock by 250,000 shares, thus making the acquisition possible. It was understood that the additional shares would be retained for future acquisitions and for additional working capital.

The acquisition became effective November 1, 1944. As was customary, the new companies maintained their established names and their management structure, but the umbrella International-Stacey Corporation's overseeing function was no longer needed, and that framework was dismantled. Havekotte retained his executive position as president of Ideco operations, and he also joined the Dresser board of directors. Until now Dresser's remarkable progress of recent years had escaped coverage by the mass media. News of the International-Stacey merger, however, prompted *The Wall Street Journal*'s Thomas M. Foristall to describe it in his column, "The Inquiring Investor." Few if any companies will have changed more after the war's conclusion than Dresser Industries, he wrote.

> Pre-war Dresser was a $5 million corporation principally engaged in the manufacture of couplings and related products for pipe line systems. Post-war Dresser will be a $35 million corporation serving almost all phases of the basic gas, oil and water industries. . . . In fact, Dresser Industries, Inc., will be a corporate family, as distinguished from a corporation. . . . It is seven companies, not one— seven companies with kindred interest, serving the same fields. Each functions as a separate unit with its own engineering, manufacturing, technical, service and other staffs; but all are joined together under common ownership, operating under a fixed management pattern providing for group planning and pooling of resources.

The reason for this outstanding growth, according to Foristall, was "extensive research and . . . a soundly conceived, long-range program of property acquisition, plant expansion and product diversification." An accompanying chart showed that between 1925 and 1943 net sales had increased from $2.9 million to $62.4 million. The future appeared even brighter to Foristall, who quoted Mallon's picture of the postwar era as including "developments of tremendous importance" in the gas, oil, and water industries; large-scale housing projects that would require heating systems; and the emerging petrochemical industry, which was only beginning to explore its "almost limitless possibilities."

Fifteen years earlier Mallon had declared his intention to build an industrial empire. He now presided over such an empire. He could count ten member companies whose activities he expected to be integrally involved in an anticipated postwar boom. And while these subsidiaries maintained their own identities and managements, their overall operations and planning were required to fit into the grand scheme as envisioned by Mallon, O'Connor, and Reimer in tiny Bradford and by the directors who lived on all sides of the continent.

As the number of subsidiary companies had grown, so had the demand for overall planning. Although autonomy was encouraged, an increasingly heavy work load was developing for those in Bradford. There thus gradually emerged in the early 1940's a "headquarters" team whose time was taken up more and more with planning and consultation with member companies. Perhaps the first visible step in formalizing a team whose responsibilities concerned the Dresser companies as a whole was in hiring industrial relations specialist Tom L. Moody. Mallon, of course, already was immersed in broad planning, and Reimer as treasurer also occupied himself with the overall fiscal picture. Another addition to this team inevitably was O'Connor, whose activities and broad acquaintances throughout the oil and gas industries opened opportunities beyond his scope as sales manager of Clark Bros. By 1943 O'Connor was concerning himself with overall management, and that year his broader responsibilities were recognized by his election as executive vice president of Dresser Industries. George Pfefferle as technical director, Richard Porter Brown as personnel director for salaried employees, Robert Kelley as purchasing supervisor, Orville Anderson as public relations officer, Richard L. Brummage corporate controller, and J. Douglas Mayson as head of the legal and tax department were other executives whose duties in the mid-1940's concerned all the companies.

This group, its responsibilities ranging from Toronto to Texas to California, had one particular problem in performing its job. Bradford, isolated from major urban centers, suffered from a lack of good air or rail connections. Valuable time was lost simply in coming or going to Bradford, not only for Dresser officials but for visitors as well. This problem became more acute as the company grew, and on October 6, 1944, in a meeting at the Lunch Club on Wall Street, the directors acted to alleviate it. First came approval to purchase a company airplane that could carry Dresser officers wherever and whenever necessary, saving time and money. The airplane was a C18S Beechcraft, bought from the Army Air

Force for $70,000. The directors also authorized the contribution
of $15,000 to the City of Bradford for its airport improvement
program. The airport, which served both Bradford and Olean, had
been constructed originally for military purposes, and it had been
given to Bradford for conversion to civilian use.

The next item on the directors' agenda was more significant.
While there had been no previous official discussion concerning
the matter, for some time there had been in the air a feeling that
the headquarters group should locate in a larger city more conveniently located. Mallon now asked the directors for a decision.
New York City and Cleveland, both of which offered excellent
transportation and banking facilities, were the best possibilities.
After considerable discussion over the relative merits of these
cities, the decision was made to move to Cleveland, which was
much closer to the various subsidiaries than New York.

While details for this move were being worked out, officers of
the ten Dresser companies came to Olean in December for their
third annual conference. These conferences presented an opportunity for top officials and salesmen of the subsidiaries to share
ideas, discuss common problems, and work with the headquarters
group in planning overall goals for the following year. The size
of the meeting was expanded considerably that year with the addition of the International-Stacey companies, and Mallon was inspired to answer the question that was being asked more and more
in those days in business and financial circles: "What is Dresser
Industries?" Mallon, cerebral-looking in his rimless glasses, balding, a bachelor, and in as trim physical shape as ever at the age
of forty-nine, stressed his underlying philosophy of decentralization. Dresser Industries, he said, was no more than

> a group of related companies in related industries. To be a member
> of the group, each member company must contribute something to
> the whole so that the group is stronger because of that member
> company's contribution . . . [It] must be so related to the group that
> it itself gains by membership in the group. In other words, our
> Dresser Industries organization makes sense only if it can offer
> advantages to each operating company and, if at the same time, each
> operating company adds strength to Dresser Industries.

Each of the member companies was thought to be of a size
best suited for efficient management—"not too large to be un-
wieldy." The men in authority were close enough to operations
to know what to do once a problem arose, and they had "full
authority" to act without consulting headquarters. "No one has

to wait for the Dresser Industries' headquarters staff to take some action," Mallon declared. The staff, he explained, was a "service group" ready to help when called upon.

Much of his talk dealt with the approaching postwar era. He foresaw a boom of impressive dimensions in the two primary industries Dresser served, oil and gas. Large amounts of new equipment would be needed for the production of new fields as well as to accommodate changing techniques in refining oil. As for natural gas, Mallon believed it would be the ideal fuel to heat the anticipated "tremendous wave of home construction."

Of course, he acknowledged, there were other companies in advantageous positions to capitalize on the expected economic boom. The different degrees of success would lie in the people involved.

> You have the right to know what is expected of you. I will try to tell you. . . . We expect of you things that other companies do not expect. We expect things of you that our competitors do not expect. Salesmen talk about getting their share of the business. I don't know what that means. If we have a product and a salesman that together persuade a customer that our product is best for his needs, then that same product and sales effort should win out in all like opportunities. We want everyone to prefer our product. We want everyone who is in the market for our equipment to be sold with the same enthusiasm. If we get all the business we are not getting more than our share of the business.

There was another aspect of Dresser Industries even dearer to Mallon than aggressive sales effort: his conviction that research and development held the keys to the future. The company expected even more, he said, from its engineers and technicians than from its salesmen and production experts. "If you do research in time, it prevents emergencies later on. Good engineering today keeps the business going tomorrow. Let's pioneer."

Mallon's plan of decentralization, of course, was not a new phenomenon in American business. The Du Pont Company in 1919 had set an important pattern when it decided that its highly centralized operation could be improved by granting greater autonomy to its divisions. Division heads were granted a certain investment and were held accountable for reaching annual goals determined by a system of financial controls that included detailed forecasts of sales, cash needs, working capital, major expenditures, and profits. A headquarters group set overall policies, and a high-level group of experts provided specialized services for all divisions. Division heads assumed authority for all day-to-day decisions. Du Pont's success with this "staff-and-line" organization was notable, and Alfred Sloan in the 1920's patterned General Motors' operation after the Du Pont plan. Mallon did not consciously emulate these two pacesetters, but the Dresser organizational plan followed their pattern.

Three days after Mallon's "What Is Dresser Industries?" speech, the firm's directors met at the Yale Club in New York City and authorized the acquisition of three more companies! The International-Stacey transaction, so smooth as to be almost effortless, had left in the treasury a bonanza of 147,000 shares. Stockholders had been told that these shares were planned for future acquisitions, and Mallon was not one to delay opportunity. His goal this time was to broaden the company's line of products in the gas heating field, and two of the three acquisitions did just that.

The company that first had emerged as the most accessible and promising was a Monrovia, California, firm founded in 1909 by an imaginative young engineer named William J. Bailey and incorporated two years later as the Day & Night Solar Heater Company. Its name aptly described the product devised for the sunny California market. By the turn of the century, Californians already were using the sun's rays to heat their household water, but at nightfall their heat source vanished. Bailey developed an insulated tank to keep the water hot during hours of darkness. By 1944 the company was a leading manufacturer of automatic gas water heaters; its founder was growing old; and although its products were proven and popular in California, for further growth it needed the national marketing system Dresser's resources could provide.

Still another firm emerged at the same time as an interesting prospect: the Payne Furnace Company of nearby Beverly Hills. In 1915, just a few years after Bailey had begun Day & Night, D. W. Payne and his son Elroy founded a company to manufacture high-quality furnaces. Their firm was the Pacific Coast pioneer in inaugurating the idea of zoned, or unit, heating. It now was well entrenched in the Los Angeles area with four sales and service centers, but its market was similar to Day & Night's in that it reached no farther than the West and South. Payne's gas-fired heating equipment was of sufficient quality that a national marketing effort seemed certain of success.

Both these companies were desirable acquisitions and two and two obviously made five. Their sales programs could be integrated easily into the Bryant Heater framework; Dresser's line of products would be broadened; and there was an almost certain possibility of merging some of the Bryant, Day & Night, and Payne manufacturing facilities to eliminate duplication. Negotiations began almost simultaneously with both companies, and agreement was reached without difficulty. Day & Night was obtained for 17,283 Dresser shares; Payne Furnace, for 22,077 shares. Since the Dresser treasury held 147,000 shares this was accomplished without strain. The approval of both transactions came on December 8, 1944.

The third acquisition on this day was that of still another California company, Kobe, Inc. Kobe was an oil-well pump company located in Huntington Park, near Pacific Pumps, and founded in 1923, the same year as Pacific. The company attracted Dresser's attention because its unique hydraulic oil-well pumping system was gaining rapid notice in the oil industry. Invented by the company's founder and principal owner, Clarence J. Coberly, the Kobe pump system had the advantage of working ten to fourteen wells from a single power source instead of having individual surface power units for each well. Kobe's subsurface pumps were connected by hydraulic power lines to a single "Triplex Pump" and were activated by the force of oil under pressure. This was an expensive system to install, but for a producing field of some size it offered substantial savings through the elimination of so many surface power units. The company was available for 34,594 shares of Dresser stock, and the directors readily gave their assent to this promising acquisition. Kobe and Payne Furnace officially became a part of the Dresser family on February 1, 1945, and Day & Night's acquisition became official on April 2, 1945.

Business Week magazine, noting this splurge of acquisitions and the announcement of Dresser's planned move to Cleveland, printed a two-page feature story about the company entitled "E Pluribus Unum," with the subtitle, "Method whereby a small business can acquire benefits of bigness is being demonstrated by Dresser Industries, Inc." The article cited Dresser as introducing a new trend in the corporate world in which "small to medium-size companies" mobilize on equal footing under a single corporate umbrella. Dresser's growth to thirteen member companies and its increase in sales by a hundredfold in nineteen years was credited largely to Mallon, who was shown in a photograph with Lyle Harvey, O'Connor, and Boncher as they sat at a banquet table during the December 1944 meeting in Olean. The article quoted Mallon's speech there detailing how the autonomy retained by member companies enhanced fast decision making, and how experts at the headquarters staff provided overall planning, financing, and special skills. Dresser was described as an "older company" assiduously engaged in adding recruits and simultaneously tightening its lines for the postwar competition that lay ahead. The article amounted to a glowing recommendation for the corporate structure favored by the company.

On March 19, 1945, the new headquarters offices in Cleveland opened. Some forty employees from Bradford, augmented by clerical assistance hired in Cleveland, reported for work that day in the eleventh-floor Dresser offices of the city's tallest and finest building, the Terminal Tower. On the next day Dresser's shareholders held their annual meeting there. They authorized a 2-for-1 split of the company's 600,000 shares of common stock and an additional issue of 1,200,000 shares, which brought the total number of authorized shares to 2,400,000.

Another significant move occurred that same month. The several Dresser companies with separate sales offices in New York City were brought together in the Chanin Building on East 42nd Street. This consolidation of facilities, aside from obvious benefits, meant that a Dresser headquarters executive might begin his day by riding the rapid transit from home and getting off at the station beneath the Terminal Tower. A few minutes later he might descend from his eleventh-floor offices to the ground floor again, board a New York-bound train, get off in Grand Central Station, walk along an underground passageway to the Chanin Building across the street, conduct his business there with New York sales officials, and then return to Cleveland the same way—all this without stepping outdoors a single time.

Amidst all the excitement at Dresser in 1944 and 1945 the war was bringing news of great moment. All Dresser's manufacturing endeavors, including those of the new subsidiaries, were devoted to bringing about V-Day. Ideco in Columbus, Ohio, improved and redesigned in three months a "Knockdown" transportable nose hangar for airplane repair in the Pacific theater, delivering ninety-six of them to the U.S. Navy and managing to reduce the price from the original $9,500 to $8,170. Ideco in Beaumont buckled down to meet the late war need for bombs, tooling up to deliver 41,110 semi-armor-piercing bombs weighing 1,000 pounds each. Stacey Bros. in Cincinnati supplied pontoons designed specifically for the landings in the Pacific islands and for the anticipated invasion of Japan. Roots-Connersville, through the Lend-Lease program, developed and manufactured six different types of blowers urgently needed in Russia for speedy rebuilding of its war-devastated gas, steel, chemical, and synthetics plants and refineries. Day & Night was called upon by the government in late 1944 to design and begin production on a fuse for the M-74 incendiary bomb. Nearly two and a half million of them were produced before the war's end. Day & Night produced the M-69X incendiary bomb used in air raids on Tokyo. This bomb had delayed-action fuses that caused intermittent explosions after the initial impact and created areas too dangerous for fire fighting. Kobe developed the remarkable Fleet Star Gage, an unbelievably precise instrument used to measure the bore of three- to sixteen-inch naval guns. These seventy-foot-long gauges, measuring to within twenty-millionths of an inch, were responsible for the accuracy of shellfire in all naval theaters of operation. The gauges permitted quick and exact measurement of rifling barrels to detect signs of wear and to permit compensations in sighting these powerful weapons on target. As American forces moved to the offensive in the Pacific, Bryant Heater adapted its production on medium-tank suspension units to manufacture similar units for the amphibious weapons needed in that critical campaign, thus playing an unseen and unheralded role in sending Japanese forces into retreat.

In May, 1945, Germany collapsed. The nation's attention focused on the Pacific theater, where massive numbers of incendiary bombs—75 percent of which were estimated to have come from Day & Night—fell with impunity on Japanese cities. In August the world was jolted by the detonation over Hiroshima and Nagasaki of two atomic bombs secretly made at Oak Ridge. The war was over. A new age began.

7

Peacetime Prosperity

When Japan surrendered in formal ceremonies aboard the U.S.S. *Missouri* on September 2, 1945, more than twelve million Americans were serving in the various branches of the armed services. Demobilization began immediately, and before 1945 ended, more than half of these servicemen were discharged. Whether a peacetime economy could absorb this many ex-GI's and several million more without severe disruption was uncertain. A renewal of the depression, with as many as eight million people out of work, was not out of the question. Manufacturers, including Dresser Industries, faced massive cancellations of government contracts at the same time that they had to retool for their customary domestic products. The cancellations of wartime contracts had begun even before the end of the war. For Dresser this meant in practical terms the abrupt loss of $15 million in business, but those businessmen with wisdom long since had been preparing for the postwar era.

In making their own projections for the postwar period, Dresser officials had not shared the pessimists' views. The company based its plans on a conviction that the natural gas, oil, petrochemical, and housing construction industries, as well as the general economy, would boom as never before. The *Oil and Gas Journal* predicted without reservation that demand for oil in the first five postwar years would break all records despite the unusually high wartime levels. Expectations for the gas industry were almost as exciting because more than twenty thousand miles of new pipeline had been laid before 1944 and surveys showed that more than 50 percent of contemplated new housing would use gas heating as compared to 15 to 20 percent before the war. It was estimated that residential construction in the three postwar years would exceed a million dwelling units annually, a sure bonanza for the company's gas appliance operations.

Of course, as events soon proved, those who had held the most optimistic views of the postwar economy were correct. Wartime shortages and rationing had prevented American consumers from spending their swollen paychecks. The result was a postwar buying spree that reverberated from one section of the economy to another. The intense demand for automobiles created a mammoth boom for the petroleum industry; the sudden expansion in housing construction boosted heating appliance sales; plastics and other synthetics emerged from the basic work of the petrochemical industry and became common elements of everyday life; and the energy needs of home and industry drew more and more on the cheap and seemingly endless supply of natural gas. All these things—so visible in the everyday lives of all Americans—required for their production less visible drilling equipment, pipelines, pumps, compressors, blowers, and other products offered by the Dresser companies.

These were capital goods items, heavy pieces of equipment with long lives. A customer might buy an expensive drilling rig, a compressor, a blower, a pump, and not need a replacement for ten or twelve years. And in that period of time he might be lost forever. In their planning sessions Dresser officials readily perceived a need for some products that were expendable, that yielded repeat sales and kept their customers coming back. Thus began a search for an expendable item.

One of the most important expendables in the oil and gas industries was the drilling bit, the critical instrument that cut through the earth's formations. The market for this item was so important that Dresser officials decided they had no choice but to enter it if they were to serve the industry as they hoped. The best bit sold was the three-cone rolling cutter rock bit offered by Hughes Tool Company and protected in the United States by many patents. A lawyer and inventor named Howard R. Hughes, father of an even more famous son who by now had expanded the family enterprises into the motion picture and aircraft industries, had invented this unique bit, with three revolving cutting elements, before World War I. It was one of the most important contributions of the century to the art of drilling. The company he formed, Hughes Tool Company, now controlled some 80 percent of the bit business. Dresser inquired into the possibility of acquiring the company, sought persistently but in vain to win an audience with the younger Hughes, and finally realized that the firm was not available under any circumstances. Neither was the second most important company in the field, Reed Roller Bit, although a deal had seemed imminent until its principal owner balked at the last

The acquisition of Security Engineering Company in 1945 placed Dresser in the drilling bit business and added a needed expendable product to the company's list.

moment. Finally, a small firm, Security Engineering Company, Inc., located in Whittier, California, emerged as a prospect. Security, founded in 1931, manufactured a drilling bit and related products, such as reamers, casing scrapers, and tubing, as well as the item that had launched Dresser sixty-five years earlier, the packer. The packer, casing, and tubing were made of a special aluminum alloy with properties approaching those of steel but which could be removed more easily from the well with a drilling bit or special "fishing" tools. War had inflated Security's recent profits, but the company's average annual net profits between 1937 and 1941 had been $128,000.

Negotiations for this acquisition began in the spring of 1945, and the agreement ultimately reached was an exchange of one share of Dresser stock for one and three-fourths shares of Security stock. A total of 35,078 Dresser shares was required for the transaction. On November 1, 1945, Security Engineering joined the Dresser family.

———————

Dresser Industries was becoming an increasingly complex organization, yet there continued to be a unifying purpose. "The function of our company is easy to define," Neil Mallon wrote in the fall of 1945. "We serve the oil and gas industries primarily—and we aim to do so all along the line." The company's success in this goal already had caused one brokerage firm to call Dresser "one of the most complete and logical aggregations of equipment and services yet put together in the service of oil and gas requirements." Indeed, the company's rapid transformation from one that offered basically a single product was breathtaking.

While oil and gas activities constituted the principal market for Dresser products, other industries finding uses for them included chemicals, mining, water, iron and steel, electric power, marine power, industrial building, aircraft, foods, refrigeration, sewage disposal, paper, radio, and rubber. The 1946 annual report provided a "condensed list" of 163 separate products.

A map showed seventy-seven sales offices and seventeen plants across the nation. Most of the sales offices were part of Ideco's chain of oil-well-supply outlets. California, especially the southern part of the state, had become the center of most Dresser activity, being home to five factories and fifteen sales offices. Next was Ohio, whose borders encompassed five factories and three sales offices, and then Texas, where thirteen sales offices and two plants existed. One of the Texas plants was the Ideco facility in Beaumont, and the other was an entirely new plant in Tyler—the first built for Dresser since 1907 (not including, of course, those constructed by various member companies prior to their acquisitions). High expectations existed for this new facility, for it manufactured not only Bryant heaters, but also units for Payne and Day & Night. The consolidation of facilities for these three companies and the integration of sales and merchandising activities promised considerable economies and a demonstration of how Neil Mallon's axiom—"two and two must make five"—could work.

The manner in which Dresser aligned itself internally for its broader purpose was illustrated by the 1945 organizational chart. Under the board of directors, executive committee, and president were three primary branches: the general staff (identified as "a group of specialists serving all operating companies") headed by Reimer; the Oil and Gas Equipment Division presided

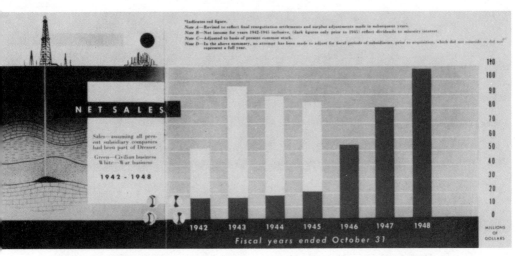

NET SALES

Sales—assuming all present subsidiary companies had been part of Dresser.

Green—Civilian business
White—War business

1942 - 1948

Fiscal years ended October 31

This chart shows the remarkable growth Dresser experienced between the years 1942 and 1948.

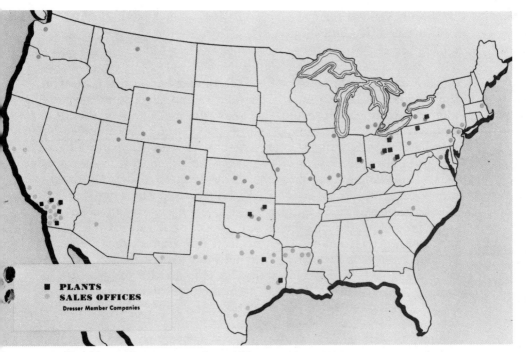

PLANTS
SALES OFFICES
Dresser Member Companies

This map indicates the extent of Dresser's operations in all parts of the nation by the close of World War II.

over by O'Connor; and the Gas Appliances Division under Lyle C. Harvey.

Dresser did not release for the public the sales or earnings of individual companies, but corporate headquarters' figures at the close of fiscal year 1946 showed that the Oil and Gas Equipment Division, paced by Clark Bros. and Ideco, accounted for sales of $41.5 million, and the Gas Appliances Division, led by Bryant, had sales of $17.5 million. The breakdown for 1946 follows:

Clark Bros., Inc.	$12,248,000
International Derrick & Eqpt. Co.	10,322,000
Bryant Heater	9,155,000
Day & Night Mfg. Co.	5,254,000
Dresser Mfg. Division	4,123,000
Pacific Pumps	3,171,000
Payne Furnace Co.	3,161,000
Roots-Connersville	2,969,000
Bovaird & Seyfang	2,383,000
Kobe, Inc.	2,071,000
Stacey Bros.	2,069,000
Security Engineering	2,028,000
Dresser Mfg. Ltd. (Canada)	114,000

Any manufacturer who catered to the oil and gas industries in the middle of the twentieth century faced a constant need to upgrade its line of products or else watch a competitor gain a distinct edge in efficiency or costs and capture the market. To stand still in this struggle meant certain eventual defeat. Mallon's approach to this problem was not merely to look to tomorrow's needs; he wanted Dresser to be creating the products and techniques that would take giant steps in setting the pace for the distant future. The radial engine and compressor had been one such project; the Gulf Plains adventure another. Now another far-reaching plan emerged. It involved the dramatic idea of converting natural gas from its normal state into a liquid. Such a conversion, achieved by lowering the temperature of gas to 250 degrees Fahrenheit below zero, reduced the volume of space required for storage by a factor of 600. The liquefied natural gas, known as LNG, could be stored at convenient locations in large volume, regasified, and distributed via new or existing pipelines. Such a procedure would be especially helpful in solving "peak load" demands common in urban centers; that is, those times such as midwinter when the demand for gas can exceed the capacity to deliver it through pipelines or, in the case of manufactured gas, to produce it.

Once again it was Howell C. Cooper, the man who had inspired the radial engine and compressor, who intrigued Dresser officials with the possibilities of this idea. Cooper, Mallon, O'Connor, Paul Clark, and other Dresser officials and engineers began studying its feasibility as early as 1942, when the East Ohio Gas Company already was building the world's first liquefaction plant in Cleveland. Liquefaction seemed so logical that it appeared certain to become a widespread practice in the near future.

Dresser's plans contained several unique elements. They involved the construction of a liquefaction plant in South Texas or Louisiana, far away from the major markets but where the gas was plentiful and cheap. The LNG, an extremely volatile liquid, then would be shipped via specially constructed 300-foot-long barges to a facility on the East Coast. There it would be reconverted to gas and transmitted through existing pipelines to coastal cities to solve their peak-load problems. Soon it was concluded that the natural gas should be obtained in Venezuela, where it was even cheaper. Another element added to the plan was the idea to transport the LNG up the Mississippi River by barge to a point near Chicago, sell the refrigeration normally lost in regasification to a large meat-packing company for its meat lockers, and distribute the natural gas to urban centers in the Midwest. Also, some of the barges could be diverted to the Ohio River and deliver their load to a regasification facility at Pittsburgh.

Considerable thought, effort, and planning were devoted to this potentially far-reaching project, and the amounts scheduled to be spent were enormous. One of the least expensive contingencies required an original investment of $5.9 million, which would pay for a liquefaction plant, barges, regasification facility, pipeline, and field station. Annual operating expenses were projected as $1.3 million.

Despite the obvious potential benefits that might have been derived from this futuristic plan, the project had to be dropped. The East Ohio Gas Company facility in Cleveland had hardly begun operations than a great calamity occurred in 1944. A storage tank containing LNG failed, causing a widespread and devastating fire with great loss of life. With this holocaust still fresh in its imagination, the federal government denied Dresser permission to send barges carrying LNG up the Mississippi River. The expressed fear was that a barge failure would result in the spreading of LNG far down the river with untold damage. As a result, Dresser dropped its liquefaction project, and not until the 1960's would ocean shipments of LNG begin.

It was stimulating and important to plan for the distant future, but obviously a company had to be concerned as well with the immediate question of profit making. The first postwar year for Dresser as for all American business was one of adjustment. Profits declined from $1.9 million in 1945 to $1 million in 1946. Part of the decline could be attributed to labor unrest throughout the nation, for the numerous strikes of 1946 caused shortages in materials. In February Mallon told the directors that several factors had "seriously jeopardized" the company's profit position. A national steel strike had caused a shortage of steel; strikes had closed three Dresser plants; and the Office of Price Administration still had not lifted its ceiling on the prices Dresser and other manufacturers could charge.

The most distressing of the Dresser strikes was one of fifty-five days' duration in Bradford by the International Machinists and the Blacksmiths, Drop Forgers and Helpers. At its worst moment pickets attempted to prevent cars from entering the Fisher Avenue plant on two consecutive days. Hec Boncher, now the plant manager, had been among those forcibly blocked. One of the pickets had lifted the hood of Boncher's car and jerked the wires from the spark plugs. Concerned over what they felt was a failure by policemen on the scene to maintain order and protect life and property, Dresser officials placed a full-page advertisement in local newspapers decrying the situation and asking their own office workers not to attempt to report for work because of the threat of "indignities and possible body harm." The company also went to court and obtained a preliminary injunction restraining further mass picketing. Within a week the strike ended when the two unions accepted an offer of a pay raise of 17½ cents per hour instead of the 18½ cents sought. Such problems were short-lived, for throughout the postwar period Dresser's relations with organized labor were predominantly cordial and were typified by a spirit of cooperation on the parts of both management and union.

The following year, however, was a turning point. Earnings surpassed even those of the busy war years, and Dresser was launched on a clear and uninterrupted long-term growth period. Net profits of $4.4 million were four times those of 1946; the profit per share of common outstanding stock jumped from 74 cents to $3.85; and net sales of $80 million were up from the previous year's mark of $54.7 million.

"The plan that we embarked upon several years ago—that of building the equipment and rendering broad engineering service for the restless, and ever-changing oil and gas industry—is today well along the road to accomplishment," Mallon told the shareholders. The good earnings, he continued, were the result of the company's willingness in depression and war to invest funds for research, product improvement, engineering exploration, and consolidation of member company activities. "The strength which these factors are adding to our market and earnings possibilities may be expected to continue for years to come."

More and more of the company's profits these days were coming from sales across the face of the globe. As nation after nation aspired to match the high standard of living achieved by the United States, each realized the essential importance of petroleum to this goal. Wherever oil or gas was produced, transported, refined, or sold there was a market for Dresser products. Dresser equipment, so necessary for the development of these industries, was being shipped after the war to the British Empire, China, Mexico, Russia, Poland, Arabia, France, Venezuela, and Argentina. Almost 10 percent of the company's business resulted from foreign exports.

The key figure in developing foreign markets continued to be O'Connor, well on his way to acquiring the eventual tag as "the world's most traveled executive." Headquarters office workers followed his foreign travels through his picture postcards, which he invariably inscribed with witty comments. From Acapulco he wrote to his longtime secretary, Beatrice Kilcoin: "Beautiful spot—no phones—and only one mail a day—some days. People here just swim and fish and some don't even fish." As a Roman Catholic, O'Connor visited the Vatican and sent his secretary a postcard saying: "Just talked with the boss and he sent you his best regards." No oil or gas field of significance opened anywhere in the world that O'Connor did not visit. In eastern Turkey he discovered that the only way he could reach one remote field was across a high railroad trestle. O'Connor casually balanced the risks against the potential rewards and promptly bounced his jeep across the narrow trestle.

In the spring of 1947 he renewed his connections in Russia by heading a three-man delegation there in search of new business. Soviet officials had become intrigued themselves, despite the disastrous end to the Cleveland facility, with the idea of building an LNG plant outside Moscow. The Russians recently had completed through the Lend-Lease program a 475-mile pipeline from the Saratova field to Moscow, where a peak-load problem existed

The man who carried
Dresser's name to the far
corners of the earth
was John B. O'Connor,
the energetic salesman who
became president of
the company.

similar to that in American cities. O'Connor was eager to discuss
this proposition with them, for the Dresser companies had the
expertise to do the job and Hydrocarbon Research,* a research
firm in which O'Connor and Dresser held a controlling interest,
could design the facility. Accompanying O'Connor were Warren
Meyer, of Stacey Bros. Construction's process engineering department, and Dr. Frank Jenny, head of the same department for
Hydrocarbon Research. For nearly five weeks negotiations continued—replete with late-night banquets and vodka toasts—and
on April 22 agreement was reached. Russian officials signed a $6
million contract for designing and equipping a liquefaction plant,
storage tanks, and regasification facility to be completed by 1949.
The plant would liquefy about 4½ million cubic feet of natural

* Hydrocarbon Research, Inc., was the joint brainchild of O'Connor and
P. C. (Dobie) Keith, the former M. W. Kellogg engineer-executive who had
directed the construction of the gaseous diffusion plant at Oak Ridge,
Tennessee. The company's purpose was to chart new paths for the natural gas
industry. O'Connor, Keith, and Dresser Industries each owned a one-third
interest.

gas a day, and the tanks would store the equivalent of forty days of production. Storage units would be underground rather than above as in Cleveland, and they were to consist of one hundred cylindrical vessels contained in vapor-tight, sheet-metal-clad boxes insulated on all sides by thirty-inch widths of cork.* Hydrocarbon would design the plant; Clark Bros. and Pacific Pumps would provide compressors and pumps; and Stacey Bros. would provide storage tanks. The contract was reported by the American press to be one of the largest signed with the Soviet Union by a United States company since the war's end.

At this point in postwar international politics the uneasy alliance formed between the United States and the Soviet Union during World War II hung together by the slenderest of threads. Relations were deteriorating as problems arose over spheres of influence in Europe. Advocates of a cutback in trade with the Russians were becoming more and more vocal. Neil Mallon earlier had recommended after the war that the U.S. government guarantee commercial transactions with the Russians to eliminate the "immediate pocket book hazard" that would harm American manufacturers if a ban should be imposed unexpectedly. The government, however, had let business proceed at its own risk in any dealings with the Russians. As work toward the liquefaction plant moved forward in 1947, Dresser and other major companies, such as Ford Motor Company, which had contracts with the U.S.S.R., began to be concerned about increasingly negative public sentiment. Mallon asked Washington for a clarification of policies toward the Soviet Union. "If accepting further business from those people is inimical to the over-all interest of the United States, then we do not want any part of such business," Mallon wrote to Secretary of Commerce Averell Harriman in late September 1947.

Mallon's earlier fears that a sudden ban on trade might be enacted were realized on March 31, 1948. The Commerce Department decided to terminate the Lend-Lease program and suspend licenses authorizing exports to the Soviet Union. By then Dresser had provided most but not all of the equipment needed for the liquefaction

---

* The detailed contract stipulated a complete design of the facility according to standards existing in the United States; spare parts sufficient for one year of normal plant operation, and spare piston rings for the Clark compressors sufficient for two years of operation; the dispatch to the Soviet Union of men experienced in the erection, welding, and heat treatment of the alloy steel storage vessels. Everything was to be shipped in prefabricated form to the port of New York, ready for delivery to the U.S.S.R. by Technopromimport, the Soviet agency that executed the agreement.

plant, including five 600-horsepower, 300-rpm Clark Bros. compressors with six-engine cylinders and two compression cylinders for compressing the natural gas, ethylene, and ammonia. The Russians also had received most of the equipment needed for the gas purification and drying units, as well as the cascade liquefaction section. Dresser, in turn, had received payment for everything shipped. What the Soviet Union did not yet have were the storage vessels and pumps needed for regasification, and there was no way for Dresser to send them.

With an Iron Curtain now descending between the two world powers, Dresser and others in the natural gas industry who were watching this LNG project with great interest heard no further word about the plant. Only years later was it learned that the Soviet Union had managed to bring the works into operation in mid-1954, some five years later than originally planned.

Meanwhile, cold war tensions also threatened the termination of Dresser contracts with Rumania and Czechoslovakia. O'Connor had negotiated to sell some $17 million in equipment for rebuilding the war-torn oil industry in those nations. Under the plan, Rumania would purchase $12 million in oil-field equipment and Czechoslovakia would buy $5 million in materials for the construction of a synthetic oil plant. After the agreement had been signed, however, the United States government adopted a requirement that export licenses were necessary for all shipments to Eastern Europe. Dresser had assembled most of the material and it was ready for delivery, but now the licenses were denied. The situation was complicated further by the fact that Rumania already had deposited its payment in gold in Switzerland and now, of course, would retrieve it. Dresser was unwilling to lose its significant investment in this contract without some redemption, and O'Connor initiated an unusual three-way swap to save the sale. He knew that Argentina desperately needed the same oil-field equipment assembled for Rumania, but had no money to pay for it. Rumania, besides needing oil-field equipment, needed commodities in its continuing effort to recover from the war. Sensing the possibilities of a barter, O'Connor hopped plane after plane for some fast, high-level negotiating. The three-way deal he worked out satisfied all parties. Argentina's Juan Perón agreed to take the oil-field equipment and to pay for it by giving Rumania a substantial amount of hides, beef, and grain; Dresser kept the Rumanian gold.

———

In 1947 Stacey Bros. Construction Company engineers built in Elizabeth, New Jersey, this ten-million-cubic-foot wet-seal gas holder, the largest all-welded unit in the world.

The year 1948 was by far the greatest in Dresser's history. Net sales of $108.6 million represented a distinct advance over the previous year—a record one itself—of some 35 percent; net profits of $8 million were nearly 50 percent better than those of the previous year; and earnings per share of $7.14 were nearly double those of 1947 and almost ten times those of 1946. Employees now numbered almost 9,000, an increase during the year of 19 percent. Average wage-hour rates were up 7 percent.

Four out of every five dollars in revenue came from the sale of equipment for the production, transportation, refining, and supply of petroleum and natural gas. The other side of the business, the gas heating appliance companies, generated the remaining volume. More significantly, the profit ratio from the capital goods sector was more favorable. This was the aspect of business in which Mallon, O'Connor, Reimer, and other top officials felt much more comfortable. Indeed, that sector's future as well as its recent past appeared brighter. Consequently, when in early summer of 1948 a partner of the investment banking firm of Reynolds & Company inquired as to whether Dresser might be interested in selling its entire Gas Appliances Division the answer was a cautious yes. Reynolds & Company proposed to purchase Bryant, Day & Night, and Payne for cash, organize them into a new company, and sell stock to the public. The sale would place Dresser in an exceptionally strong cash position; it would enable the company to concentrate its effort in manufacturing and selling equipment for the oil and gas industries; and it would come while the Gas Appliances Division's earnings were up and its value high. These favorable factors seemed to outweigh the fact that disposal of the division would reduce, at least for the short term, Dresser's earning power.

After an audit and appraisal of the Gas Appliances Division, its value was determined to be $10.8 million. This was the amount Reynolds & Company paid to Dresser officials for the division.* Dresser officials never regretted their decision to sell; their total attention now could be concentrated on the area they knew best.

And this area, the manufacture of equipment essential to the all-important search for oil and gas throughout the world, seemed limitless in its prospects. The United States alone produced two-thirds of the world's supply of oil, and it was estimated that only one-eighth of the nation's potential sources had been discovered. Yet, there was even greater long-range opportunity for international growth, and Dresser's foreign sales still were in their infancy. The oil and gas industries were becoming, Mallon told shareholders at the end of 1948, two of the most important industries in the world.

> As [postwar] reconstruction continues and other countries, who have become exposed to new techniques and acquired new ideals from wartime experience, try more earnestly to follow the American pattern of better living, who knows to what extent foreign petroleum resources may be developed? . . . The underlying characteristic of the petroleum industry . . . is one of necessary and perpetual expansion. Its needs are more urgent—and therefore, it must always continue to extend its efforts to find, to transport, and to refine more oil, and to utilize natural gas, which is a partner-product of oil drilling.

Despite this forecast, there remained one weakness in the Dresser line of products: its emphasis on capital goods continued to make the company vulnerable to shifts in economic winds. Security's bits had helped in this regard, but expendable items still accounted for less than 12 percent of overall sales. The company needed to augment its line of expendables.

In late summer of 1949 such an opportunity arose when Mallon learned that the nation's second-largest manufacturer of drilling mud might be available. The company was the Magnet Cove

---

* The new company formed by these units was Affiliated Gas Company, Inc., which six years later was acquired by Carrier Corporation.

As the oil and gas industries moved into South America after World War II, so did Dresser products. Here, at a booster station in the middle of Lake Maracaibo, Venezuela, Clark compressors control pressure on the gas in oil wells beneath the water.

Barium Corporation of Houston. One of its partners wanted to sell his approximate one-third interest, and in trying to determine the most satisfactory arrangement, it was realized that the best profits could be made by selling the entire company. Dresser, having enhanced its cash position through the sale of the heating appliance division, undertook a thorough examination of Magnet Cove. "This company has had a phenomenal growth," Reimer reported. "It was organized in 1940 with an original investment of $3,200 and has grown to produce $10,685,000 sales in 1948 with a net profit after taxes of $748,875." Reimer's report was confirmed by an independent engineering firm's analysis, which showed that the commercial value of the company's barite (the principal ingredient for drilling muds) operations was $3,450,000; its reserves constituted 30 percent of the known U.S. deposits of barite; and the 5½ million tons of recoverable barite should last thirty-eight more years at the present level of operations. The company had current assets of $3.2 million and current liabilities of $909,000.

When it was learned that all of Magnet Cove's common stock could be acquired for $2.8 million in cash, the directors unhesitatingly approved the transaction on October 28, 1949. Five days later the deal was consummated, and a bright new company with an essential—yet expendable—oil-field product was added to the Dresser Industries family.

Several years later Mallon described in broad terms why Magnet Cove clearly seemed to be a desirable acquisition.

> Dresser knew that in the drilling for oil the search . . . would go to deeper horizons below the surface of the earth, because much of the oil in shallow depths had already been found. As the well goes to deeper depths, the pressures encountered are greater and barite is a heavy material, one of whose purposes—one of whose functions —is to hold the pressures in the well while drilling proceeds.

> With our knowledge that heavier pressures would be encountered in the development of the oil industry, we thought that more and more barite would be used. So in considering Magnet Cove we realized that we would be getting into an expanding business so that the development of that company in the years ahead would probably be greater than it had been in the years immediately preceding, so it looked like a fine business opportunity.

Magnet Cove brought a fascinating though little-known element of the oil industry to Dresser. The company had started when Willard Johnson, a young, small-town Tennessee banker, began authorizing loans to a fifty-year-old prospector named Harry B. Brown for mining by wheelbarrow and shovel a small barite deposit on the Wolf River in Fentress County, Tennessee. "At that time, I didn't know what barite was," Johnson later recalled. "But he showed me a piece of the rock . . . and he brought this check in and anything that would bring money into a bank in those days was very interesting. So I became interested." Johnson became so interested that he became partners with Brown and started working the deposit by hand with him on his days off from the bank. On weekends he began making sales trips to potential barite customers—primarily the glass and chemical industries—throughout the southern part of the United States.

Johnson and Brown soon realized that their deposit of barite was being depleted, however, with every sale. Once it was used up, their promising enterprise would come to an abrupt halt. As this unhappy eventuality loomed ever more imminent, Brown encountered an intriguing geological report issued by the State of Arkansas. It told of a large barite deposit near Malvern, Arkansas, that had been known since the turn of the century but that could not be mined because it was only about 60 to 70 percent barium sulfate (the scientific name for barite) instead of the more than

Willard Johnson, cofounder of Magnet Cove Barium Corporation, was an important individual not only for Dresser but for the entire drilling industry.

90 percent purity needed by the markets. Desperate to find new reserves, they decided to investigate this deposit despite the discouraging report. Obtaining samples of this low-grade ore, they took them to a young metallurgist named Leonard McMurray of the Tennessee Valley Authority at Knoxville. Was there any possible way, they wanted to know, to upgrade this ore to make it usable? One by one McMurray exhausted the standard techniques for beneficiating barite—which, in this case, meant removing finely ingrained silica and pyrite—but all of them failed, as they had failed for everyone else who had experimented with the Arkansas barite. McMurray was not one to give up easily, and he decided to attempt a flotation process sometimes used with other minerals to remove impurities, but never before with barite. To his relief—and perhaps surprise—the process worked. The upgraded ore still did not fit the requirements of Johnson and Brown's customers in the glass and chemical industries, however, but there was emerging a new use for barite for which it did seem

suitable. This was its use as the principal ingredient of "mud" to insert into oil wells during drilling. But there remained still another problem. The drilling mud business was dominated by the National Lead Company, and to attempt to compete with limited resources against this company seemed foolhardy. Johnson and Brown took their hats in hand and approached National Lead to see if it might be willing to market this plentiful new supply of barite. National Lead politely declined; the quality of the Arkansas ore simply was too low, it believed, to meet industry standards.

Undaunted, the two partners plunged ahead, attracted a number of brave investors, and organized on January 5, 1940, their own company, which they called the Magnet Cove Barium Corporation. Joining them as stockholders were three brothers named Gernst and a Malvern, Arkansas, man named Joe W. Kimsey. Authorized capital stock was $25,000.

Johnson, who still had not yielded his position at the bank in Tennessee, was president; Brown became vice president in charge of production. Six months later the world's first barite-processing plant utilizing the flotation method for beneficiation went into production. Its effectiveness was proved at once beyond any doubt. The oil industry's standards, which National Lead had believed the Arkansas barite could never meet, were surpassed with ease. Magnet Cove's production from the beginning averaged a specific gravity of 4.35, or 95 percent barite, considerably higher than industry standards of 4.0 specific gravity, or 84 percent barite. Johnson and Brown, through their determination and faith, added fifteen million tons of reserves to the country's supply of usable barite at a time when its need as a drilling mud was mushrooming into immense proportions. The company adopted the trademark of "Magcobar" for its production, a name by which the company itself ultimately became known. By the time Dresser acquired the company, its remarkable growth already had made it a close second to National Lead. It was destined soon to surpass that once-dominant company.

The acquisition turned out to be one of the most profitable ever made by Dresser. Over the years it proved to be a consistent money-maker, and Willard Johnson, who remained as the company's president and became a Dresser director, was an important addition. Magnet Cove already had a modern laboratory and a trained staff for product development and quality control, a complete line of various mud materials in addition to barite to meet various drilling needs, field engineers and laboratory-equipped

The barite deposit that enabled Magnet Cove Barium Corporation to become the dominant firm in the drilling mud business was this one at Malvern, Arkansas, shown in the early 1950's.

cars to assist at the drilling rig, and a dealer organization offering day and night service from more than 250 warehouses.

The company's product, an essential part of every modern drilling operation, was little known to the general public, yet drilling mud was of critical importance to the successful completion of a well. Forced down through the drill pipe and up again between the pipe and the well wall, it performed several key functions. It lubricated and cooled the drilling bit; it "floated" the cuttings to prevent their accumulation at the bottom of the hole; it built up a mud cake on the wall of the well and eliminated the need to halt drilling to run casing; it supported part of the weight of the drill pipe and casing; and its density prevented high-pressure formation fluids—oil, gas, or water—from flowing into the well or "blowing out," with a possible loss of the well and drilling equipment. Before adoption of drilling mud by the industry, beginning in the mid-1920's, these needs had been served inadequately by water and actual mud obtained at the site. Now, with the certainty that the search for oil would go to deeper and deeper depths of the earth, the need for mud was more critical.

While the term implied a certain simplicity, drilling mud had become anything but that. By 1949, specialists known as "mud engineers" (and Magcobar itself had more than forty trained engineers who operated over the Southwest) analyzed individual wells from their portable laboratories and recommended complex and carefully controlled mixtures for the particular formation and conditions encountered. The mixtures, prepared on the spot, varied not only from well to well but even during different stages of drilling. The principal material was barite, but additives were bentonite, kaolin, native clay, various phosphates, oil-base muds, crude oil, water, and sometimes even unusual substances such as shredded cellophane or plastic flakes. Total mud requirements for a well in 1949 ranged from one hundred barrels to upward of fifteen hundred barrels with an average weight of ten to eleven pounds per gallon. These amounts were destined to escalate in coming years.

As 1949 ended, Dresser's goal of serving the oil and gas industries "all along the line" was closer than ever to realization. Revenue for the year was down, primarily because of the sale of the gas appliance companies, but the program of plant improvement and modernization, for which some $3.7 million had been spent, was to continue at a high rate. Expenditures for research and development remained high too. And while the bitter steel strike and other work stoppages of 1949 caused that year to be one of the most strife-ridden ever in the nation's industrial history, Dresser operated without a single man-hour being lost because of labor disputes.

The annual report called 1949 a "year of teamwork," citing examples in which effective cooperation of the various companies had proved mutually beneficial. A mud pump engineered by Clark was built by Bovaird & Seyfang and was sold by Ideco's oil-well-supply stores. Kobe, Inc., threaded and slotted pipes for Security

Ideco's construction of derricks for the petroleum industry inevitably carried it over into the making of many of the nation's television antennas.

Engineering. A series of illustrations showed bags of Magcobar mud being loaded onto a ship for delivery to an offshore drilling operation in Louisiana and then being dispatched by a Clark-Ideco pump into the well, where a Security drilling bit "made hole." Another series of photographs related contributions by five Dresser companies to the gas industry. In a single gas booster station one could see ten Clark centrifugal compressors moving gas through long-distance pipelines from field to city, an all-steel booster station constructed by Ideco, and a dry seal holder built by Stacey Bros. Roots-Connersville's turbine-driven centrifugal boosters were shown in a large city gas station, and its gas meters were tied together with Dresser couplings. Other sections of the annual report portrayed still other examples in which Dresser products united in a common effort to serve the oil and gas industries.

And, for the first time, the report told of an expansion of Ideco's rig-building enterprise to accommodate a growing American phenomenon—television. A 595-foot self-supporting Ideco television tower rose high above an Atlanta, Georgia, station beaming to thousands of viewers popular programs such as the Tuesday-night antics of Milton Berle. A company that could build a steel oil-well derrick had no difficulty in building the same sort of tower, though much taller, for television. The horizon for Dresser products seemed forever expanding.

S

A Time of Maturing

If in April of 1950 a person happened to glance over the array of magazines at his corner newsstand, there was a good chance that he would see the studious, shy visage of Dresser's president, Henry Neil Mallon, on the cover of *Business Week*. The story inside asked:

"What makes a thriving industry turn nomad?

"How can a big company get the advantages of smallness?

"How can a small company get the advantages of size?

"How can a dying company in a booming industry slough its obsolete line and get back on its feet?"

The answers, the magazine declared, could be found by studying the actions of Dresser Industries under the leadership of Mallon, whose calm exterior seemed to contradict the internal man who was "full of ideas—and ready to go to bat for them."

Mallon's latest idea, the one that inspired the article, was to move Dresser's headquarters again. The five years in Cleveland had been satisfactory and comfortable. Yet, the Southwest now was indisputably the center of the oil and gas industries, and with the sale of Bryant, Dresser had no manufacturing plants in Cleveland nor any particular reason to be there.

In May 1950, the move was complete. Headquarters was on the third floor of the small but new and attractive Atlantic Building, located in the heart of downtown Dallas. Mallon and O'Connor had adjoining offices, with a connecting doorway, and Reimer was situated just a few feet away. A professional decorator furnished the offices in impressive fashion.

Perhaps no one was happier about the move than O'Connor and his Oklahoma-born wife of Indian descent, Sansa. For years Sansa had yearned to return to the Southwest, and now the O'Connors bought a farm with a white, two-story country home near

Neil Mallon and some
of the symbols of Dres-
ser's recent growth ap-
peared on the cover of
Business Week on April
22, 1950, coinciding with
the company's move
to Dallas.

Richardson, some twenty miles north of downtown Dallas. O'Connor promptly dubbed it Haderway Farm, signifying that Sansa
had "had her way." In years to come Haderway Farm would
be the site of annual Dresser employee picnics, and years later it
would provide a lovely setting for the campus of Richland College.
Mallon, still a bachelor, similarly bought a country place some
twenty miles northwest of town at Farmers Branch and transformed it into a gorgeous setting with artificial lakes* and a
tennis court. Reimer, who had married a Bradford woman in
1934 and now had two sons, settled more conveniently in fashion-
able North Dallas.

* For a while Mallon's landscapers struggled vainly to build lakes that
would hold water. The bottom of the lake beds seemed determined to permit
the water to seep away. Mallon finally ordered a large shipment of bentonite
from Magnet Cove, being aware of its peculiar swelling properties. With a
layer of bentonite applied, the water could not escape and the problem was
solved.

During the 1950's, office workers at corporate headquarters enjoyed annual picnics at the spacious grounds of John B. O'Connor's Haderway Farm north of Dallas.

One month after the move to Dallas the cold war that had curtailed Dresser's business with nations behind the Iron Curtain suddenly became hot. Communist forces from North Korea crossed the 38th parallel to invade the Republic of Korea, where U.S. armed forces, stationed in limited numbers, retreated along with the South Korean army. The resulting war, or "police action," as it came to be called, was an agonizing experience for the American nation and destined to end in a stalemate in 1953. Dresser stood ready, as did other manufacturing enterprises, to retool once again its facilities for the war effort, but this time few defense contracts arrived and the company maintained in almost all respects its normal activities. Dresser inevitably was affected on the home front, however, through higher corporate taxes in the form of income and excess profits taxes, wage and price controls, and new federal regulations concerning production. Despite the uneasiness engendered by the Korean conflict, the cold war, and increased federal taxes and regulations, the decade of the 1950's was to be a period of tranquility for American society and a prosperous time for industry. The company that Solomon R. Dresser founded was seventy years old at midpoint twentieth century. One of the member firms—Roots-Connersville—was only four years short of celebrating its centennial anniversary. Thus, the Dresser Industries of 1950 was really a new combination of companies with different, if related, overall goals.

The company's rapid expansion had raised anew the question to which Mallon had addressed himself in 1944: "What is Dresser Industries?" This was the theme for the company's most ambitious advertising campaign to date. It consisted of a series of two-page, full-color advertisements highlighting each of the Dresser companies. The advertisements appeared month after month in the nation's leading oil and gas publications during 1952 and 1953. They were especially attractive because the company had commissioned an artist to create eye-catching paintings showing the company's products in use. For Kobe, for example, a helmeted oil-field worker, accompanied by a handsome collie, was depicted wading knee-deep through snow to reach a Kobe pump in a scenic mountain area. The advertisement for Dresser Manufacturing Division showed a natural gas pipeline being repaired by a group of workers on a big-city street. The careful detail and varied settings portrayed in the ten advertisements, plus the simple, uncluttered content of the written messages explaining the kinship of the Dresser companies and their roles in the oil and gas industries, made them a truly memorable series.

While such efforts sought to explain to the public the unity in the company's energy-related activities, new attention was being paid to promoting internal cohesion as well. For one thing, a plan was needed to prepare young executives to assume top leadership roles. On several recent occasions, confronted by the loss of high-level executives, it had been necessary to recruit replacements from other companies. This was harmful for morale at the junior executive level, and Mallon recommended in the summer of 1951 that a program be instituted to train executives of member companies to qualify for positions of broader responsibilities. "Unless we get going soon we will be at the end of the parade instead of at the head where we belong," he warned. Agreeing with this sentiment, the board of directors passed a resolution for Mallon to appoint a committee to study management training programs of other businesses and "to develop a Dresser plan for selecting and training top executive personnel replacements."

Boncher, who still was in Bradford as general manager, was named committee chairman. Other members were Richard Porter Brown, director of personnel for salaried employees; Tom L. Moody, industrial relations director; and A. R. Weis, president of Pacific Pumps. Boncher and his committee reviewed the training programs of sixty of the nation's foremost companies before recommending a plan for Dresser. The one finally adopted centered around conferences planned every quarter in various sections of the country where Dresser plants could serve as laboratories. Each meeting would stress a different theme, such as sales, production, accounting, or engineering. The first conference, held February 20–22, 1952, at the Town House in Los Angeles, was attended by thirty-five Dresser employees. Its general theme was sales. Talks by various officials, panel discussions, and question-and-answer periods were interspersed with field trips to the Dresser plants in Southern California. This new emphasis on executive training would increase with each passing year.

The streamlining of the company's operations assumed other forms too. As Dresser had expanded through acquisitions, the new units generally retained their corporate structure even though virtually all outstanding shares were owned by Dresser. This was deemed a satisfactory arrangement, for there was a desire to maintain for those companies the identity and goodwill built up over the years. Moreover, there were small tax advantages in having separate charters. An alternate status was typified by Dresser Manufacturing and Clark Bros., both of which had become divisions rather than corporations. Under this scheme there were no separate boards of directors or separate charters. The question of which of the two plans was better generally was academic, but in light of the remarkable postwar success of the Dresser Manufacturing and Clark Bros. divisions, it was decided to convert Roots-Connersville to divisional status. As far as federal income taxes were concerned, Roots would lose its surtax exemption, but that would be offset by a savings in Pennsylvania state taxes. In January 1952, the Roots-Connersville Blower Corporation was liquidated and became the Roots-Connersville Blower Division. In the years to come all Dresser's member units were to be converted to divisional status, a change that was not intended to de-emphasize the autonomy of the units.

International Derrick & Equipment Company presented another situation that needed clarification. Among the company's operations was a chain of sixteen oil-field-equipment stores. Sixteen stores were hardly enough to provide adequate coverage if Dresser was to service the entire oil-field industry, yet they required a substantial amount of working capital for inventories and accounts receivable. A conclusion was reached that the capital would generate more profits if transferred to other Dresser companies. Thus, on March 2, 1951, the Ideco supply stores were sold to the H. K. Porter Company, Inc., for approximately $1.6 million. This represented a loss of some $250,000, but the freeing of the capital involved made the action worthwhile.

Ideco operations next were divided into two separate and distinct units, each maintaining the word "Ideco" in its name. Ideco Division, Dresser Equipment Company, with offices in Dallas and Beaumont, concentrated on oil-field equipment. Ideco Division, Dresser-Stacey Company, located in Columbus, specialized in steel towers, prefabricated steel buildings, airport equipment such as landing beacons, and similar products. Ideco's manufacturing facility in Torrance, California, was sold.

The company that had appeared so promising because of its novel approach to oil-field pumping, Kobe, Inc., seemed as far removed as ever from realizing its anticipated potential. The hydraulic pumping system Coberly had designed required a large initial investment, and its potential thus was limited to the biggest fields. The equipment was so sophisticated that it was likened to a Swiss watch, and this intricacy did not seem compatible with oil fields. After just two years as a part of Dresser Industries, Kobe had become a profit maker. But profits had not been substantial, and in 1954 the company was sold for $2.6 million to a new corporation organized by Coberly.

Indeed, it was now determined that merely to return a profit was not enough. Dresser established an earnings-before-taxes goal for all units of 30 percent on the invested capital. Recent studies had shown that firms comparable to Dresser earned in 1953 an average of 37 percent on invested capital before taxes. Dresser had earned 14.7 percent, and this, despite the larger-than-average investment on research and capital improvements, did not satisfy headquarters in Dallas. Even the company's average earnings from 1948 through 1953 had been hardly better: 17.2 percent. Dresser's top officials became convinced that the company could earn approximately twice its present earnings. "This poor showing is the result of very poor planning or no planning at all, and little or no control over our operations," Reimer told Dresser officials in 1954 at the fourth Management Development Conference in Mineral Wells, Texas. "It is just this sort of situation that we must correct, and we think we can correct it with the right kind of profit planning." To accomplish the 30 percent profit goal announced by Reimer, the company instituted careful planning sessions before the beginning of each fiscal year. Top officers of Dresser's divisions prepared elaborate blueprints for the approaching year. Once agreement with headquarters was reached on the goals, the individual managers were free to make the decisions necessary to attain them. The profit-planning sessions became increasingly detailed and sophisticated in future years, and formed an integral part of the Dresser system.

A continually growing proportion of Dresser's sales was international. Between 1950, when the total was approximately $9 million, and 1955, Dresser's foreign sales doubled. The United States, the world's largest producer and consumer of petroleum, was relied upon by areas of the world such as the Middle East and South America to furnish the technology they needed to develop their own industry. American firms were ready and eager to comply, but international dealings were complicated by the difficulties involved in exchanging currencies. The inequities in the balance of trade meant that foreign nations invariably lacked the American dollars they needed to buy American products. Practically the only way Dresser and other American manufacturers could meet the international demand for their equipment was to grant licenses for manufacturing their goods to foreign firms who could be paid with their own currency. Of course, the grantor of the license reaped a percentage of the profits, and the problem of conversion to American dollars was not entirely eliminated.

In 1952 Dresser conceived of a way to alleviate this problem through the creation of its own foreign company. Located in the town of Vaduz, Liechtenstein, it was named Dresser A. G. Vaduz. Liechtenstein, being a neighbor to Switzerland, was a convenient site because it was a party to all trade or payment agreements made by Switzerland with other nations. International forms of currency could be converted in Liechtenstein without restrictions. The man chosen to head the operation was a Swiss corporate lawyer named Hans Berger. Berger had first worked with Dresser when he assisted O'Connor in arranging the three-way trade in 1948 with Rumania and Argentina. Berger, who worked closely with J. D. Mayson and Reece Hatchitt of the Dallas legal staff, was charged with negotiating, executing, and monitoring the performance of the various license agreements; alerting the Dallas headquarters to technical developments in Europe; and offering other general services in the international arena to member companies. A further benefit of the foreign company, a considerable one, was the fact that no American taxes had to be paid on international earnings until the money was returned to the United States. Thus, profits from international operations could be funneled into Dresser A. G. Vaduz and used to expand overseas ventures. The establishment of Dresser A. G. Vaduz brought needed stability and order to this rapidly growing sector of the company's business.

Berger's earliest undertakings indicated the global nature of Dresser A. G. Vaduz's operations. First, he executed a license agreement with an Italian company, Cantieri Navali Riuniti, for the manufacture of Clark Bros. compressors. Next came a license agreement in Britain for the manufacture of Ideco products. Then he investigated and cleared up questions concerning license agreements executed in the late 1940's by Pacific Pumps with firms in England, France, and Holland. Involvement in Asia, South America, and the Middle East soon followed.

Dresser equipment could be found wherever oil and gas were

produced—in the Arctic Circle, the Middle East, North Africa, or the jungles of Burma. Plants in Italy, Venezuela, Mexico, Argentina, and Canada were manufacturing or assembling products bearing the trademarks Dresser, Clark, Pacific, Ideco, Magcobar, and Security. Sales offices were located in Africa, Australia, India, Europe, the Middle East, and South America. The 1952 annual report devoted an entire section to these expanding international activities. One illustration showed an Ideco Hydrair Hoist in the forests of Venezuela as part of a Shell Oil Company exploration project. A long line of Pacific process and slurry pumps was seen in a catalytic cracking unit in the Netherlands, the first such modern unit in continental Europe. A Roots-Connersville three-stage exhauster for handling gas was portrayed in a Latin-American industrial plant; ten Clark Bros. right-angle compressors were operating in a petroleum refinery in Scotland; multistage pumps made by Pacific Pumps were irrigating rice fields in the Orient; and a Dresser-coupled water line carrying fresh water to Singapore was guarded by a large, bearded Sikh policeman bearing a sawed-off shotgun and a long knife.

One of the most promising areas in foreign sales was in drilling equipment. O'Connor, who had come to know Argentina's Juan Perón in the three-way deal with Rumania, executed a contract with that nation to provide its government-owned oil company with more than $500,000 in Ideco equipment to develop the prolific oil and gas fields there. A decision also was made to extend credit for the first time to Mexico's Pemex Company to enable that company to buy Ideco rigs for its oil fields.

Part of the business of streamlining Dresser's operation in the early 1950's was in making certain that its services to the oil and gas industries kept pace with technology. Two areas of service not performed by any Dresser company were the important and technically sophisticated areas of perforation, a method of increasing the productivity of wells, and logging, a means of analyzing underground strata. Both practices had progressed immeasurably from the days when Solomon Dresser used Rackarock to loosen oil-bearing sands and followed Angell's "belt" theory to interpret what lay below. One of the leading firms in offering modern, technical oil-field services of this nature was Lane-Wells, a company with headquarters in Huntington Park, California, and with current assets in 1954 of $8.9 million and net income of approximately $2.5 million. Such a company could add substantially to that portion of Dresser sales represented by expendable products and services as well as enhance the goal of service "all along the line." In late 1954 friendly negotiations commenced between Mallon and the chairman of the board of Lane-Wells,

Tom L. Moody became Dresser's first industrial relations director before World War II.

Rodney S. Durkee. By mid-December they reached a tentative agreement. Dresser would exchange four shares of its common stock for five shares of Lane-Wells, an amount totaling 576,000 shares of Dresser stock. Lane-Wells would retain its staff of officers; Mallon, O'Connor, and Reimer would join Lane-Wells's board of directors; and three of Lane-Wells's directors would be invited to sit on the Dresser board.

In recommending the merger to his company's shareholders, Durkee explained that Dresser's greater financial strength would make it possible to accelerate Lane-Wells's programs of construction, capital equipment, and research and development. Moreover, Lane-Wells's shareholders would enjoy a broader market for their new Dresser shares. The arguments were persuasive, and effective March 1, 1955, Lane-Wells and its subsidiaries, Well Surveys, Inc., and Petro-Tech Service Company,* joined Dresser Industries.

* Petro-Tech, the larger of these subsidiaries, had California headquarters but operated in South America with an early emphasis on Venezuela which soon shifted to Argentina. Its equity in net assets was $2.4 million at the time of acquisition.

Lane-Wells's historical emphasis on creative research especially pleased Dresser's top management. The company's founders, oil equipment salesmen Wilford E. Lane and Walter T. Wells, when they started their company in California in 1932, had introduced the practice of "gun perforating" oil wells to increase their production. Gun perforating was the novel art of actually shooting bullets through the steel well casing into the producing formation, facilitating the flow of oil and gas. The two men, inspired by reading about the unsuccessful efforts of a man in Rumania to do the same, bought a patent for perforating from an American who had not been able to develop a workable gun himself. After many failures, they finally devised a gun that discharged by an electric current, and in December 1932 they perforated their first well at the Montebello field in Los Angeles County. The well's owner, Union Oil Company of California, was ready to abandon it as depleted, but after Lane and Wells perforated it with eighty-seven shots, the well began producing forty barrels of oil a day and continued to do so for several years. The practice spread rapidly thereafter to both new and old wells, and by the 1950's it was a common technique. Lane-Wells had never lost its lead in this important practice, introducing many new refinements to the art.

The company's other important pioneering effort, introduced in 1940 under license from Well Surveys, Inc., was in radioactivity well logging. In this practice, subsurface formations were analyzed by a sensitive instrument that measured the radioactivity of different strata through the casing and rendered unusually precise identifications. Another Lane-Wells breakthrough had been the introduction of the MS Neutron Log, which bombarded the formation along the bore hole with neutrons and measured the intensity of the resulting gamma-ray activity. This technique was particularly valuable for secondary recovery or in seeking new producing zones in existing wells, for unlike electric logging, it could penetrate the existing casing. To perform these specialized services Lane-Wells had an extensive network of skilled technicians, many of whom operated out of specially equipped trucks, around the globe. The company slogan, "Tomorrow's Tools—Today," seemed especially fitting.

One important effect of the Lane-Wells acquisition was the substantial addition to Dresser's expendable business. Mainly because of the impact of Magnet Cove, some 36 percent of the sales volume had consisted of such expendables as mud, drilling bits, and repair parts. Now that figure climbed suddenly to approximately 50 percent, and the effect was a virtual guarantee of greater stability in sales and profits.

Service Car No. 1 helped launch Lane-Wells into the perforating business in the early 1930's.

Not the final—there would never be a final step in such matters—but the culminating move in the streamlining of Dresser in the postwar period was a restructuring of the organizational chart. Previously, all companies had reported directly to O'Connor in his capacity as executive vice president. Aside from the fact that O'Connor was the perennial globe-trotting supersalesman for the company, with little time for administrative matters, Dresser's enterprises now were too vast and complicated for any one individual to oversee. Consequently, the company's member units were divided into two groups and placed under the responsibility of two new vice presidents in charge of operations. One of those men was Boncher, who was moved from Bradford to Dallas to become the vice president responsible for Clark Bros., Dresser Manufacturing, Pacific Pumps, Roots-Connersville, and Dresser-Ideco in Columbus. W. D. Miller, a former oil-field superintendent in the mid-continent area and Venezuela, was hired from a subsidiary of Standard Oil Company of New Jersey to be the operating vice president in charge of Magnet Cove, Lane-Wells, Security Engineering, and the Ideco Division. Both of these new vice presidents reported to O'Connor.

In announcing the reorganization, Mallon was eager that it not be interpreted as a deviation from the overall philosophy of decentralization. He underlined the fact that "local company managements will continue to have final responsibility for their own operations and for the combined success of their own companies." His description of the vice presidents' duties reiterated the point, listing their duties as guiding "local managements" in building sales through improved techniques and new-product development, reducing manufacturing and other controllable costs through encouraging greater operating efficiency, and aiding in executive development and organizational activity.

Change was a sign of vitality, and Dresser was full of change. A constant infusion of new ideas and projects kept the company from falling into a routine pattern. The staple products—compressors, pumps, mud, couplings, drilling bits, blowers, and rigs—systematically were being refined and new versions introduced as the search for oil went deeper and deeper into the ground and offshore into the ocean. Other novel projects expanded the reach of Dresser into new areas.

Roots-Connersville, which celebrated its one hundredth anniversary in 1954 with a gala ceremony, was working that year with the National Advisory Committee for Aeronautics in the development and construction of blowers for supersonic wind tunnels and engine test facilities. Some of the blowers, the biggest in the world, provided higher flow capacities and pressure ratios per stage than ever before achieved. Their pumping capacities were more than twice those of commercial machines. One government contract for large centrifugal blowers was so big that it required a plant expansion costing $903,000 to accommodate it. These powerful blowers were absolutely essential for the testing of experimental aircraft as the United States sought to maintain its lead in superiority in the skies.

Another important new Roots product that gained immediate acceptance was the Spiraxial compressor, revolutionary in principle and design. Instead of conventional rotors the Spiraxial compressor employed two screw-type rotors that rotated in opposite directions. This new compressor required no internal lubrication, needed a minimum of servicing, operated smoothly, and was comparatively lightweight. It was helpful for such varied activities as asphalt tank oxidation, fly-ash conveying, bacterial tank aeration, burner air supply, turbocharger testing, filter cake removal, and catalyst aeration.

Magnet Cove's geologist-explorers constantly searched the world over for new reserves of basic ingredients for drilling mud. They located approximately a million tons of commercial quality bentonite—the largest high-quality deposit in the world—in Wyoming's Big Horn Basin near Greybull. A processing plant costing approximately $330,000 was erected at the site in 1952. The use of bentonite as a component of drilling mud was increasing rapidly, and projections showed that the Wyoming plant would generate enough profits to pay for itself in only two and a half years of operation. Barite remained the principal ingredient of drilling mud,

J. D. Mayson, who joined Dresser in 1945, was instrumental in the formation and operations of the international firm, Dresser A. G. Vaduz, and also served the company as vice president, general counsel, and secretary.

and large amounts had been added to the company's reserves. Commercial lodes were discovered in 1952 in northern Mexico, near Salinas, and at Galeano, south of Monterrey. A foreign subsidiary, Magcobar de Mexico, was organized to mine the barite there, and in 1953 a new processing plant for it was constructed at Brownsville, Texas. Another new plant was built the same year at New Orleans to serve the heavy demand for barite in the increasingly deep drilling occurring in southern Louisiana. Barite from both Magnet Cove and Mexico was shipped to the plant for processing, and in the following year a second plant was constructed near Lake Charles, Louisiana.

Still another barite deposit was located in 1954 near Battle Mountain, Nevada, and the next year a processing plant was built there to serve the California and Rocky Mountain markets. Yet another huge deposit of barite was located and secured in 1954 on the colorful little Greek island of Mykonos, in the Aegean Sea. From that distant location the barite was transported by freighter to the New Orleans plant for processing.

This ongoing search for new deposits was, of course, critical to Magnet Cove's continuing prosperity. It was even more difficult than one might imagine to discover good reserves, for the unusually heavy weight of barite meant high shipping costs. Usable deposits thus had to be convenient to rail or waterway, preferably near intensive drilling activity, and of high quality if the expensive beneficiation process was to be avoided. The high shipping costs were illustrated by the fact that it was cheaper to send barite from Greece to New Orleans by freighter than to send it there from nearby Malvern, Arkansas, by rail.

Willard Johnson and his aides not only succeeded in replenishing but also in enlarging their reserves so that they were the most substantial in the world. These men's remarkable success in every sphere of endeavor was very evident. By 1954 the company enjoyed a 47 percent share of the drilling mud market, having surpassed the one-time monolith in the field, National Lead.* The company had almost 800 employees that year; some 150 of them were salesmen. This constituted the biggest sales force of any Dresser company. That same year the company opened an impressive new building in the suburbs west of Houston to serve as a center for research, production, distribution, and engineering activities. Oil company engineers and executives from throughout the world began coming to the center for special courses on the effective use of drilling mud. Specialists at the facility's laboratories analyzed difficult problems sent to them from around the globe. The company also developed a fleet of flying mud engineers assigned to waterlocked locations in southern Louisiana. By traveling in a laboratory-equipped seaplane, a mud engineer could service as many as eight locations a day instead of the two customarily done by car over the same area.

Dresser-Ideco in Columbus, Ohio, had found new prominence in these changing times by shifting its emphasis from oil-well derricks to communications towers. As television blossomed into a national phenomenon in the 1950's, the company became the leading producer of tall television antenna towers. Every year new towers reached higher into the sky to expand the range of the television signals. In 1950 Dresser-Ideco built the industry's first 1,000-foot tower, and five years later it was responsible for more than 40 percent of the country's television towers over 1,000 feet tall. This was twice the number of the nearest competitor's total. In 1954 the 1,572-foot tower built by Dresser-Ideco for KWTV

---

* The use of barite by the drilling industry increased from 154,760 tons a year in 1941 to 913,147 in 1954, and the rate still was climbing.

in Oklahoma City was the tallest man-made structure in the world, exceeding the height of the Empire State Building by 100 feet and the Eiffel Tower by nearly 600 feet. This structure permitted KWTV to broadcast to an audience over a 70,750-square-mile area. Triangular in shape, the tower was supported by nine guy wires 4¼ inches in diameter anchored in concrete pads a sixth of a mile from the base. The following year Dresser-Ideco built southwest of Dallas the earth's second-tallest man-made structure, a 1,521-foot "candelabra" multiple-antenna tower for television stations KRLD (now KDFW) and WFAA. The unique multiple-antenna platform at the top of the structure permitted as many as three broadcasting stations to place their individual antennas on a single tower, achieving a considerable economy. Dresser-Ideco's efforts in this endeavor expanded the broadcasting range of television to reach millions of additional Americans.

The company also was involved in solving a growing urban problem for shoppers and office workers: finding a downtown parking space. Its unique contribution was the Park-a-Loft system, a mechanical parking garage that stacked cars on multiple levels of open steel framework.

Another interesting outgrowth of Dresser-Ideco's former derrick business was a $4 million contract for the construction of towers for radar outposts in Arctic regions to detect possible surprise air attack from the north. This DEW (distant early warning) line received extensive publicity in the nation's press as an integral part of the defense system.

Ideco in Texas continued to serve the drilling industry by offering the most complete line of rigs and related equipment. Having been a leading manufacturer of steel derricks since the time they began in the 1920's to replace the traditional wooden structures, Ideco now was the leading manufacturer of portable rigs too. The company's Rambler rigs, mounted on self-propelled tractors, could be moved from site to site and made operational within hours. Some of the bigger rigs by the mid-1950's were capable of drilling to depths of more than twenty thousand feet and of hoisting almost a million pounds of "down-hole" equipment. Ideco's 1350-S was the world's largest torque-converter-equipped drilling rig.

Clark Bros., still the largest of Dresser's divisions, showed no willingness to relinquish its lead in compressors. Its line included reciprocating, centrifugal, and axial-flow compressors, and in 1955 it produced the most powerful gas-engine-driven compressor unit ever developed. This turbo-supercharged compressor, used for underground gas storage service in Michigan, developed 3,400 horsepower in ten seventeen-inch cylinders. The company also built a line of balanced-opposed electric-motor-driven compressors for a synthetic ammonia plant in Formosa. The production of synthetic ammonia, integral to the world's growing agricultural requirements, was an important new market for the compressor and one that had broad ramifications in the battle against hunger.

Security Engineering embarked in the 1950's on a grand project. The company was ready to make a serious challenge to Hughes Tool Company's dominance in the drilling bit business. Approximately 80 percent of the rotary drilling in the United States used Hughes's three-cutter bits. This was a lucrative business, for nearly four bits were required for each thousand feet drilled. With about 200 million feet drilled in the world in 1953, the market clearly was enormous. Learning that major Hughes patents were expiring in the early 1950's, Security made plans to manufacture its own three-cutter bit and capture a broader share of that market.* Company projections showed a possibility of winning at least a 12 percent share. The facilities in Whittier, where Security headquarters remained, were not adequate for a major expansion in production, so a new $2 million plant, equipped with the most modern machine tools and heat-treating equipment available, was constructed in 1952 on a twenty-acre tract in Dallas. An advantage of the Dallas location was its proximity to the active mid-continent fields.

Problems inevitably occurred in such a major new undertaking. By 1955 Security had lost approximately $5 million, with a deficit that year alone of $1.5 million. One of the major obstacles was Hughes Tool's willingness and ability in the face of Dresser's vigorous competition to hold down the price on its own bits. Dresser's expenses for research, engineering, and sales necessarily were much greater in proportion to Hughes's, and it was difficult to compete in price. Yet there seemed little option but to make a determined bid to get into this market, for to be a supplier of equipment "all along the line" one had to offer competitive drilling bits—preferably three-cone bits. The decision to continue in this undertaking in the face of losses was a difficult one. Still, the problem was not one of lack of acceptance, for by 1955 more than three thousand bits a month were being produced by the Dallas facility with annual sales of approximately $9 million. Confident that the major metallurgical and marketing problems had been

* A small beginning had been made in 1949 when three-cutter bit parts were manufactured at the Whittier plant and shipped to Canada and Mexico for assembly.

Security Engineering's new Dallas plant was placed in operation for the manufacture of drilling bits in 1952.

solved, Dresser directors authorized a five-year $7 million program of expansion of the Dallas plant to permit the ultimate production of fourteen thousand bits a month with a goal of $27 million in annual sales and a profit of 15.7 percent before taxes. The Dallas plant increased in size from 62,000 square feet to 165,000 square feet with space for a headquarters office building, research laboratory, and experimental section. Almost a decade was to pass before these large outlays began returning profits.

The struggle to gain a larger share of the drilling bit market had to be conducted on a worldwide front, so when Hughes began construction of a plant in Ireland and Reed Roller Bit was known to be considering a plant in Holland, Dresser acted too. The company purchased for $448,000 a Manchester, England, bit manufacturer named EDECO Rock Bits, Ltd. EDECO's name was changed to Security Rock Bits, Ltd., and the company began manufacturing Security's bits for the European market.

Especially cheering in the light of other difficulties was the news that Security's new S3P rock bit, introduced in Canada, demonstrated a substantially longer life than competing bits and also faster rates of penetration. This bit was enhanced by the application of wear-resistant metals to the gauge surfaces. From twelve to fifteen bits previously were required to drill a typical

4,000-foot well, but only five to seven S3P bits were needed to reach that depth.

———————

Dresser's board of directors was an unusually compatible group. It was also a *working* group. Either the full board or the executive committee met on an average of once a month, alternating from Dallas to New York to Los Angeles and occasionally to other cities. The executive committee, presided over by Mallon, was remarkably stable. Next to Mallon, the man who had served longest on that committee was the very capable Prescott S. Bush of Brown Brothers Harriman & Company, who had become a director in 1930. Bush, of course, had known the company intimately since he had helped reorganize it in 1928 and 1929. Another outside member of long tenure was William A. McAfee, the corporate counsel who was senior partner in a Cleveland law firm. McAfee, elected to the board in 1933, had been on the executive committee since the late 1930's. O'Connor and Henry P. Isham were the remaining committee members. O'Connor became a member early in World War II, and Isham, president of the Clearing Industrial District, Inc., of Chicago, joined the committee in 1950, the same year he was elected a director.

The number of board members fluctuated, usually between ten and twelve. The more important Dresser units, such as Clark Bros. or Magnet Cove, always had board representation, and an effort was made to have directors representing the various industries served by Dresser. Board members in 1951 who were affiliated directly with Dresser were Mallon, O'Connor, Arthur R. Weis, Willard M. Johnson, and C. Paul Clark. Outside directors included Bush, Isham, McAfee, Norman Chandler, and William V. Griffin. Griffin, president of Brady Security & Realty Corporation of New York, was the senior man, having been elected on January 3, 1929, the same day as Mallon.

Several notable changes occurred in board membership in the first part of the 1950's. In November 1952 the voters of Connecticut elected Bush to the United States Senate. He resigned from his directorship after twenty-two years of service. Dresser's directors, paying tribute to him, cited his "tolerance and understanding, respect for the feelings and opinions of others, concern for his country, wise judgment, and . . . ability to fight vigorously and effectively for his convictions." Bush's own regard for Dresser had been passed on to his son, George, who, following World War II, had worked for Reimer in the Cleveland headquarters,

The two Bush families pose in front of a Dresser company airplane in West Texas. George Bush, center, an oil-field-supply salesman for Ideco, is with his wife, Barbara, and son George. Prescott Bush, right, a long-time director for Dresser, is with his wife, Dorothy.

then for Pacific Pumps and Ideco before becoming an independent oil producer in Texas.*

Another prominent individual who joined Dresser's board was Everette L. DeGolyer of Dallas. DeGolyer enjoyed international renown as a petroleum geologist. This scholarly and literate man had gained a different sort of public attention a few years earlier by buying the struggling *Saturday Review of Literature* and saving it from an uncertain future. Elected to Dresser's board on July 8, 1954, DeGolyer had less than three years to serve before his death.

Another well-known American who joined Dresser's board in this period was former Secretary of the Navy Robert B. Anderson. Anderson was given the additional titles of vice president and chairman of the executive committee upon his election in December 1955. Prior to his work in the nation's capital, this native Texan had had experience in the petroleum business, and it was believed that he would be particularly effective in the company's interna-

* George Bush later would become a congressman from Texas, national chairman of the Republican Party, delegate to the United Nations, director of the Central Intelligence Agency, and the nation's first diplomatic representative to the People's Republic of China.

tional operations. In less than two years, however, President Eisenhower nominated Anderson to be Secretary of the Treasury, and he resigned his Dresser positions upon assuming that office.

Dresser's most important affairs continued to be supervised largely by the troika of Mallon, O'Connor, and Reimer. As one brokerage firm's analysis noted, the company was unique in that these three leading executives had worked together for nearly twenty years. "This long and close association has naturally resulted in all three individuals possessing the overall, broad approach toward Dresser's corporate policy." The team was expected to continue for several more years since Mallon was 61; O'Connor, 59; and Reimer, 51. "It is commonly accepted that Management is the most important single factor in the success of any industrial enterprise, and Dresser appears to be unusually blessed with an able, experienced, and aggressive management team," the analyst concluded.

The headquarters group, numbering now approximately seventy-five persons, became in these early years in Dallas a close-knit group. It was small enough so that one employee could know all others. A favorite festivity enjoyed by all was the annual company picnic hosted by the O'Connors at their spacious Haderway Farm. Employees and their families donned casual clothes on that one day of the year to participate in such summer activities as sack racing, rowboat racing, horseback riding, singing, and novelty contests such as the "tray race" in which contestants balanced food and drink as they ran. A photographic summary of this fun was produced each year in the "Dresser Picnictorial Review," prepared by the Systems Planning and Public Relations departments.

———————

As fiscal year 1955 ended, Dresser could be proud of its record. Sales and net earnings of $164.7 million and $10.3 million, respectively, represented an all-time high. "The Company's growth is so closely linked to the rapidly growing oil, gas and chemical industries, that further growth seems almost inevitable," Mallon told the shareholders. But as Mallon would be the first to point out, "inevitable" growth was not really satisfactory. What he wanted, what Reimer and O'Connor wanted, and what the directors wanted was extraordinary growth.

9

The Turbodrill Adventure

America in the 1950's: expanding suburbs, ducktail haircuts, drive-in movies, hi-fi, Davy Crockett coonskin caps, transistor radios, galloping capitalism, time payments, "I like Ike," rock 'n' roll, television, cold war jitters. For most Americans it was a happy, prosperous time.

Between the late 1940's and 1955 the median income for a family rose 50 percent. American workers were producing half of the world's goods. The United States was a prosperous nation whose unusually high standard of living and thriving industry were supported by what appeared to be a boundless supply of energy.

There were few if any obvious reminders for the average American of Dresser Industries' basic role in helping to support this affluent age. Indeed, Dresser's products were not directly intended for the consumer. Yet, the company indirectly had an impact on a remarkable range of daily activities. The most obvious and important of these was its role in converting energy sources into goods and services that touched almost everyone. Foremost was Dresser's historic participation in the petroleum industry. The company was critically involved in almost every aspect of this endeavor—exploration, drilling, production, refining, and distribution. The businessman who drove daily to work from the suburbs or the teen-ager who cruised the streets in his hot rod was powered by a fuel that inevitably had touched a Dresser product somewhere in its complicated journey from the earth's interior to the gas tank. The same crude oil that was refined into gasoline also served as the basic material for such varied items as lipstick, nylon hosiery, and plastic shopping bags. Dresser's compressors and pumps were essential to all such conversions.

Even the housewife's flicking of a light switch could involve a Pacific boiler feed pump, a product widely adopted by the nation's electric utility plants. The electric current itself may well have flowed through lines suspended from Dresser-Ideco towers, and the family who watched Sid Caesar and Imogene Coca in television's popular *Your Show of Shows* quite likely received the signal from an antenna high atop a Dresser-Ideco television tower. Dresser Manufacturing, skilled for so many years in producing precision rings, now manufactured them for products as diverse as jet engines, washing machines, and gasoline pumps, not to mention ten thousand couplings every day. Chances were good that the tap water used in the average home got there through Dresser-coupled mains. The paper stock for such items as the afternoon newspaper or the mail-order catalogue may have emerged from a paper mill that utilized Roots's blowers, and the nation's highly acclaimed atomic submarines, the U.S.S. *Nautilus* and the U.S.S. *Seawolf,* used Roots's rotary bronze compressors.

Thousands of schools, restaurants, churches, office buildings, industrial plants, and other structures were heated and cooled by natural gas pushed through Dresser-coupled lines by Clark compressors. Hardly anyone realized it, but the natural gas used in a single year in the United States weighed twice as much as the annual tonnage of steel produced in America, and the pipelines carrying it underground extended farther than even the nation's railroad network.

In the midst of this abundant life an ominous note had already sounded for those few who examined the situation with care. Dresser's 1957 annual report emphasized the problem: a growing disparity between demand and discovery of oil and gas. The report cited some salient comparisons. Before World War II sixty-three barrels of new oil reserves were discovered for every foot of wildcat drilling in search of new fields. From 1947 through 1951 this figure declined to twenty-one barrels for every foot of wildcat drilling, and from 1951 through 1956 it dropped to less than ten barrels. It was obvious that increasingly sophisticated exploration and drilling equipment was required as crews in search of new fields crisscrossed the globe from the Arctic to the Sahara and from the jungles of South America into the ocean itself.

The acquisition of Lane-Wells in 1955 had given Dresser a substantial position in providing services for this search as well as for increasing the productivity of existing fields. In January 1956 Dresser acquired another company involved in exploration activities: Southwestern Industrial Electronics of Houston. S.I.E., as the firm was known, was acquired for $750,000 and 50,000

Every U.S. nuclear submarine in the 1960's, such as the U.S.S. *Nautilus,* was equipped with Roots compressors. (Department of the Navy)

shares of Dresser common stock. The company was a leading manufacturer of electronic seismograph, or "shooting," instruments used to reveal the location of subsurface structures suggesting the existence of oil deposits. The technique involved exploding dynamite in shallow holes in the ground and recording sound waves that bounced back from subsurface formations. S.I.E. had been founded in 1945, and in the five years prior to its acquisition, its annual revenues had jumped from $600,000 to $6 million. The company and its five affiliates also manufactured auxiliary equipment such as geophysical field party equipment and components for general electronic instrumentation—transformers, magnetic recording systems, voltmeters, and electronic potentiometers.

Still another acquisition, in August 1956, added depth and breadth to Dresser's line of equipment for oil-well production, drilling, and servicing. This was the purchase of the Guiberson Corporation of Dallas for 109,375 shares of Dresser common stock. Guiberson's current assets were $2.5 million. While this company, founded in 1919, did not specialize in any one product,

A jaunty crew of oil-field workers in the 1920's poses with a Guiberson rotary disk bit. Guiberson, a Dallas-based company, was acquired by Dresser in 1956.

it was a major supplier of basic drilling equipment such as swabs, packers, tubing blocks, rotary swivels, blowout preventers, and oil savers. Most of these products were of a relatively short life span, and they not only rounded out the company's line for the petroleum industry but enhanced that portion of sales from expendables.

Dresser clearly was capturing a larger share of the oil and gas industries' exploration and drilling market. From 1949 through 1956 the company's sales to this segment of the industry—excluding production, refining, and transmission—increased by 186 percent while total footage drilled climbed just 52 percent. Nearly 50 percent of the total volume of the company business resulted from sales and services for exploration and drilling.

Dresser's steady flow of acquisitions automatically brought it many new products, but the firm continued to rely no less on heavy research expenditures to achieve the same result. The overall research budget for 1955, for example, was approximately

$3 million, and capital expenditures totaled $10 million. The ultimate value of these continuing expenditures could be seen in the fact that at least one-third of the sales volume for 1955 resulted from products developed since 1950. A few of these included a Clark 3,400-horsepower gas-engine compressor unit; Dresser-Ideco's rigid frame truss for use in school gymnasium and auditorium construction; Dresser Manufacturing's gigantic new couplings, approaching seven feet in diameter, for water lines in Venezuela, Chile, and Peru; and Lane-Wells's MS Neutron Log, called the world's smallest atom smasher.

The extent to which Dresser was involved in the all-encompassing search for the 5.8 billion barrels of oil used annually throughout the world can be seen in an imaginary scenario for drilling a wildcat well. Initially, of course, a driller took every precaution to find a place where oil was most likely to be. This was where S.I.E.'s seismic equipment was used to record sound waves.

Once these seismic operations were satisfactorily concluded, a drilling rig had to be set up to begin "making hole." A new depth record of more than 22,500 feet was set in 1955, and if this particular well was expected to match or even better that mark, a

Magnet Cove's drilling mud, being inserted here into a well through a pipe, is a product little known to the general public but essential to the oil industry. Magnet Cove eventually became known simply as Magcobar.

driller could choose no better rig than Ideco's "2500" draw works, capable of reaching those depths and of lifting almost 1.25 million pounds of "down-hole" equipment. Or, if a shallower well was indicated, Ideco's new Super 7-11 rig could be separated into units for easy transportation to the site and rapid reassembly. The central purpose of the rig, of course, was to rotate the drilling bit to penetrate the various formations encountered underground. Security Engineering now was the world's second-largest producer of rotary drilling bits. The pressures these bits were designed to withstand were unbelievably intense, and to insure the ruggedness of Security bits, pressures of up to sixty tons were applied to them in tests. The rapid rotation of these bits against hard rock created high temperatures, and it was partly to cool the bit that drilling mud was inserted through the pipe from above. Magnet Cove, with mines located in the United States, Nova Scotia, Greece, Ireland, and Mexico, was the nation's leading producer of drilling muds.

As drilling operations progressed, occasional halts would be made to check the formations for producing potential. Here, Lane-Wells was the industry pioneer and recognized leader in radioactivity logging, which, in contrast with electric logging, could be used after the steel casing had been placed. The information gained told precisely where another Lane-Wells service—perforation—should should be utilized. The casing and adjacent formations were penetrated with bullets or high-velocity jets to facilitate the flow of oil or gas into the well. At this point, the long drilling process over, the well was ready to produce.

If the drillers were fortunate, there might be sufficient underground gas pressure to cause the crude oil to flow to the surface without mechanical assistance. (For this to occur the gas pressure would have to be about 3,500 pounds per square inch.) Even if this condition existed, however, as it did in about one out of every ten wells, at some point the natural flow would cease and artificial lifting measures would be required. This could call for the installation of a Pacific plunger pump at the bottom of the well. Or, if sufficient formation gas were available, the well might be restored to vigor by drilling nearby and reinjecting natural gas to make the well flow once more. Clark Bros. compressors long had been the favorite of the industry for this purpose.

All the above were only the basic steps in drilling and producing, and a more elaborate description could have included the uses of many other Dresser products. Refining the crude oil into its various end products represented a different aspect of operations in which Clark Bros., Pacific, Roots-Connersville, and Dresser Manufacturing played integral roles. Transmission and distribution of the oil or gas was yet another aspect in which Dresser products were thoroughly involved.

All these activities were becoming more common to the international scene, where Dresser continued to grow at an ever-increasing rate. Between 1950 and 1956 the company's percentage of foreign sales and services doubled, from 10.9 percent to 21.4 percent, and O'Connor predicted that by 1959 even that figure would be redoubled.* The network of foreign licensees and offices continued to expand, too, with the 1956 annual report listing nineteen foreign affiliates. Clark Bros.' foreign companies were the most numerous, being located in London, Calgary, Rome, Milan, Buenos Aires, Caracas, and Mexico City.

It was somewhat ironic that as foreign sales were booming, international tensions showed few signs of relaxation. One mildly encouraging indication that an era of greater cooperation lay ahead was the interest shown in the spring of 1956 by American business in trading with Iron Curtain nations. The Commerce Department reported that it was getting about twenty applications a week for licenses to export goods to the Soviet bloc, a 100 percent increase in a few months' time.

Dresser Industries, and in particular Clark Bros. (whose powerful compressors were essential items for all nations seeking to build strong industrial bases), had been dealing with the Russians since the 1930's. Government restrictions imposed in the late 1940's had curtailed that trade, but now, with the continued expansion in foreign sales and Washington's new tone of "competitive coexistence," it was inevitable that Dresser again would look in that direction. And it was just as inevitable that O'Connor would be the looker.

Of course, there was no reason to renew trade unless substantial benefits for Dresser could be foreseen, and O'Connor thought he saw those benefits in a unique Russian drilling device called the turbodrill. In this drill, the power unit was placed at the bottom of the hole, over the bit, rather than at the surface. In the conventional drill used throughout most of the world, the surface power unit had to rotate the entire length of the drill stem. This wide separation between power source and drill, growing wider every year with deeper wells, inevitably caused the loss of considerable energy. The turbodrill, in contrast, revolved only the bit at the bottom of the hole. The turbine was powered by drilling mud pumped from the surface through the drill pipe. From information O'Connor gathered, the turbodrill was many times faster than the rotary drill.

* He was overoptimistic. The percentage in 1959 was 26 percent.

Americans had sought unsuccessfully for years to perfect such a device, and now with drilling activity reaching a peak that would continue for many years, the time for it seemed riper than ever.

O'Connor had first learned of the Russians' success with the instrument in 1947, when he negotiated the contract for the natural gas liquefaction plant near Moscow. He tried then to learn more, but his Soviet hosts were unwilling to discuss it. His interest again was whetted in 1948 when he visited Rumania and heard further stories of the turbodrill's speed and efficiency. Seven years later Argentine engineers who had visited Soviet oil fields provided him with enough details for him to believe that this was the kind of revolutionary product Dresser should have. Still further details surfaced at the 1955 Petroleum Congress in Rome, and O'Connor wrote afterward to Anastas I. Mikoyan, with whom he had dealt in 1947. Mikoyan referred him to V. I. Rodnov, the president of the Soviet agency that produced oil-field equipment, Machinoexport. O'Connor, pleased at the now cordial reception of his inquiries, flew to Russia and watched the turbodrill perform in snowy fields. What he saw convinced him that the instrument seemed destined to be just as significant in the art of drilling as the introduction of the rotary drill had been early in the century. On March 2 he signed a contract with his Soviet hosts obtaining American rights to produce the turbodrill. In return, Dresser was to provide data concerning the design, production, assembly, and operation of rotary rock bits as well as a number of finished bits. At the government ceremony in Moscow for the signing, the Soviet trade minister said, "I hope this is the beginning of a new relationship between us." Tass, the Soviet press agency, widely circulated news of the trade in an apparent attempt to encourage further East-West trade.

Less than three weeks later the Dresser board of directors, meeting in the Chanin Building in New York City, heard O'Connor exclaim over the turbodrill's revolutionizing potential. It was the turbodrill, he told them, that had been largely responsible for the Soviet Union's recent increases in oil reserves. "New drilling records have been established, and yet costs are being reduced," O'Connor said. This was a trend that contrasted sharply with the United States' own experience of rising drilling expenses. The directors ratified the contract that day.

Dresser and O'Connor had made headlines. *Forbes* dramatically entitled its story "Cracking the Iron Curtain." Norman Cousins, editor of *Saturday Review*, wrote a page-long editorial praising the turbodrill as an instrument that "could bore a hole ten times faster than existing equipment" and that rendered competing methods "virtually obsolete."

John B. O'Connor's negotiations with the Soviet Union concerning the turbodrill carried him to the southern Urals, where he posed near the wintry Ufa oil field with the two Soviet officials at right.

There remained, of course, one important technicality before the deal could be consummated: the granting of an export license by the U.S. Department of Commerce. To the surprise of Dresser officials, their request for a license was denied. Secretary of Commerce Sinclair Weeks cited as justification for the refusal a need to preserve the national security. He claimed that the drilling bits to be turned over to the Soviet Union were "highly important" to the security not only of the United States but of fourteen other Western nations. He explained in a public statement that the

United States government maintains stringent control on the shipment of goods and technical data to the Soviet bloc which have strategic significance to our national security. Under our national policy, no exception can be made unless a net security advantage to the free world can be clearly demonstrated. The proposed exchange in technical data is not justified within this policy.

More specifically, *The New York Times* in a page-one story quoted anonymous government officials as citing several practical reasons for vetoing the deal. These were the essential ones: granting the license would have weakened the United States' position with allies who against their own judgment had placed embargoes on shipments of many products even though they preferred a relaxation of trade restrictions with the Soviet Union and the People's Republic of China; the Russians wanted "far more" in technological information than they were giving Dresser; the United States needed to maintain its "virtual monopoly" on oil-well drilling and oil-field supplies in supplying 95 percent of such equipment for the free world; and the Russian turbodrill would contribute little to the knowledge of American industry.

These official statements, Mallon and O'Connor believed, were inspired mostly by a need to project an unyielding public stance in cold war rhetoric rather than by a genuine concern for national security. But they both refrained from making unseemly responses. Dresser's only public response was Mallon's statement contending that the proposed arrangements would have given the Russians "nothing they did not already have and would have given us technical information of value and many years of extensive field experience." The government's action, he said, would temporarily deprive the petroleum industry of an important tool for certain types of drilling. Nevertheless, Dresser Industries would abide by the decision.

Several days later, *Pravda*, the official organ of the Soviet Union's Communist Party, entered the debate by assailing the United States government for hampering trade relations despite earlier public claims that the Commerce Department actually was seeking to ease controls. The newspaper deplored recent testimony before congressional committees advocating a halt to all trade between the nations. It cited as an example of harmful propaganda a newspaper headline stating that "Trade with Communists Is Trading with the Enemy."

The Commerce Department's veto and the ensuing publicity inspired *Business Week* to publish an assessment of the entire question under the title "Trading with the Communists." The article pointed out that the American Businessman, encouraged by the so-called new era of "competitive coexistence," was showing increasing interest in trading behind the Iron Curtain. But the "kind of troubles he will be in for," the magazine stated, "were exemplified by the government's veto of the Dresser-Soviet Union agreement." The central figure in the article was O'Connor, portrayed standing in the Russian snow in a remote field with two Soviet officials at the time he witnessed the turbodrill in action. "Though this swap failed (now) to go through," the article concluded, "O'Connor apparently intends to keep up Russian contacts for the day when such deals may be possible."

Actually, O'Connor had not given up on the turbodrill. In July he again was in Russia, renegotiating the deal by substituting cash in place of technical data and bits. To the surprise of almost no one at Dresser, he succeeded, and this time the Commerce Department approved the modified terms.

In the fall of 1956 Dresser received in its Dallas offices forty

Russian turbodrills, carefully packed in heavily reinforced cases. The Russian news agency, Tass, announced that a team of Russian engineers would follow them to Texas to demonstrate their use, an announcement that upset Mallon and O'Connor because federal approval had not yet been obtained. "It is not very agreeable for our authorities in charge of visas to find out through the newspapers that the visa is to be granted when it has not yet had formal consideration," O'Connor complained to Rodnov. As it turned out, the government denied Dresser's request to permit the Soviet engineers to come to the United States. O'Connor and Mallon both went to Washington and appealed the decision, first to the Commerce Department and then to the State Department, but to no avail.

The difficulties over the turbodrill did not end here, for when the Soviets read a press report indicating that Dresser would create its own turbodrill Rodnov sent a sharp protest. Mallon explained that newspaper reports had "garbled" O'Connor's earlier comments that before Dresser could manufacture the turbodrills it would be necessary to convert Russian drawings and designs from the metric system to American standards.

In business matters and as business people we should disregard newspaper articles such as those to which you refer. . . . Mr. O'Connor has stated over and over again in talking to the oil industry, with newspaper representatives present, that Dresser is accepting the Russian design. You and your fellow engineers in Moscow are getting full credit for a fine mechanical product and a new engineering achievement.

As the months progressed, a series of lengthy, detailed letters ensued between Dresser and Soviet officials over interpretations of the nature of the agreement and technical details, punctuated occasionally by misunderstandings that required involved, tactful responses. As promising as the turbodrill itself appeared to be for Dresser and for the drilling industry, and as difficult as its acquisition had been, it was destined to be a source of further problems in development.

O'Connor's constant crisscrossing of the globe in the midst of these and other negotiations now caused him to log more than 160,000 miles annually. The oil industry's Nomads Club voted him the title of "the world's most-traveled executive." Dresser's board was no less mindful of his zeal, and in October 1956 the directors recognized his many contributions by naming him president of

Dresser Industries. Mallon was advanced at the same time to chairman of the board, a position authorized by the bylaws but unfilled since Fred A. Miller's resignation in 1938. Mallon would continue to be the chief executive officer. The third member of Dresser's ruling triumvirate, Reimer, was promoted to executive vice president and a member of the board of directors.

Time magazine noted O'Connor's ascent to the presidency in a brief profile by calling him a "man smitten by wanderlust" whose assumption of the new position was one of the most important moves of his career. Actually, as O'Connor himself pointed out, the title change signified little real difference in his responsibilities. "My duties will be the same," he said. "I'll still be out hustling business around the world, while Mallon continues to set top policy. As usual at Dresser, everybody will work just a little harder." *Time*'s article covered Dresser as well as O'Connor with praise, observing that since 1929 the company had been "farsighted enough to acquire the best and newest equipment that the oil world has to offer." Mallon received credit for having built up the company from a specialized firm that produced "only flexibles for plain-end pipes" into one that served the entire gas and oil industries. The company's philosophy of decentralization, its unusual record of outstanding acquisitions, and its increasing profitability were portrayed in generous terms. The article concluded with a direct quotation from O'Connor: "I'll continue to spend most of my time in an airplane. You can't run this kind of company from a swivel chair in Dallas."

The toll in physical terms on O'Connor for all this activity could not be denied. He was now a distinguished-looking, gray-haired man of fifty-eight years, and he had not permitted himself to slow down as much as a single step in two decades. On Thanksgiving Day, 1956, having returned that afternoon from a trip to South America to be with his wife and grown children at Haderway Farm, O'Connor was stricken by a heart attack. He was carried to the hospital in an emergency midnight trip by ambulance, with siren wailing, and he remained there until two days before Christmas, when he was released to go home for further rest.

Friends from around the world besieged him with so many cards that he printed a response filled with humorous illustrations of his hospital experiences. The episode had scared the "bejabbers" out of his family and friends, and "some even broke down and vouchsafed compliments normally deferred until rigor mortis sets in." As for those who had advised him to stop working so hard, burning the candle at both ends, and chasing blondes, he responded: "The truth is I have not chased blondes for many years. Not more than a block anyway."

On March 1 O'Connor returned to the office—prematurely. Before the end of April he was back in the hospital, where he stayed for two and a half more weeks. In late summer he visited Greece, Switzerland, and Sweden, then returned to the hospital once again in September for five weeks.

At the end of the year Mallon announced to him that the first objective of 1958 was to return him to "health and effectiveness." He must make no more than one or two out-of-town trips a month, work no more than six hours a day, and schedule frequent periods for rest. His areas of responsibility, Mallon said, were to be confined to customer relations, long-range planning, and acquisitions. "You must be relieved of all other business details. Important activities which only you can do are to be your responsibility. Nothing else." O'Connor, however, was not one for slowing down. Five months later his itinerary showed out-of-town trips to Bradford, Olean, New York City (twice), Shreveport, Oklahoma City, Tulsa, Houston, and Fort Worth.

His visit to Bradford and Olean coincided with a special honor. St. Bonaventure U., located on a beautiful campus near Olean, presented him with the honorary degree of doctor of commercial science. He was cited as "a man whose leadership in the field of Business and Industry has gained world-wide recognition. . . . [He is] a symbol for international trade and good will . . . [who] stands strong for the principle of the brotherhood of man regardless of national boundaries."

O'Connor had carefully prepared his acceptance speech. As he stood under the scholarly adornments of cap, gown, and multicolored hood, he urged the nation's businessmen to be soldiers in the war of the international marketplace, to sell not just American goods but American ideology. The nation had fared poorly in this regard in the past, he said, citing as an example a Parisian who recently had told him that "the things which America has offered the rest of the world can be summed up in three words—dollars, Coca-Cola and nylons." The Frenchman was right, O'Connor said.

> The truth is that we have gone abroad only as hucksters, with something to sell, or as bargain hunters, trying to buy something more cheaply. . . . In contrast, our competition is merchandising a philosophy, a political outlook, and a good bit of clever diplomacy with each sale they make. This upsets us, and it should. Not because our competitors are so sly. What should upset us is the fact that we have turned out to be such low-caliber salesmen.

Foreign capital, he said, had been instrumental in building up American industry, a fact that too many Americans had forgotten.

Now it was time to show the United States' faith in the future of other nations. "With private American capital we should now finance and build the dams, the steel mills, the communications systems and the factories which other nations so sorely need to improve their standard of living." Implying clearly that ideological differences should not prevent international trade, he quoted Pope Pius XI's famous remark that he would "bargain with the devil himself if the souls of Italian schoolchildren were at stake." This, he said, must be the attitude of American businessmen, who must "come to know and understand other peoples according to their own values." Differences must be recognized without making the moral judgment that what was not American was inferior.

O'Connor's firsthand experiences in international trading in these years when foreign affairs assumed priority in the minds of many Americans caused considerable demand for him as a speaker. Of particular interest was his knowledge of the Soviet Union. As an avid amateur photographer, he had a large collection of slides that he used to accompany his talks about the U.S.S.R. In these appearances he sought to correct any mistaken notions that the Russians were some kind of subhuman monsters. "Except for the cut of his clothes, the man on the street in Moscow is substantially the same as the man on the street in Shreveport, or Dallas, or Mexico City," he would say, noting that the primary difference was that the Soviet citizen looked to the state for daily sustenance.

At home, on Haderway Farm, O'Connor enjoyed the good life. He and his wife had filled their house with collector's items from around the world, including a 250-year-old handloomed French rug. A favorite cartoon hanging on a wall showed two Texas cowboys looking at the Eiffel Tower in Paris with one pointing to it with a snort: "I've been coming here for fifteen years and they ain't struck oil yet." O'Connor sought to make his expanse of land productive through farming, and he developed a special interest in raising unusual varieties of birds, such as African white guineas, pheasants, and chukars. He marketed some of these birds to a specialty food store. Nearly half a hundred white-faced cattle roamed the grounds of the farm. The frequent overnight guests at the farm would hear O'Connor smilingly refer to his origins in a "log cabin" at Augusta, Georgia, though in truth his father had been a stockbroker, who, with his wife, had reared his son in a handsome home boasting gracious white pillars.

While O'Connor was a citizen of the world in a very practical sense, Mallon was thoroughly involved in international affairs in a more cerebral way. In Cleveland he had been an active participant in that city's Council on World Affairs, an organization whose

A famous figure, Charles de Gaulle of France, is pictured beneath an Ideco mast in France.

primary purpose was to educate Americans in foreign affairs by sponsoring discussions, entertainment of international visitors, and lectures by distinguished speakers. When Dresser moved to Dallas, Mallon had been concerned over the city's lack of such an organization, and he initiated a drive to found a chapter of the Council. He enlisted some of the city's foremost businessmen, such as Stanley Marcus of Dallas's famed specialty store, Neiman-Marcus, and brought to the city the national director of the Foreign Policy Association, Brooks Emeny, for a series of conferences. The result was the formation in 1950 of the Dallas Council on World Affairs. This organization had become since then Mallon's chief outside interest, and by the spring of 1957 its success was so apparent that *News-*

week featured an article on it with a picture of Mallon cutting a
cake to celebrate the birthday of the "durable Dallas council." The
organization by then had grown to a membership of 2,500; it had
held 660 meetings; and it had sponsored discussions of foreign
affairs before a combined attendance of some 160,000 persons.

Mallon, now past sixty, had remained a bachelor, but his
widowed sister and her children had lived with him and provided
a family environment. As one of Farmers Branch's most successful
citizens, he was elected for several terms to serve on that city's
council.

Reimer's life in Dallas had assumed more typical dimensions
than either O'Connor's or Mallon's. He and his Bradford-born wife,
Cleone, lived in a comfortable home in the north part of the city
where they had reared two sons. It was Reimer who at the office
provided a practical, realistic balance to Mallon's emphasis on
visionary goals and to O'Connor's penchant for grand scale with
an occasional neglect of necessary details.

The company that these three men had guided for so many
years had become in the mid-1950's a favorite topic for the media.
One of the most thorough of the many articles was *Business Week*'s
April 5, 1958, cover story entitled "Building an Empire on an Oil
Supply Package." A color photograph on the cover showed Mallon
and O'Connor examining a bit at a testing facility. The image the
article portrayed of Dresser and its top leaders was compelling from
its first paragraph:

"Start talking about Dresser Industries, Inc., with anybody who
does business with the company, and you'll get any of a dozen re-
actions ranging from 'tough operators' to 'swell guys to do business
with.' One thing is sure: The reaction will rarely be neutral." The
magazine credited the company's "ruling triumvirate" of Mallon,
O'Connor, and Reimer as the masterminds behind the strategy and
tactics that had lifted Dresser from a company that in fifteen years
had climbed in annual sales from $28 million to $275 million.

Mallon was the "guiding genius"; O'Connor the "beguiling salesman and world operator"; and Reimer a "fast man with a pencil."
Even those who were not fans of these men, the article stated,
admitted that " 'these boys are sharp—and they don't get into any
game for marbles.' " Of the approximately twenty acquisitions they
had made over the past two decades, they had "lopped off without
qualms almost half of them that did not fulfill early promise for

Rudy E. Reimer, brought to Dresser in 1929 by Neil Mallon as controller, was a top executive from then until his retirement forty years later.

growth."* The article's subtitle summarized its general theme: "Dresser Industries combines artful timing with timely products to expand sales of its equipment and services here and abroad."

The thing that had catapulted Dresser into headlines more than anything else was the turbodrill transaction. Since the earliest publicity, a Turbodrill Division had been formed under the direction of Otto Hammer for the development of that product, with actual research conducted at the Guiberson Corporation plant in Dallas. In July 1958, two years after the deal had been made, Dresser introduced its version of the turbodrill in a demonstration at Herscher,

---

* An example of this had been the sale in 1957 of Stacey Bros. Construction Company for only $73,029. The company's primary product, holders for manufactured gas, no longer had a good future since manufactured gas was diminishing in importance. Also, the anticipated move to liquefaction plants requiring large-capacity holders obviously was not to occur in the foreseeable future.

Illinois, before some eighty oil and gas news writers and broadcast journalists. Some twenty-four television stations as well as Fox Movietone News carried sound film of O'Connor explaining the turbodrill's importance. The results of the demonstration were highly encouraging. The turbodrills were operated by the Moran Brothers Drilling Company of Wichita Falls, Texas, in a project to store natural gas underground for use in Chicago. Eight turbodrills were matched against two rotary drills. Drilling time for the turbodrills was from 35 to 37 hours, while the rotaries required some 110 hours to reach the required depth. It was shown that fluid pumped through the turbine rotated the turbodrill bit at 600 rpm, ten times the speed of the rotary drill. *Oil and Gas Journal* called these early results "spectacular." Six weeks later, with more results from the field available, the publication labeled Moran Brothers' use of the Dresser turbodrills as a gamble that now was "paying off handsomely."

Conditions at Herscher had been perfect for the turbodrill, for it thrived on the hard rock formations encountered there. As Otto Hammer acknowledged at the demonstration, however, Dresser's tests had shown that the turbodrill was not as efficient as the rotary in some softer formations. A more serious consideration was the ironic fact that the turbodrill was so fast that no bit was strong enough to withstand the pressures for any length of time. The result was a frequent need to change bits, thus causing the total drilling time involved to be greater than for the rotary drill except under special circumstances such as at Herscher. Tom Slick, a Texas oilman and Dresser director, went to the Soviet Union in 1958 and reported back that the Russians' success stemmed from their peculiar technique of drilling with practically no load on the rock bit bearings. If only more details could be gathered about the Russians' techniques, he felt, the problems now being encountered with the turbodrill in Dresser's tests might be overcome. But Dresser officials were concerned about the negative public opinion that might arise if they made too many trips to that Communist-ruled nation, and Soviet engineers still were being denied permission by the U.S. government to come to this country. The central research effort by Dresser in trying to improve the turbodrill was in developing a tougher bit that could withstand great speeds. By October 1958 the company had invested more than $2 million in the turbodrill, and 1959 was expected to bring losses as high as $500,000. A number of oil companies were experimenting with the instrument—notably Shell—and by the fall of 1958, rentals of the turbodrill were returning approximately $20,000 a month. To reduce further losses Mallon recommended a "more conservative long-range program" in which sales emphasis would stress the turbo-drill's use for specific situations such as offshore drilling in the Santa Barbara area and for drilling the large holes required for underground gas storage. At the same time, he emphasized the need for research to develop the proper bit. Thus, the high hopes for the turbodrill already were fading by 1958 despite glowing press reports.

One of the reasons the turbodrill had seemed so promising was the continuing growth of the drilling industry. Intensified drilling meant greater sales for almost every one of Dresser's divisions, and the result was that sales and earnings achieved that year set levels not to be matched for eight years. Sales revenues totaled $275 million and earnings reached $33.6 million. Obviously,

A group of delegates to the Independent Petroleum Association of America convention in Dallas sees a demonstration of the turbodrill.

Dresser prospered as the oil and gas industries prospered. What would happen, though, when and if drilling activity slowed down? The answer, it seemed, was to continue to intensify the company's efforts at diversification so that its fortunes would not be inextricably linked to those of oil and gas.

In these flush times a company Dresser had courted for several years as a possible acquisition once again emerged as a prospect: Gardner-Denver of Quincy, Illinois, a firm heavily involved in the manufacture of pneumatic equipment for the coal-mining industry. This was an area of energy—the only major source of energy—in which Dresser was not intimately involved. In addition to its involvement in mining, Gardner-Denver manufactured such products as compressors, pumps, drills, and pneumatic tools for the oil, construction, and general industrial markets. The company was approximately a fourth the size of Dresser. It ranked 482nd in *Fortune* magazine's list of the five hundred largest manufacturing corporations, but it was sixth in return on invested capital and forty-second in net profit as a percentage of sales. Three years earlier serious but unofficial talks had been held between Mallon and O'Connor and Gardner-Denver's chairman of the board, Ralph G. Gardner, and its president, Gifford V. Leece, but nothing had come of them. In March 1956 Mallon renewed his pursuit of the company in a letter to Leece in which he declared that he was "more than ever convinced" that a combination of Gardner-Denver, Clark Bros., Pacific Pumps, and Roots-Connersville would constitute a powerful division with nearly limitless possibilities for expansion. In the following months more letters from Mallon, O'Connor, and Reimer spelled out their plan in increasingly minute detail.

The first public notice of the negotiations appeared in the July 3, 1957, edition of *The New York Times*, in which Gardner-Denver's president, G. V. Leece, played down the possibility by calling Dresser's offer "not at all attractive." It was, Leece claimed, Dresser's fifth proposal in the past three or four years and his company was inclined to treat it as another routine offer from a "merger-minded" company.* In fact, on the day Leece made his statement to the reporter, he wrote a three-page letter to Mallon in which he proposed a one-to-one exchange of stock as the basis for the merger. He cited the "many advantages Gardner-Denver offered Dresser." Dresser officials were just as eager to discourage public attention,

---

* Dresser officials did not at all consider themselves to be "merger-minded." They prided themselves for never having acquired a company simply for growth, and indeed they had declined countless opportunities with well-known companies.

and in August *The Wall Street Journal* quoted unidentified company spokesmen as saying there was "absolutely nothing" to rumors in "some quarters" that their firm was taking over Gardner-Denver. The only news for public consumption that Dresser had to offer that month was to tell of the opening of a new barite-processing plant at Mykonos, where O'Connor presided over ceremonies. The plant would enable Magnet Cove to ship processed drilling mud directly from that Greek island instead of hauling it all the way to Louisiana for beneficiation.

In October 1957 Mallon officially advised his board of directors of the negotiations with Gardner-Denver. The acquisition would be desirable, he told the directors, because more than 75 percent of Gardner-Denver's sales were to the mining, construction, and general industrial markets, and would be a further step in broadening and diversifying Dresser's operations. If the acquisition did occur, Gardner-Denver would be aligned with Clark Bros., Ideco, Pacific Pumps, and Roots-Connersville in a new corporation to be called Gardner-Dresser Company with Leece as president. Initial annual sales volume of this division would be approximately $200 million, and within five years it was expected to reach $350 million. This alignment would bring savings and efficiency in selling and manufacturing through the integration of many functions. Terms had been agreed upon with Gardner-Denver: an exchange of stock on a share-for-share basis for Gardner-Denver's 1,800,000 shares. Dresser's board unanimously approved the plan, and, in anticipation of the new grouping, converted Pacific Pumps from corporate to divisional status. Gardner-Denver's directors similarly approved the plan unanimously. On October 24, 1957, Mallon, Gardner, and Leece jointly announced in New York City the proposed merger, subject to shareholders' approval.

The details remaining to be worked out, aside from the vote of the shareholders, were questions involving relationships between the new corporation of Gardner-Dresser and Dresser Industries and the nature of the new organizational structure. Dresser envisioned a continuation of its overall philosophy of decentralized management with retention of the distinct identities of the companies moving into the new Gardner-Dresser unit. Gardner-Denver felt just as strongly about the efficacy of strong central authority with the new Gardner-Dresser name receiving primary and immediate emphasis. A second point of disagreement arose over the possibility of future acquisitions, Dresser favoring them to a greater degree than Gardner-Denver. Throughout November long memos were sent back and forth in an effort to reach mutual agreement on these points, but they proved futile. On December 3, 1957, Leece informed Mallon

Penstock lines taller than a man and carrying large amounts of water commonly are joined by Dresser couplings, as is this line for the B. C. Electric Company in Canada.

by letter that he now believed that "the growth psychology of our two companies is not at all compatible. . . . I think I misjudged the lesser degree of importance the Dresser organization might have placed on the consolidation understandings of this Gardner-Dresser group as compared to the importance Dresser might place on additional acquisitions, and the independence of each operating unit." Two days later Mallon announced to the press that the proposed merger had been canceled. Investors saw the cancellation as bullish, for Dresser stock opened that day at $38⅜ and closed at 41.

As so often proved to be the case in such ventures, the lengthy negotiations—aside from adding to the Dresser files a 600-page notebook of correspondence and data related to the proposed acquisition—were not without significant indirect benefit. In anticipation of the added headquarters executive responsibilities the acquisition was expected to bring, Dresser had made arrangements to hire an executive vice president who had excellent experience in the manufacture of mining equipment. He was John Lawrence, a vigorous man in his mid-forties who loved tennis and mountain climbing, and who had been president and chief executive officer of Joy Manufacturing in Pittsburgh, a leading manufacturer of coal-mining equipment. Dresser's top officials had come to know and to respect him when they had tentatively explored the possibility of acquiring Joy. Lawrence was a native of Vermont and a graduate of the Massachusetts Institute of Technology. As executive vice president he was charged with general supervision of the capital goods group of subsidiaries. Another change was the promotion of J. D. (Doug) Mayson to corporate secretary. Mayson, who had been with the company for thirteen years, also was in charge of the tax, legal, insurance, and patent affairs departments.

Expansion in the number of officers seemed inevitable given the company's rapid growth and additional burdens on the headquarters group. In August 1958 a third executive vice president, J. P. Gasser, formerly executive vice president of the Seaboard Oil Company, was hired. Gasser, who also became a director, assumed responsibility for the company's drilling, oil tool, and technical service companies. Just beneath the executive vice presidents in authority in 1958 were three operating vice presidents: Boncher, who had been in that position since 1955; and Hammer and H. A. Herzig, both having held their positions since 1956. Moody, still in charge of industrial relations, had been a vice president since 1957. The company's two other vice presidents in 1958 were Willard M. Johnson and Arthur R. Weis, both of whom worked out of their companies, Magnet Cove and Pacific Pumps. The three other company officers in 1958 were J. C. Freeman, controller since 1953, and assistant treasurers C. C. Hill and Paul E. Brodrick, both of whom had been elected in 1957. Perhaps it was inevitable that with this growing list of headquarters executives there would arise in some of the subsidiaries casual complaints that the Dresser operation was becoming less and less decentralized—despite Gardner-Denver's complaint. But in the 1958 annual report Mallon emphasized that management changes were "designed to accommodate Dresser's basic operating philosophy of decentralized operations" in which "the day-to-day responsibility for operations of the various Dresser companies rests entirely with the managements of these companies." He added, however, that since the ultimate responsibility for growth in Dresser's sales and earnings necessarily fell upon the top management of the parent company, it had become increasingly important to provide for "direct, effective liaison between the parent and the operating units."

Indeed, the size of Dresser was such that capital expenditures in 1958 alone amounted to $10.9 million, and 20 percent of that was devoted to the expansion of foreign facilities. And acquisitions were becoming so routine that at the same December 1957 directors' meeting at which negotiations with Gardner-Denver were announced as terminated, four additional acquisitions were approved. These were the Elgen Corporation, a Dallas-based company specializing in electrical logging; Mud Supply Company, Inc., a Louisiana company that sold drilling mud and various additives and chemicals from thirty-two warehouses or stocking points in the Louisiana Gulf Coast area; Andike Corporation, another Louisiana company that owned and operated a fleet of supply vessels for delivering mud to offshore and inland water locations; and a small Texas corporation that acted as operating agent for various oil companies to which some of the Andike vessels were leased. The acquisition of all these companies save that of the latter firm, which was deemed unnecessary, occurred early in 1958.

The late 1950's was a period of transition for the nation and for Dresser. In 1957 the entire world was startled by a Russian achievement of monumental proportions—the launching by rocket of a satellite that went into orbit around the earth and began transmitting signals from outer space to Soviet listening posts. Where had America's vaunted technological superiority been? Embarrassed but generally too proud to admit the significance of the Soviet accomplishment, the United States redoubled its efforts to catch and surpass the Soviet space lead. Massive amounts of federal funds began being allocated in the form of contracts and grants to private enterprise and universities. A huge new federal agency, the National Aeronautics and Space Administration, was created to oversee and to inspire the nation's attempt to achieve superiority in the new frontier of space. Dresser Industries was eager to be a part of this national effort.

No more than a month after Sputnik had gone into orbit, Dresser had founded a new company, Dresser Dynamics, a small group of specialized scientists with the aim of developing improved missile navigational aids and special apparatus for high-speed measurement and instrumentation. Its vice president and general manager, Dr. Frederick F. Liu, was former senior research scientist for the Rocketdyne Division of North American Aviation. Other Dresser companies that were in a position to answer the nation's call to service in conquering space included in particular S.I.E., with its

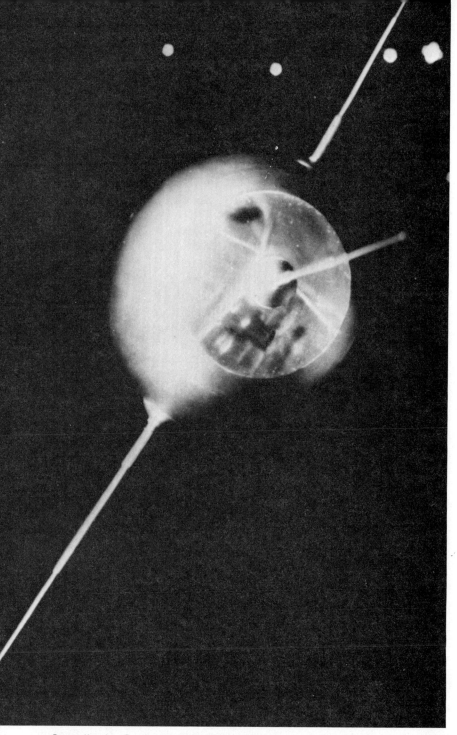

Sputnik, the Soviet satellite that spurred the United States into redoubling its own space effort, inevitably had an impact on the nature of Dresser's business. (Wide World Photos)

electronics expertise; Dresser-Ideco, with its communications towers; and Clark Bros., with its compressors and gas turbines.

Another unrelated development made this period one of transition for Dresser: a sudden decline in drilling activity. The peak year had been 1956, when nearly sixty thousand wells were drilled in the United States, and this rate had continued into 1957 before turning down. The decline did not come soon enough to prevent Dresser from achieving record sales and earnings in 1957, which were not to be matched for nearly a decade. The decline in drilling activity was accompanied by a minor recession in the general economy. The result of this was that fiscal year 1958 assumed troubled outlines before even the first quarter was over.

Despite the huge earnings of 1957, Mallon evidently knew at the beginning of 1958 that the stage had been set for trouble in the remaining three quarters of the fiscal year. In the first week of 1958 he told O'Connor that "1957 was a year highlighted by top level mistakes in judgment . . . a year which revealed many weaknesses." The year 1958 "must not repeat these same errors," he said. Mallon did not specify the mistakes, but he was convinced generally that some of the firm's top executives had "lost the competitive drive necessary for success." As one remedy he suggested "better COMMUNICATIONS" as a "MUST" for 1958. He wanted a twice-monthly Monday meeting of the officers and a few key men to last from morning through lunch. O'Connor would preside, and "searching inquiries and pointed comments" would be expected.

As 1958 progressed, it became apparent that the year-end fiscal statement would contain distressing figures. Mallon began sending memoranda to O'Connor, Reimer, and Lawrence in which his alarm was evident. "The situation is serious," he told O'Connor in the fall. "Each month, we run way behind our estimated profits, even though these estimates are recent downward revisions of earlier forecasts." He wondered if Dresser had not overexpanded. "For example," he told O'Connor, "we went into the bit business on too big a scale," a fact that was "evident in retrospect." The company had sunk $20 million into that ambitious effort, and it was destined to lose more than a half million dollars on it in 1958. "Another example of our overbuilding due to too much enthusiasm and optimism is the very expensive Dresser Center in Houston—the carrying charges of which are a severe drag on our business."* An-

---

* The Dresser Electronic Center was a huge complex for S.I.E.'s manufacturing and research activities. It consisted of more than 300,000 square feet on a 146-acre tract.

other subsidiary operating at a loss, destined to be some $2 million for the year, was S.I.E., which Mallon termed "one of our worst problem children." Not counting the elaborate Dresser Center, S.I.E. "owed" the parent company some $6 million. The turbodrill endeavor was costing Dresser some half a million dollars in losses annually. "This is because the repeated field runs really prove nothing, because they all come up with exactly the same answer, namely, that the bits won't stand up." These expensive field trials were generating neither new customers nor new information, and the isolated success in Illinois could be duplicated only occasionally around the country. The company already had invested more than $2 million in the turbodrill, and a bit that could withstand its high speeds under all conditions still was not in sight. Finally, Mallon felt that overhead costs at the Dallas headquarters office were becoming inordinately expensive. He hoped to cut some $500,000 to $600,000 from the 1959 budget for that category.

Always concerned about any appearance that Dallas headquarters enjoyed undue lavishness at the expense of overall earnings, Reimer—the "fast man with a pencil"—earlier in the year had

The Dresser Electronic Center at Houston was one of the most modern plants of its kind when it went into operation in the late 1950's.

compiled an analysis of headquarters expenses in proportion to sales. He found that while expenditures had tripled, from $1.3 million in 1951 to $4 million in 1957, the percentage of management expenses to total sales had increased insignificantly, from 1.3 to 1.5 percent. But the 1958 proposed budget showed 1.8 percent of projected sales devoted to management expenses, so at Reimer's direction this was reduced in midyear by some $900,000 to 1.5 percent. The most significant reduction was in cutting the advertising budget from $1 million to $600,000.

At the end of fiscal year 1958, sales and earnings totals were worse than anyone had expected. Sales dropped nearly $50 million from the previous year (from $275 million to $225 million) and earnings dropped even more precipitously from $33.6 million to $14 million!

"This kind of setback is not exactly a new kind of experience for Dresser, but it is a rare one," commented *Forbes*. Actually, the only setback approaching it in severity had been the general decline during the 1930's depression, a decline that had been sharper but on a lesser scale. *Forbes* explained the decrease in profits this way: "Closely tied to petroleum industry activity, Dresser Industries' profits tend to gush up when well-drilling is booming, dry up when exploration and production slip."

In times of crisis Mallon liked to re-emphasize the need for research and development. This period was no exception. In the summer of 1958 he sent a broad, far-reaching memo to O'Connor, Reimer, and Lawrence outlining some basic future considerations.

> Technology is advancing at a frightening pace.
>
> Scientific breakthroughs are creating new industries.
>
> The Atomic Revolution is about to break over our heads.
>
> Electronic and Chemical developments will revolutionize the oil industry.
>
> Foreign scientific competition is something to be reckoned with.
>
> To the alert American firm, foreign developments can be made an ally, not a competitor.

To meet these challenges of the future Mallon said that Dresser must: keep abreast of the times technologically by learning about all new ideas and scientific progress; choose with knowledge and discretion the potential leaders of the "scientific 60's"; evaluate new developments from the company's point of view and its ability to handle them; and move toward the acquisition of those companies that fit the overall scheme before their prices got too high and the

In 1953 this Dresser coupling was uncovered in New York's Allegheny State Park, and was found to be still tight and in excellent condition after fifty years of service.

bidding too competitive. He suggested the formation of a team, or committee, to evaluate each company's ability to fulfill these goals.

The drilling business and the general economy were certain to revive at some future date, and Dresser once again was determined to be prepared to capitalize on that moment. As one financial publication commented, "Sometimes you can't make business but you can be ready for it when it inevitably comes. That's Dresser Industries' tactics."

10

End
of an Era

Company policy dictated that Neil Mallon retire immediately after
his sixty-fifth birthday on January 11, 1960. Could Dresser shareholders afford to lose their still-zestful leader at this critical junc-
ture? The question nagged at the minds of the directors. As the end
of fiscal year 1959 approached, their concern heightened, for it wor-
ried them to see that earnings and sales would fall far short of the
most careful profit plans the company yet had devised. Two weeks before the fiscal year ended, the directors met and heard two of their
most influential members, Henry P. Isham and William A. McAfee,
urge that Mallon's retirement be postponed. Their reasoning, as the
secretary summed it up in the minutes, was that the company was
"currently passing through a rather difficult period, due to internal
problems and economic conditions in the oil and gas industries."
The other directors concurred; Mallon agreed to remain; and Dresser maintained as chief executive the man who had been largely
responsible for its spectacular transformation and growth over the
past thirty years.

The "internal problems" noted by Isham and McAfee were nothing that would not be solved by a spurt of renewed activity in the oil
and gas industries. This was a matter, however, that was out of
Dresser's hands. Still, one could isolate certain other factors that
had exacerbated the situation. Lane-Wells and S.I.E., intimately involved in exploration and drilling, both were losing money. Reimer's
studies pointed to another reason: a startling increase in overall
"capacity costs"—that is, expenses merely of being in business,
such as salaries, depreciation, insurance, and pensions. These costs
totaled $80 million for 1959. This, he declared, was a "prime rea-
son" for the profit decline of recent years. More immediate factors
affecting 1959 were two strikes, one of which shut down the largest
operating unit, Clark, for much of the summer. The second strike
interrupted production at Security for several weeks.

One of the most frustrating aspects of the decline was profit planning's failure to predict the situation with any degree of accuracy. The company had relied too heavily, as had many other firms in the oil business, on the enthusiastic projections of an economic analyst who asserted that the 1956–57 boom in the oil industry was merely the beginning. Dresser spent many dollars preparing itself for this anticipated demand, and when the boom failed to materialize, a financial crunch inevitably occurred. The company's 1959 plans had been the most elaborate ever. Each division prepared notebooks containing several hundred pages of analyses and forecasts. These projections pointed to an increase in sales of $17.7 million, or a year-end total of $243.7 million; yet, sales reached only $232 million. Net earnings had been expected to hit $13.6 million; in fact, they came to $9.2 million.* Such was the complicated situation facing Mallon, his headquarters staff, and the operating units as the decade of the 1960's got under way.

Magnet Cove Barium Corporation faced another kind of problem. It was, in essence, a problem of success. Having been launched as a fledgling company amidst giants, Magnet Cove in fourteen years had become the drilling industry's chief supplier of mud with a market share of 47 percent in the United States. The seemingly insatiable demand for its product had caused the company to undertake in the mid-1950's an aggressive expansion program to insure sufficient reserves to accommodate the needs of such customers as Texaco, Gulf, Humble, Shell, and Phillips. Magnet Cove and its chief competitor, National Lead, controlled between them more than 80 percent of the total sales of crushed and ground barite.

Such situations did not go unnoticed in Washington, and in April 1958 the Federal Trade Commission charged that Magnet Cove and its parent company, Dresser Industries, as well as National Lead, were in violation of the antitrust laws as stated in Section 5 of the Federal Trade Commission Act and Section 7 of the Clayton Act. The companies were accused of restraining trade by hindering or preventing competition and seeking through acquisitions to achieve a monopoly in the producing, processing, buying, and selling of barite. For Magnet Cove and Dresser the FTC had specific reference to the acquisitions of Canadian Industrial Minerals, Ltd., in Canada in 1955, Superbar Company of Missouri in 1957, and leases obtained in 1955 and 1956 from two individuals in Missouri. The complaint concerning the acquisition of the Canadian firm was significant from a legal standpoint because it marked the first time the FTC ever had challenged a foreign acquisition under the anti-

* Adjustments in later years would reflect slightly higher year-end totals.

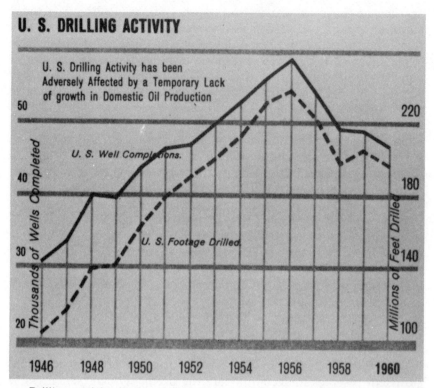

U. S. DRILLING ACTIVITY

U. S. Drilling Activity has been Adversely Affected by a Temporary Lack of growth in Domestic Oil Production

Thousands of Wells Completed

Millions of Feet Drilled

U. S. Well Completions.

U. S. Footage Drilled.

50   220
40   180
30   140
20   100

1946   1948   1950   1952   1954   1956   1958   1960

Drilling activity in the United States declined significantly in the late 1950's for the first time since World War II. Dresser's earnings were affected adversely as a result.

merger statute. Section 7 of the Clayton Act, the principal weapon of the FTC in the case, had been strengthened in 1950, but no case had yet been decided by the United States Supreme Court.

Dresser and Magnet Cove officials, confident the government's charges could not withstand the scrutiny of an impartial hearing, responded immediately. O'Connor acted as spokesman. The allegations, he insisted, were "completely without foundation." Acquisition of the two companies and other expansionary activities were undertaken "solely to make it possible for Magnet Cove to meet the increasing demands of its customers for barite." Magnet Cove, he pointed out, had been hard-pressed in recent years to fulfill the petroleum industry's need for drilling mud. The only way to accommodate this demand was to acquire additional reserves. "Dresser is proud of the role it has been able to play in successfully meeting the present needs of the vital oil and gas industries in a manner which was neither designed to, nor resorted in, the alleged restraints of trade nor in a tendency toward monopoly," O'Connor stated.

Dresser's own legal staff and its outside counsel, board member William A. McAfee's Cleveland law firm of McAfee, Hanning, Newcomer, Hazlett & Wheeler, were satisfied that no violations had occurred. Yet, one could never predict confidently the outcome of any courtroom battle, and, as feared, the case turned out to be lengthy, aggravating, and very expensive. Dresser's attorneys had some solid refutations for the complaints, including figures proving that since 1954 Magnet Cove's share of the market actually had declined. *"If Magnet Cove had an ounce of monopoly power,* direct or indirect, could any reasonably minded person expect that in a drastically declining total market, its market share would decline from 47% to 31%?" the attorneys asked in a brief. Moreover, the number of suppliers of ground barite to the industry had more than

A Magcobar boat delivers mud to an Ideco rig drilling in the Louisiana offshore area.

doubled since 1954. In fact, Dresser's attorneys contended, Magnet Cove could hardly have "market control" over customers who were "principally the large and financially powerful major oil companies, each with sales and assets in excess of the sales and assets of Magnet Cove."

Before the complicated case was to be concluded, Mallon, Johnson, and many other Dresser officials were obliged to testify and undergo cross-examination; the set of transcripts and documents would balloon to fill several filing cabinets; and expenses would reach astonishing sums. But five years after the original accusations, the five-member Federal Trade Commission in 1963 dismissed the government's complaints. It was the last time for almost a decade that the government lost an antitrust case under the stregthened Clayton Act. Dresser and Magnet Cove were cleared of all allegations. But the Commission issued a vague warning: "Any future acquisitions in this industry would raise questions of utmost gravity."

Such comments, of course, attested to the fact that Dresser had fulfilled its long-declared mission to serve the oil and gas industries "all along the line." To serve any more fully was likely to get the attention of the antitrust division of the Justice Department. Moreover, the government's action was a reminder that future acquisitions must broaden, not concentrate, the company's range of activities.

Still another legal matter was pending at the end of the 1950's, and for this one the conclusion was nowhere in sight. Lane-Wells and its research arm, Wells Survey, Inc. (WSI), were convinced that two competitors, McCullough Tool Company and Welex, were infringing at least three WSI patents in radioactivity logging. For six years, even prior to Dresser's acquisition of Lane-Wells in 1955, WSI had been negotiating with McCullough to persuade its officers to take a license under its patents. Finally, on June 15, 1956, Wells Survey filed a suit in the U.S. District Court for the Northern District of Oklahoma, alleging patent infringement.

In the spring of 1960 the case went to trial. The result, while as in many civil cases not decisive on every point, was in Mayson's opinion a "clear victory for Dresser." WSI now was able to launch a diligent program to license all infringers of its patents, particularly the Swift Casing Collar Locator patent, which was believed to be infringed by "almost everyone in the industry." It was expected that total recoveries from McCullough and Welex would be about $635,000—not even enough to pay legal expenses—but that was not the point of Dresser's determination. The idea was to serve emphatic notice that the firm was willing to protect its rights at all costs. This would reinforce its patent position, prompt others to obtain the license, and assure good royalty collections for years to come.

A basic ingredient of the program to reverse Dresser's declining earnings was to involve the company more thoroughly in new fields that were attracting so much attention in the 1960's: space, atomic energy, and electronics. This was not especially difficult since the activities of many Dresser units already were related to those endeavors. Dresser-Ideco was involved in the nation's effort to orbit the first man in space through its fabrication of forty-eight communications towers for NASA's Project Mercury. The intensity of the effort could be seen in the fact that the forty-eight towers were built in just fifty-two days. The company also constructed launcher buildings for thirty-five BOMARC missiles. These buildings had special roofs that slid open to permit the missile to be raised into firing position. Dresser-Ideco also provided key elements for Strategic Air Command antennas for use in worldwide communications, as well as the supports for the giant radar antennas at the Thule, Greenland, ballistic missile early warning site.

The unit also continued its involvement in the construction of tall towers. The 1,675-foot structure it built for Station KFVS of Cape Girardeau, Missouri, in 1960 surpassed the one in Oklahoma City as the tallest man-made structure anywhere in the world. Two years later Dresser-Ideco erected for the Atomic Energy Commission a 1,527-foot-high tower in Nevada that held an unshielded nuclear reactor for studying radiation effects from air explosions of atomic bombs. The completion of this tower meant that by 1962 the company had built the three tallest man-made structures anywhere on earth. The involvement with towers led in still another direction: the design of tall "space needles" with revolving platforms on top that might contain restaurants or observation rooms. In fact, the space needle constructed in 1962 at Seattle's Century 21 Exposition was based on a design the contractor obtained from Dresser-Ideco. Dresser officials held preliminary talks with a group in Philadelphia and with State Fair of Texas officials in Dallas about building futuristic needles for those cities, but none resulted, and this projected avenue for profits never materialized. Despite such attention-getting projects, Dresser-Ideco was not one of the more profitable subsidiaries. In 1960 it lost nearly half a million dollars.

Roots-Connersville's involvement in the new space technology included the production for NASA of a three-stage vacuum pumping system for simulating extremely high altitudes for the testing

Among Dresser-Ideco's many steel structures was this radar antenna tower under construction at Mount Hebo, Oregon.

of missiles. The firm's Spiraxial compressors were used for ventilation and blast blowing on every one of the nation's nuclear submarines, and in 1960 England installed the Spiraxial compressor on its first nuclear submarine, the H.M.S. *Dreadnought*.

Clark touted its industrial gas turbine system as the most satisfactory backup power system for the nation's missile sites. A two-color, ten-page brochure showed the gas turbine's application for the multitude of endeavors associated with the launching of a Nike-Zeus or Atlas missile. Clark compressors were used for compressing air or gas at missile launching pads for the fuel delivery system.

While American eyes focused largely on space technology, a somewhat antipodal effort also received some attention. This was the Mohole Project, a government-sponsored effort to penetrate the depths of the earth and retrieve a sample of the earth's mantle. A number of major companies formed consortiums in the bid for this potentially lucrative government contract. Dresser joined the Zapata Off-Shore Company and General Dynamics Corporation in a proposal. By late 1961 the Dresser consortium had survived along with four other bidders for the final round of competition, and company officials were optimistic at their chances. The others remaining were groups led by Socony Mobil Oil Company, Shell Oil/Global Marine Exploration/Aerojet General, General Electric Company, and a little-known Houston contracting firm, Brown & Root.

To the surprise of almost everyone, the contract went to Brown & Root.*

Ironically, Dresser earlier had turned down an opportunity to acquire Brown & Root for approximately $35 million. O'Connor had reported to Mallon and Reimer that the company could be bought, and the possibility was intriguing. However, such an acquisition would raise the specter of Dresser becoming a competitor with some of its major customers, for Brown & Root often laid pipelines itself. After deliberation over the possible ramifications of such an acquisition, the opportunity was not pursued. Another manufacturer of oil and gas equipment, Halliburton, did buy the company, and the acquisition was destined to play a prominent role in Halliburton's rapid growth during the 1960's, especially because of the large number of government contracts won by Brown & Root during the Vietnam war.

Dresser's involvement in electronics emerged initially through S.I.E.'s applications of electronics to the oil and gas industries. By the end of the 1950's Mallon envisioned broader if uncertain possibilities for other Dresser companies in this field. He observed in 1958 that "a great deal of money is going to be lost in the coming year by electronic companies. [But] occasionally a combination of scientific abilities and business management will produce very large profits in this industry. The difference between profit and loss will rest with the wisdom and business foresight of the man in charge." An example of a company which thus far had exemplified wisdom and foresight, Mallon said, was the Dallas-based firm of Texas Instruments. Having started originally in seismographic work, it now was a "high earning company with further meteoric expansion under way."

A second Dresser subsidiary involved in electronics was Hermetic Seal Transformer Company, Inc., located in the Dallas suburb of Garland. HST, as it was known, had been acquired in 1957, just five years after its founding. The company's chief products were magnetic components for a wide variety of electronic applications. Principal among them were transformers, filters, chokes, reactors, amplifiers, and toroidal and subminiature components.

In the effort to enlarge its share of the growing commercial and military electronics market, Dresser formed in 1960 a new unit, Dresser Electronics, which encompassed both S.I.E. and HST. Both divisions of this company energetically began pursuing and

---

* But the project ended in 1966 before completion when Congress refused to allocate more money.

This huge water irrigation pipeline near Mount Bantai, Japan, is connected by 100-inch Dresser couplings.

winning government contracts. S.I.E., while continuing to emphasize its seismic equipment for oil and gas exploration, obtained a number of especially exotic contracts. For the Office of Civil and Defense Mobilization's Project ARMS, the company developed a prototype automatic radioactivity-monitoring system. This system was to be employed in case of nuclear attack, at which time it would plot the radiation intensity of fallout within a populated area and point out the safest escape routes. Another S.I.E. space-age project was in developing seismic instruments to detect the point of impact for missiles landing too far away for direct observation. Field work for this U.S. Army Signal Supply Agency contract was done at the Army's White Sands Missile Range in New Mexico. A contract from the U.S. Air Force involved the use of S.I.E. electronic systems in tracking the flight of missiles fired from Cape Canaveral. S.I.E. equipment also was sold to the government for detecting underground nuclear blasts and distinguishing them from earthquakes, for recording systems used in underwater submarine communications, and for guidance systems of the Polaris missile fired from a submerged submarine.

The HST division of Dresser Electronics became involved in the sophisticated areas of producing traveling-wave tubes in a coast-to-coast microwave system being built for Western Union; Doppler radar systems important to the control of manned aircraft; sonic test installations; and power supplies for small radar systems in commercial aircraft.

Perhaps Dresser's goals for the rapid expansion of its electronics capabilities were too broad and immediate, for while its work in this area was highly significant and specialized, it was never to reach the level of expectations. During 1960, Dresser Electronics lost more than $2 million, and in the struggle to achieve profitability, significant changes occurred in personnel. Three years later Dresser Electronics was to be disbanded, S.I.E. becoming part of the Exploration & Production Group and HST a part of a new Communication & Control Group.

Aside from the internal broadening of product lines into new markets, there remained, of course, the distinct possibility of acquiring companies for this purpose. One interesting company that emerged in John Lawrence's studies of possible acquisitions was a Chicago, Illinois, firm named Podbielniak, Inc., a manufacturer of laboratory distillation instruments and centrifugal contactors. The company's contactor was highly efficient in separating liquids, a function particularly applicable to the petrochemical, pharmaceutical, vegetable oil, soap, and other chemical process industries. The company had been organized in 1928 by Dr. Walter J. Podbielniak, still the president and controlling stockholder. Its annual sales had been as high as $3.5 million in 1958, and in 1960 they were at the $2 million level. More than half of these sales were from the foreign market. Marketing areas that showed promise of rapid future development for the contactor included lube oil refining, uranium and other metal recovery and refining, decontamination of waste liquors, processing of plastics and detergents, and vegetable oil refining.

Perhaps the most interesting aspect of Podbielniak was its role in making possible the mass production of penicillin. The Podbielniak contactor worked through a series of perforated drums that operated at a speed sufficient to exert a centrifugal force ranging from five hundred to five thousand times the force of gravity, and in the case of penicillin, removed the pure antibiotic from the broth in which the penicillin was created.

Lawrence and F. W. Laverty, the president of Clark, under whose aegis Podbielniak would be placed, both examined closely the company's circumstances and possibilities, made a presentation to Dresser's directors in favor of the acquisition, and on October 1, 1960, Podbielniak became a Dresser division, having been obtained for 36,000 shares of Dresser stock worth more than $700,000. Dr. Podbielniak remained as president. An interesting property among the company's assets was a 106-foot yacht on Lake Michigan. Having no use for such a luxury item, Dresser promptly sold it.

In November 1961 the company achieved further diversification by acquiring for approximately $6 million the M&H Valve & Fittings Company. Purchased from the Walworth Company, this subsidiary manufactured products for the water and sewage industries, including large gate valves and hydrants. It was a logical complement to Dresser Manufacturing Division, under whose authority it was placed. The acquisition backed up the company's belief that one of the most important and rapidly growing markets in coming years would be centered around the country's "greatly increasing requirements for water; the treatment of pollution, whether industrial or otherwise; and other elements bearing upon a need for water."

Dresser sought to highlight in the 1960 annual report the

The acquisition in 1961 of M&H Valve & Fittings Company proved to be a profitable move. M&H was a prominent manufacturer of valves and fittings for the water industry, such as those seen in this water treatment plant.

A group of Dresser officials poses in the 1950's: left to right, front, John B. O'Connor, Willard Johnson, and Neil Mallon; rear: C. Paul Clark, Rudy E. Reimer, William McAfee, and Henry Isham.

new directions it was taking. The traditional emphasis on oil and gas was played down, and the message on the cover said that the company was "Serving Growth Industries: Chemical/Gas/Industrial/Defense/Oil/Electronics/Power." Inside, the role of each of these industries was described with equal space given for each.

As the company sought to regain lost sales and earnings in this new era, a more formal approach to planning was evolving. The twice-monthly Monday-morning sessions of top officers were one obvious manifestation of this emphasis. There also were occasional Saturday-morning meetings at Mallon's home attended by Mallon, O'Connor, Reimer, and Lawrence. These were not coffee klatches, as Mallon's memo for one of these occasions illustrated. After a list of important items for discussion, the final note read: "*Excluded from discussion:* Politics—world affairs—weather." In a 1960 memorandum to the twelve officers who customarily attended the Monday-morning sessions, Mallon asked them to consider these questions:

Should we start a program of long-range planning within Dresser at the headquarters level? Should we bring in a new Vice President of Planning to lead this activity? What present staff executives should play a part in this planning program? How can it be conducted so that it will be of maximum assistance to the line executives in Dallas and to some degree within the local companies? What comments would you like to make, especially as to the leadership in this planning program and where you yourself would fit in, if at all? What sort of problems do you feel should come within the planning effort?

Before the year ended, an official planning committee consisting of Mallon, O'Connor, Reimer, Lawrence, economist Fred M. Carlson, and a new executive vice president named Francis G. Fabian, Jr., had been designated to meet once a month to discuss substantive issues and to set priorities, not only on long-term goals but also on handling immediate problems and opportunities. Carlson was in charge of coordinating the meetings. Some of the earliest topics discussed included the strategy for exploiting the potentially lucrative market in India, a survey of the market for amusement towers, acquisition policy and procedure, and Iron Curtain trade. Notebooks containing background information on all topics on the agenda were prepared beforehand and distributed to the committee members. The new executive vice president, Fabian, had been promoted to his position in May 1960 from the presidency of the Dresser Manufacturing Division in Bradford. He had been especially aggressive there in promoting the need for formalized planning and goal setting. He was the company's third executive vice president, joining Reimer and Lawrence, and also becoming a director.

One of Mallon's primary objectives in the twilight of his long leadership was to create as a legacy a strong and visionary management team. A series of appointments, including Fabian's, was made in this regard. Another significant addition to the headquarters office in 1960 was that of John V. James as controller. James was advanced from financial vice president of Clark, still Dresser's largest operating unit. A year later, three other major headquarters appointments were made. John P. Cartwright, formerly a colleague of Lawrence's at Joy Manufacturing Company, was elected vice president with supervising responsibilities over the machinery companies. Dan M. Krausse, formerly senior vice president of Cosden Petroleum Company, was named vice president to oversee the group of companies primarily identified with supplying products and services to the drilling industry. J. V. Holdam, a nuclear physicist who was a cofounder and vice president of Laboratory of Electronics in Massachusetts, became a Dresser vice president with

Four thirty-year Dresser men, the same ones who came together in Bradford in 1929, were honored at a company celebration in 1959. Left to right are George Pfefferle, Neil Mallon, Rudy E. Reimer, and Hector P. "Hec" Boncher.

responsibilities over electronics activities. An addition to the board of directors was that of a familiar figure, Robert B. Anderson. Anderson, who had resigned as Secretary of the Treasury with the advent of the new Democratic administration, resumed his directorship in 1961.

At the same time that diversification and long-range planning were prime topics in Dallas headquarters, it was not forgotten that the company's principal business remained with the oil and gas industries. In fact—and this was somewhat ironic in view of recent diversification efforts—a bigger percentage of the company's business came from oil and gas in 1960 than had been the case six years earlier.*

While the oil and gas industries declined domestically, international activity remained on a steady upward path, and Dresser's involvement there continued to increase year after year. The proportion of foreign sales climbed from 10 percent in 1951 to 28 percent in 1960. Dresser could count twenty-three foreign

* In 1960, 71 percent of sales resulted from the activities of oil and gas exploration and drilling (which accounted for 43 percent of that figure), oil and gas production (12 percent), and gas transmission and distribution (16 percent). This left 19 percent from the industrial and government markets, and 10 percent from the refining, petrochemical, and chemical markets.

The tornado that struck Dallas in 1957 and cut a devastating swath through the Oak Cliff section of town barely missed the Security Engineering plant at right.

affiliates in 1960, and the network of licensees represented virtually every important industrial nation of the world. These licensees were responsible for some 15 to 20 percent of the business done abroad.

As part of the re-evaluation of Dresser's operations, Mallon asked the company's general counsel to review foreign operations as they pertained to tax advantages. The conclusion soon reached proved the worth of the international company, Dresser A. G. Vaduz. Between 1953, the year of its formation, and 1959, the international company had been responsible for tax deferments of nearly $6 million. While federal taxes would be paid ultimately upon the return of these sums to the United States, until that day this money added significantly to the funds available for foreign operations.

One of the company's most significant international ventures of this period was tied to Argentine ruler Juan Perón's determination to achieve self-sufficiency in oil and gas for his nation. To do this he needed American experience and equipment. In light of Argentina's wealth of reserves, Perón was embarrassed by the fact that his country imported much of its oil requirements. Argentina simply did not have the technical knowledge or equipment to develop the potential of its existing fields. O'Connor, having dealt for

many years with Perón and his state oil agency, Yacimientos Petro-
liberas Fiscales (YPF), helped devise a strategy to achieve Perón's
goal. Since Dresser had a firm policy against competing with its
customers in the search for and production of oil, O'Connor recommended a number of American firms that were capable of performing the various tasks involved. One of these companies was
Southeastern Drilling Company of Dallas (now SEDCO), headed
by William P. Clements,* which drilled some one thousand wells.
Dresser sold to Southeastern Drilling some $10 million in equip-
ment for this mammoth job. It was the largest supply contract ever
awarded by a single drilling firm. The contract's biggest single
element was Southeastern's purchase of twenty drilling rigs from
Ideco. Dresser companies also were furnishing much of the equipment used for new pipelines, refineries, and the expansion of established refineries.

Another foreign project of note was a joint venture with an
Iranian group to mine and process barite in that country to serve
the heavy drilling activity in the Middle East. Dresser invested
$100,000 in the venture for 50 percent ownership and lent an
additional $400,000 to launch operations of the company, which
took the name Sherkat Sahami Magcobar Iran. The plant commenced commercial production in December 1960, and first-year
earnings alone were forecast to be $375,550. Formal dedication
came on May 9, 1961, and the Shah of Iran was among the digni-
taries present who heard O'Connor speak at the opening ceremony.
A United States Voice of America radio broadcast praised Dresser's
participation in this program as important to the industrial progress
of Iran. As the broadcast stated, until the new plant and mine were
developed, farmers in nearby villages worked hard to scratch a
meager living from the desert soil. It was obvious that some kind
of industry was necessary if the local economy was to be stimulated
and living conditions improved. The establishment of Sherkat
Sahami Magcobar Iran did much to achieve this goal. It employed
about 250 workers from the start and was expected to save about
$2 million a year in foreign exchange for the Iranian economy.
With this part of the world now becoming the most active center
for drilling anywhere, the Iranian plant was essential for augment-
ing barite processed on Mykonos† for the huge Middle East market.

Dresser's push for foreign sales had never as a policy excluded

* Later to become Deputy Secretary of Defense under President Richard
Nixon.

† In 1959 Dresser became sole owner of the Mykobar Mining Company
on the island of Mykonos.

His Imperial Majesty, the Shah of Iran, right, was on hand with John B. O'Connor, center, when the Magcobar barite-processing plant was dedicated in Iran in 1961.

the Soviet Union or other Communist-ruled nations. The turbodrill deal, however, had focused critical attention on the company for doing business with a country generally deemed to be a threat to the security of the United States. Mallon and O'Connor had suffered considerable abuse as a result.

Dresser had had no transactions with an Iron Curtain country since the turbodrill contract. Government policy made such trade difficult if not impossible. But in 1960 a change in policy by the Commerce Department made it permissible for U.S. component parts to be used in drilling rigs imported by Communist-bloc nations. Should the foreign licensees attempt to win some of this market? Many competitors of Dresser's foreign licensees were finding these markets lucrative, and considerable sentiment existed to permit the Dresser licensees to enter these markets. The board of directors wrestled with the problem, considered the adverse effect that such trade might have on Dresser's relations with many major domestic customers, and decided finally against competing in such markets. The question of whether the company should deal with Communist-ruled nations had never before undergone formal consideration, for the operating assumption always had been that Dresser would sell its products and seek a profit wherever a market existed unless government policy prohibited it. With this new declaration, however, that assumption ended.

When Neil Mallon arrived in Bradford on that wintry January day in 1929 to assume the leadership of Dresser Manufacturing Company the sales for the previous year had been less than $4 million. The company produced couplings, sleeves, fittings, and other accessories for the construction and operation of pipelines. It was an age in which the boyish Charles Lindbergh was lionized wherever he went for his solo flight two years earlier across the Atlantic. In the intervening years the visionary Mallon had presided over the transformation of the company into one whose member firms and affiliates spanned the globe and one that was numbered among the nation's two hundred largest corporations. Annual sales in 1961 were $235 million, and the company's services and products were essential ingredients throughout the oil and gas industries as well as in other important areas of industry. Lindbergh's flight across the Atlantic now seemed to be part of another age entirely. The world's attention was focused on the United States' preparations to send a man to the moon! Even in this romantic goal, seemingly so far removed from the oil and gas industries, Dresser Industries was prepared to play a role.

Since the postponement of his retirement, Mallon, his top aides, executives, and personnel throughout Dresser had worked diligently to reverse the decline in earnings that had begun in 1958. There had been painful self-analysis, a strengthening of the headquarters management team, added diversification, a push for new revenue from electronics and government contracts, a reduction of overhead, added emphasis and attention to annual profit planning, and the institution of a planning committee. Unfortunately, the decline in oil and gas activity and a lagging general economy had persisted, and sales and earnings had remained in a decline since the drop in 1958. As far as current assets and working capital were concerned, however, the company was in its best shape ever. The future was bright.

In early 1962, having celebrated his sixty-seventh birthday, Mallon announced his retirement effective March 19. O'Connor, who would turn sixty-five in December 1962, would retire on the same date. The announcement was made jointly.

"Both Mr. O'Connor and I have been planning for our respective retirements for some time, and with this in mind we have greatly strengthened the Dresser management team and have complete confidence in its ability," Mallon said.

Mallon had been the company's chief executive officer for thirty-three years, a longer period than founder Solomon R. Dresser or Fred A. Miller. O'Connor had served the Dresser name nine

John Lawrence, left, as chairman of the board, and Francis G. Fabian, Jr., as president, assumed managerial leadership of Dresser in the early 1960's.

years less, but his service with Clark and Dresser extended for thirty-six years. If Mallon was "Mr. Inside," O'Connor was a distinctive "Mr. Outside," the man who more than anyone else was responsible for the growth of the company's foreign business.

Who would be the fourth chief executive officer of the corporation stemming from Solomon Dresser's enterprise? It had been envisioned at one point that Robert B. Anderson would succeed Mallon, but that notion had vanished when Anderson became Secretary of the Treasury for Eisenhower. Willard Johnson, who had done so well with Magnet Cove and whose business acumen always had been valued on the board of directors, earlier had declined to entertain a notion that he move to Dallas and assume the position. Since then the strengthening of the headquarters executive group had added new choices for this important role.

On March 29, 1962, the board of directors met in a special session in New York City to make their decision. The nominating committee, chaired by William A. McAfee, recommended that both Mallon's and O'Connor's positions be filled, and that they be filled from within the company. The man they nominated as the new chairman of the board and chief executive officer was John Lawrence. For president they presented the name of Francis G. Fabian, Jr. The directors unanimously elected these executives to those offices. A new era began for Dresser Industries.

11

Broadening Horizons— Rising Profits

John Lawrence was the fourth chief executive officer of the company that bore Solomon R. Dresser's name. A trim, athletic man with wiry, close-cropped hair marked by a distinctive streak of gray, he had demonstrated as an executive those qualities so frequently associated with his native state of Vermont: integrity, hard work, and taciturnity. As a boy he once packed his meager belongings and ran away from home, managing to stay away for twenty-four hours. When at last he returned, his parents pretended not to have missed him. It was a good lesson in self-reliance, one he never forgot. He attended Exeter Academy and then studied engineering at Massachusetts Institute of Technology. Upon graduation in the depression in 1932 he began looking for a job and did not find one for eight months. The job was on the night shift at Jones & Lamson Machine Tool Company in Springfield, Vermont; ten years later he was the factory manager. Married by then, and with the first three of his eventual five children, he soon moved to SKF Industries, Inc., in Philadelphia, where he advanced to vice president of factory management, engineering, and research. From there he went to Joy Manufacturing Company, where he had become president and chief executive officer. Then he joined Dresser in 1956. As Dresser Industries' new chairman of the board, he was expected to exhibit the same traits that already had carried him so far in industrial management: a penchant for planning and goal setting, stress on good engineering, and a knack for handling men. His salary, excluding bonuses and other perquisites, was $75,000 a year.

The company's new president, Francis G. Fabian, Jr., attended the exclusive boys' preparatory school Choate and was a 1937 graduate of Yale University with a bachelor of science in industrial engineering. He served with the U.S. Navy during World War II and worked with the management consultant firm of Booze, Allen, and Hamilton before joining Dresser Manufacturing Division in Bradford. His first job there was as assistant to Hec Boncher, the general manager. When Boncher was promoted to Dallas, Fabian succeeded him in the presidency of that unit. After establishing a fine record there, he had been a logical choice to become executive vice president in Dallas, and now he seemed to be just as fine a choice to be president. While Lawrence was an engineer by profession, Fabian was identified as a management specialist. The combination of these two men with their complementing skills seemed ideal for the leadership of Dresser Industries.

They would not operate without the benefit of the accumulated wisdom of Mallon and O'Connor, for both these men were retained as consultants and they remained directors. Mallon, in fact, became chairman of the executive committee. Reimer, the third leg of the triumvirate that had guided Dresser for so many years, remained as senior vice president, treasurer, and chairman of the finance committee.

An analysis of the company at this moment of transition in leadership showed its continued ties, despite efforts at diversification, to the oil and gas industries. Its dependence on drilling activity, however, had lessened. The percentage of income derived from exploration and drilling had declined from the peak of 48.7 percent in 1956 to 36.4 percent in 1962. The combined percentage from exploration and drilling, oil and gas production, and gas transmission and distribution was 64.3 percent. An additional 13.5 percent of sales came from the refining, petrochemical, and chemical fields. The remaining 22.2 percent of sales was derived from the industrial and government markets.

There were still other broad perspectives from which to view the company. A total of 77.4 percent of the business originated from domestic sales and 22.6 percent from foreign activity. The biggest change of the past decade had been the addition of expendables to supplement the capital goods sector. In 1950 seven out of every ten dollars earned had come from the sale of such capital goods items as compressors, pumps, blowers, and drilling rigs. By 1962 that figure had been reduced to five out of ten dollars, the remaining dollars resulting from expendables such as drilling muds and geophysical and other services. Sixteen domestic units were included in the Dresser stable of companies, and twenty-seven foreign affiliates were owned wholly or in majority.

The company still had not regained the peak it had reached in 1957, although the $16 million in earnings gained in 1962 was up substantially from the recent low of $13 million in 1959. Nevertheless, only a month after Lawrence succeeded Mallon, it was apparent that the projected earnings per share of $2.44 for 1962 would not be achieved. They fell short by 42 cents, reaching only $2.02 per share. This seemed meager indeed compared with the rosy mid-1950's when earnings between 1954 and 1957 had been $2.77, $2.58, $3.97, and $4.60, only to be followed by annual figures of $2.14, $1.95, $1.94, and $2.16.*

These statistics had not endeared Dresser to investors. The price commanded by its shares declined from $58 in 1957 to $16 in 1962 (figures adjusted). Despite recent efforts to revive the company in the midst of economic slowdown, the turnaround in fact had not been achieved.

Lawrence clearly was confronted with a difficult task. Yet, he had no plans to "revolutionize" the company. Its circumstances had been dictated by external events. "It seemed to me that Mr. Mallon and Johnny O'Connor had pointed the company in the right direction and it was merely a matter of sharpening up some of the management techniques," Lawrence recalled years later. Business had a way of ebbing and flowing over the years, and there was no doubt but that the company's fortunes would turn up again if management did not boggle the opportunity. "We didn't know where the bottom was going to be," Lawrence said. "We all felt it [the company] was going to come back but we didn't know when."

Part of the initial need was in defining the separate areas of responsibilities for Lawrence and Fabian. Little distinction in their job descriptions appeared in the company bylaws other than the fact that the chairman was the company's chief executive and as such the president reported to him. Lawrence elected to concentrate on the broad picture: long-range planning, shareholder relations, key decisions concerning products and markets, and government relations. Fabian would be the chief *operating* officer, whose concerns would be more of the day-to-day nature.

One of Fabian's first undertakings was to prepare a set of objectives for the company. All the objectives were based on the overriding goal of increasing profits for the shareholders. He outlined three basic approaches: (1) by achieving through operations a more effective marshaling of capabilities than the competition; (2) by outperforming competitors in providing superior

* Data as reported in the years involved, adjusted for 2 for 1 split in 1957.

engineered products and services; and (3) by serving through marketing an increasing spectrum of world business.

He elaborated on the operating objectives as follows:

> We are dedicated above all to *profitable* growth. . . . We recognize that an *improvement* in present operations (i.e., product cost, market penetration, etc.) can be more immediately valuable to profitable growth than a new undertaking. . . . But we are always willing to invest in outside acquisitions when these will extend our capability more effectively than by building the business internally.

The objectives for achieving product superiority stated:

> We will strive for the highly-engineered, proprietary and preferably patented products and services that require the management disciplines inherent in this type of high investment. We find these situations more nearly fit our concept of management and our dedication to the task of providing a better product, and give us more opportunity to pay out the company's investment.

As for the market objective of servicing an increasing spectrum of world business, the guidelines stated:

> We consider the world to be our opportunity. We must design, manufacture, sell, manage or even headquarter wherever our long-term profitable growth can best be achieved. In doing this we will strive for operating units of practical and effective size.
>
> And this is a global concept, including all countries. The promising opportunities must be defined with the best long-run strategy to win, including such tools as credit, foreign ownership, etc. But remembering always that Dresser Industries proprietorship and control in foreign fields must be maintained, strong enough to prevent the cub's returning to devour the mother.
>
> Recognizing that advances in research, in products, in processes and in business practice are available throughout the world, and [that] we must have an intelligence function alert to find them, wherever the source.
>
> Recognizing also the opportunities in government markets, not only for present products but for R&D [research and development] contracts that develop advanced knowledge and capability to serve our customers.

In this last regard there was the reminder that top priority must be given for growth and strength in existing markets. "What they lack in glamour will normally be far exceeded by the compound profit they can provide."

If the above were the objectives, what would be the administrative practices, or, in Fabian's words, the "rules of the game," to follow in pursuing them? These policies, Dresser's executives were told, were a "distillation of experience which we believe in now, but which should be further improved as we learn." The company's basic credo was that it would be a "results organization," one in which performance would be measured by profit results rather than internal politics. All executive jobs would have "clear-cut definition of functions to be performed to achieve agreed upon results." The goals must be set by the superior and agreed upon by the subordinate, but the "subordinate must then have the authority, as well as the responsibility, to determine how he will achieve these results." In this relationship the superior would "coach" rather than order, pressing his advice, based on logic and broader experience, rather than on authority. The ultimate decisions as to *how* the agreed-upon goals would be achieved belonged to the man responsible for getting the results. During the process, however, the subordinate had "a clear responsibility to keep his superior fully and forthrightly informed on his problems, plans, and progress." Only through this communication could the superior render maximum assistance to facilitate the subordinate's success.

All these directives, of course, were not new to Dresser. They simply represented a clear-cut outline of the decentralization that had been the company's credo since its first acquisition nearly thirty years earlier. The idea was to delegate responsibility downward to the nearest point where intelligent decisions and action could be taken. As always, headquarters would coordinate and control overall plans and stand ready to render expert assistance in specialized areas, such as industrial relations, legal matters, taxes, insurance, or finance. In this scheme of things, it was pointed out, committees could "never be used or held accountable for responsibility, decision, action or results." Committees, it was stated, occasionally proved effective, if time-consuming, in various types of "wolf-pack" approaches to auditing plans, in inciting "group hysteria," or in "brainstorming," but all these were lacking as effective business practices. It was observed that "a disorganized committee effort to solve a problem may indicate lack of the mental guts to think it through."

This tone of no nonsense was characteristic of the new guidelines. All "team members" were told that they would be charged, measured, and rewarded on an equal basis. No favorites would be played. Complaints or criticisms of others would be made only in their presence, or at least with their full knowledge so that they could present a rebuttal. This did not apply in the case of a superior reporting on a subordinate. The reason for this policy was stated plainly. "The private cup of poison and political knife-wielding will destroy the teamwork and change the motivation of any organization from profits to politics. If we mean what we say —that we are a *results* organization—this takes men, not cats." There finally was a strong statement to insure that the listed guidelines would be followed carefully: "We must recognize that contrary behavior will categorize itself as 'disloyalty' to the company purpose and policies."

This was only the first in a series of guidelines formulated by the new executive team for such areas as acquisitions and financial relations. While they were not intended to detract from Dresser's traditional decentralized form of management, the idea soon emerged in the operating companies that their relationships with headquarters were destined now to be much closer.

At the same time these hard-spoken directives were being formulated, headquarters also compiled a more generous executive compensation plan. As adopted by the board of directors, it basically provided for headquarters executives to be paid 4 percent of consolidated earnings before taxes, and for operating executives to receive 6 percent of their companies' earnings before taxes. These funds would be administered for headquarters office by an executive compensation committee composed of three or more directors, and for operating units, the compensation committee would consist of Lawrence, Fabian, and one or more persons of their choice. The object of the plan, of course, was to inspire the company's top officers to their peak performance by giving them a vested interest in earning profits. A deferred compensation plan, adopted less than a year later, permitted executives for the first time to defer portions of their bonuses until retirement or their departure from the company.

While administrative policies thus were being formulated more concisely than ever before, Lawrence also was eager to emphasize long-range planning. In his first few months as chairman of the board he was joined by Fabian, Mallon, and O'Connor in projecting Dresser's future. "In general across the country, the outlook seems to be for industrial companies and equipment manufacturers like Dresser, to be facing somewhat of a profit squeeze," they concluded. Dresser's own profit picture was clouded further by the fact that it faced "another year or two of curtailment of drilling and weakening of prices" in the oil industry. While this economic squeeze would affect Dresser's profits, it would harm—perhaps to an even greater extent—other companies, too. And here would be opportunity for well-managed companies like Dresser: acquisitions on favorable terms! The opportunities would be further enhanced if Dresser could build up its cash position, and, as Lawrence mused, there was one certain way to do that:

"As a result of all this forward thinking, we are adopting a somewhat different philosophy in regard to our dividend policy and are considering omitting our quarterly dividend payment until we build up a cash position adequate to meet the challenge of these acquisition opportunities." The board of directors agreed that in the long run such action would improve the stockholders' position. The cash purchase of M&H Valve Company six months earlier had demonstrated anew the rewards of such acquisitions, for M&H was earning profits at an annual rate of $500,000 after taxes. Of course, acquisitions could be made by using Dresser stock, too, but the stock's market value at present was too low to be used to advantage for this purpose.

While the contemplated temporary omission of dividends seemed far-sighted to top-level planners, many stockholders would not welcome a company's decision not to pay expected dividends. Thus, before the plan could be instituted, it was reconsidered and dropped.

Another kind of problem faced by Dresser in 1962 lay not within the company but in Washington, D.C., where Congress was considering the Revenue Act of 1962. This bill included provisions to tax foreign earnings of American multinational corporations. The current policy of taxing foreign earnings only upon their return to the United States had been extremely helpful to Dresser as well as to other multinational corporations in financing further foreign ventures. Secretary of the Treasury Douglas Dillon viewed this, however, as a tax haven that should be removed. Dresser officials joined other companies in speaking against the proposed change, arguing that the present policy helped accomplish precisely what the Kennedy Administration desired—an expansion of U.S. exports. Meanwhile, however, as many as thirteen agents at a time from the Internal Revenue Service were combing Dresser's records thoroughly, and Mallon feared that the Democratic administration hoped to use the company's foreign earnings as an example of what the Revenue Act would prevent.

The eventual result of the debate over the provisions of the Revenue Act of 1962 was the enactment of the Export Trade Amendment, introduced by Senator Robert S. Kerr of Oklahoma. This amendment permitted the creation of "export trade corporations"—largely as proposed by Dresser. Such corporations received tax advantages so long as the reinvestment of their earnings in foreign nations met certain criteria. When the act became effective in 1964, Dresser established Dresser International, S.A., a company that qualified as an export trade corporation. Its purpose was to promote in foreign markets the sale of products made in the United States by Dresser's operating units, a function formerly performed by Dresser A. G. Vaduz. The latter company, in contrast, now performed general services for the foreign subsidiaries and licensees.

Dresser's struggle to reclaim its former high level of sales and profits was long and difficult, but, as it turned out, steady and sure. At the end of fiscal year 1962, sales were up over the previous year by $10 million, but earnings per share declined from $2.16 to $2.02. (Except for $1.05 million in foreign exchange losses, earnings would have improved slightly.) A year later the picture brightened considerably, for in the face of a slight decline in sales, attributable to a degree to the company's withdrawal from military contracts, earnings before taxes increased by $4 million. This amounted to a climb in earnings per share to $2.36. It was not a remarkable recovery, but it was significant. How had it been achieved? Lawrence and Fabian explained it as the elimination of unprofitable product lines, including especially certain military products, a reorientation of important marketing efforts, and an improvement in the general efficiency of operations. "We view 1964 with a growing determination to achieve our goal—a steady improvement in earnings from Dresser's world-wide operations," they said in the 1963 annual report.

Several items of note had occurred during 1963. One was the acquisition of a Canadian oil-well-servicing firm, Eskimo Fracturing & Well Servicing Ltd., for slightly more than $1 million. ("Fracturing" is a technique that involves the breaking up of subsurface formations to facilitate the flow of crude oil.) A well-known Texan, Allan Shivers, who had served three terms as governor of the state, was elected to the board of directors. Shivers, chairman of Champlin Oil's executive committee, was familiar with all aspects of the oil industry. The directors also elected a new assistant secretary who was the first woman in the company's history to hold an officer's position. She was Lillian B. Edwards, an attorney in the legal department who had joined Mayson's staff in 1950 in a clerical capacity upon graduation from Southern Methodist University law school.

Charles A. Moore was one of Edward Ashcroft's leading gauge salesmen, and in 1880 Moore joined Henry S. Manning and Eugene L. Maxwell in forming a new company to buy Ashcroft's interests.

While Dresser in recent years had added a number of small companies to its roster, it had been almost a decade since the last major acquisition, that of Lane-Wells, had occurred. That situation was to be changed in late 1964 when Dresser acquired its most diversified company yet, Manning, Maxwell & Moore, Inc., of Stratford, Connecticut. The acquisition of this corporation, whose net sales in 1963 were $54 million, started in a modest enough fashion. Charles Kuhn, Fabian's successor as president of Dresser Manufacturing in Bradford, originally envisioned only the acquisition of MM&M's valve division, with Consolidated and Hancock valves as prominent products, as a logical supplement to the coupling line. In preliminary discussions it suddenly dawned on him that the entire company seemed to be available. This included a crane and hoist division, an instrument division that manufactured pressure gauges, temperature regulators, and other specialized instruments, and the valve division. The company had nine manufacturing plants across the nation, a wholly owned Canadian subsidiary, and a wholly owned Swiss subsidiary that owned stock in other foreign affiliates. Kuhn alerted Lawrence to the possibility of this acquisition, and Lawrence began negotiating with Charles A. Moore, MM&M's chairman of the board and grandson of the firm's first president. MM&M was agreeable to such talks because the company seemed to have stalled in its progress. The market price of its shares, Moore said, was not what it should be, and in common with other medium-sized companies, MM&M was having difficulty in "attracting and retaining management in depth in the face of increased competition from larger companies." By August 1964 an agreement had been reached for Dresser to acquire MM&M for $35 a share, or $27.7 million. Shareholders readily assented, and on November 1, 1964, MM&M became a part of Dresser Industries.

The company brought with it an extremely interesting historical aspect to that of Dresser. Its origin stemmed from the founding of the Ashcroft Company in 1852 by Edward H. Ashcroft of Lynn, Massachusetts, to manufacture pressure gauges for steam engines.*

Ashcroft, who had taken American rights to Frenchman Eugene Bourdon's gauge, adapted that useful instrument for locomotives, steamships, and boiler rooms of American mills and factories, and thereby played an important role in the widespread adoption of steam power in America, especially through locomotives. Probably Ashcroft's most important work was his role with George W. Richardson of New York in developing a spring-loaded safety valve. In 1880 Ashcroft sold his interests in the two manufacturing companies he had formed to a new company, Manning, Maxwell & Moore. Charles A. Moore had been Ashcroft's salesman, and Henry S. Manning and Eugene L. Maxwell were partners in a firm that sold industrial mill supplies. Headquarters were established on Liberty Street in New York City, and as the nation's railroads prospered so did Manning, Maxwell & Moore. Farsighted acquisitions of companies that manufactured other products for steam boilers followed, and in 1905—the same year of incorporation—the company acquired the Shaw Electric Crane Company of Muskegon, Michigan, a firm for which it previously had operated as selling agent. This company's founder, Alton J. Shaw, had designed and manufactured the nation's first three-motor electric traveling crane.†

One of MM&M's top salesmen of this period was the fabulous James Buchanan Brady, otherwise known as "Diamond Jim" Brady because of his impressive collection of diamonds. Brady, a lavish

---

* See Chapter 1, p. 17.
† See Chapter 1, p. 31.

Since 1852 the Ashcroft gauge has performed essential services for industries ranging from railroads to petrochemical plants. This product joined the Dresser line in 1964 with the acquisition of Manning, Maxwell & Moore.

Shaw-Box cranes perform a wide range of lifting services for industry.

Manning, Maxwell & Moore counted among its past executives a famous *bon vivant* of Broadway, James "Diamond Jim" Brady. (Bettmann *Archives*)

entertainer and prominent personality in New York's theatrical circles, became a vice president of the company in 1912.

In 1932 the company acquired the Box Crane & Hoist Corporation and combined it with Shaw Electric Crane Company as the Shaw-Box Crane and Hoist Company. Six years later, after extensive design and test work, the company introduced the first universally accepted electrically operated chain hoists, the "Budgit" line.

In World War II virtually all of MM&M's products were in heavy demand by industry and the military. Safety relief valves were important to petroleum processing and to synthetic rubber plants centered in the Southwest, and the company's gauges, valves, and instruments were relied upon by the merchant marine and naval shipbuilding programs. Other MM&M gauges for monitoring such things as oil pressure, temperature, manifold pressure, and oxygen supply systems were used in large quantities by military aircraft.

By 1964 MM&M's cranes and hoists were important especially to the steel industry, and also to foundries and metalworking plants. The company's valves and gauges were used extensively in the electric power industry, and the line of Hancock valves had been adapted to the special requirements of steam generation using nuclear fuels. Continuous-process industries such as petroleum, chemical, petrochemical, refining, and pulp and paper production were prime customers for gauges, thermometers, and gate, globe, safety, and relief valves.*

Kuhn, the Dresser Manufacturing executive who had called attention to MM&M as an acquisition, was rewarded with his promotion to vice president in corporate headquarters, where his primary duty was to oversee the Industrial Specialties Group, where MM&M operations were placed. Others in this group included Dresser Manufacturing and M&H Valve & Fittings Company.

There were now, as the 1964 annual report pointed out, "four worlds of Dresser": Industrial Specialties, Exploration and Production, Machinery, and Communication and Control. Exploration and Production, headed by Dan M. Krausse, encompassed S.I.E., Guiberson, Ideco, Lane-Wells, Magnet Cove Barium, and Security Engineering. Machinery included Clark, Pacific Pumps, Roots-Connersville, Podbielniak, and Dresser Vacuum. Communication and Control, a group whose future was uncertain because of its lack of profitability, included Dresser-Ideco, Dresser HST, and Dresser Controls.

The year 1964 saw further changes on the board of directors. As a rule, the company preferred outside directors rather than full-time Dresser men because of the extra dimensions outsiders brought to the boardroom. But in the spring of 1964 Lawrence concluded that the time had come to add additional Dresser executives to the board, and Mallon supported his position. Four new men were named. The first two, Kuhn and Dan M. Krausse, were elected on June 25; and John V. James, vice president and controller, and Edward R. Luter, vice president, finance, were elected on August 20. Luter, a graduate of Northwestern University in law and commerce, was a newcomer to Dresser, having joined the company earlier in the summer after being employed in a similar capacity at Studebaker International. The number of directors thus suddenly increased from twelve to sixteen, with eight of those sixteen employed at Dresser and two others, Mallon and O'Connor, still performing consulting services for the company. Mallon, in fact, continued as chairman of the executive committee, whose members included Lawrence, Fabian, Henry P. Isham, and William A. McAfee.

* Two years later the name Manning, Maxwell & Moore would be discontinued and its operations placed in the Industrial Valve & Instrument Division and the Crane, Hoist & Tower Division.

Mallon, while remaining in the background since his retirement as chief executive officer, had continued to be available when called upon. His years of service and his affection for his alma mater, Yale University, were recognized by the board in 1964 with the establishment of the Henry Neil Mallon Scholarship Award to be presented each year to a Yale student. Dresser endowed the scholarship with a gift of $100,000.

The annual profit-planning sessions held each fall in Dallas were one company endeavor that headquarters began making every effort to improve. Actually, by the time the hundred or so executives from the various operating companies met in Dallas, their forecasts and goals had already been worked out and presented in handsomely bound books. The October three-day planning sessions were a time for presentation of these forecasts to other Dresser executives and a chance to exchange ideas and comments. As such, presentations were expected *not* to be dull, and in this spirit each company was allotted no more than one hour for its presentation. Presidents were asked to take no more than three to five minutes in "keynoting the new spirit" and identifying the goals of their particular companies. Other key company executives were expected to tell of their own responsibilities in three-minute talks. The presentations, Fabian advised, "must have *impact and pace and brevity.*" The use of visual aids and graphics, as well as examples and personal experiences, was strongly encouraged. "Don't let your people read from the Plan. . . . Let each man, in his own words, tell what he's *trying* to do." The last fifteen minutes of the hour were reserved for questions and answers. To encourage intermingling of the various executives, a number of luncheons, dinners, and cocktail-buffets were held. In short, the annual profit-planning sessions became one of the most widely anticipated events of the year for the company's executives.

One of the recurring problems for headquarters continued to be what to do concerning trade with Communist-bloc nations. Manufacturers of competitive equipment in England, France, Switzerland, and Italy were doing booming business behind the Iron Curtain, and Dresser's European licensees still were eager to participate in this market despite the 1961 directors' decision to prohibit operating units and licensees from accepting orders from Iron Curtain countries. (An exception to this embargo was Yugoslavia, which exhibited a stubborn streak of independence as a Communist nation.) Competitors such as Hughes Tool Company had European licensees who were shipping bits and other products to Eastern European countries, and Security Engineering's C. T. Kastner was one of those who urged Dresser headquarters to reconsider the embargo.

Donald H. Hartmann, president of Lane-Wells, was another operating unit executive who believed the U.S. State Department's liberalized attitude toward Communist-ruled nations called for a re-evaluation of Dresser's policy. Still another operating unit executive who questioned the policy was Magcobar's W. W. McBrien, who in November 1964 informed Krausse that he had received requests for quotations on drilling mud from Iron Curtain countries that would amount to $140,000 in business. He had not yet responded because of Dresser policy, he said. One of the inquiries indicated that Magnet Cove's principal competitor was supplying drilling mud materials for Hungary and the U.S.S.R. Another significant order that had to be declined was one from Rumania for Clark compressors.

The result of all this discussion and lost business was a series of lively memos in which the ban on trade was reviewed and analyzed from all sides. The chief concern regarding resumption of trading activities with the Soviet bloc was a fear of reprisal from major customers, particularly a major oil company. Memories of the turbodrill controversy lingered, but proponents of trade resumption gained at least a foothold in the policy. At Lawrence's recommendation, the board of directors modified company policy to permit the shipment of non-oil-field equipment to Iron Curtain countries if permitted by the Commerce Department. "However," the minutes stated, "where practical, it was thought that orders should be filled through licensees rather than through direct shipments from the Company's U.S. Operating Units."

The original plan adopted by Lawrence and Fabian for dividing management responsibilities had worked out in practice just as they envisioned it in theory. Lawrence had removed himself from daily decision making to concentrate on broad planning and supervising functions; Fabian had taken readily to the role of "operating" officer. This arrangement worked well for a period, but as Fabian broadened his interests and began to get into matters relating to corporate tax planning and financing functions, the two men found themselves in basic disagreement. Their differences on matters relating to corporate policy became so serious that in January 1965 Lawrence, who thus far had refrained from interfering with Fabian's relations with operating unit executives, asked Fabian to resign. After unsuccessfully appealing to the directors for their support, Fabian resigned. Lawrence now became president as well as chairman of the board.

Two months later a number of other changes occurred in the Dallas headquarters offices. The most significant was the elevation of Charles Kuhn to executive vice president. His successor as vice president over the Industrial Specialties Group was William K. Downey. John V. James, formerly controller and vice president, became vice president in charge of the Machinery Group. Replacing him as controller was R. J. Donachie.

The complexion of Dresser Industries, the management of which so long had been identified with three men—Mallon, O'Connor, and Reimer—obviously was changing rapidly. Only Reimer remained on the payroll as senior vice president and treasurer. Mallon, who continued to function as chairman of the executive committee, had taken an important step in his personal life. After living and working beyond retirement age as a bachelor, in early 1964 he married a widow from Cleveland, Mrs. Ann Thayer, whom he had known since Dresser's headquarters were in that city.

O'Connor, who also continued to be on Dresser's board of directors, left his beloved Haderway Farm (though he continued to own it) for a commodious high-rise apartment with a spectacular view of the Dallas skyline. He and his wife, Sansa, decorated the apartment with exquisite furniture and accessories collected throughout the world, particularly the Orient and the Near East. So spectacular was their place that the *Dallas Morning News* devoted an entire front page of a section to a pictorial spread of its interior and described the apartment with yet another half page of words.

It had been nine years since O'Connor, now sixty-eight, had suffered his first heart attack in 1956. On Friday night, April 16, 1965, O'Connor again was stricken, at his high-rise apartment, and this time the attack was fatal. Obituaries appearing in the nation's newspapers cited him for his leadership in developing foreign markets and his pioneering work in the development and use of high-speed compressors for boosting natural gas through pipelines. Dresser's board of directors lamented his death as a "great blow to all of us." O'Connor, they declared, was a man who

> combined with his charm an unlimited energy. He traveled widely and in doing so spread around the world a fine image of Dresser

Industries and its products. Like many men of great energy and business drive combined with an enviable *joie de vivre*, John O'Connor lived a life overflowing with varied interests, satisfying pursuits and fine friends. . . . We shall miss his business judgment and his cheerful presence at our Directors' Meetings and the warm and glowing brightness of his friendship.

By 1965 the turnaround in Dresser's progress was confirmed. Sales and earnings for every quarter topped the marks of the previous year, and quarterly earnings climbed from 29 cents in the first quarter to 76 cents in the final quarter. At the end of the year, sales of $353 million and earnings of $38.9 million were easily the highest in history, topping the long-standing 1957 mark by almost $78 million in sales and more than $5 million in pre-tax earnings. Contrasted with 1964, sales were up by $94 million, a jump of 36 percent. Manning, Maxwell & Moore had contributed significantly to the sizable increase, being responsible for approximately $60 million of the $94 million gain. The prosperous year was duly noted by investors. From a low per share of $16 in 1962 the stock reached $55 by the end of the 1965 fiscal year. At this point it was split two for one. Dresser stock again was being mentioned in superlatives.

In the annual report Lawrence resisted the opportunity to boast of the year's results. It was, he wrote, "a year of significant development." He stressed the increased amount of time and investment put into new and improved products and services, such as centrifugal compressors for fertilizer plants and oxygen compression, ultramodern fire hydrants and a new line of valves for the water distribution industry, portable digital seismic recording systems for oil-field exploration, and new salt-water muds and additives for offshore drilling. The list of Dresser's assets cited in the annual report was impressive: there were 15 operating companies with 16,000 employees, 22 manufacturing plants, 17 mines and mills, 38 foreign subsidiaries, 73 engineered product lines, and 500 sales and service outlets. Eight major markets were identified as being served by the company: chemical processing, general industry, exploration and drilling, oil and gas production, gas transmission and distribution, water and sewage, electric power generation, and materials handling. Significantly, Dresser's upturn had been brought about without benefit of an increase in drilling activity. The drilling industry, while as dependent as ever on Dresser products, no longer held the company's fortunes in its hands.

Although Dresser earlier had stopped manufacturing oil-well packers, that product re-emerged after World War II as one of a long list of company staples for the drilling industry with the acquisition of Guiberson.

Such success generated many new projects for the following year, and many of them were international in nature. One of the most significant international projects was the formation with a French company of a joint manufacturing venture, Dresser-Dujardin, Société Vallourec, on an equal basis. Dresser-Dujardin purchased for approximately $4.1 million a huge plant at Le Havre to manufacture Clark compressors and Pacific pumps. The Le Havre plant accommodated a growing demand on the European continent for compressors and pumps that were identical in every way to those manufactured by U.S. divisions.*

* In 1971 Dresser acquired full ownership of the company.

The Dresser-Dujardin joint venture indicated a growing preference to establish arrangements of this nature rather than operating
as in the past through licensees or wholly owned subsidiaries. A
worldwide surge of nationalism made joint ventures seem more
acceptable and promising because of the more significant participation by local companies.

In another expansionary move Dresser purchased a thirty-acre
tract on the Houston Ship Channel to build a $2.5 million facility
to package, test, and assemble Clark products prior to shipment by
sea. The tract, purchased for $730,950, was located across the
channel from the historic San Jacinto battlefield where Texas won
its independence from Mexico in 1836. At its principal facility at
Olean, New York, Clark began a $4 million modernization pro-
gram for its machine and testing facilities in the Large Reciprocating and Turbo Products Division. Still another significant Clark
project soon to be undertaken was a $15 million capital improve-
ment program for a gas turbine development program.

Lane-Wells's declining earnings had been boosted in 1964 by
an important breakthrough—the Neutron Lifetime Log, which
represented a distinct improvement over radioactivity logging.
Rather than emitting a continuous bombardment of radioactive
elements through the well casing, the Neutron Lifetime Log
utilized bursts of neutrons every 1/1000 second. This permitted
the measurement of their rate of decline and indicated rather
precise knowledge about the formations encountered.

With this distinct success ongoing, the company embarked on
another venture in 1966. This was an attempt to provide first-rate
servicing of the offshore wells that began to be drilled after World
War II in the waters off the coasts of Texas and Louisiana. Lane-
Wells purchased for more than $1 million two self-contained,
self-propelled vessels for performing services on these oil and gas
wells. Each unit contained living quarters for twenty workers and a
4,500-square-foot mobile platform. These unusual vessels could
propel themselves to offshore wells and then be elevated and
stabilized above water level by sending down retractable columns
to attach to a submersible pontoon resting on the ocean floor at
depths as great as sixty feet. These self-contained vessels, out-
fitted jointly and fully by the various Dresser service companies,
eliminated logistical problems involved in collecting miscellaneous
service equipment at a point of embarkation and having it towed
by barge or tug to the well site. The men and equipment aboard
were capable of performing total completion and workover service,
including logging, perforating, cementing, acidizing, snubbing,
tubing removal, and other jobs.

The rigs gained immediate industrial acceptance since previously available equipment had been grossly inadequate, causing many operators to shut down their offshore wells rather than pay the high costs required in servicing them. Construction began a year later on two additional rigs, and a new operating unit called Dresser Offshore Services, Inc., was established to develop this activity. Dresser achieved an early lead in this promising field, but competitors quickly began striving to gain a foothold in a market that was virtually untapped around the world. From an original two employees, Dresser Offshore progressed by the end of the decade to two hundred workers who operated six self-propelled rigs and six platform rigs. From a first-year loss of $9,000 its earnings reached $1.8 million in 1969.

Another ambitious project undertaken in 1966 was an effort to acquire the Chicago Pneumatic Tool Company, a company half the size of Dresser. This firm was desired especially for its pneumatic, hydraulic, and electric tools, and it also had a line of compressors, drilling bits, and diesel engines. Chicago Pneumatic would be Dresser's biggest acquisition yet. Promising though the move appeared to be for both companies, negotiations were dropped after several months because routine checks with the Department of Justice revealed "irreconcilable antitrust problems." Other possible acquisitions, as always, continued to be studied by Dresser's top executives, particularly by Luter.

The year 1966 showed that Dresser's turnabout in the preceding year had been no fluke, for sales and earnings reached even higher plateaus. Sales of $401 million showed an increase of nearly $50 million; earnings before taxes of $48 million represented a climb of almost $10 million; and earnings per share of $2.70 were up by 76 cents. The dramatic turnabout of the past two years reflected more than anything Dresser's growing diversification. Industrial and government sales for the first time accounted for the biggest portion of revenues—31.6 percent. The proportion of business represented by oil and gas exploration and drilling had declined from 36.1 percent in 1964 to 29.1 percent; oil and gas production accounted for 11 percent (down from 18.3 percent in 1964); gas transmission and distribution sales of 10.8 percent had not changed significantly; and refining, petrochemical, and chemical sales were up from 12.5 percent in 1964 to 17.5 percent. The ratio of revenue between foreign and domestic sources remained basically unchanged, 77 percent originating from the United States and 23 percent coming from the rest of the world. With such fine earnings, investors continued their recent infatuation with Dresser stock, its price now having climbed 110 percent in five years.

The key to this success, Lawrence told stockholders, lay in stressing new basic goals. First, Dresser sought to anticipate the products and services its customers *must have* to operate. Then, the charge was to design, develop, and test these products *in advance* of customers' needs to assure an early and sound position in the marketplace. Wherever possible, patent protection was obtained to insure a proprietary position, and executives always had to be willing to commit the capital necessary to become and remain the low-cost producer in the field. A final aim was to work diligently toward worldwide acceptance of these products. That these goals were not idle ones was indicated by the fact that the company's product research and engineering program had been expanded in two years from an annual figure of $10 million to $18 million and capital expenditures for 1967 were to be $25 million, almost double the 1956 figure.

There continued to be other reminders in these mid-1960's that the company had entered a new era. Aside from the fact that Mallon no longer was chief executive officer and O'Connor was dead, other familiar executives were nearing the end of long and distinguished business careers. Art Weis, one of the founders of Pacific Pumps and chief executive of that firm since it had joined Dresser in 1940, reached his sixty-fifth birthday in 1965 and was able to continue as president for another year only with the consent of the directors. Near the end of 1966 Willard M. Johnson of Magnet Cove Barium Corporation retired after being the chief executive of that company since its founding in 1940. During these twenty-six years, Magnet Cove's net earnings had exceeded $45 million. Johnson's rather fantastic achievement was summed up by the board of directors in a glowing testimonial. "Starting with a new company in a highly competitive field, Willard Johnson guided Magcobar from nothing to the undisputed leader of the mud business. . . . His unique grasp of the industry problems and his foresighted sagacity in meeting them have made him the outstanding business leader in this essential field." The directors sent an engraved copy of their testimonial to Johnson.

The year 1967 was destined to bring even greater changes to Dresser. Flush with recent profits, the company aggressively pursued several important acquisitions and gained headlines on business pages throughout the country.

The initial goal was to acquire the large, diversified firm of Link-Belt, whose principal products pertained to power transmission, materials handling, and materials processing. Link-Belt's sales in the previous year had been $245 million, with earnings after taxes of $12 million, or $4.20 per share. Its customers represented different industries, and the company's sales thus were not dependent upon any one segment of the economy. Link-Belt had no long-term debt, and while its products were compatible with the Dresser line, there were no similarities likely to arouse the attention of the antitrust division of the Justice Department.

The critical question was how did Link-Belt's management view this idea? Dresser's offer to the company's chairman of the board, Robert C. Becherer, was that the merger be achieved through the exchange of one and a half shares of Dresser stock for each outstanding share of Link-Belt. Becherer's initial response was cordial but not enthusiastic, and after the offer was repeated, Lawrence in late February received the same response and withdrew the proposal. This did not mean that Dresser's interest in Link-Belt had decreased. There was more than one way to acquire a company, and while Dresser had never yet taken over a firm whose management opposed the idea, it was decided that this was the time to try it. The technique was to approach Link-Belt's shareholders directly by offering to buy their shares at a price higher than the current market price—a tender offer. Dresser would purchase as many as 1.3 million shares from Link-Belt stockholders at $48 a share, and since Link-Belt shares then sold for $43.75, many shareholders could be expected to take the quick and easy profit.

Link-Belt's management, as expected, did not view Dresser's offer with favor. "They felt I was a raider, and I was," John Lawrence recalled a decade later. "In those days it was not the popular thing to do." In fact, Link-Belt officials had been negotiating with another company concerning a merger, and Chairman of the Board Becherer announced that fact, making it clear that he favored the unnamed company's proposition over Dresser's. This merger, he said, could be accomplished through an exchange of stock that would be tax-free. In a four-column advertisement in *The New York Times* and other newspapers, Link-Belt management urged its shareholders not to sell to Dresser.

> Link-Belt's consistently good record, plus substantial growth prospects for the immediate and long-range future, are evidence that there is nothing to be gained by a switch in ownership. . . . The company's record and the knowledge your directors have of Link-Belt's pending developments have resulted in their refusal to sell any of their holdings. . . . We suggest that you also carefully evaluate this offer and support our decision. . . . It is important to note that there is no guarantee that Dresser will purchase any stock offered due to conditions qualifying their offer. We also

SWACO exhibited its products to potential customers at a Lafayette, Louisiana, oil show in the late 1950's. Left to right are R. L. O'Shields, Joe Baker, R. W. "Woody" Erwin, and an unidentified customer. Erwin was the inventor of the D-Gasser.

want to remind you that any sales of shares to Dresser will be subject to income tax considerations. We urge you not to act on this offer, about which information is incomplete.

Lawrence responded immediately with a telegram to Link-Belt demanding a retraction for "grossly misleading" statements. At issue was the Link-Belt claim that Dresser was not guaranteeing purchase of the stock "due to conditions qualifying their offer." This statement, he pointed out, was in error because the early proviso that at least a million shares must be offered for the sale to be effective already had been canceled. As to the claim that Dresser's information was "incomplete," the company contended that this was true only because Link-Belt refused to mail to its stockholders material supplied by Dresser. "Also your diversion of company personnel all over the country from profit-making activities to contact shareholders amazes us as it will no doubt amaze your shareholders," Lawrence concluded. The message was not a private one, for its contents were released to the press and resulting news stories told how "the battle for control of Link-Belt Company grows hotter."

The next day the identity of Link-Belt's second pursuer was revealed as the FMC Corporation. Becherer recommended that shareholders approve FMC's offer of exchange for a new cumulative convertible preferred stock redeemable in five years at $50 a share. In the face of this competition Dresser raised its tender offer from $48 to $52, after which FMC countered by offering to buy any number of Link-Belt shares at $58. A week later it became evident that Dresser's drive had fallen short. Just 27,148 shares of Link-Belt had been acquired at $52 a share. (The earlier offer at $48 was superseded by the higher price.) But the answer as to what to do with these shares was obvious—sell them to FMC at $58 a share. This was done, and Dresser's profits of better than $150,000 more than offset the costs of the unsuccessful campaign. Meanwhile, Link-Belt's merger with FMC was consummated in mid-summer.

Undaunted by the rebuff, Lawrence by that time already was eying another company, Symington-Wayne Corporation, a manufacturer of service station and railroad equipment and hand tools. The movement to acquire this large company was precipitated in an unusual way while a preliminary examination of a possible merger had just gotten under way. This happened when a recently resigned member of Symington-Wayne's board of directors unexpectedly called Lawrence and offered to sell 140,000 shares, or 7 percent of the company's stock. Dresser promptly bought it, leaving open the possibility of acquiring a greater interest if the examination indicated such a step.

This Salisbury, Maryland, corporation, Dresser's study revealed, was not as large as Link-Belt, but its 1966 sales of more than $100 million and profits before taxes of better than $9 million made it a significant objective. Moreover, the company's gasoline-dispensing pumps, a major product, and related service station equipment tied in nicely with Dresser's position as a producer of equipment for the oil and gas industries. Symington-Wayne's other major products included automotive lifts, specialty steel castings and equipment for the railroad industry, hand tools, and portable pneumatic tools. The company employed more than six thousand people in its six manufacturing facilities in the United States and England.

Lawrence told his board that Symington-Wayne had unusual growth possibilities, its sales were not cyclical, and the pursuit of additional shares for a merger should prove worthwhile. The directors authorized the move, and Lawrence approached Symington-Wayne's president, W. H. Bateman, in June 1967 with a proposal to merge the companies. Days later Bateman advised him that his directors had rejected Dresser's proposal and had agreed in principle to a merger with another company, Universal American Corporation, a manufacturer of heavy equipment. Lawrence,

The acquisition of Symington-Wayne in 1968 prominently placed Dresser in the gasoline pump business.

who was becoming accustomed to such messages, was unperturbed. Dresser was a Symington-Wayne stockholder itself, and the proposed merger with Universal American was not in *Dresser's* best interests! After reviewing alternatives on strategy, the directors voted to extend a tender offer for as many as 400,000 shares of Symington-Wayne stock at $40 per share. If achieved, Dresser would own about 30 percent of the company. With this hot pursuit of Symington-Wayne shares from two sources, its stock jumped 5⅛ points in a single day's trading.

As expected, Symington-Wayne's management opposed the tender offer. Bateman told the company's shareholders that they would profit far more from a tax-free exchange of stock with Universal American Corporation than they would from Dresser's bid to purchase their shares at $40. "We strongly recommend that the Symington-Wayne stockholders do not tender their stock to

Dresser," he said. Five days later Symington-Wayne officials filed suit in a United States district court in New York City to enjoin the company from proceeding with its tender offer. Lawrence, Luter, and Mayson flew to New York City immediately to appear at a preliminary hearing in U.S. District Judge Dudley B. Bonsad's court. Symington-Wayne's attorneys argued there that Dresser had failed to state properly its "present plans and intentions" concerning the method of carrying out the acquisition and that it "deceptively sought to create the false impression that a Symington-Wayne shareholder who sells his stock to Dresser pursuant to the tender offer would be in as good a position as a nontendering shareholder." Judge Bonsad, however, promptly denied Symington-Wayne's request for an injunction, and his ruling was destined to be upheld less than a month later by the U.S. Circuit Court of Appeals. Meanwhile, Universal American and Symington-Wayne revised the terms of their proposed merger to make their respective plans more attractive.

When Dresser's tender offer expired on July 24, the company had bought 396,376 shares, or about 20 percent of Symington-Wayne's outstanding shares. Its objective was not yet accomplished, but the ultimate goal drew closer when the Symington-Wayne and Universal American deal collapsed after Gulf & Western Industries took over the latter company in October. Subsequently, in November, Dresser, as *The New York Times* wrote, "backed up to the Symington-Wayne gas pump . . . and filled up with about 300,000 shares." The price was $45 a share. Dresser now owned 38 percent of the company, or 808,361 shares. It thus had effective control of Symington-Wayne. One last strategy remained for Symington-Wayne. The company proposed to issue sufficient convertible preferred stock to dilute Dresser's ownership to less than a controlling percentage. When Dresser announced its intention to buy the entire issue, however, Symington-Wayne at last yielded.

Four months later shareholders of both Dresser and Symington-Wayne voted their approval of a merger of the two companies, and on the last day of April 1968 operations were combined. Bateman and other top Symington-Wayne executives were retained in their usual capacities, and Bateman and Otis E. Kline, a Symington-Wayne director, were added to Dresser's board of directors.

Symington-Wayne was in reality, as was Dresser, a combination of companies that had merged over the years. Its product with the longest history was one that had not been very profitable in recent years: coupling links for railroad cars. This aspect of the company originated with the efforts of a former Buffalo, New York, customs collector named Charles A. Gould, when in 1887 he became owner of the Buffalo Steam Forge, a company that made forgings for locomotive and railroad car construction. Five years later he constructed a huge plant outside Buffalo, at Depew, New York, for manufacturing automatic railroad car couplers. Soon the couplers produced by his newly named Gould Coupler Company were pronounced by many to be the best available anywhere. Another individual who figured in a different aspect of the company's multiple origins was T. H. Symington, a machinist apprentice at the Baltimore & Ohio Railroad shops in New York in the same pre-1900 era. Symington, especially aware of inadequacies in railroad equipment, designed a freight car journal box that was greatly superior to those in general use. He leased a small foundry in Corning, New York, to manufacture his product, and as orders began pouring in from all over the United States and Europe, he purchased it outright in 1901. Eight years later, with business continuing to boom, Symington constructed a fine new

A group of Symington-Gould engineers poses before a test car at the Depew, New York, works. Symington-Gould ultimately became a part of Symington-Wayne, predecessor to Dresser's present Transportation Equipment Division.

manufacturing facility in Rochester, New York. The T. H. Symington Company became the largest manufacturer in the world of malleable-iron journal boxes. Other related products were added to the company list, and in 1925 the firm acquired a controlling interest in Charles A. Gould's coupler company at Depew. Eleven years later the firm's name was changed to Symington-Gould. During World War II Symington-Gould's plants operated day and night turning out steel castings for tanks, ships, heavy-duty guns, and various parts. In 1957 a merger occurred with the Wayne Pump Company, and the company name became Symington-Wayne. The Wayne Pump Company had originated in 1891 when W. H. David and J. T. Becker devised a pump dispenser for kerosene.* This modest original product soon was converted into something far more ambitious by the automobile revolution and the firm's kerosene pumps became gasoline pumps for cars. Since that time Wayne Pump had been at the fore of practically every advance in gasoline dispensing, and its operations were worldwide. By the time of Dresser's acquisition, Symington-Wayne had added still other companies to expand its product lines into hoists, hand tools, and pneumatic tools, and it had interests in nineteen foreign companies that manufactured its products.

While the attempts to acquire Link-Belt and Symington-Wayne were the year's headline makers for Dresser, yet another highly significant acquisition had been quietly proceeding. This was the purchase of Harbison-Walker,† the nation's leading manufacturer of firebricks for lining the interior walls of industrial high-temperature furnaces. The company's products fulfilled a vital though unheralded function for basic industry, especially iron and steel. Lawrence had known since his pre-Dresser days that Harbison-Walker was a fine company and now he initiated a study to see if it might be a good acquisition. "It was a top-notch company, and the fact that a high-grade company with a relatively restricted stock ownership was available—and it was a significant company— made us look real hard, and the harder we looked the better it looked," Lawrence later recalled. Harbison-Walker's net earnings in 1966 had been $11.8 million, making it a bigger and more profitable enterprise than Symington-Wayne. Fifty-nine percent of its refractory products went to the iron and steel industry, 17 percent to the cement, glass, lime, and other mineral industries, and the remaining 24 percent for other uses. The company owned

* See Chapter 1, pp. 33–35.
† See Chapter 1, p. 23.

majority interests in subsidiaries in Canada, Australia, Peru, and
Chile, and it had 250 authorized agents and dealers around the
world. Twenty-five Harbison-Walker manufacturing plants were
located in nine states and four foreign countries. The terms of the
merger centered around the exchange of a new series of Dresser
preferred stock on the basis of 1.1 share for each Harbison-Walker
common share, or a total cost of approximately $150 million. On
October 26, 1967, Harbison-Walker officially joined Dresser as
the largest acquisition the company ever had made. Three of
Harbison-Walker's directors joined Dresser's board. They were A. B.
Bowden, president of Mellon National Bank and Trust Company,
Pittsburgh; Richard G. Croft, chairman of the finance committee of
the Great Northern Paper Company, New York; and A. Brent
Wilson, president of Harbison-Walker.

Harbison-Walker brought yet another dimension to Dresser
Industries. After being founded as the Star Fire Brick Company
in 1865, the company soon became known as Harbison and
Walker, and captured and maintained the lead in making high-
quality refractory bricks. In 1902 it organized the consolidation of
a group of refractories under the Harbison-Walker name, and the
result was easily the dominant company in the industry. This
huge new company then owned twenty-seven plants in Pennsylvania, four in Ohio, and two in Kentucky, as well as prime mineral
property in those three states as sources for fireclay. Harbison-
Walker's size made it briefly a target of opprobrium in common
with other consolidations in this age of large-scale mergers, but
throughout the remainder of the century the company was identified with almost every technological advancement in refractories.

The acquisitions of Harbison-Walker and Symington-Wayne
alone increased Dresser's annual revenue by more than 50 percent.
Excluding these two companies, Dresser's sales in 1967 totaled
$417 million. *Forbes* magazine contrasted the company's change
in fortunes this way: "When Lawrence took over in 1962, Dresser's
earnings were lower than they had been ten years before. Its stock
sold at 8, down from 29 in 1957.* The company's loose collection of
16 companies, predominantly serving the oil and gas industries,
was in a shambles, and Dresser was in danger of being raided."
Since that time the company's stock had risen more than 200
percent in comparison to 26 percent for the Dow-Jones industrials;
its sales had more than doubled; and earnings per share had
nearly tripled from $1.01 to $2.86.

* Data adjusted for 2 for 1 stock split in 1965.

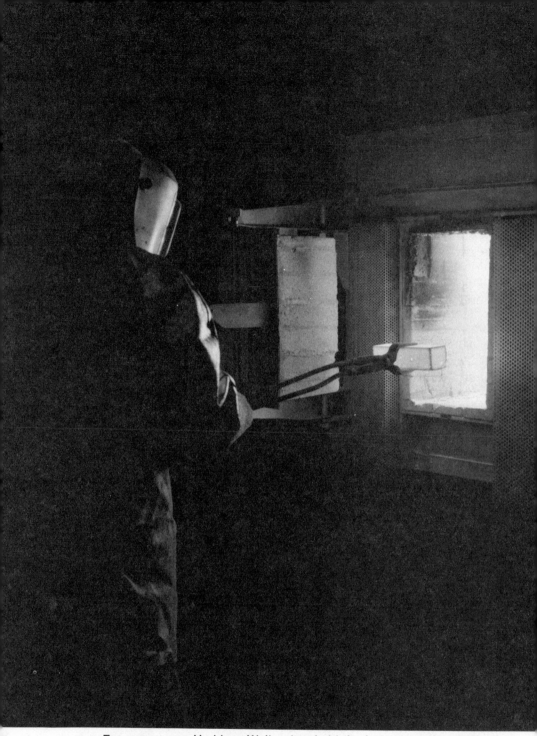

For many years Harbison-Walker has held the largest market share as a manufacturer of refractory bricks for use throughout heavy industry. Here, a brick is tested in a furnace for strength and durability.

The new diversification did not mean that Dresser was seeking to lessen its role in the oil and gas industries, but merely that it wished to expand its horizons in ways that were compatible with the company's general objectives. In fact, Dresser continued to solidify its ties to the oil and gas industries. Two additional acquisitions, overshadowed by the more spectacular deals, augmented Dresser's role in that endeavor. SWACO, Inc., a Texas company that manufactured such items as degassers, desanders, clayjectors, and adjustable chokes used in connection with drilling mud systems, was purchased for $7.4 million in 1967 and was integrated into Magnet Cove's operations. Pan Geo Atlas Corporation, which engaged in electrical logging and oil-well perforations, was purchased for $6 million in 1968, together with the company's interests in seven foreign countries.

———————

At the end of 1967 Neil Mallon completed his thirty-eighth year of service with Dresser. Since his retirement as chief executive officer in 1962 he had continued to play a part in the company's affairs as chairman of the executive committee of the board of directors. In January 1968, at the age of seventy-three, he resigned that post. Still in the best of health, he would continue as a member of the executive committee and the board of directors. The new chairman of the executive committee was Richard S. Morse, senior lecturer in the Sloan School of Management at the Massachusetts Institute of Technology, who had been a director since 1966.

Several high-level promotions were made in 1968. Charles Kuhn became president and chief operating officer, having served as executive vice president since 1965. Kuhn, whose special strengths lay in marketing, had joined Dresser in 1948 as vice president for sales of Dresser Manufacturing in Bradford. Kuhn's successor as executive vice president, administration and planning, was John V. James, whose climb in the Dresser ranks had been rapid after he left Corning Glass Works in Corning, New York, in 1957 to join Clark Bros. in Olean as assistant controller.

Still another milestone was passed in 1969. R. E. Reimer, whose tenure with Dresser Industries had lasted for more than forty years—every one of them in an executive capacity—reached the mandatory retirement age of sixty-five. His last day of service as Dresser's senior vice president, treasurer, and a director came on May 31.

The company's organization, and coincidentally its impact on American life, now was far more complicated than even a half dozen years before. As fiscal year 1969 began there were four major subdivisions of the Dresser companies: a Petroleum Group, a Machinery and Transportation Equipment Group, a Refractories and Minerals Group, and an Industrial Specialties Group. More than twenty-one thousand Americans could claim partial ownership of the company's more than nine million common shares, and more than sixteen thousand others owned the five million shares of preferred stock.

Despite the company's remarkable earnings record and overall growth and diversification during recent years, or perhaps because of it, Dresser was perceived by its top executives in late 1968 to have an image problem with stockbrokers, who understandably had had a difficult time staying abreast of its changes. A public opinion research firm, engaged to study the company's image among stockbrokers throughout the nation, sought to determine what sort of response a potential investor would get if he inquired about Dresser Industries. The result was disconcerting, for nearly three-fourths of the brokers interviewed had "no recommendation" about Dresser. Only one in ten rated Dresser as a "buy." This lack of interest was combined with a low level of knowledge concerning the fields in which Dresser operated. The company's involvement with the oil industry was known, but four out of five brokers had no knowledge of its diversification.

Dresser seldom made substantial efforts to attract the attention of the financial community. Member companies, each of whom had its own markets and different customers, conducted their own advertising programs in specialized trade publications. Public recognition of Dresser Industries as an institution largely had arisen through headlines connected with such newsmaking episodes as the turbodrill and acquisitions. The most significant institutional advertising program to date had been the early 1950's campaign under the theme "What Is Dresser Industries?" which had been directed to the oil and gas industries. Now, however, the awareness study indicated that a new campaign directed at the financial community was necessary to raise the consciousness level of brokers.

The result was a series of full-page advertisements appearing in The Wall Street Journal under a bold caption, "Today at Dresser," followed by a specific date in equally big letters. The advertisement itself consisted of a collection of pertinent facts, accompanied by sketches, concerning the many diverse things done on that day by Dresser. Typical was the March 11, 1969, advertise-

The nearest Dresser came in the 1970's to serving the immediate needs of the average consumer was through its complete line of S-K Tools, brought to the company with the Symington-Wayne acquisition.

ment that included such items as: "Today Dresser high-purity refractories, especially designed for ammonia process applications, are en route to São Paulo, Brazil, for a petrochemical plant there." Other events cited as occurring that day included the designing of a 981-foot candelabra tower to support antenna systems for eleven television and twelve radio stations near San Francisco; the introduction of a commercial bimetal thermometer for temperature control systems in new hospitals, schools, and apartments; the testing of a new line of jet-turbine-driven compressors; the installation of a master supervisory control system to help automate control of producing oil wells on four man-made islands in the harbor at Long Beach, California; and placing in service the company's newest truck-mounted unit for furnishing technical oil-field services. These events, readers of the *Journal* were told, were "only a small part of a Dresser day." They also learned that the company had 850 products and services, 31,000 employees, 56 operating units and 50 foreign subsidiaries, and 118 plants and mines. The tag line for the advertisements was "Dresser Industries Gets a Lot Done Every Day." The campaign was buttressed in the spring of 1969 with a meeting in which Lawrence, Kuhn, James, Luter, and other top Dresser executives met over cocktails and lunch with brokers from around the country to discuss the company's present operations and goals, and to answer questions. These sessions, in previous years a routine practice, now were resumed with regularity in an effort to keep the Dresser name visible to stockbrokers.

This was a good time for calling attention to the company, for the final year of the decade was another exceptional one. Sales of $700 million again were the highest in history. Especially encouraging was a resurgence in the petroleum aspect of company endeavors, which accounted for 36 percent of the sales and 33 percent of the $38 million net earnings. Dresser's products for the industry were, as usual, ubiquitous—found around the world in the North Sea, in the Middle East, in South America, and on the continental shelves of Indonesia, West Africa, Texas, and Louisiana. While the level of domestic drilling activity had not reached that of a decade before, nor did it seem likely ever to do so, the wells being drilled in the United States were going deeper and deeper and were requiring more and more services. From 1967 to 1969 the average well depth increased from just under 4,300 feet to nearly 4,800 feet. For the growing offshore service market, Dresser was well equipped by virtue of having pioneered the concept of self-propelled, jack-up vessels that moved from well to well to perform services, and it now had six of these vessels operating in the Gulf of Mexico. Industry sources expected the world demand for oil and gas to double in the next fifteen years, and Dresser's Petroleum Group seemed certain to continue to play an essential role in meeting this need.

The Machinery and Transportation Equipment Group had accounted for 26 percent of Dresser's sales in 1969 but only 16 percent of the profits. It was expected to show a return to higher profits within the next year because substantial expenditures had been made on new product development. During the year, this group entered into a broad agreement with Mitsubishi Heavy Industries, Ltd., to manufacture a line of compressors for Japan and the Far East. Thus, throughout Asia a greater number of compressors in industry would bear the Mitsubishi-Dresser label. Other notable achievements for the year included the successful marketing of the new Roots "Whispair" blower, which was more compact and up to 75 percent quieter than conventional blowers; the development and delivery of new automatic couplers for the

Metroliners in the northeastern corridor of the United States; the completion and delivery to the gas pipeline industry of four newly developed 12,500-horsepower jet-turbine compressor packages at a price of approximately $1 million each; and the development of unique electronic alarm devices for signaling trouble on running gears of freight cars.

The Refractories and Minerals Group accounted for 21 percent of the company's sales and 28 percent of its profits. Perhaps the most significant event for the group was the opening in 1968 of a lead mine in Bixby, Missouri, jointly owned with the operator, Cominco American, Inc. The new facility represented a Dresser investment of $9 million, with the annual output of lead amounting to about 25,000 tons.

The most diversified of Dresser's operations was the Industrial Specialties Group, whose sales accounted for 17 percent of the overall total and whose profits represented 25 percent. A new addition to this group in 1969 was the Cleco Industrial Tool Division, a manufacturer of pneumatic tools, bought from G. W. Murphy Industries, Inc., for approximately $26 million. With Cleco came interests in Cleco de Mexico, S.A.; Cleco International, Inc.; and Cleco International, G.m.b.H. Cleco was added to product lines ranging from couplings to gauges to hand tools to hoists. The Industrial Specialties Group was not tied to any one industry; its products were useful for the creation of such basic essentials as electricity, food, fuels, drugs, chemicals, paper products, water, and natural gas.

Before the decade ended it appeared briefly that Dresser's size would be doubled through a spectacular merger with Santa Fe Industries, Inc. In September 1969, executives of both companies signed memoranda of intent for an exchange of stock valued at about $500 million. One of Santa Fe's subsidiaries was the famous Atchison, Topeka & Santa Fe Railway. Further investigation, however, revealed that the expected benefits of merger were not as certain as imagined, and in November the proposal was called off by Dresser.

The new decade of the 1970's was dawning. John Lawrence told Dresser's shareholders that "we move into 1970 with confidence." As it turned out, his confidence was well placed.

12

An Age
of Energy Crisis

"Suppose when you wake tomorrow morning and flip the light switch, no lights come on," mused Dresser Industries in its 1971 annual report. "And, just suppose your heating and cooling thermostat, your coffee maker, radio, television and the 29 other appliances you depend on for living don't work. And, your automobile sits on the driveway immobile as a piece of iron sculpture." This frightening possibility probably would not happen tomorrow morning, the report continued, "but *some* morning, sooner than you think, it *could* happen." The nation, Dresser warned, was facing "a serious energy crisis" in which productive capacity was falling behind needs. Yet, a singular complacency existed among citizens who saw energy, next to air and water, as the "most taken-for-granted commodity" in life.

Dresser and others intimately involved in the business of finding and providing energy for daily American life knew that a crisis was approaching. Since 1950 the consumption of energy in the United States had doubled. It was expected to double again by 1985. In an effort to focus attention on this potentially dire situation Dresser inserted in its 1971 annual report the ten-page transcript of an interview with a noted specialist in the energy field, Dr. John J. McKetta, chairman of the Advisory Committee on Energy to the Secretary of the Interior and a distinguished professor of chemical engineering at the University of Texas at Austin.

Dr. McKetta stressed certain undeniable, alarming facts: Oil was becoming harder and more expensive to find. New fields tended to be smaller and deeper. Higher costs, higher taxes, lower real prices for crude oil, and uncertain government policies on imports and ecological pressures had resulted in a low rate of return on investments. The number of wells being drilled in the United States continued to decrease, and drilling costs continued to escalate. Those involved in natural gas exploration and discovery faced the same problems as well as the additional constraints of government regulations, which suppressed the prices producers could obtain. All these factors contributed to a growing reliance on foreign imports, and as Dr. McKetta pointed out, this could result in eventual threats to American economic and national security.

"Since our standard of living goes hand in hand with energy availability, we simply have no alternative but to solve the energy dilemma," Dr. McKetta said.

> An enormous amount of money will have to be spent on technology and tools at a steadily increasing pace in the year ahead. . . . It seems clear that equipment and service suppliers to the energy industries who have a record of competence in these markets will have challenging and exciting years ahead.

The average American was not ready in 1971 to consider the serious implications of these remarks. The full import of the "energy crisis" was not to burst into consciousness until two summers later when Americans encountered the startling experience of having to wait in long lines to fill their automobiles with gasoline. Then, too, they could feel their pocketbooks and purses grow lighter as the result of the concerted action by Arab OPEC nations to raise the prices of the crude oil that they exported. Thus,

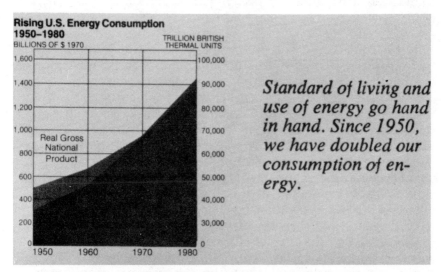

Rising U.S. Energy Consumption 1950–1980

Standard of living and use of energy go hand in hand. Since 1950, we have doubled our consumption of energy.

America's high standard of living during the mid-twentieth century made the development of new sources of energy one of the nation's most critical concerns if that level of life was to be maintained.

the questions that Dresser sought to highlight in 1971 for its shareholders and anyone else who would listen were destined to become perhaps the central concern of the decade.

As the 1970's began, it was a concomitant issue that concerned Americans most of all. A George Gallup poll revealed that 70 percent of Americans placed the environmental issue first among the nation's domestic problems. The problem had been highlighted by an offshore accident in 1969 six miles west of California's beautiful beaches at Santa Barbara. As a drilling bit was being replaced in a high-pressure pool of petroleum and gas, the well suddenly erupted and spewed oil for eleven days. Forty miles of beaches were temporarily despoiled and marine life suffered severely, resulting in a spate of national publicity. In reality, the two concerns of environmental protection and dwindling production of energy were related. To increase the supply of energy meant that more efficient methods of discovery and production had to be conceived, wasteful practices eliminated, and an appreciation for the nation's vanishing natural resources awakened. Together, these joint concerns meant that for the first time serious questions were being raised about the possibility of mankind's extinction or certainly a reduction to a living standard in which the quality would be severely restricted.

There was also to be in the 1970's a growing concern over the power of "multinational" corporations whose operations transcended boundaries. Was there a possibility that these huge corporations would become "supranational," immune to the laws and customs of a single state? How could they adopt policies that were compatible with the conflicting aims of the many diverse nations in which they operated? How could the laws of one nation be applicable to the multinational corporation's activities in another land? Dresser, with 28 percent of its 1970 sales coming from outside the United States and having some ten thousand employees in foreign nations, was among the many American corporations that had to face these questions.

Because of the seriousness of matters such as energy sufficiency, preservation of the environment, and the role of the newly dubbed multinational corporation, it was incumbent upon all responsible Americans to join in the growing dialogue concerning them.

Unlike so many corporations that were reluctant to participate in such dialogue for fear of alienating present or potential customers, Dresser Industries was destined to contribute to this exchange of ideas in a meaningful and vigorous way.

John V. James, seated, and John Lawrence provided management leadership for Dresser in the first half of the 1970's. James became president and chief executive officer in 1970; he assumed the additional title of chairman of the board upon Lawrence's retirement in 1976.

A number of prominent changes occurred in the top levels of Dresser's management and administration to coincide with the beginning of the 1970's. At the end of 1969 Charles Kuhn resigned as president and director of the company, and six months later John V. James was elected as his successor. James, however, was given the additional title of chief executive officer. Lawrence had desired for some time to relinquish his duties as chief executive officer to insure an orderly succession of top management. He retained his position as chairman of the board, and was given additional responsibility as chairman of the executive committee. With James assuming the chief executive's position, Lawrence now had additional time for planning and the coordination of research and development.

James, a native of Wilkes-Barre, Pennsylvania, was from a family that had owned and operated anthracite coal mines for several generations. He had graduated from the University of Pennsylvania with a bachelor of science degree in economics, spent the war years as an Army intelligence officer with Eisenhower's D-Day strategists, and afterward earned a certificate of management from the Wharton School of Finance at the University of Pennsylvania. Before joining Clark in 1957 he had been manager of budgets and procedures at the Corning Glass Works in Corning, New York, and prior to that was controller of the Carr Consolidated Biscuit Company. He was fifty-one years old upon assuming the chief executive's job, a stocky, square-shouldered man with the ability to turn a clever phrase. He was a history buff who liked to read European economic history; he was the author of several articles related to industrial accounting; and while his early training was in finance, his recent experience at Dresser had been in operations and administration.

Probably his key contribution to date had come during the 1960's through his leading role in the company's establishment of uniform measurement and control procedures across the world. The process included the determination of both short- and long-range objectives for each operation; the development of a workable plan toward attaining those objectives; the establishment of policies to govern actions taken; the translation of paper plans into operational programs; and an efficient way of measuring results at any time against the plans. The goal of this accounting and control system was to be able to identify problem areas immediately so that corrections could be made without delay. Elements of this system included the annual profit plan, a five-year plan, a monthly outlook from the various units projecting the next two months' earnings, a report on each month's results, which was compared against the plans, quarterly recapitulations that updated the annual profit plan, an annual cost-price study, and an annual analysis identifying investments not providing the required minimum return. James's idea was to force planning down to the lowest level of supervision and to make every manager accountable for specific and highly detailed targets. This system permitted Dallas headquarters to monitor results so closely that on the fourth business day of every month it knew the net return for three hundred different "profit centers" in one hundred countries. Any product or operation that dropped below a 25 percent return on investment was subject to instant scrutiny.

As the fifth chief executive officer of the company that bore Solomon R. Dresser's name, Jack James inherited a thoroughly revised board of directors. Six of the seventeen directors had not stood for re-election at the annual spring shareholders' meeting, largely because of a new policy stipulating retirement at the end of a director's term upon reaching seventy years of age. Those affected by the policy included those of longest experience and most influence, foremost being Neil Mallon. The others were Norman Chandler, who had been a principal shareholder of Pacific Pumps at the time it was acquired and who had served as a Dresser director for twenty-six

In 1971 Dresser's board of directors' executive committee included, left to right, George C. Scott, Richard S. Morse, John V. James, John Lawrence, and Otis E. Kline.

years; Willard M. Johnson, whose tenure stemmed from the acquisition of Magnet Cove Barium in 1949 and who had continued to serve as a Dresser director after his retirement from Magcobar in 1966; William A. McAfee, who had been elected to the board in 1933 and who had ably represented the company as outside counsel during those eventful years; A. Brent Wilson, whose service as a director extended only from 1967 but who had thirty-three years' experience with Harbison-Walker, beginning when he had taken a laborer's job there; and William H. Bateman, who had become a director in 1968 with the acquisition of Symington-Wayne. Such men, their cumulative experience as Dresser directors numbering 130 years, could not be easily replaced. Their retirements, especially those of such longtime directors as Mallon, McAfee, Johnson, and Chandler, signaled a decisive change in tone if not in direction.

It was decided not even to attempt to replace all these men, for a reduced number was deemed more efficient. The one new director elected at the time was James D. Davis, a partner in the Cleveland law firm of Squire, Sanders & Dempsey,* the same firm with which McAfee had been associated for so many years and which still represented the company. Of the twelve directors who now served, seven of them were "outside" directors. Four of the remaining directors were full-time Dresser employees, and the other one, Charles A. Moore, formerly of Manning, Maxwell & Moore, was retired.

* The firm's name now was different as a result of a merger.

A constant challenge to this newly constituted administrative and managerial team was in overseeing manufacturing and sales for the world market. In 1969 about 26 cents out of every dollar of Dresser's revenue originated from foreign sales and services, and in the following seven years those figures would be enhanced to about 30 cents out of every dollar. A number of significant steps were taken to account for this growth.

The extent of the company's international commitment could be seen in the 1971 capital expenditures budget. Nearly half of the amount, or 44 percent, was allotted to foreign operations. Of this sum, 18 percent was spent in Canada, 17 percent in Europe, 3 percent in Latin America, and 6 percent in other areas. The officer primarily responsible for international activities was Rex A. Sebastian, senior vice president, operations.

One of the most significant expenditures was toward a new $10 million refractory plant for the West German Ruhr district in a joint venture with a West German refractories producer, Martin & Pagenstecher G.m.b.H. This plant, designed to manufacture high-quality magnesite refractories primarily for use in basic oxygen steelmaking processes, was destined to give Harbison-Walker a firm base for the lucrative German market. The new facility was one of the most modern refractory plants in the world. Construction began three years later on a similar joint venture in Iran, and by 1976 Dresser's Harbison-Walker Refractories Group would have joint-venture operations in Mexico, Chile, Peru, Venezuela, Canada, and Australia. The importance of these refractories, which generally escaped the gaze of the mass media, was indicated by the vital role they played in the production of most of the world's basic raw materials—steel, copper, aluminum, glass, cement, paper, and the like. Refractories additionally were essential to electric power plants and refineries. Underdeveloped nations seeking to build industrial bases had a critical need for steel mills, and as the world's leading refractory manufacturer, Harbison-Walker played an essential role for developing nations.

The site of one of Dresser's operations had a peculiar problem. The Greek isle of Mykonos, where a productive barite mine existed, had been home for sixteen years to a solitary pelican that had alighted during a storm to recover from injuries. A Mykonos fisherman nursed the huge bird back to health, after which it wandered freely about the island as everyone's pet and became a tourist attraction. "Nothing has happened here for five thousand years," one Mykonian observed, "then our pelican came." Residents became concerned, though, because Petros, as they named the pelican, had no mate. In October 1961, the mayor of Mykonos approached

Dresser officials for help. Sixteen years of solitude was more than enough for man or beast, he declared. Petros needed a companion. Since in all these years no one had discovered Petros's gender, Dresser obliged the mayor's request by arranging to send not one but two pelicans, one of each sex—Barry and Benny—to assure progeny. The new pelicans were greeted on their arrival by a large group of Mykonians, and in a short welcoming address the mayor charged the long-beaked birds to "remain faithful unto each other forever after and to let no Aegean shrimp put them asunder."

Another interesting location for a Magcobar operation was in Nigeria, where Nigerian chief Dennis N. Chukwu was a 30 percent partner in Dresser-Magcobar Minerals. In August 1973, Charles Hooper, a Dresser vice president of the oil-field products international department, brought Chukwu to Houston for his first visit. The Nigerian chief arrived in a gold brocade tunic carrying a lion's-tail fly whisk, and he was accompanied by the favorite of his three wives. The Chukwus cut a broad swath through Houston society as they were entertained with a special party and visits to the Astrodome for a baseball game and to the NASA facilities south of Houston.

Virtually all the acquisitions of the early 1970's brought additional international dimensions to Dresser. One of the most interesting new companies was Boyles Industries, Ltd., a Canadian subsidiary of Inspiration Limited. Boyles had its own foreign subsidiaries in Australia, the Philippines, and Singapore. This company, purchased in April 1970 for $6.1 million, had a full line of diamond core drilling equipment and thus gave Dresser additional products for the mining industry. The company had been founded in 1895 by Elmore and Page Boyles to provide diamond drilling service for the mines of British Columbia. Its growth was a rags-to-riches story, for the two brothers had been left alone in Iowa to provide for themselves before they were even teen-agers. Through perseverance that would be remarkable for anyone, much less for two youths, by the time they were thirteen and fifteen, the Boyles brothers had earned enough money from farm work to pay their way to Arizona in 1886 to work in the Silver King Mine. When they started work at Silver King, 155 men were on the payroll; by the time they quit, in 1891, there were only two—the Boyles brothers! In Spokane, where they moved after Arizona, they conceived the idea of buying a diamond drill to probe some of their own claims, but they wound up contracting their services to others and establishing a prosperous contracting business that they ultimately located in Vancouver, British Columbia. The familiar figure of the bearded prospector with pick and mule was destined soon to disappear as a result of

Boyles's diamond drills were the instruments primarily responsible for converting prospecting in the Klondike from a pick-and-shovel operation to a mechanized one. Boyles's drills soon were in use throughout the world.

this drilling mechanization. As the turn-of-the-century Klondike gold rush reached gigantic proportions, the Boyles brothers followed it throughout the western wilds. Later, in 1930, with both brothers dead, the company built a plant in Vancouver and began manufacturing lightweight surface and underground diamond drills that became accepted around the world.

Only two weeks after the acquisition of Boyles, Dresser gained another foreign company with an entire different but equally interesting background. This was the Swedish firm of Aktiebolaget Ljungmans Verkstader. The company had been founded in 1924 by Jakob Ljungmans to develop and manufacture equipment for the storage and distribution of petroleum products. Its first product created a sensation. It was a coin-operated, automatic gasoline dispenser, the first of its kind. A motorist inserted one Swedish crown, pumped up the gasoline, and opened a valve to receive about five liters of fuel through a hose. Heretofore, Swedish motorists bought gasoline by the can. Since this early beginning, Ljungman's had maintained a comprehensive program of product development aimed primarily at making self-service easier, and it especially prospered during the rapid expansion of automobile sales following World War II. The Ljungman line was viewed by Dresser as a valuable complement to its Wayne pumps.

A third acquisition in 1970 bolstered still another aspect of Dresser's business—that of providing exploration services for oil and gas. This was the Olympic Geophysical Company, purchased in October, along with its Canadian subsidiary, Canwest Geophysical, for 165,539 shares of Dresser common stock. Olympic, a Texas corporation, specialized in offshore seismic surveys through the operation of uniquely equipped vessels. These vessels worked primarily off the Texas-Louisiana coasts, while the Canadian subsidiary employed entirely different techniques by operating from wheeled and tracked vehicles in the arctic areas of northern Canada.

The acquisition in the same year of the National Equipment Leasing Corporation (completed in 1970 although an initial stock purchase was made in 1968) placed Dresser in an entirely different line of business. As its name implied, this company leased industrial machinery, railroad cars, trucks, and automobiles to commercial accounts throughout the United States. The firm was acquired for 75,000 shares of Dresser common stock.

Dresser's 1970 warning of an impending energy crisis had been recognized in its own research long before the report was issued. One line of inquiry that seemed particularly attractive as early as 1968 was a new form of carburetion promising significant fuel economies. The Stanford Research Institute was hired to evaluate the system, and laboratory work by Robert D. Englert and Lester P. Barriman led to a method of carburetion that combined fuel economies with pollution control, a particularly attractive and unique blending of assets. Named the "Dresserator," it provided atomized fuel and air at mixtures leaner than possible with a standard carburetor. It promised to enable automobiles of all sizes and weights to meet stringent new exhaust emission standards without using catalytic convertors. The principle of the Dresserator was to crash the gasoline at sonic speeds into a diffuser that broke it into tiny droplets. A pressure-flow system then sent the uniform fuel-air mixture into the intake manifold and on into the combustion chambers. Development and testing of the Dresserator became a high priority at the Research Institute.

In early 1970, shortly before his retirement as chief executive officer, John Lawrence determined that Dresser should have its own corporate research facility to complement programs carried on by the separate operating divisions. It was decided to locate it in Southern California and to give it the Dresserator as its top priority. In July 1970, the Environmental Technology Division, later changed to Dresser Advanced Technology Center (DATeC), began operations with the aim of concentrating on environmental control systems and devices. The basic concept was for DATeC to consist of a small but exceptionally creative group of engineers and scientists who would use outside research organizations to supplement their own specialized work.

Lawrence, as he had planned, began to spend more of his time after his retirement as chief executive officer in coordinating research. To make certain that the operating units, where primary research and product development responsibilities lay, were giving this vital element sufficient attention, he began monitoring their progress himself. He made a practice of meeting twice a year for in-depth sessions with each major research and development facility to review progress.

This was an endeavor critical to the success of the company. It was understood at Dresser, and even calculated as precisely as possible, that every product would become obsolete at some date, and at that time a new Dresser product should be ready to succeed it. Thus, at any given time, the life cycle of a particular product was considered to be at a certain stage, and so was the research toward a successor. Dresser's products were protected in 1972 by 3,224 patents, and 1,241 patents pending. Research and engineering costs incurred annually were more than $26 million.

The public's emphasis on pollution controls in the 1970's was not without effect on Dresser's own operations, for any company engaged in manufacturing and mining on such a broad scale inevitably had pollution control problems of its own. New state and federal laws passed in 1970 imposed substantial liabilities on companies whose activities created certain levels of pollution. Bringing the various Dresser activities into compliance with these laws was an expensive task, but one that the company unhesitatingly sought to fulfill. In August 1970, James promulgated the company's own pollution control and compliance policies, indicating its readiness to preserve and improve the environment. The policies established a chain of responsibility and directed that a plan of action for pollution control by each operating division be submitted for corporate review and approval. The area of Dresser endeavors that seemed most potentially hazardous was in offshore services, where accidental oil spills might reach nearby beaches. To compound the risks, Dresser's insurers withdrew protection on November 1, 1970, against the pollution risk from offshore oil spills. As a result, James and a Dresser negotiating team initiated a series of agreements with offshore customers in which liabilities would be shared proportionately. The company's customers were basically sympathetic and responsive to Dresser's position, and agreements were signed that balanced the risks equitably.

The Petroleum and Minerals Group went a step further in insuring that its operations complied with the highest standards of pollution control. Its Environmental Control Department in Houston developed and put on the road a custom-built truck to inspect pollution levels at the group's plants and mines around the country. Equipment within the truck's van permitted its engineers to sample smokestack emission, liquid waste disposal systems, the flow and quality of air, temperature and humidity within work areas, and the purity of water released into municipal sewer systems. A typical plant visit required two days of work to fully assess pollution levels.

The company's involvement in pollution control activities was emphasized in an even more direct way in 1972 when it acquired a recognized leader in the manufacturing of pollution control equipment. This was Lodge-Cottrell Ltd. of Birmingham, England (a subsidiary of Simon Engineering of Manchester), purchased for approximately $2 million. Lodge-Cottrell's principal activity was designing, building, and installing highly effective pollution control devices, particularly electrostatic precipitators. Included in the acquisition were Lodge-Cottrell's subsidiaries in the United States, South Africa, and Australia.

This company's background and the principle of electrostatic precipitation were remarkable. Since at least 1600 it had been known, as Queen Elizabeth's court physician, William Gilbert, wrote, that "everything rushes towards electricks excepting flame

A Lodge-Cottrell electrostatic precipitator is being installed in a TVA electric generating plant in Tennessee.

and flaming bodies, and the thinnest air. . . . Bodies are borne towards the electricks in a straight line towards the centre of the electrick." Experiments based upon this phenomenon were common in the latter half of the eighteenth century, and in 1824 Hohlfield demonstrated that a smoke-filled jar could be cleared by suspending in it an electrified wire. Not until the early 1880's, however, did commercial possibilities begin to be recognized with the work of Professor Oliver Lodge (who subsequently was knighted), who demonstrated the effectiveness of electrical precipitation in the elimination of fogs, mists, and smoke, and the improvement of agricultural crop production by electrifying the atmosphere immediately above the soil. In 1909 the Agricultural Electric Discharge Company was formed to employ Sir Oliver's method in agriculture. A network of electrically charged fine wires, suspended and spaced about twelve yards apart over an agricultural field, was reported to increase productivity by 49 percent in oats and comparable amounts for other crops. Meanwhile, in 1913, Sir Oliver formed his own company, the Lodge Fume Deposit Company, Ltd., and its first significant job was to recover valuable potash from gases emitted in blast-furnace operations. The fact that the gas was cleaned in the process was secondary to the recovery of potash. Business rapidly expanded to include precipitation of lead and tin smelter fumes, and in 1920 the company installed a precipitation plant at the Royal Mint Refinery to recover gold released in the refining process. In the years to come, Lodge's company made several structural changes, one of the most significant being a 1922 agreement with International Precipitation Corporation of America for an exchange of patents and technical information. At that time the name of Dr. F. G. Cottrell, whose experiments with precipitation in America had roughly paralleled those of Lodge's, was added to the company name, which became Lodge-Cottrell Ltd. In the years to come, Lodge-Cottrell's equipment was installed in plants the world over, and by the time Dresser acquired the company, its products were effective for water purification as well as for the cleaning of gases emitted from virtually every industrial or power activity. Despite its remarkable growth in its more than fifty years' existence, its greatest years seemed to lie ahead, for Dresser's information indicated that Lodge-Cottrell's electrostatic precipitators were superior to anything on the United States market in pollution control.

The high quality of Lodge-Cottrell's electrostatic precipitators was to be affirmed in 1975. The company won a 15-percent-of-contract bonus from the Tennessee Valley Authority for attaining a 98 percent efficiency of operation on four units installed at the

TVA's Colbert steam power plant in Pride, Alabama. By that date more than twenty-seven precipitators were in operation in the United States and another twenty-two units were being installed. Approximately two thousand precipitators based on Lodge-Cottrell's designs and technology existed around the world at electric power plants, blast furnaces, open-hearth furnaces, steel converters, cement kilns, chemical processing plants, lead smelters, and large commercial incinerators.

Other acquisitions in 1971 and 1972 continued to round out the Dresser line of equipment for the energy and industrial markets. The company's new emphasis on products for the mining industry brought a well-known manufacturer of pneumatic drilling equipment into the Dresser fold. This was the Pneumatic Equipment Division of Westinghouse Air Brake Company of Pittsburgh, purchased for approximately $6.6 million. The division was better known for its old name—Le Roi—used prior to its acquisition in 1968 by Westinghouse. The company had been founded in 1913 as the Milwaukee Machine Tool Company to manufacture small gasoline engines for automobiles and light trucks. Upon incorporation it had taken the distinctive name Le Roi—"the king" in French. In 1921 the company began a transition to industrial and construction applications for the gasoline engine by introducing the first multicylinder engine for use in concrete mixers, portable saws, and pumps. In 1926 it began manufacturing a portable air compressor, and here Le Roi achieved its greatest success. During World War II Le Roi supplied thousands of truck-mounted, portable air compressors to the Corps of Engineers, and thousands more generator sets. In fact, it had been a Le Roi generator set that powered the radar unit that gave the first warning in 1941 at Pearl Harbor. After the war Le Roi purchased a line of air tools from the Cleveland Pneumatic Tool Company, and by 1972 the company had a broad line of compressed air tools that were especially important in mining to accompany its line of air compressors. Dresser, recognizing the value of the old name, renamed the company Le Roi and returned to it the familiar lion emblem.

Still another company acquired in the fall of 1971 added a different dimension to Dresser's capabilities for serving industry. This was the Bay State Abrasives Division of Avco Corporation in Westboro, Massachusetts, purchased for $26.8 million. Bay State manufactured a complete line of grinding wheels and bonded abrasive products. The company was founded in 1922 when three Massachusetts men, Orello S. Buckner, Leonard M. Krull, and George H. Bullard, leased an abandoned power plant for operating trolley cars and converted it into a plant for manufacturing grinding

Le Roi portable compressors bearing the familiar lion insignia became part of the Dresser family in 1972.

wheels. The conversion of this dilapidated structure occurred in the midst of Westboro's coldest winter in memory, and somehow the kiln was built despite the fact that the water used for making mortar froze every night and a sheet of ice frequently covered it during days. By the time Dresser bought Bay State, it had acquired a manufacturing subsidiary in Brantford, Ontario; a California subsidiary that produced metal-bonded diamond wheels and machines for the masonry, concrete, stone, and construction fields; and a Luxembourg subsidiary that offered a full line of bonded abrasive products for the European market. Bay State was the third-largest manufacturer of grinding wheels in the nation with total assets of $29 million.

Dresser now had eighteen domestic operating units and sixty-one foreign subsidiaries and affiliates that offered more than one thousand products and services. The policy, following Mallon's precedent, had been to stress the distinct and separate identities of the various units. Names such as Pacific, Harbison-Walker, Roots, Bay State, Le Roi, and others did not automatically call to mind an image of Dresser Industries. This problem was one that concerned John V. James, and at his direction a "corporate identity program" was devised and implemented in 1972. The program was based upon a visual graphics system that tied the name Dresser to those of its operating units identified in its logotype, so that all displays gave equal space to Dresser and the particular unit. The word "Dresser" appeared in the stylized version within the familiar oval, and the operating unit maintained its own distinctive name. The program was flexible enough to permit many variations within this basic framework.

Not being in the business of retail sales, Dresser had never been particularly concerned about its impact on the general public. While it had gained more than its share of attention in the press, the company had never pursued a distinctive public image. Its manufacturing plants typically were located by preference in small towns where a steady and congenial work force was available: Bradford, Olean, Connersville, Depew, Sidney, Muskegon. Even the corporate headquarters in Dallas was virtually anonymous to the public because of its location high in the Republic National Bank Building. There were no distinctive architectural structures bearing the Dresser name, but a decision recommended by John Lawrence and approved by the directors in early 1970 would soon change this in a spectacular fashion.

A forty-story building to be called the Dresser Tower was to be constructed in downtown Houston as a joint venture with Cullen Center, Inc. The responsibility for negotiating with Cullen, planning the design, and supervising the construction of the building was assigned to Duane Rost, senior vice president. The modernistic structure was to be a part of the six-block Cullen Center, a complex that would include a hotel, restaurants, shops, banking facilities, and landscaped malls with fountains. The Dresser Tower, a $30 million office building and the tallest structure in the complex, was to be headquarters for three Dresser operating groups: Petroleum and Minerals; Machinery; Mining and Construction; and other offices as well. The building would be connected by air-conditioned overhead walkways to other buildings in the Cullen Center.

By 1936, fourteen years after its founding, Bay State Abrasives had enlarged its facilities from the original abandoned power plant to this complex of buildings.

A Bay State Abrasives diamond wheel resharpens a carbide-tipped saw.

In June 1973 the sparkling white structure with dark vertical lines extending from top to bottom was ready for some five hundred Dresser employees who moved from twelve different locations to occupy the twenty-eighth through thirty-fourth floors. Their move was said to have been one of the most complex in Houston's history, and it was done in one remarkable Friday afternoon and Saturday after six months of planning. The building was so beautiful and so satisfactory that many employees believed Dallas headquarters would transfer there. But this was not to be the case, for the old principle of decentralized management that had carried Dresser so far remained. To have the corporate headquarters in close proximity with the operating headquarters might offer temptations for direct involvement in those affairs that would be unproductive in the long run. Houston, however, was home for ten thousand of the company's forty-five-thousand employees, and no other location had so many Dresser workers.

Certain functions logically could be coordinated best from central offices, and one of these was Dresser's growing reliance on computers. In 1971 nineteen computers were being used throughout the Dresser operating units with considerable duplication. It seemed logical to concentrate this equipment in strategic locations, eliminating duplication and permitting the operation of far more sophis-

The Dresser Tower, forty stories high, added a sparkling new dimension to the rapidly growing Houston skyline upon its completion in 1973.

ticated equipment. The company chose to do this in two locations, establishing a Southwestern Computer Center in Houston at a cost of more than $2.5 million and an Eastern Computer Center in Pittsburgh for more than $1.8 million. The equipment at these centers handled far more complex tasks than did the smaller units previously used, and by 1974 thirty-one Dresser units had terminals connected to one of the two computer centers by direct telephone line.

The year 1973 was a landmark one for the company. Sales for the first time topped a billion dollars. Earnings reached $44.2 million. In their joint letter to Dresser shareholders at the end of the year, Lawrence and James cited several reasons for the bonanza year: (1) an investment during the past six years of nearly a quarter of a billion dollars in capital expenditures for modernizing and expanding operations; (2) the outlay in the same period of more than $150 million on research and engineering programs; (3) an acceleration of programs to identify and eliminate marginal products and obsolete or inefficient facilities; (4) a significant broadening of the company's marketing base by expanding worldwide sales and distribution networks; and (5) the establishment of a comprehensive management control system and flexible organization structure that enabled the company to respond more effectively to changing business conditions.

"Although these long-term programs have been costly and time consuming," the two executives reported, "we resisted the temptation to dilute them in order to increase the earnings performance of recent years. . . . Today, as a result of these programs, the Company is in a position to serve existing and developing markets with the broadest range of technologically-oriented products in its history." They predicted that the energy crisis, now recognized generally, would give new impetus to "finding and producing oil and gas, to building fossil-fueled and nuclear power plants, pipelines and refineries, and synthetic fuel plants." Such activities would require increasing quantities of specialized technological products and services of the type provided by Dresser. "We are prepared to benefit from these emerging opportunities. . . . We have well-developed definite plans and innovative marketing strategies for the 1970's and in some cases into the mid-1980's to help guide the Company toward its long-term improvement goals."

Two additional steps already had been taken to assure continued emphasis on planning. One, as planning director J. B. Graves reported to the directors in 1973, was the separation of long-term planning meetings from annual profit-planning sessions. The other was the implementation of Wharton econometric models as a new method of forecasting long-term sales. This marketing model, developed at the University of Pennsylvania, provided computerized projections of sales based on the economic environment, industry sales and price levels, and management decision variables. Long-range financial, marketing, and production plans had become so complex that it now was impossible for the human mind to comprehend all relevant variables in making decisions regarding long-range plans and strategies. Thus, econometrics, or computerized model building, was being used by firms like Xerox, IBM, and Motorola, and was destined to play an increasingly large role for Dresser.

Another increasingly sophisticated area of operation was in executive training. The program established in the early 1950's was cited by *Dun's Review* in 1973 as one of the fifteen outstanding in the nation. An important part of the training program was an arrangement with Hillsdale College in Michigan to conduct management training seminars for Dresser employees. There was an unusual bit of irony in the arrangement, for neither Hillsdale nor Dresser executives had been aware that the company's founder had attended that small college.

"I am convinced Dresser is more properly organized now to pursue growth than ever before in its history," James told a group controller's conference in 1973 in Dallas. He announced a goal of $1.5 billion in sales by the end of 1975.

One of the newly opened markets for the company resulted from a relaxation of both public opinion and the government's foreign policy toward the Soviet Union and other Communist-ruled nations. The once-suspended trade between Dresser and the Soviet Union had resumed in 1969 when John J. Murphy, a young Clark executive, flew to that country to negotiate a license agreement permitting the Soviets to manufacture centrifugal compressors for their ammonia and petrochemical plants and refineries, particularly in connection with developing rich natural gas fields in Siberia and their petroleum resources there and in the Arctic Ocean. The Russians, Murphy learned, still remembered John O'Connor with high regard. Murphy, whose father had worked in the Clark Bros. foundry when O'Connor was that company's top salesman, negotiated patiently with the Soviets for three weeks. At the end of that frustrating period, in which the Soviets seemed to object to every Dresser condition, Murphy abruptly began gathering his papers and declared that they obviously could not reach an agreement. At this point Murphy's counterpart smoothly switched from Russian to English and began talking directly across the table to Murphy.

Suddenly the barriers dissolved and agreement was reached. It proved to be a rewarding arrangement for Dresser in which the company obtained a sum for the license, an annual fee, and money from the sale of equipment for the compressors. In 1973 the company signed another agreement with the Soviet Union, a five-year pact for scientific and technological cooperation. And in 1974 two contracts totaling $27.5 million were signed in which the U.S.S.R. agreed to buy Clark compressors to be used primarily for ammonia production. By 1976 Dresser was shipping some $30 million annually in goods to the Soviet Union, making it one of the United States' leading exporters of goods to that nation.

In 1973 an important agreement was signed with Poland whereby a government agency of that nation obtained from Dresser an exclusive license to manufacture rock bits and rock bit arms of the Security type. The agency would sell these products to the U.S.S.R., Hungary, Rumania, Poland, Czechoslovakia, Albania, East Germany, and Bulgaria.

The year 1973 was not without its unforeseen events either. In January the company's Lockheed Jetstar was totally destroyed as a result of a hangar fire at Dallas's Love Field. There were no injuries but the airplane's value was placed at $1.3 million.

In the fall a fire also hit the Pacific Pumps facility in Huntington Park, California, destroying 15 to 20 percent of the plant area with damage estimates of $1.4 million. Sixty firefighters spent nearly an hour bringing the predawn fire under control, and when they had finished, from two to twelve inches of water were spread throughout the plant. C. M. Winslow, manager of industrial relations for Pacific, described what happened next:

> We had immediate cooperation of all employees. Everybody pitched in. Not one employee was laid off. Those working in areas not affected by the fire went back to their regular assignments. Those affected by the fire started on the cleanup job. Some first shifters willingly took second and third jobs to help keep production going. We had excellent cooperation from the union. Our key personnel and their staffs forgot about such things as an eight-hour workday and five-day week.

When the new facility opened it was nearly double the size of the old building, and it was shown off to some two thousand people in the first open house ever held by Pacific Pumps.

More pleasing news that year was the announcement on June 21, 1973, by James that Dresser and Ford Motor Company had executed that day a licensing agreement for the commercial development of the Dresserator inductor. Ford agreed to test and evaluate the Dresserator system over a three-year period to see how it performed under 50,000-mile durability tests. If adopted, Ford would pay Dresser a royalty based on the number of units produced. A year later, Dresser entered into a separate license agreement with Holley Carburetor, a division of Colt Industries and the nation's largest independent supplier of carburetors.

In October 1974, Dresser's hopes for the Dresserator were encouraged by a report issued by the Environmental Protection Agency that declared: "This carburetion device is capable of achieving substantial reductions in automobile emissions, without requiring catalytic converters. . . . If no difficulties arise in attempting to mass produce the unit, it may prove to be a successful method of controlling emissions from internal combustion engines." The E.P.A.'s conclusions came after it had tested the Dresserator on a 1973 Ford Capri and a 1973 Chevrolet Monte Carlo with encouraging results.

As the 1970's progressed and the nation became more and more aware of its energy crisis, a new appreciation began to arise for the valuable coal deposits in the Appalachians. Here was a neglected source of energy plentiful enough to last the nation for two hundred or three hundred years.

Through acquisitions and product development, Dresser already had become a factor in supplying equipment and technology to the mining industry, but it wanted a bigger position in the market. An acquisition seemed in order. Through a system developed for identifying likely acquisitions, the name of Jeffrey Galion, Inc., popped up before James R. Brown, Jr., president of the Mining Equipment & Foundry Group, as a firm whose products complemented the existing Dresser line. This was a privately held company headquartered in Columbus, Ohio, with a large line of mining and construction products, and foreign subsidiaries in the United Kingdom, Mexico, Canada, South Africa, Australia, and Brazil. Its net sales in 1973, $223.5 million, were one-fifth those of Dresser's, and it had a backlog of $200 million in orders. An intensive study of the company, made prior to any contact with Jeffrey Galion officials, confirmed the assessment that it would be the kind of acquisition that followed the Mallon philosophy—two and two must make five. Jeffrey Galion officials, however, declined the opportunity at first. A year later they reconsidered because they foresaw an eventual need for greater diversification and liquidity of investment that a privately owned company would have difficulty in achieving. The owners retained an investment banking firm, Lazard Frères, to help them negotiate the sale. Dresser offered $120 million in cash and 416,350 shares of Dresser common stock (priced at $46.50 per share at the time of the offer). Lawrence and James, in recommending the bid to their directors, contended that the acquisition would "offer Dresser an unusual opportunity to expand its construction and mining equipment product lines, provide additional worldwide manufacturing facilities, and increase its overall marketing capabilities." To raise the cash, Dresser made in March a public offering of two million shares priced at $49.75 each. It was to be one of the last successful major stock operations for nearly a year, for the stock market already was declining. There was a serious question as to whether any corporation could sell two million shares at this time, but the firm's investment banker, First Boston Corporation, thought it could be done, and so did Edward R. Luter, Dresser's vice president for finance. Moreover, Luter and First Boston's Jack Wadsworth added a fillip: close the acquisition and the stock sale on the same day. Despite the apparent hazards of closing two deals of such magnitude on the same day—each dependent upon the other—the offering sold out, all loose ends of the complicated arrangement were tied neatly, and the acquisition was completed on schedule on May 31, 1974.

The transaction marked the end of ninety-seven years of the company's ownership by the Jeffrey family. "There is no question in my mind," commented R. H. Jeffrey to F. J. Durzo, president of Jeffrey Galion, Inc.,

> that the acquisition by Dresser will prove beneficial to Jeffrey Galion's business. As a large public company, Dresser has access to the financial resources which will be needed to support the rapid growth which Jeffrey Galion is planning for the future, and which would eventually exceed the limited means of a private company.

Jeffrey himself would not participate in the new management, but Durzo remained as president of Jeffrey Galion.

As was true for Dresser and for practically every large modern American corporation, Jeffrey Galion in reality was a number of companies organized under a single banner. The key units had emerged from two companies: the Jeffrey Company, founded in 1877 as the Lechner Mining Machine Company, the nation's first manufacturer of automatic coal cutters,* and the Galion Iron Works, founded in 1907 in Galion, Ohio, to manufacture cast-iron culvert pipes. The history of these and the other firms that had

---

* See Chapter 1, pp. 24–26.

Materials-handling systems such as this Jeffrey belt conveyor and stacker are in operation throughout the world.

The acquisition of Jeffrey Galion added this line of Galion hydraulic cranes, graders, and rollers.

merged through the years was intimately connected with America's industrial progress.

The Jeffrey Company had been the nation's leading producer of automatic coal cutters from 1877 to the mid-twentieth century. At that latter period its lead was lost because its owners failed to foresee a switch from rail-mounted coal-cutting machinery to rubber-tired machines. When Robert H. Jeffrey II, working at the family plant as a college student, asked his grandfather in 1949 what the company was doing to meet the competition, R. H. Jeffrey replied, "Son, we have all the business we know what to do with." Prior to that time, however, Jeffrey consistently had been the industry's leader in developing automatic coal-cutting equipment, one notable achievement having been the switch from steam-powered machines to electric ones and another being the development in 1936 of the first so-called universal coal cutter. In 1926 the firm acquired a pioneer English mining machine company, Diamond Coal Cutter, and renamed it Jeffrey Diamond Ltd.

Two years later, in search of new products to ease the cyclical nature of its own business, Jeffrey acquired the Galion Iron Works and Manufacturing Company, which since beginning in 1907 as a manufacturer of cast-iron culvert pipes had begun making road rollers and graders. The transition had an interesting origin. Soon after the company's founding, its owner, David C. Boyd, developed a corrugated steel pipe that made obsolete the cast-iron variety. Boyd somehow conceived the interesting notion of putting an axle inside his big new pipes and using them as the wheels of a steamroller. Soon a line of horse-drawn scrapers and graders was developed to level the ruts so common to dirt roads, and ultimately came the natural shift to gasoline-powered rollers and scrapers. As the nation's networks of roads expanded dramatically, Galion road graders and scrapers played an important role in improving them, and through a series of innovative products, Galion climbed firmly to the fore of the road machinery industry. As Jeffrey lost its lead in the 1950's, Galion prospered, and by 1952 Galion's net income surpassed that of Jeffrey. In the following years its profitability continued to increase in proportion to that of its parent. In recognition of this fact the company's name was changed to Jeffrey Galion, Inc.

By the time Dresser acquired the company, Jeffrey had taken an important step toward reclaiming the undisputed supremacy it once had held as a manufacturer of coal-mining equipment. Its new HELIMINER (continuous underground mining machine) boasted of mining a record 5,720 tons of coal in a single day.

There were other operations of Jeffrey Galion that also had played no small part in the industrialization of America. For one thing, the Jeffrey Company in 1887 began manufacturing steel thimble roller

Jeffrey's HELIMINER, a highly engineered continuous coal miner, provides an efficient modern system for underground operations.

chains for industry that in some years earned more money than the automatic coal cutters. Other operations originated in companies later acquired. One of these was Foote Bros. Gear and Machine Corporation, founded in Chicago in 1893 as a small machine shop devoted to cutting gears of improved accuracy and strength. Eventually the company began manufacturing gears and power transmissions for tractors, airplanes, and heavy machinery. Another important subsidiary was the Whitney Chain Company, founded in 1896 as a manufacturer of bicycle chains. Clarence E. Whitney, the founder, conceived the then unheard-of practice of using alloy steels. These chains proved to be so superior that alloy steel was adopted by practically the entire chain-making industry. Whitney's chains made possible a terrific increase in speeds and loads, and they came to be used for automobiles, agricultural machinery, aircraft, machine tools, conveyor systems, and many industrial purposes. In 1959 Foote Bros. purchased Whitney, and in 1962 Hewitt-Robins, Inc., bought both of these companies. Hewitt-Robins was a leading manufacturer of vibrating screens used in separating materials in mining operations. The founder, Thomas Robins, developed before the turn of the century the first rubber-covered conveyor belt,* and in 1912 the company developed the first vibrating screen for beneficiating ores. Other "firsts" had followed, and one of the company's more spectacular products in the early 1950's was a hose and coupling assembly for refueling high-flying aircraft in

* See Chapter 1, pp. 35–36.

Sir William Garforth, knighted
for his work in reducing the
danger of fires in mines, was
the founder of the company that
became British Jeffrey Diamond Ltd.

midair. In 1965 Hewitt-Robins and its subsidiaries were acquired
by Litton Industries and were formed into a power transmission
division; in 1973 Jeffrey Galion acquired that division; and in the
following year Dresser acquired Jeffrey Galion.

Four weeks after Jeffrey Galion became part of the Dresser
family, John V. James spoke in Houston to a group representing the
financial community. Many of his comments dealt with this most
recent feather in Dresser's cap, the largest acquisition Dresser
ever had made.

"The company's underground mining equipment seems destined
to grow at an accelerating rate, particularly in view of the outlook
for coal, oil shale, and other minerals," James said.

Jeffrey's comprehensive line of conveying, crushing and processing
equipment is expected to achieve significant growth due to the
tremendous quantities of minerals that must be mined, crushed,
moved and processed to meet growing consumption levels throughout the world.

Dresser's goal, James told those attending the meeting, was to
be the world leader in providing technology, products, and services
essential to the energy and natural resource industries. Within the
week that announced aim was furthered through still another ac-

quisition of a company less sizable than Jeffrey Galion but an important one with annual sales of approximately $65 million. This newest addition was Waukesha Motor Company, purchased from the Bangor Punta Corporation of Greenwich, Connecticut, for $20.1 million in cash. Waukesha was a leading manufacturer of heavy-duty internal combustion engines, including diesel, gasoline, and natural gas engines. The company's 750,000-square-foot main plant was in Waukesha, Wisconsin, where engines ranging from 40 to 2,130 horsepower were manufactured. Waukesha engines served three major markets: petroleum (where the engines were used for drilling and production platforms and gas-gathering repressuring systems); power generation (to provide power for hospitals, office buildings, essential municipal services, airports, irrigation and flood control systems, and industrial plants); and industry (for mining, agricultural, and construction equipment, marine use, and for materials-handling vehicles).

Waukesha, with approximately 1,800 employees, was yet another Dresser company whose birth and rise had paralleled and been tied to the twentieth-century automobile revolution. From its inception in 1906—one year after Ford introduced his Model T—Waukesha concentrated on internal combustion engines. The company's products originally were for the construction industry, and the compact internal combustion engines began replacing the cumbersome steam engines as power sources for hoists, vehicular equipment, pumps, and compressors. The benefits resulting from the Waukesha-Dresser merger became obvious right away. In its first full year with Dresser, Waukesha increased its sales by 50 percent and tripled its profits.

Waukesha Motor Company had its manufacturing plant in this pastoral setting in Wisconsin in the year 1915.

This Waukesha heavy-duty diesel engine provides power for a California sanitation plant.

———————

Dresser's advance to the $1 billion annual sales plateau, its important acquisitions, and the ongoing energy crisis that highlighted the company's importance prompted attention from the financial press. *Forbes,* in a 1974 analysis, playfully entitled its article "From Stengel to Lawrence to James," and said that John Lawrence and James had done a job that Casey Stengel of the New York Yankees baseball team would have admired. "It was John Lawrence's *acquiring* and Jack James' *structuring* that have positioned Dresser to take maximum advantage of the boom," the article stated. "Together they have converted a group of industrial specialty shops into a virtual department store for capital goods." Just as Stengel had restructured some "highly promising material" into a baseball team that claimed five world championships in quick succession, it was said that James had meshed into profitability Lawrence's acquisition of Manning, Maxwell & Moore, Harbison-Walker, and Symington-Wayne. Moreover, James had brought in Jeffrey Galion and Waukesha, and he had introduced to Dresser the notion of the multiproduct plant in which production easily could be switched from one product to another when the need arose. When gasoline pump sales slumped in Europe, Dresser's plant in Einbeck, Germany, had been able to convert to making pneumatic tools.

Industrial Specialty Products assembles nuclear valves such as this one in pressurized and air-controlled clean rooms.

Aside from the profits generated by Dresser's recent acquisitions, the company's longtime service to the oil industry was enjoying a surge in profitability. Yet, as *Forbes* quoted James, he did not expect the oil-drilling boom to last forever, and in fact thought the existing oil fields would be "well worked over" by the 1980's. James believed the development emphasis thereafter would switch to coal and other nonpetroleum fuels, and that was where Jeffrey Galion fit into plans. *Forbes* commented: "The thing about Casey Stengel was that he never stopped running hard, even when he was winning. Jack James shows every sign of being exactly the same kind of guy."

Seldom did Dresser's directors, now only nine in number, meet that they did not have some unique new project to discuss. Sometimes they were involved in selecting proper philanthropic activities for the company. In August 1974, they established an endowment fund of $50,000 at Texas A&M University to honor an outstanding professor each year with an award of $4,000. At the same meeting the company contributed fourteen acres of land to Westminster College in Fulton, Missouri, completing the earlier gift in 1966 of five adjoining acres as a site for the college president's home.* In 1975

* This small college had achieved a lasting mark in history by being the site of Winston Churchill's famous "Iron Curtain" speech after World War II.

Dresser gave $50,000 to the School of Business Administration at Southern Methodist University in Dallas; $25,000 to an imaginative project to convert a triangular block in downtown Dallas to a park to be called Thanks-Giving Square; $100,000 to John Lawrence's alma mater, the Massachusetts Institute of Technology, in his honor; and $100,000 to the building fund for St. Bonaventure University near Olean, New York. Such activities were not unusual for the company, for donations to worthwhile causes now totaled nearly a half million dollars annually. Two separate trusts had been established for this purpose—Dresser Foundation, Inc., and Dresser-Harbison Foundation. By 1975 the two foundations had combined assets of $6.2 million.

Several prominent real-estate transactions for Dresser, all of long-term significance, occurred in the mid-1970's. The most visible transaction involved a decision to find a new facility for corporate headquarters. The company's main offices in the Republic National Bank Building filled three full floors and additional space was required on four separate floors. This scattering of facilities was inconvenient, and there was no room for further expansion. The situation prompted an in-depth review of what should be done, including the question of whether the offices should even remain in downtown Dallas. The decision made was for the company to seek to buy an existing building in the central business district. Responsibility for implementing the decision was assigned to Duane Rost. The best possibility to emerge was the sixteen-story Dallas Federal Savings Building at 1505 Elm Street, hardly more than a block away from the Republic National Bank Building and in the heart of the downtown district. An agreement soon was reached, and the deal was closed in the summer of 1974 for $5.5 million, payable by $540,000 in cash and the assumption of notes totaling $4,960,000. Dresser moved its offices to the smart-looking, blue-trimmed building at the corner of Akard and Elm Streets early in 1975, occupying eight of the sixteen floors and renaming it the Dresser Building.* Jack James and the key corporate officers took spacious quarters in the penthouse floor with a fine view of the surrounding Dallas skyline. There, high above the city's bustling streets, Dresser officials oversaw their worldwide empire.

Also in 1975 Rost negotiated the purchase of two more Dallas buildings. The acquisition of the thirty-two-story LTV Tower and its adjoining nine-story parking garage, adjacent to the Dresser Building, was surprising since it occurred so soon after the latter building

---

* Dallas Federal Savings retained its prominent street-level offices through a lease agreement.

In 1975 Dresser moved its corporate headquarters into the sixteen-story Dresser Building, foreground. The building had been purchased the preceding year from Dallas Federal Savings. Adjacent, at right, is the thirty-two-story LTV Tower, acquired by Dresser in 1975.

had been bought. But the purchase made good sense as an investment, for it was obtained for approximately $5.5 million in cash and the assumption of mortgages just under $10 million. An analysis of the leasing arrangements indicated that the income generated by tenants was sufficient to pay off all notes. Moreover, the eleven-year-old building's replacement cost was calculated to be $29 million. It thus represented a genuine bargain. Even the new Dresser Building might prove inadequate for Dresser's headquarters in future years, and a move next door to the LTV Tower was a distant possibility. The purchase was made quietly by Dresser's subsidiary for the management of its property, Direlco (which also had bought the Dallas Federal Savings Building). Since no visible changes in the building's name, appearance, or tenants occurred, few Dallas residents were aware that Dresser now owned this prominent building.

The acquisition of the second building in 1975, the former Braniff Training Center, was a commentary on how far Dresser's management training program had progressed, for the entire structure was dedicated to that purpose. Located alongside Dallas North Tollway, the gleaming white structure had been used as a school for stewardesses and other personnel by Braniff International. Dresser bought the six-story building for approximately $1.9 million. Just ten minutes from downtown Dallas, it contained thirty-three bedrooms, seven visitor suites, an auditorium, four large classrooms, a dining room, and complete kitchen and recreational facilities. James declared that the building, renamed the Dresser Leadership Center, would be utilized for a "comprehensive executive and management development program second to none in industry." Responsible for the program was Thomas J. Raleigh, senior vice president for industrial relations. After minor renovations and the installation of modern audiovisual facilities, the Center first was used for a management development program in the fall of 1975. Thereafter, it was in continuous use as selected Dresser employees came to Dallas from around the world for training sessions. Dresser's agreement with Hillsdale College, which enabled employees to work toward degrees, remained in effect, but the management training program's focal point shifted emphatically to the new Center.

Meanwhile, James's restructuring of the company continued. A year after having taken over Jeffrey Galion, three new operating groups were established which integrated that company's activities into the Dresser family. The three new elements were the Construction Equipment Group, presided over by G. A. Howser and consisting of Galion Manufacturing, Le Roi, and an international section; the Industrial Equipment Group, presided over by B. R. Stuart and including Jeffrey Manufacturing, Jeffrey Power Transmission, Crane & Hoist, Roots Blower, and an industrial products marketing organization; and the Mining Equipment & Foundry Group, whose divisions were Jeffrey Mining Machinery, Mining Services and Equipment, Transportation Equipment, and JG Castings. All these operating groups reported to J. R. Brown, Jr., senior vice president, operations, who had been elected a corporate officer the year before. F. J. Durzo, former president of Jeffrey Galion, became chairman and special assistant to Brown. In addition to overseeing the new operating groups, Brown served as president of the Mining Equipment & Foundry unit.

Dresser's corporate organizational chart accordingly took on a new look. Just beneath James as president and chief executive officer were J. B. Graves, staff vice president for planning, and R. W. Shopoff, staff vice president, administration, operations. In addi-

Dresser's Leadership Center in Dallas.

tion to the three new groups that reported to Brown, there now were six other major groups. Reporting to R. F. Schnoes, senior vice president for operations, were the Industrial Specialties Group, whose president was R. R. Ringley, and the Petroleum Equipment Group, presided over by C. D. Byrd. Also part of this alignment were a Canadian Specialties Division under E. R. Carey and an Industrial Specialty Products unit for Europe headed by R. W. Ytterberg. Reporting to R. A. Sebastian, senior vice president for operations, were the Harbison-Walker Refractories Group, under D. R. De-Veaux, and the Tool Group, whose president was W. K. Downey. The president of the Machinery Group, John J. Murphy, reported directly to the office of the president, as did the Petroleum & Minerals Group, whose president was John R. Blocker.

Four other senior vice presidents also reported directly to the office of the president: Edward R. Luter, senior vice president, finance; J. D. Mayson, senior vice president, secretary, and general counsel; Thomas J. Raleigh, senior vice president, industrial and

Dresser Titan's pumping services include acidizing, fracturing, and cementing. Here, a Dresser Titan acidizing unit is ready for delivery to an offshore rig to increase oil production.

public relations; and Duane D. Rost, senior vice president, accounting and administration.

Such an organizational chart indicated the complexity of Dresser. It was a company of such size that events such as a $2 million expansion and modernization program of the old Bovaird & Seyfang plant in downtown Bradford for the coating of couplings, valves, and pipe fittings went unnoticed almost everywhere except in Bradford. The same was true for a $5 million expansion of Harbison-Walker's high-purity periclase production facilities at its plants in Ludington, Michigan, and Hammond, Indiana. The new $10 million hand-tool plant constructed at Johnson City, Tennessee, and employing some one hundred workers, was big news only in that small town.

While this size and complexity had been brought to Dresser by the happy note of success, these elements also brought attendant problems. It was difficult for potential stockholders, for example, to comprehend the scope of the company. If a couple who wanted to invest in the future considered Dresser a prospect, just what were

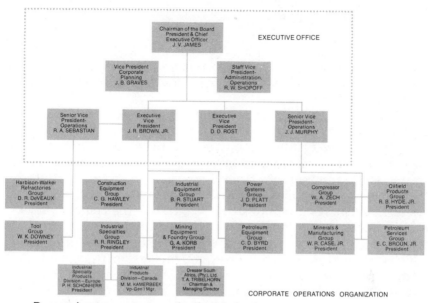

Dresser's corporate organizational chart.

they buying? This question was not as difficult, actually, as many believed. Dresser, as James and all his predecessors as chief executive officers emphasized, was *not* a conglomerate in which a group of unrelated companies were united. As the 1975 annual report declared, Dresser was dedicated to "serving energy and natural resource industries with highly engineered products and sophisticated technology." There were, the report continued, "myriad facets" to this endeavor: "Gauges monitoring a petrochemical plant . . . rock bits twisting miles beneath the surface of the earth in the never ending search for oil and gas . . . refractories controlling the high-temperature violence of molten steel . . . compressors forcing gas through pipelines." And with its decentralized approach to management, instead of being a billion-dollar monolith, Dresser was a handful of related groups, each with a clearly defined purpose. It had been so structured that James told business reporters more than once that "we can reach a decision anywhere in the world in half an hour."

To educate the financial community and in turn the general public to these basic facts, Dresser officials began placing increasing emphasis on financial and public relations. In 1974 top management made nineteen in-depth presentations to groups of security analysts in the United States and Europe. More and more analysts, investment fund managers, and members of the financial press were being brought to Dallas headquarters offices for briefings. The company also started an automatic reinvestment service that permitted shareholders to apply their dividends toward the purchase of additional Dresser stock.

The fact that Dresser's sales and earnings were increasing substantially and that the company was thoroughly involved in finding, transporting, and converting energy for the world began to be recognized by more and more investors. The level of activity for Dresser stock rose sharply from a previous average of 317,000 shares monthly to an average of 600,000 shares a month in 1975 and 904,000 shares a month in 1976. In 1975 the common stock reached a price of better than $70 per share, and a year later a two-for-one split was made. The burden of informing the financial public—shareholders, prospective investors, brokers, analysts, and the financial press—about Dresser Industries through annual reports, news releases, and seminars was that of Herb M. Ryan, director of investor relations. The most obvious manifestation of his office was the annual report, which for many years now had been an entirely different specimen from the simple foldouts of the 1930's. Annual reports of the 1970's included as a matter of course beautiful full-color photographs taken around the world, varying kinds of fine paper appropriate to the sections printed on them, special pocket inserts, detailed financial statements, and narratives that followed different themes each year.

Communicating effectively with the financial public about Dresser was one problem; communicating *internally* among the company's multitude of employees—engineers, researchers, salesmen, personnel managers, factory workers, typists, security guards, geologists, foundry workers, and a myriad of others representing almost every nationality—was a different problem. The job of instilling spirit in which all employees realized that they were pursuing the same goal was the responsibility of the company's office of Communications and Public Affairs, which also handled general as opposed to financial public relations. A variety of approaches and programs was used in this undertaking under the direction of Thomas W. Campbell. Perhaps the single most prominent means of internal communication was the *Dresser News*, a quarterly newspaper distributed to some twenty thousand salaried employees around the world. Twenty-four of the larger operating units participated in a centralized newspaper program that provided each location with a four-page quarterly newspaper also entitled *Dresser News*. Two of the pages carried general Dresser news distilled from the corporate edition, and the other pages were devoted to news of the operating unit.

Another approach designed to acquaint Dresser employees and the public with the activities and scope of the company was through the use of film. A corporate movie, *The World of Dresser,* was completed in 1974 and was shown to financial audiences and to all employees and their families. The difficulty in capturing the essence of such a constantly changing company was emphasized when in the film's final moments of preparation the company announced its biggest acquisition ever, Jeffrey Galion. Campbell inserted the necessary last-minute footage and script changes, and the 28½-minute film was completed with only a small delay, with showings commencing across the world. A sequel to *The World of Dresser,* entitled *Teamwork and Technology,* was filmed in 1977 at locations around the world. It featured Dresser employees talking to other Dresser people about their jobs, and the narration was translated into the various languages of the countries where large numbers of employees worked. "*The World of Dresser* told *what* we are and the new film tells *who* we are," said Campbell.

In addition to a need for an internal communications network, there also was a need for rapid transportation all over the world. Dresser's own fleet of five jet airplanes, stationed at Dallas's Love Field, was ready at a moment's notice to transport executives whenever the need arose. The three largest airplanes, BAC 111's, each had seating capacities for twenty-four persons. Fifteen pilots were on the Dresser payroll, and the staff for air flight activities numbered thirty-six persons. During 1976 Dresser's jets logged a total of 3,800 hours in the air and traveled 1.2 million miles.

Dresser Atlas provides wire line services in all the major oil-producing areas of the world.

It had taken Dresser ninety-three years to reach $1 billion in sales, or even longer if the earlier founding dates of some of its member companies were used. Nothing more indicated the phenomenal nature of the 1970's growth than the fact that the company topped the $2 billion mark in just two additional years. Sales for fiscal year 1975 totaled $2,011,600,000. Dresser officials, of course, were acutely aware that the 27,837 owners of its 17.3 million common shares were interested not so much in sales as in earnings. This being the case, their report glowed with good news. In 1973, the year the billion-dollar mark was achieved, the company's earnings were $44.2 million; in 1975 earnings had virtually tripled by reaching $123.9 million. Net earnings per common share jumped in the same period from $2.98 to $7.12 fully diluted, a figure that could have accommodated a hefty increase in dividends. This did not occur, for Dresser's directors elected to invest these earnings in the company's future. Cash dividends were held at $1.40 per share, the same amount paid since 1969. In 1975 the company's expenditures for new plants and equipment totaled a record of approximately $115 million. "These substantial investments in our diversified businesses are necessary if we are to remain competitive in the marketplace and continue to grow and prosper," James explained. A few of the major projects initiated or completed during 1975 were:

—A new plant constructed in Victoria, Australia, by a joint-venture company, Clyde-Galion Pty., for the production of road graders.

—Expansion of air compressor production facilities at Le Roi operations in Sidney, Ohio.

—A facility for the Industrial Valve and Instrument Division in Alexandria, Louisiana, for the manufacture of newly designed valves for the power market.

—Modernization and expansion of Waukesha's large engine assembly plant in Waukesha, Wisconsin.

—Completion of new calcium carbonate facilities at Nolanville, Texas, and limestone facilities at Damon, Texas.

—A new offshore oil-field supply base on Pelican Island, near Galveston, Texas.

The $2 billion year naturally pleased Dresser's employees and officers as well as its shareholders. For one thing, the company's minimum goal of 25 percent pre-tax return on investment had been surpassed by half of 1 percent. The ultimate goal of 35 percent, which Lawrence and James reported in the 1975 annual report, seemed attainable. The 1974 pre-tax rate of return had been 16.7 percent. The dramatic improvement, according to Lawrence and James, reflected the market's acceptance of "new and improved product introductions stemming from our strong research and development programs, the favorable impact on costs of record capital expenditures, and the enterprise and ability of the Company's 'results-oriented' management."

The company's rapid growth prompted still further realignments in organization. The nine previous groups were divided into twelve groups as a part of the continuing effort to hold these units to manageable sizes.* Each group consisted of two or more operating units having similar products, markets, and technological capabilities, all of which served the company's five lines of business: petroleum (oil field and marketing), energy processing and conversion, refractories and minerals, construction and mining equipment, and industrial specialty products. The proportion of profits generated by these five areas ranged from 15 percent for refractories and minerals to 30 percent for petroleum.

In February 1976, John Lawrence became sixty-five. In accordance with company policy, he retired as chairman of the board. He had served Dresser in an executive capacity for nineteen years, during which time the company's annual sales climbed from less than $275 million to more than $2 billion. This dramatic growth, the directors declared in a resolution, "is attributable in no small part to John Lawrence's imaginative participation as an officer and key executive." Lawrence's association with the company was to continue through his service as a director and as a special consultant. Aside from the gains made in sales and the diversification of the company through acquisitions, Lawrence had emphasized the important roles of engineering and research. He had played a major part in the formation of Dresser Environmental Technology Division,* in the continuing development of the Dresserator fuel inductor, and in the establishment of technical task forces.

Lawrence, having lost none of his vigorous appearance, departed with keen optimism for the company's future. At a Dresser

---

* The groups and their presidents were: Petroleum Services, E. C. Brown, Jr.; Mining Equipment & Foundry, J. R. Brown, Jr.; Petroleum Equipment, C. D. Byrd; Minerals & Manufacturing, W. R. Case, Jr.; Harbison-Walker Refractories, D. R. DeVeaux; Tool, W. K. Downey; Construction Equipment, G. A. Howser; Oilfield Products, R. B. Hyde, Jr.; Compressor, J. J. Murphy; Power Systems, J. D. Platt; Industrial Specialties, R. R. Ringley; and Industrial Equipment, B. R. Stuart.

* Later to be called the Advanced Technology Center.

Planners' and Controllers' Conference he boldly predicted sales of $4.5 billion by 1980. It was not an estimate to be taken lightly, for in 1970 at a similar conference he predicted that sales by 1975 would be $1.5 billion. He, of course, had been on the low side, for sales had reached $2 billion. "It looked next to impossible at the time," he commented about that prediction, "but look at the results —our 1975 sales topped $2 billion and our after-tax earnings totaled nearly $124 million! Now, in spite of all the problems on the horizon, I predict that by 1980 Dresser will be doing a $4.5 billion business with after-tax earnings in the $250 to $300 million range!" One thing was certain: Dresser's confidential projections for future sales were carefully recorded in corporate headquarters, and while variables beyond Dresser's control could alter the situation, at least a theoretical path toward $4.5 billion was charted.

"Dresser's future could never be brighter. We are in the right markets. We have a well-directed, highly motivated group of managers who have been tested under fire. In Jack James we have at the top the best, most professional manager of any industrial company in the U.S.," Lawrence said.

James, who had been president and chief executive officer of the company since 1970, assumed the additional position of chairman of the board effective March 1, 1976. Other changes at this time in corporate headquarters included the promotions of James R. Brown, Jr., and Duane D. Rost, who had joined Dresser in 1967, to executive vice presidents, and the election of B. D. St. John, a sixteen-year employee, to vice president, accounting.

In October 1975, four additional members joined Dresser's board of directors: John J. Adams, a partner in the Cleveland law firm of Squire, Sanders & Dempsey, which had represented Dresser for more than forty years;* J. Rawles Fulgham, president of First National Bank in Dallas; and two of Dresser's corporate headquarters officers, Brown and Rost.

All of Dresser's chief executives had brought unique personalities and preferences to the position. Solomon R. Dresser was the entrepreneur who created a manufacturing empire in the heart of the Pennsylvania oil patch through determination and perseverance; Fred Miller was the "genial general" who maintained high-level relations with important customers in the natural gas industry; H. Neil Mallon was the Yale-educated "big idea" man who applied

* The law firm's name had changed during these years.

This unusual-looking construction is a British Jeffrey Diamond Auto-Shredder at a metal plant in London, England.

scientific management concepts to Dresser and transformed it into a modern corporate giant; John Lawrence was the engineer who masterminded the essential acquisitions of the 1960's that loosened Dresser's longtime dependence on the fortunes of the oil and gas industries and broadened the company's markets; and John V. James was a dynamic "numbers" man who combined an accountant's desire for order with an adventurer's love of discovery.

One of James's interests, as it had to be for any top-level Dresser executive, was in the area of international trade. In 1974 he had been the moving force behind the founding of the Center for International Business, a nonprofit organization whose purpose was to promote a better understanding of critical issues in this field. James, as the Center's chairman of the board, led the association into an energetic series of conferences, briefings, publications, and books that provided a source of expertise and professional growth to all participants. Members of the Center included senior business, government, and educational leaders from throughout the nation and the world. Their activities continued to grow in the years after the organization's formation.

As for James's background in accounting, he realized in the midst of Dresser's prosperity that its "numbers" did not have the ideal mix. From the late 1960's to the early 1970's the convertible, or short-term, debt had swelled out of proper proportion. Because the company had a high debt level and also a large number of preferred stocks, bond agencies did not rate Dresser highly, giving it a BAA. (AAA was the best rating, followed by AA, A, and

BAA.) Higher ratings enabled a company to have a more favorable interest rate for its bonds and a wider market for selling them.

James initiated several key steps to transform this state of affairs, including a redemption of $230 million in preferred stock (one of the largest ever made by a U.S. corporation) and the sale of two million shares of stock in early 1976 to generate $142.6 million in cash. The ultimate result was a substantial reduction in short-term debt, an increase in working capital, a low 27 percent debt-to-capital ratio, and the earning of an A rating by bond-rating agencies.

As Dresser's balance sheet thus was put in good order, Jack James was quietly preparing for an attempted takeover of a company of equal size. His target was Signal Companies, a conglomerate headquartered in Beverly Hills, California, with annual sales of $2.1 billion generated from a variety of enterprises. Two of Signal's lines were particularly attractive to Dresser: Garrett Corporation's aerospace turbines and Mack Trucks, Inc. Garrett's turbines would tie in nicely with Dresser-Clark compressors, and the familiar Mack Trucks seemed to complement the line of heavy construction equipment. Less compatible were Signal's interests in Southern California real estate, broadcasting, and the California Angels baseball team.

James made Dresser's intentions known in a bold manner. In a letter to Signal's headquarters he announced that Dresser was interested in obtaining every one of the company's 19.7 million shares outstanding—a $470 million deal! The transaction would involve an exchange of three-tenths of a Dresser share for each share of Signal. In more direct terms, Signal's shareholders who responded to the offer would get approximately $24 a share. This offer was all the more interesting in its timing. Signal's own management, in conjunction with Gulf & Western, already had offered to purchase 6.4 million of its own shares from stockholders at $20 each, $4 less than Dresser's proposed bid. The stunned Signal directors threatened to sue if Dresser made the offer. Amidst a spate of commentary by the financial press, the matter was left pending. News stories inevitably focused on James's personality and Dresser's prosperous circumstances, which permitted it to consider such a takeover.

James, according to *Business Week*, was the "enigmatic . . . devilishly cool poker player" who was "holding the aces" in one of the "cagiest poker games around" and keeping all options open. Although he was said to be little known in the "merger-and-acquisition game," *Business Week* termed him a "top-flight manager and finance man" who was employing at Dresser two principal weapons: a detailed system of cost controls and financial planning, and a thoroughgoing redesign of Dresser's capital structure. He was a "master of both financial and management techniques" whose cost control and corporate planning systems were "without a doubt among the most sophisticated in the U.S."

In the weeks that followed, James remained uncommitted as to whether Dresser would pursue an unfriendly tender offer or let the matter rest quietly so that events would take their own course. As it turned out, James and Dresser's directors elected to do nothing. James had decided that to pursue the acquisition without having an opportunity to review in detail Signal Companies' assets and earning potential would be an unwarranted risk to the Dresser shareholders. The matter quietly subsided.

A year later, however, Dresser acquired a company based in Marion, Ohio, that substantially supplemented its position in surface mining. One of the state's oldest privately owned companies, Marion Power Shovel Company, Inc., was bought for approximately $126 million in cash and senior debt securities. Marion's principal products included the largest mobile land machines ever built. They were designed primarily for loosening, excavating, and moving materials in the surface-mining industry. The company's solid position in its market could be discerned by the fact that as of 1977 its figures indicated that it had built more than 45 percent of all walking draglines in operation or on order, 75 percent of all stripping shovels, and approximately one out of every three mining shovels having eight yards or more capacity.

Since its origin in 1884—which could be traced to Ohioan Henry M. Barnhart's design of a superior steam-powered, rail-mounted shovel—the company had made innovation after innovation in its products.* In the next years a complete line of ditching machines was developed, including the first ever built with a full-circle swing. By the turn of the century, Marion's steam shovels and dredges had helped transform vast tracts of swamp into fertile, productive land, irrigated arid lands of the west, and deepened and widened canals and harbors from coast to coast. In the twentieth century the company continued to pace the field. In 1906 Marion shovels helped build the Panama Canal; in 1908 the company introduced the first three-motor electric shovel; in 1910 it manufactured the world's first stripping shovel, thereby opening the way for open-pit mining of coal, metal, and other materials. The innovations continued steadily through the years. In 1962 Marion's 8800 walking dragline, used at Peabody Coal's Homestead mine,

* See Chapter 1, pp. 28–31.

Marion Power Shovel's earliest models bore the name of inventor and company founder Henry M. Barnhart.

The acquisition of Marion Power Shovel in 1977 added this gigantic plant in Marion, Ohio, to the Dresser family.

was the world's largest, its 85-cubic-yard bucket being two and one half times as big as that of any previous walking dragline. In 1974 Marion introduced the SuperFront, a radically new mining shovel incorporating the first major change in front-end .geometry since the power shovel's invention nearly 150 years earlier. One of Marion's specially designed crawler transporters was used for the Saturn rockets and Apollo spacecraft at the Kennedy Space Center as well as for carrying the launch tower and Saturn vehicle into position for the historic Apollo-Soyuz space linkup in 1975. That year, through a licensee in Japan, the company received one of the largest single mining shovel orders in history: ten SuperFront shovels to be used for coal-mining operations in the Yakutsk coal-mining project in Siberia.

By 1977 Marion had 2,800 employees; seventeen sales offices in the United States and Canada; full-time agents in Australia, Latin America, and Europe/Africa; manufacturing affiliations and/or subsidiary operations in France, India, Australia, and Japan; and more than fifty-five distributors in Africa, Asia, Australia, the Middle East, Europe, and Latin America. The overseas market accounted for about 20 percent of Marion's sales volume. The size of the company's primary manufacturing facilities in Marion was especially impressive, the largest of them being big enough to contain three football fields.

An interesting if relatively minor aspect of the acquisition was the reunification of Marion and a Dresser company obtained in 1974 in Brazil under the name Huber-Warco. "Huber" referred to Edward Huber, a nineteenth-century Marion manufacturer who largely had financed Marion's founding and whose extensive manufacturing interests had led to a Huber company in São Paulo. The Brazilian company built HWB-Galion road graders under the Construction Equipment Group.

Ohio now was home for eleven Dresser operating units employing approximately 6,600 people in the state and generating annual sales of approximately $244.5 million. Only Texas had more operating units.

――――――――――

It was difficult to imagine any American institution that could escape the impact of the important moods and trends of the 1970's. Business institutions, and certainly Dresser Industries, were no exception. The issues that concerned the American public—preservation of the environment, the energy crisis, corporate responsibility —were issues that inevitably touched Dresser. Corporations of the

1970's, more so than ever before, had to consider their social responsibilities as well as profit making, for their actions at home and abroad were subject to intense scrutiny. Generally, American business institutions were reluctant to enter into the public dialogue on such vital issues. Yet, viewed from the perspective that the democratic system required issues to be explored from a multitude of viewpoints, this reluctance was unfortunate, for as one of the most vital elements in society, business needed to add its voice to the dialogue.

Dresser Industries was one of the few corporations willing to speak its piece in the last half of the 1970's, and it did so in several attention-gaining ways. One of the areas in which corporations feared to tread openly was in politics. James and other key Dresser executives concluded in 1976 that this was a mistaken notion. James's reasoning appeared in the *Dresser News*.

"Most of us in industry in the past have concentrated on minding our stores," he said.

> We have channeled most, if not all, of our efforts into keeping our business growing, on maximizing the investment of our shareholders, on providing new opportunities and security for our employees—all activities which contribute substantially to the basic underlying strength of our economy and nation. We felt that these efforts would be respected and encouraged.

Such had not been the case, he continued. "In recent years an antibusiness mood has developed within our political process that must be countered if free enterprise, the highest standard of living in the world and the life style and freedoms that most Americans have come to enjoy are to survive."

In October, with the presidential campaign between incumbent Gerald R. Ford and Democratic challenger Jimmy Carter revealing what James believed to be "dramatically different" attitudes toward business, James sent a letter to Dresser's more than 27,000 shareholders urging the re-election of Ford. James cited Ford's attitude that with a minimum of interference business could achieve "full productive and profitable potential" as one of the key reasons for favoring him. The endorsement received more attention than anticipated when a Democratic Tennessee state representative complained to the Federal Election Commission that this communication amounted to a corporate contribution "in kind" and should be investigated. But while federal election laws did prohibit direct contributions to candidates, the law clearly permitted corporations to seek to influence the vote of their own stockholders. Thus, there were no improprieties. Dresser, with a modest expenditure of $5,200 for this mailing, was one of only four corporations willing to exercise its important prerogative in this presidential election, according to the Federal Election Commission.*

In a related move Dresser decided to encourage salaried employees to participate in political processes by forming the Dresser Industries Political Action Committee (DIPAC).† Its objectives, according to James R. Brown, Jr., chairman of DIPAC, were the "preservation and furtherance of the private enterprise system" and in particular the "protection and advancement of the industries and other types of business in which diversified multinational energy, mining and manufacturing companies may be engaged." Contributions to DIPAC were confidential. A DIPAC committee was established to determine which candidates should receive support. As part of DIPAC's actions, a special insert in the fall 1976 edition of the *Dresser News* listed U.S. House and Senate candidates and their voting records as rated by five special-interest groups (Americans for Democratic Action, Americans for Constitutional Action, the AFL-CIO's COPE, the Chamber of Commerce of the U.S., and the Independent Petroleum Association of America). DIPAC also began issuing the *DIPAC Report*, an occasional publication that discussed pending legislation and stated Dresser's opinions concerning it.

Another issue of central concern to all Americans in this period was deciding how best to cope with the energy crisis. Dresser had demonstrated in its 1971 annual report its own eagerness to grapple with this issue through its interview with Dr. John J. McKetta, former chairman of the Advisory Committee on Energy to the Secretary of the Interior, in which he had alerted Dresser shareholders to an impending energy crisis. Dr. McKetta's dire observations about the situation had proved to be frightfully accurate, and the 1976 annual report included a booklet with more of his comments under the title "The Energy Crisis Revisited." Dr. McKetta, as James wrote in an introductory note, had been one of the first to call attention to the gravity of the nation's inefficient energy resources policies. His observations in 1976, however, were far more alarming, for he foresaw "deep and painful disruptions" in the economy, and by 1985 the worst recession in history marked by a severe energy shortage with an intensity difficult to imagine.

---

* The others were Libby-Owens-Ford with an expenditure of $13,100; Cooper Industries, $5,100; and Pepsico, Inc., $4,500.

† Federal law prohibited corporations as such from contributing money to political parties or to candidates, and hourly employees and their immediate supervisors were ineligible for such organizations as DIPAC, according to the Federal Election Act.

If we allow our energy programs to drag on as they are today, I predict the government, by 1985, will have on its payrolls a large number of "regulators" who will appear at our homes to make certain that we maintain low temperatures in the winter and high temperatures in the summer, and that our clothes dryers are permanently disconnected. Air conditioners in automobiles will be banned and we will drive on Saturday and Sunday for emergency purposes only.

I further predict that escalator use will be prohibited, elevator use severely limited, that unemployment will be as high as 14 per cent and that we will have the worst recession in the history of the country.

These alarming statements were supported by a series of careful calculations showing how the import gap was widening and how demand was outstripping supply. Dr. McKetta proposed ideas of his own about steps needed to alleviate the situation—basically that the national strategy should be to increase domestic production and reserves of oil and gas over the short term to gain time for the development of alternate energy resources. This would entail the removal of price controls from oil and gas, which would have the double effect of slowing demand because of higher prices and spurring further domestic drilling. "Time is running out," Dr. McKetta said. "No matter what we do we are going to feel the adverse effect of the energy crisis on our living standards."

Dr. McKetta's knowledgeable comments and his prediction of an impending crisis inspired Dresser to promulgate his views to a wider audience. The medium chosen was *The Wall Street Journal*, where, on March 17, 1977, a two-page advertisement containing a reprint of Dr. McKetta's message appeared under the bold headline "The Energy Crisis: Why the country's over a barrel, and what you can do about it." What readers could do about it, an accompanying editorial comment explained, was to insist to their elected representatives and senators that they get busy and help develop a comprehensive federal energy policy. Meanwhile, readers were urged to conserve energy in every way possible through their daily living habits. Dresser itself was identified as the sponsor of the advertisement in an inconspicuous manner. Those who wanted a reprint of Dr. McKetta's comments were advised in small type to write to Dresser headquarters in Dallas, where a limited number were available. The response was little short of overwhelming; requests for more than thirty-two thousand reprints arrived from other corporations, educational institutions, government agencies, utility companies, publications, trade associations, and individuals.

Thus began a series of "public awareness" advertisements in 1977, all following precisely the same format and all addressing major issues of the day in which Dresser had a vested interest. The campaign was directed by Edward R. Luter, senior vice president, finance, and Thomas W. Campbell, communications and public affairs director, with the support of James.

The second advertisement in the series addressed the highly sensitive matter of boycott legislation then pending in the U.S. Congress. This legislation, it was believed, would make it difficult for Dresser and other American corporations to do business with Arab nations where the rich oil fields required the extensive use of Dresser equipment. The advertisement appeared on April 14 under the title "500,000 American jobs hanging in balance as Congress considers more boycott legislation." Once again the content was the transcript of an interview with a recognized authority, Dr. Richard D. Robinson, professor of international management at the Sloan School of Management, Massachusetts Institute of Technology. Dr. Robinson forcefully argued that the legislation was counterproductive to peace negotiations, and would make it difficult or impossible for the United States to compete with the Europeans and Japanese in the Middle East. The net result could be the loss of some 500,000 jobs in the United States. Reprints again were made available, and more than sixteen thousand were mailed to interested parties.

The third advertisement quoted remarks by Professor Henry P. deVries, director of the Inter-American Law Center at Columbia University, over the passage of federal laws regulating the conduct of multinational corporations which in his estimation sought to impose American law on foreign countries. Instead, he believed that the United States "must take into account the broad spectrum and shades of opinion expressed in the laws and attitudes of other countries." In the case of "sensitive payments," he proposed that all questions could be handled through treaty agreement among nations, including a comprehensive system of disclosure, a defined class of payments, and enforcement methods.

The fourth advertisement in the series sought to dispel fears raised about the dangers of nuclear power as a source of energy. Two recognized authorities, Dr. Petr Beckmann of the University of Colorado and Dr. Bernard L. Cohen of the University of Pittsburgh, declared nuclear power to be the *safest* of all large-scale energy conversion, and discussed in rational, scholarly terms questions concerning its dangers. This advertisement attracted a more immediate response than any of its predecessors, for all Americans were acutely concerned about alternative energy sources. Within

Dresser initiated in 1977 a series of advertisements alerting the public to issues the company deemed important for American society as a whole.

three weeks more than a thousand individual responses from housewives, businessmen, government employees, professors, and others arrived at Dresser's headquarters, and nearly seventeen thousand requested reprints were mailed. The contents of the letters reassured Dresser officials in their belief that a need existed for responsible parties to speak directly and factually to this critical public issue. "It's about time somebody started discussing the *FACTS*," wrote a Californian. A Kansas research consultant thanked the company for its attention to a matter that "desperately needs to be brought to public attention in this age of technophobia." A reader in St. Louis was inspired to send President Jimmy Carter a clipping of the two-page advertisement with a letter advocating the development of a nuclear policy. He provocatively suggested that "promulgation of a national energy policy based on nuclear power is the kind of energy policy that will put that President on the next new coin series of the United States."

These advertisements were not intended to win new friends for Dresser. Company officials *did* believe that they were performing a public service by presenting these viewpoints to a wide, influential audience.

Another matter that unexpectedly received treatment in the nation's press in 1978 concerned Dresser's international operations, particularly its trade with the Soviet Union. Such trade followed the expressed international priorities of the executive branch of the U.S. Government, and the Export Administration Act as passed by Congress in 1969 and amended in 1977.

Following a week-long industrial symposium by Dresser representatives in Moscow in February 1978, an agreement was reached for the company to construct a $144 million drill-bit plant in that country. The contract was approved routinely by the departments of Commerce, State, Defense, and Energy, and a validated export license was issued on May 30 1978. However, in July the Carter administration sought to express its disapproval of Soviet treatment of dissidents, and when the news was leaked that certain of President Carter's advisers and U.S. Senator Henry M. Jackson favored canceling the contract as a show of force, headlines reminiscent of the Cold War of the 1950's appeared. It was also charged that the technology of certain equipment in the plant would help the Soviets militarily.

Reaction from Dresser officials was immediate. Pointing to the United States' unfavorable balance of trade, John V. James expressed grave concern over the advisability of using exports as a "lever" in foreign policy. He pointed out that the technology involved was readily available to the Soviets from suppliers outside the United States, and that four federal departments had reviewed and approved the transaction. Moreover, insofar as the defense interests of the United States might be concerned, James noted that none of the technology in the Dresser plant was on the list of critical technologies compiled by the Department of Defense, and added that it might be better to assist the Soviet Union to develop its own oil resources rather than face the possibility of a showdown with that nation in the future over the resources of the Middle East. On August 6, the White House announced that President Carter had personally reviewed and approved the sale.

———

As Dresser Industries approached its centennial anniversary in 1980, one thing was certain: the role that its many operating units had played in the industrial development of the nation was destined to become even larger as the critical question of obtaining and providing energy for the world's needs was confronted. The company's line of products and services encompassed every known form of potential energy—oil, natural gas, coal, hydro, geothermal, nuclear, and others.

As a report from one prominent brokerage firm stated: "Dresser Industries, Inc.[,] is the world's largest multinational company geared to supplying total technical systems and highly engineered systems. It is also the world's largest producer of preventive and remedial ecological and environmental products and services." The uniqueness of the company's position was indicated by an interesting fact. While Dresser competed with hundreds of corporate entities, no one company competed in areas representing more than 15 percent of Dresser's total revenue. The company's position also could be seen in the fact that in each of its major products the Dresser line ranked from first to third as the largest supplier of either the service or the product. "It is our belief," the report stated, "that Dresser Industries, Inc.[,] is the only publicly-owned company that has the capability to supply products and technical services to the entire gamut of world energy markets whether they be oil, natural gas, coal, nuclear or synthetics." And, as the report went on, the dramatic growth of recent years seemed certain to continue, considering new products, capital expenditures, and the status of U.S. and world energy requirements. Since 1974 the company had spent some $318.2 million on modernization, expansion of existing production facilities, and the construction of new plant capacity with emphasis on products with high profit margins. During the same period, an additional $150.2 million was spent on research and development.

Dresser's operations now were divided into five major reporting groups: Petroleum Operations, whose sales accounted for 28 percent of total company revenues in 1976; Industrial Specialty Products, 21 percent; Energy Processing and Conversion, 24 percent; Construction and Mining, 15 percent; and Refractories and Minerals, 12 percent.

All these groupings were prospering, but none more so than Petroleum Operations, whose profit margins increased from 9.6 percent in 1971 to 16.8 percent in 1976. This reflected careful expansion into areas with better margins and market potential. The components of Petroleum Operations were Drilling Fluid Systems; Bits, Tools, and Rigs; Petroleum Services; and Dispensing Systems. Magcobar continued to be a shining light, for its drilling fluids and engineering services accounted for a significant share of the total world market. SWACO, another unit that manufactured drilling-fluids mixing equipment, enjoyed a strong position of leadership in the market.

The Bits, Tools, and Rigs component consisted of Security, SWACO, Guiberson, Ideco, and an International Division. The ambitious plans laid two decades earlier for Security's bits were at last being realized, for they now accounted for 15 to 20 percent of the world market, following Hughes Tool and vying for second with Smith International, Inc. By 1980 the share was expected to be larger because of the opening in the fall of 1977 of a new facility at Eunice, Louisiana, which would increase production capacity by 40 percent.

The operating divisions of Petroleum Services were Dresser Atlas and Dresser Titan, which offered, respectively, well logging and completion (acidizing, perforating, and cementing) services. These services combined accounted for about 5 percent of the total world market, but Dresser's internal projections forecast a doubling of that percentage by 1980.

The final unit of Petroleum Operations was one around which considerable popular interest revolved—Dispensing Systems. The largest single product line was the Dresser gasoline pump with ancillary equipment such as changemakers, automatic blending pumps, digital readout equipment, remote-controlled pumps (which used keys, credit cards, coins or currency), and prepay and postpay systems. Dresser-Wayne had developed equipment that would eliminate vapor pollution of the atmosphere at the gasoline pump, and if the Environmental Protection Agency's view prevailed, it was possible that the government might mandate installation of this equipment. If so, Dresser would be a prime benefactor.

In terms of sales, Dresser's Industrial Specialty Products Group was second in size to Petroleum Operations. It consisted of the Controls product line, Industrial Equipment, and Tools & Abrasives. Dresser Manufacturing Division, still a distinct and direct successor to Solomon R. Dresser's original company, was one of the operating units, and indeed was doing as well as ever. It held a major share of the coupling market, and its most recent achievement had been the development of Al-Clad, a special coating that made parts impervious to corrosion. The diverse Industrial Equipment sector included products designed for mining; ore processing; conveyor systems; gear boxes; cranes; hoists; railroad castings, couplings, and cushioning devices; pneumatic tools; and hand tools.

The third-biggest reporting group in Dresser was Energy Processing and Conversion, whose operating units contributed 24 percent of the corporation's total income. The dominant products in this line were compressors and pumps, which accounted for nearly one out of every six dollars of Dresser's total revenues. Clark and Pacific remained the key components here. Dresser Clark, as that division now was called, had manufacturing plants in Olean, New York; Lethbridge, Alberta, Canada; and Le Havre, France; and accounted for a significant share of the world's energy demands for compressors. Pacific Pumps' share of the market was smaller but more specialized, being more highly concentrated in petroleum processing, nuclear, and public utilities.

The other two lines of products in Energy Processing and Conversion were Power Systems and Environmental Systems. Power Systems' operating divisions were J. G. Power Transmissions and Waukesha, both of which manufactured products that generated and transmitted power for use in the field with drilling platforms, gas gathering systems, mining and construction sites, irrigation and flood control systems, and as a standby power source for hospitals, airports, office buildings, and other such facilities. Waukesha's gas and diesel engines, with up to 2,500 horsepower, were being concentrated more and more on energy markets. The Power Transmission Division's products included a wide range of chain drives, speed reducers, and gear motors.

Environmental Systems was composed of just one unit—Lodge-Cottrell. Lodge-Cottrell was the fifth-largest factor in the pollution control market, but its efficient electrostatic precipitator systems held great promise for dramatic growth. And in the event that public utilities burning oil or natural gas were required to shift to coal, the company could expect immense new demands. Dresser's involvement in pollution control extended beyond Environmental Systems, for in Santa Ana, California, the Environmental Technology Division carried out research in air, water, and solid waste pollution abatement, and advised the company on all environmental concerns. Dr. Robert D. Englert, formerly executive director of the Stanford Research Institute—Southern Laboratories, was head of these operations.

The fourth-largest of Dresser's five major groupings in 1976 was Construction and Mining. This area generated 15 percent of the overall revenues. Construction equipment included Le Roi's air compressors and air tools and Galion's motor graders, road rollers, mobile hydraulic planes, and cold road planers. For the mining industry Jeffrey's continuous coal-mining machines had set new standards for underground productivity and between 1973 and 1975 catapulted the company's share of the market from an insignificant level to a leading one. Jeffrey's new machines were designed for the "longwall" mining technique, which generally provided an opportunity for removal of 80 to 90 percent of the coal in place rather than the 50 to 60 percent from room and pillar methods. Moreover, the longwall mining method appeared to afford closer compliance with health and safety regulations. To complement its continuous mining machines, Jeffrey also offered highly flexible hauling equipment and conveyor systems. In another aspect of serving the mining industry, a line of Security's rock bits—adapted for mining insert bits—had become the world leader with a market share of between 30 and 40 percent.

The smallest of Dresser's five major groups was Refractories and Minerals, responsible for 12 percent of the company's revenues. This represented a decline from earlier years, but it was expected to be short-lived since Harbison-Walker was the world's largest producer of refractories and was in the fore of coal gasification research. Of some eighteen coal gasification plants recently constructed, Harbison-Walker had helped design fifteen of them. Also, with the envisioned transition from oil and natural gas to coal as an energy source, major refractory usage would be essential. As for its mineral properties, Dresser operated twenty mines over the world. They produced barite, bentonite, sand, kaolin, calcium carbonate, lignite, lead, zinc, and copper. The company's barite deposits, obtained from ten mines, were processed at eighteen locations, making Dresser one of the world's largest producers and processors of barite. Second in importance were the deposits of bentonite, with Dresser again being among the world's largest producers. The company had a staff of seventeen geologists whose jobs were to locate and identify potential ore bodies anywhere in the world. Indeed, Dresser was in virtually every aspect of its operations a global enterprise.

As Dresser Industries' management, fifty-three thousand employees, and twenty-seven thousand shareholders looked to the company's second hundred years, they could reflect on a heritage encompassing almost every aspect of the energy, natural resources, and industrial markets. Theirs was a heritage that summed up in many ways the broader story of American technological progress and the struggle to find new and better means of utilizing the natural resources of the world. Such ongoing endeavors seldom are visible to the average American, and when he does happen to encounter them they may seem far removed from daily life. Nothing could be further from the truth, for it is difficult to imagine any of these activities that do not have a real impact on daily life. Solomon R. Dresser's leakproof coupling alone enriched the lives of millions of people by enabling natural gas to be sent to their homes from fields far away. Such a list goes on and on to encompass the efforts of other early men like Edward H. Ashcroft, who helped solve the problem of steam engine explosions with his safety valves; Francis M. Lechner, who invented the first automatic coal cutter and thereby multiplied significantly the amount of coal that could be mined each day and thus made available to industry; Alton J. Shaw, who devised the first three-motor electric overhead crane; and Henry M. Barnhart, who designed and manufactured an efficient power shovel that helped dig the Panama Canal.

Today, efforts continue at Dresser toward other important breakthroughs, and because of dwindling sources of energy, there is a new urgency about them. The company's engineers and technicians seek to improve or to find revolutionary new techniques for such operations as exploration and drilling, oil and gas production, gas transmission and distribution, oil and gas processing, coal mining, coal gasification and liquefaction, electrical and mechanical power conversion, and many others. Additional research funds are allocated toward improving or devising techniques for deriving energy from nuclear, hydro, geothermal, wind, fusion, solar, and tidal sources.

Unless breakthroughs are made in these areas, the comforts brought to civilization from the achievements of the past will diminish. The burden of devising the means to prevent this promises to be one of the most challenging in the history of mankind. For Dresser this means that the next century promises to be even more exciting and demanding than the company's first hundred years as an American business institution.

APPENDICES

Appendix A

Dresser Industries
Major Plants and Mines, 1978

U.S. Plants and Mines

ALABAMA

Anniston: Anniston Operations, Dresser Manufacturing Division
Bessemer: Bessemer Works, Harbison-Walker Refractories Division
Eufaula: Eufaula Works, Harbison-Walker Refractories Division
Fairfield: Fairfield Works, Harbison-Walker Refractories Division

CALIFORNIA

Anaheim: Electra Motors Operations
Glendale: Glendale Plant, Tool Group
Huntington Park: Pacific Pumps Division
Long Beach: Globe Pacific Hoist Plant, Petroleum Equipment Division
Santa Fe Springs: Pacific Pumps Division
Torrance: Felker Operations

CONNECTICUT

Hartford: Whitney Chain Operations
Newtown: Heise Plant, Industrial Valve & Instrument Division
Stratford: Industrial Valve & Instrument Division

GEORGIA

Calhoun: Calhoun Operations, Harbison-Walker Refractories Division

ILLINOIS

Chicago: Chicago Plant, Tool Group
Chicago: Foote-Jones Operations

Downers Grove: Foote-Jones Operations
Franklin Park: Hand Tool Division

INDIANA

Connersville: Roots Blower Operations
Hammond: Hammond Works, Harbison-Walker Refractories Division

IOWA

Clinton: Clinton Plant, Waukesha Engine Division

KENTUCKY

Berea: Berea Operations, Industrial Valve & Instrument Division

LOUISIANA

Alexandria: Alexandria Operations, Industrial Valve & Instrument Division
Dubberly: Dresser Minerals Division
Eunice: P&M Manufacturing Division
New Orleans: Dresser Minerals Division
Westlake: Dresser Minerals Division

MARYLAND

Baltimore: Baltimore Works, Harbison-Walker Refractories Division
Grantsville: New Savage, Harbison-Walker Refractories Division
Northeast: Hile Works, Harbison-Walker Refractories Division
Salisbury: Petroleum Equipment Division

MASSACHUSETTS

Westborough: Bay State Abrasives Division
Worcester: Anderson Division

MICHIGAN

Ludington: Ludington Works, Harbison-Walker Refractories Division
Muskegon: Crane & Hoist Operations

MISSOURI

Fulton: Fulton Works, Harbison-Walker Refractories Division
Fulton: Fulton-Vandalia Mines, Harbison-Walker Refractories Division

Potosi: Dresser Minerals Division

Vandalia: Vandalia Works, Harbison-Walker Refractories Division

NEVADA

Battle Mountain: Dresser Minerals Division

NEW JERSEY

Cape May: Cape May Works, Harbison-Walker Refractories Division

NEW YORK

Depew: Transportation Equipment Division
Niagara Falls: General Abrasive Division
Olean: Dresser Clark Division

OHIO

Columbus: Engineered Systems Operations
Columbus: Jeffrey Mining Machinery Division
Defiance: Defiance Plant, Tool Group
Delaware: JG Castings Operations, Transportation Equipment Division
Galion: Galion Manufacturing Division
Marion: Marion Power Shovel Division
Portsmouth: Portsmouth Works, Harbison-Walker Refractories Division
Portsmouth: Portsmouth-Brinegar-Riggs Bear Run Mines, Harbison-Walker Refractories Division
Sidney: Le Roi Operations
Springfield: Springfield Plant, Tool Group
Windham: Windham Works, Harbison-Walker Refractories Division
Worthington: Jeffrey Manufacturing Division
Worthington: Power Transmission Division

OKLAHOMA

Tulsa: P&M Manufacturing Division

PENNSYLVANIA

Bradford: Dresser Manufacturing Division
Clearfield: Clearfield Works, Harbison-Walker Refractories Division
Mineral Springs: Clearfield-Woodland District Mines, Harbison-Walker Refractories Division

Mount Union: Mount Union Works, Harbison-Walker Refractories Division
Templeton: Templeton Works, Harbison-Walker Refractories Division
Wellsboro: Wellsboro Operations, Dresser Manufacturing Division
West Mifflin: Garber Research Center

SOUTH CAROLINA
Belton: Conveyor Components Operations
Woodruff: Processing Equipment Operations

TENNESSEE
Johnson City: Johnson City Plant, Tool Group
Morristown: Jeffrey Chain Operations
Russellville: Dresser Transportation Division

TEXAS
Austin: Spenco Systems Division
Beaumont: P&M Manufacturing Division
Brownsville: Dresser Minerals Division
Dallas: Mining Services & Equipment Division
Dallas: P&M Manufacturing Division
Fort Worth: Screw Conveyor Operations
Galveston: Dresser Minerals Division
Houston: Dresser Atlas Division
Houston: Dresser Measurement Division
Houston: Dresser Minerals Division
Houston: Dresser Titan Division
Houston: Guiberson Division
Houston: Ideco Division
Houston: Industrial Tool Division
Houston: Lodge-Cottrell Operations
Houston: Magcobar Division
Houston: Modular Systems Division
Houston: Pacific Pumps Division
Houston: Security Division
Houston: SWACO Division
Kosse: Dresser Minerals Division
Nolanville: Dresser Minerals Division
Zavalla: Dresser Minerals Division

WISCONSIN
Waukesha: Waukesha Engine Division

WYOMING
Greybull: Dresser Minerals Division

International Plants and Mines

AFRICA
Apapa, Lagos, Nigeria: Wayne (West Africa) Ltd.
Port Harcourt, Nigeria: Dresser Magcobar Minerals, Ltd.
Warri, Nigeria: Magcobar Minerals, Ltd.
Wadeville, Germiston, Transvaal, South Africa: Dresser Engineered Products, Dresser South Africa (Pty.) Ltd.
Maitland, Cape Town, South Africa: Dresser Wayne Division, Dresser South Africa (Pty.) Ltd.

AUSTRALIA
Bayswater (Perth) Western Australia: WEPCO (Pty.) Ltd.
Campbellfield, Victoria: Galion Pty. Ltd.
North Pole, Western Australia: Dresser Minerals International, Inc.
Port Hedland, Western Australia: Dresser Minerals Division, Dresser Products Australia (Pty.) Ltd.
Unanderra, New South Wales: Harbison, A.C.I. Pty. Limited

CANADA
Brantford, Ontario: Bay State Abrasives Operation, Industrial Products Division, Dresser Industries Canada, Ltd.
Calgary, Alberta: P&M Manufacturing Division
Cambridge (Galt), Ontario: Industrial Products Division
Edmonton, Alberta: Dresser Titan Division
Grenville, Quebec: Canadian Refractories Division
Kilmar, Quebec: Canadian Refractories Division
LaSalle, Quebec: Jeffrey Manufacturing Division
Lethbridge, Alberta: Lethbridge Plant (Dresser Industries Canada, Ltd.
Mississauga, Ontario: Industrial Products Division
Niagara Falls, Ontario: General Abrasive Canada Operations
Orillia, Ontario: Industrial Products Division
Rosalind, Alberta: Dresser Minerals Division
St. Thomas, Ontario: Galion Manufacturing Division
Walton, Nova Scotia: Dresser Minerals Division

MEXICO
Guadalajara, Jalisco: Jeffrey Manufacturera Mexicana, S.A.
Monterrey: Refractarios H-W Flir, S.A.

Mexico: Refractarios H-W Flir de Mexico, S.A.
Nuevo Leon Linares: Magcobar de Mexico, S.A.
Nuevo Leon Monterrey: Magcobar de Mexico, S.A.

PUERTO RICO

San Juan: Dresser Industries, Puerto Rican Branch

EUROPE

BELGIUM

Familleureux: Galion Europe, S.A.

ENGLAND

Birmingham: Lodge-Cottrell Limited
Bracknell, Berkshire: Dresser Wayne Division
Openshaw, Manchester: P&M Manufacturing Division
South Gosforth, Newcastle: Boyles Bros. Operation
Skelmersdale, Lancashire: Dewrance & Co. Ltd.
Wakefield, West Yorkshire: British Jeffrey-Diamond Division
Wirksworth, Derbyshire: Dresser Minerals International, Inc.

FRANCE

Le Havre: Dresser (France) S.A.
Paris: Dresser Wayne Division

GERMANY

Baesweiler: Industrial Specialty Products Division
Einbeck: Dresser Wayne Division
Oberhausen: Magnesital-Feuerfest GmbH

GREECE

Milos: Mykobar Mining Co., S.A.
Mykonos: Mykobar Mining Co., S.A.

IRELAND

Foynes, County Limerick: Foynes Manufacturing, Ltd.
Nenagh, County Tipperary: Magcobar (Ireland) Limited

ITALY

Milan: Dresser Wayne Division

LUXEMBOURG

Steinsel: Bay State Abrasives, S.A.

NETHERLANDS

Helden-Panningen: Dresser Manufacturing Division
Vlaardingen: Air Tool Division

SWEDEN
Malmö: AB Ljungmans Verkstader

SWITZERLAND
Kloten, Zurich: Dresser Wayne Switzerland

FAR EAST

INDONESIA
Djakarta: P. T. Dresser Magcobar Indonesia

MALAYSIA
Kuantan, Pahang: Malaysian Barite Sdn. Bhd.

THAILAND
Bangkok: Thailand Barite Co., Ltd.

MIDDLE EAST

IRAN
Isfahan: Iran Refractories Company
Parandak: SSK Magcobar Iran

KUWAIT
Kuwait: Dresser Kuwait, S.A.K.

LIBYA
Benghazi: Magcobar Libya, Ltd.

SAUDI ARABIA
Dammam: Arabian Minerals & Chemicals, Ltd.

SOUTH AMERICA

BRAZIL
Mogi das Cruzes: HWB Galion Division
Resende: HWB Galion Division
Rio de Janeiro: Wayne Division
São Paulo: Manometros Willy Division

CHILE
Santiago: Refractarios Chilenos, S.A.
Santiago: Triconos Mineros, S.A.

PERU
Lima: Refractarios Peruanos, S.A.

VENEZUELA

Matanzas: Ceramica Carabobo, C.A.
Valencia: Ceramica Carabobo, C.A.

The above list refers to international manufacturing and/or assembly plants and mines. Other operations, administrative and sales offices are listed in corporate directories.

Appendix B

Major Acquisitions

Year	Company or Operation	Headquarters Location	Major Products
1933	Bryant Heater Company (sold in 1949)	Cleveland, Ohio	Gas-fired furnaces and boilers for residential heating
1937	Clark Brothers Company	Olean, New York	Large capacity gas-engine-driven compressors for pipelines, refineries, and petrochemical plants
1940	Pacific Pump Works	Huntington Park, California	Engineered centrifugal pump for refineries and petrochemical plants
1941	Bovaird & Seyfang Manufacturing Company	Bradford, Pennsylvania	Oil field tools and equipment
1944	International Stacey Corporation (International Derrick Equipment Companies of Texas, California, and Ohio; Stacey Bros. Gas Construction Company [sold in 1957]; and	Columbus, Ohio / Columbus, Ohio / Beaumont, Texas / Torrance, California / Cincinnati, Ohio	Oil field drilling and producing equipment / Gas holders, high-pressure tanks, storage tanks
	Roots-Connersville Blower Corporation)	Connersville, Indiana	Blowers, compressors, meters
1945	Kobe, Inc. (sold in 1954)	Huntington Park, California	Hydraulic pumping system for producing oil
1945	Payne Furnace & Supply Company (sold in 1949)	Beverly Hills, California	Gas-fired furnaces and space heaters for residential use
1945	Day & Night Manufacturing Company (sold in 1949)	Monrovia, California	Gas-fired hot water heaters and space heaters for residential use
1945	Security Engineering Co., Inc.	Whittier, California	Rock bits for drilling oil and gas wells
1949	Magnet Cove Barium Corporation	Houston, Texas	Drilling mud for oil and gas wells

Year	Company or Operation	Headquarters Location	Major Products
1955	Lane-Wells Company	Los Angeles, California	Perforation, logging and completion services for drilling industry
1956	Southwestern Industrial Electronics Company (sold in 1973)	Houston, Texas	Seismograph instruments
1956	The Guiberson Corporation	Dallas, Texas	Oil-field production tools and equipment
1961	M&H Valve & Fittings Company	Anniston, Alabama	Valves, fittings, fire hydrants
1964	Manning, Maxwell & Moore, Inc.	Stratford, Connecticut	Valves, gauges, cranes, hoists for general industrial use
1967	Harbison-Walker Refractories Company	Pittsburgh, Pennsylvania	Refractories
1968	Pan Geo Atlas Corporation, and PGAC Development Company	Houston, Texas	Logging, perforating, and completion services
1968	Symington-Wayne Corporation	Salisbury, Maryland	Gasoline dispensing pumps, steel castings for railroad industry, hand tools, pneumatic tools
1968	National Equipment Leasing Corporation	Pittsburgh, Pennsylvania	Leasing of cars, trucks, railroad cars and machinery
1969	Cleco Pneumatic Division of G. W. Murphy Industries, Inc.	Houston, Texas	Industrial pneumatic tools
1970	Boyles Industries, Limited	Vancouver, Canada	Drilling equipment for mining industry
1970	Aktiebolaget Ljungmans Verkstader	Sweden	Gasoline service station equipment
1971	Bay State Abrasives Division of Avco Corporation	Westborough, Massachusetts	Abrasive products
1972	Lodge-Cottrell, Ltd., and Lodge-Cottrell, Inc.	Birmingham, England Birmingham, Alabama	Environmental systems
1972	Pneumatic Equipment Division of Westinghouse Air Brake Company	Sidney, Ohio	Construction pneumatic tools
1974	Jeffrey Galion, Inc., and subsidiaries	Columbus, Ohio	Underground coal-mining equipment, graders, rollers, conveyor systems, chains
1974	Waukesha Motor Division of Bangor Punta Operations, Inc.	Waukesha, Wisconsin	Heavy-duty engines
1977	Marion Power Shovel Company, Inc.	Marion, Ohio	Power shovels, walking draglines
1977	Anderson Corporation	Worcester, Massachusetts	Rotary power brushes, hole saws, maintenance brushes
1978	General Abrasive Division of U.S. Industries	Niagara Falls, New York	Abrasive grain products

Appendix C

Directors Since 1905 Incorporation

	Dates Served
SOLOMON R. DRESSER Founder, president, Dresser	1905–1911
FRED A. MILLER General manager, president, chairman of the board, Dresser	1905–1938
GEORGE P. BOOTHE Superintendent, Dresser	1905–1917
CAROLINE K. DRESSER Wife of S. R. Dresser	1905–1917
ROBERT A. DRESSER Son of S. R. Dresser	1905–1929
IONE DRESSER MILLER Daughter of S. R. Dresser, Wife of Fred A. Miller	1911–1928
S. RICHARD DRESSER Son of S. R. Dresser	1917–1929
CARL K. DRESSER Son of S. R. Dresser	1918–1928
HAMILTON PELL Harriman Brothers & Co.	1928–1930
HENRY NEIL MALLON President, chairman of the board, Dresser	1929–1970
MERRILL N. DAVIS Vice president, Dresser	1928–1943

W. FRANK MILLER   1929–1935
    Corporate secretary, Dresser

FLOYD W. PARSONS   1929–1941
    Editor, *Gas Age Record,* New York

GEORGE L. OHRSTROM   1929–1947
    G. L. Ohrstrom & Co., New York

WILLIAM V. GRIFFIN   1929–1958
    Brady Security & Realty Corp.,
    New York

WILLIAM T. SMITH   1929–1931
    Brown Brothers & Harriman, New York

PRESCOTT S. BUSH   1930–1953
    Brown Brothers & Harriman, New York

WILLIAM A. MCAFEE   1933–1970
    McAfee, Hanning, Newcomer, Hazlett &
    Wheeler, Cleveland

T. G. WILKINSON   1936–1938
    Chicago

JOHN B. O'CONNOR   1938–1965
    President, Dresser

G. A. TOMLINSON   1936–1937
    Tomlinson Fleet, Cleveland

GEORGE A. BALL   1936–1937
    Ball Bros. Co., Muncie, Indiana

G. PAUL CLARK   1937–1958
    President, Clark Bros.

LYLE C. HARVEY   1940–1948
    President, Bryant Heater Co.

ARTHUR R. WEIS   1940–1958
    President, Pacific Pumps

NORMAN CHANDLER   1943–1970
    Times Mirror Co., Los Angeles

O. M. HAVEKOTTE   1944–1949
    President, Ideco, Columbus

WILLARD M. JOHNSON   1950–1970
    President, Magnet Cove

HENRY P. ISHAM   1950–1967
  Clearing Industrial District, Inc., Chicago

TOM SLICK   1952–1962
  Slick-Moorman Oil Co. and
  Slick-Urschel Oil Co., San Antonio

RODNEY S. DURKEE   1955–1958
  Chairman, Lane-Wells Co.

E. L. DEGOLYER   1954–1957
  DeGolyer & MacNaughton, Dallas

ROBERT B. ANDERSON   1955–1957;
  Ventures, Ltd., Toronto   1962–1968

R. E. REIMER   1956–1969
  Executive vice president, Dresser

JOHN LAWRENCE   1958–present
  Chairman, Dresser

LEWIS W. MACNAUGHTON   1958–1969
  DeGolyer & MacNaughton, Dallas

GORDON G. GUIBERSON   1958–1961
  President, Guiberson Corp.

JAMES P. GASSER   1958–1960
  Executive vice president, Dresser

FRANCIS G. FABIAN, JR.   1960–1965
  President, Dresser

ALLAN SHIVERS   1964–1972
  Austin, Texas

DAN M. KRAUSSE   1964–1965
  Vice president, Dresser

CHARLES KUHN   1964–1969
  President, Dresser

JOHN V. JAMES   1964–present
  Chairman, Dresser

E. R. LUTER   1964–present
  Senior vice president, Dresser

CHARLES A. MOORE   1965–1971
  Chairman, Manning, Maxwell & Moore

RICHARD S. MORSE   1966–present
    Massachusetts Institute of Technology

GEORGE C. SCOTT   1967–present
    First National City Bank, New York

A. BRUCE BOWDEN   1967–present
    Mellon National Corporation, Pittsburgh

RICHARD G. CROFT   1968–1971
    New York, New York

A. BRENT WILSON   1968–1970
    Pittsburgh, Pennsylvania

W. H. BATEMAN   1969–1970
    President, Petroleum Equipment
    Division, Dresser

OTIS E. KLINE   1969–present
    Scottsdale, Arizona

JAMES C. DAVIS   1970–1976
    Squire, Sanders & Dempsey, Cleveland

DONALD H. HARTMANN   1969–1971
    Executive vice president, Dresser

JOHN J. ADAMS   1975–present
    Squire, Sanders & Dempsey, Cleveland

JAMES R. BROWN, JR.   1975–present
    Executive vice president, Dresser

RAWLES FULGHAM   1975–present
    First International Bancshares,
    Dallas

DUANE D. ROST   1975–present
    Executive vice president, Dresser

A Note on the Sources

Two opposite problems emerged concerning the sources for this book. The first was one of scarcity; the second, the happier problem of overabundance. Records concerning Dresser's history from 1880 to 1929, when it was a relatively small, family-owned business, consist of no more than a handful of early catalogues and two volumes of minutes of the board of directors. These early minutes give only the barest details from incorporation in 1905 to the company's conversion at the end of 1928 to a publicly held corporation. Most of the other information concerning the Dresser company for these early years was pieced together from patents, old newspaper and magazine advertisements, newspaper stories, recollections of Solomon R. Dresser's descendants, courthouse records, interviews with former employees long since retired, and the few extant letters written by Dresser himself or members of his immediate family.

Beginning in 1929 the company documents concerning its history become far more voluminous. Especially helpful are the more detailed minutes of the directors' meetings, the annual reports, which began to be printed in the early 1930's, advertising brochures, interviews, news releases, news stories, miscellaneous internal company documents, retired files, and sundry documents. These materials become so numerous after the World War II period that the problem becomes one of sorting out the relevant and interesting data from an overwhelming flood.

In the summaries of the chapters that follow I have avoided in most instances citing the obvious sources for basic facts readily available concerning such things as sales, earnings, personnel changes, and products. These are easily found in annual reports and in the minutes of the directors. I have cited in the acknowledgments the great debt owed to many people for interviews and assistance, many of whom are mentioned again in the summaries below.

CHAPTER 1

Early-day packers are described in the *1884 Illustrated Catalogue of Oil Well Supply Co., Limited* (Bradford and Oil City, Pa.), as quoted by J. E. Brantly in *History of Oil Well Drilling* (Houston, 1971), p. 174. Dresser's first advertisement appears in the *Bradford Era*, May 11, 1880, p. 4. Information on Ashcroft is from *Scientific American*, August 14, 1852, and July 23, 1853, and from *Manning, Maxwell & Moore, Inc., 1880–1961* (Stratford, Conn., 1962). Roots's background is thoroughly covered in miscellaneous studies made by the U.S. National Park Service in 1973, copies of which are in the company's files in Connersville, Ind., and the Dresser archives. Pertinent items include Edwin F. Schievely, *Biographical Memoir of Francis Marion Roots* (Philadelphia, 1893); an advertising brochure entitled "Illustrated Circular of Roots' New Iron Blower," 1880; an article from the *Connersville* (Ind.) *News Examiner*, October 19, 1937, p. 6; "American Industries, No. 32," *Scientific American*, February 28, 1880, p. 127; and the obituary of Francis M. Roots, which appeared in the January 4, 1890, edition of *Scientific American*, p. 6.

Harbison-Walker's early days are from James E. MacCloskey, Jr.'s *History of Harbison-Walker Refractories Company* (Pittsburgh, 1952). Lechner's coal-cutting machine and other early machines of Jeffrey and other manufacturers are found in Edward W. Parker, "Coal-Cutting Machinery," *Transactions of the American Institute of Mining Engineers*, XXIX (1900), and A. B. Parsons, ed., *Seventy-five Years of Progress in the Mineral Industry, 1871–1946* (New York, 1947), pp. 227–29. A brief and informal history of the Jeffrey Co. is found in Robert H. Jeffrey II, *A Short History of the Jeffrey Company* (Columbus, Ohio, 1975). The patent number for Lechner's first machine is 172,637.

Information concerning Clark Bros. Co. came from an interview with C. Paul Clark, grandson of one of the founders and a former company president himself; "Forty Years of Industrial Progress," *Belmont* (N.Y.) *Dispatch*, February 2, 1906, p. 1; and a typewritten company script entitled "75 Years of Service to Industry: The Story of Clark Bros. Co. 1880–1955." Marion Steam Power Shovel Co.'s origin is related in a company brochure entitled "Marion Steam Power Shovel . . . 90 Years of Doing It Better," and in a typewritten script prepared for the company in 1932 by L. C. Morley. Alton J. Shaw's invention of the electric three-motor overhead crane is described in the previously cited *Manning, Maxwell & Moore, Inc.*, and in Carl Edward Schirmer, P.E., *History of the Overhead Crane & Hoist Industry of the United States of America,* prepared in typescript in 1967 for the Crane Manufacturers of America. Shaw's original patent is No. 430,487. The longevity of Shaw's crane at Cheyenne, Wyo., is confirmed by G. Edward Sencabaugh, Union Pacific Railroad, in a letter to the author, September 7, 1977.

The description of Wayne Pump Co.'s founding comes from that company's January 1967 edition of *Peptalk* and from an unpublished manuscript by Argus Leidy entitled "History of Dresser Petroleum Group," written in 1971. Thomas Robins, Jr.'s development of the rubber-covered conveyor belt is described in an undated brochure, "The Story of Hewitt-Robins: 1891 to Now," published by Hewitt-Robins Co., and from Theodore Waters, "Edison's Revolution in Iron Mining," *McClure's Magazine,* November 1897, pp. 75–94; and Matthew Josephson, *Edison* (New York, 1959), pp. 373–74.

CHAPTER 2

Early details of the Dresser family in America are related in a genealogy prepared in 1913 by Mrs. Jasper Marion Dresser and privately printed as *Dresser Genealogy, 1638–1913*. The letter from Hannibal Dresser to Parker Dresser, February 17, 1851, was reprinted that year in the *Jonesville* (Mich.) *Independent*. I am indebted to L. L. Dresser for calling it to my attention. Vesta Stimson's childhood was related in a handwritten memoir by her daughter, Ione Dresser Miller, and now held among many other Dresser family papers by Mrs. Cornell N. Pfohl, Jr., of Bradford, Pa., who is Mrs. Miller's daughter and Solomon R. Dresser's granddaughter. Miss Lillian A. Comer, archivist, Hillsdale College, provided attendance records of Dresser and Vesta Stimson.

Details of Dresser's life in Lafayette, Ind., are virtually unknown, but early biographical sketches that mention his work as a clerk there include Vernelle A. Hatch, ed., *Illustrated History of Bradford* (Bradford, 1901), and *History of McKean, Elk, Cameron and Potter Counties, Pennsylvania* (Chicago, 1890). Information concerning the courtship and early married life of Dresser are in a letter from Jane Hoyt to Vesta Stimson Dresser, August 31, 1863; in several letters to Vesta Dresser from "Auntie"; and in an 1883 privately printed memorial to Vesta Dresser upon her death. All these items are in Mrs. Pfohl's papers.

The early oil industry in Pennsylvania and West Virginia is

described in Harold F. Williamson and Arnold R. Daum, *The American Petroleum Industry*, I (Evanston, 1959), *Romance of American Petroleum and Gas*, II (New York, n.d.); Writers' Program, Works Progress Administration, *West Virginia: A Guide to the Mountain State* (New York, 1941); and the indispensable *Derrick's Hand-Book of Petroleum* (Oil City, Pa., 1898).

The ledger book for the Peninsular Petroleum Co., later adopted by Vesta Dresser as her notebook, is in the Pfohl papers. In it appear her descriptions of life in the oil regions and her personal thoughts and observations, including the essay "A Glimpse of Oildom."

Dresser's participation in the debating society in Millerstown was mentioned by Vesta Dresser in a letter to a relative named Ione (not Vesta's daughter) on January 24, 1877, Pfohl papers. Her admonitions to the children appear in an undated letter to them, Pfohl papers. The anecdote concerning the piping of natural gas into the Dresser house is from Mrs. Pfohl and Mrs. J. Martin Kelly of Milwaukee. Mrs. Kelly is the granddaughter of Dresser and the daughter of Robert Dresser. Dresser's producing wells are described in *Derrick's Hand-Book of Petroleum*, pp. 205, 213.

The early history of the natural gas industry is related in Alfred M. Leeston, John A. Crichton, and John C. Jacobs, *The Dynamic Natural Gas Industry: The Description of an American Industry from the Historical, Technical, Legal, Financial, and Economic Standpoints* (Norman, Okla., 1963). Details about Bradford come mostly from 1878 editions of the *Bradford Era*, and also from Herbert Asbury, *The Golden Flood: An Informal History of America's First Oil Field* (New York, 1942). Dresser's residences are listed in various editions of the Bradford city directory. The first mention of Dresser in the *Era* appears on May 4, 1878, p. 2. His agreement with Conners is recorded in the "Miscellaneous Records" book, McKean County Courthouse, Smethport, Pa.

Mrs. Pfohl related the Christmas anecdote, and the relative who wrote to Dresser about Jasper's success was Clarence P. Dresser, October 3, 1880, Pfohl papers. The March 24, 1880, patent for the packer is U.S. Patent No. 227,419. The packer advertising war raged daily in the pages of the *Era* in early 1881. Dresser's advertisement offering to buy used packers appeared in the August issues of the *Era* in 1881. Dresser's armor packer patent, No. 258,565, is dated May 30, 1882.

B. J. Stimson commented on Solomon Dresser's victory over poverty in a letter to Vesta on February 22, 1882. This letter is in the Pfohl papers.

Nina Dresser's death and details of her life are in a privately printed memorial in the Pfohl papers. A notice of her death appears in the *Era,* April 6, 1881. Vesta Dresser's death and the circumstances surrounding it are in Mrs. E. L. Huntington to Vesta Dresser, January 22, 1882; Ione [?] to Ione Dresser, March 11, 1883; and a privately printed memorial to her. Parker Dresser's death is related in a privately printed memorial to him. All of these items are in the Pfohl papers.

Details concerning the use of nitroglycerine in the oil fields come from Williamson and Daum, *The American Petroleum Industry,* I, pp. 149–56; *Derrick's Hand-Book of Petroleum,* p. 365; and various issues of the *Era* in the summer of 1883.

Dresser's telephone number first appears in his September 14, 1883, advertisement in the *Era.* An example of his advertisement for Rackarock appears on January 3, 1884. The legal dispute over the explosion is *John P. Zane* v. *S. R. Dresser,* Court of Common Pleas, Case No. 116, February 1890 Term, McKean County Courthouse, Smethport, Pa.

The advertisement listing Dresser's branch offices and boasting of the superiority of the "cap packer" appears in the *Era,* January 3, 1884. Dresser's first coupling patent is No. 350,421; it is mentioned in the *Era* on October 6 and 7, 1886. The patent numbers for Dresser's 1887 inventions are 381,916, 389,797, and 400,644. Methods of achieving tight joints are described in "Making Petroleum-tight Joints," *Scientific American,* April 25, 1896, p. 267. Also useful is B. E. V. Luty, "Development of Pipe Manufacture," *Oil and Gas Journal,* June 5, 1930, p. T85.

Dresser Genealogy erroneously lists the year of Dresser's marriage to Caroline Kirsch as 1883. Caroline Kirsch Dresser's comments on developing the physical side of the children is in an undated letter to Ione Dresser Miller, Pfohl papers.

Dresser's property transactions in this period are found in Deed Records, Vol. 33, pp. 343, 345, 349, McKean County Courthouse, Smethport, Pa. The various leases taken by Dresser in Ohio are recorded in Volume B, Morgan County's Oil and Gas Leases, McConnelsville, Ohio. His purchase of the Patent Alley property is in Vol. 54, Deed Records, December 18, 1889, McKean County Courthouse, Smethport. His home on S. Mechanic Avenue is pictured in Hatch, *Illustrated History of Bradford,* p. 245.

The anecdote concerning Dresser's bet with Lewis Emery, Jr., is related by Mrs. Kelly. A brief biographical sketch of Fred A. Miller, as well as of Dresser, appears in Joseph Riesenman, Jr., ed., *History of Northwestern Pennsylvania,* III (New York, 1943), pp. 69–70.

Newspaper references to Dresser's activities in the Malta-McConnelsville, Ohio, area are found in the *Morgan County Demo-*

crat editions of October 9, 16, and 30, November 6, 13, and 27, and December 18, 1891; March 11 and 18, June 10, and October 7, 1892; and May 5, 1893. The Malta city council actions are recorded in the minutes for July 15 and September 15, 1891.

Letters from Caroline Kirsch Dresser to Ione Dresser Miller concerning activities around Malta include one written apparently in the fall of 1891, and others dated September 29 and October 12, 1892. Dresser's letters to Ione Dresser Miller are dated August 4, 1890, and October 23, 1891. All of these letters are in the Pfohl papers. A map in the McConnelsville office of the Columbia Gas Co., No. 4389-I, dated December 4, 1974, shows that Dresser's original 5⅝-inch line still carries natural gas under Main Street (formerly Centre Street).

Dresser's civic services are recorded in the various Bradford city directories. The newspaper advertisement carrying his picture is in the *Bradford Evening Star*, May 29, 1895, p. 3.

Earliest sales of the Dresser coupling are listed in the 1904 catalogue, which also reprints the letters from C. P. Sloan and E. Strong. The patent for the insulated coupling is No. 625,155. Early natural gas pipelines are described briefly in Leeston et al., *The Dynamic Natural Gas Industry*.

William L. Graham's remarkable memories are recorded in his letter to Austin F. Platt of Dresser Manufacturing Division on December 2, 1974, a copy of which is in the Dresser Archives. Graham also granted the author an interview in the fall of 1976 when he, a resident of Glenview, Ill., was a very spry 101 years of age.

The quotation from *Metal Worker* appears in "Joints for Cast Iron Pipes," *American Gas Light Journal*, September 18, 1899, pp. 454–55.

CHAPTER 3

Details of the natural gas industry come from Leeston et al., *The Dynamic Natural Gas Industry*, and Louis Stotz, *History of the Gas Industry* (n.p., 1938).

Dresser's products and their prices are from the 1904 catalogue, which also describes his displays at the expositions, reprints Brophy's report, and contains a list of customers.

Dresser's property purchases are recorded in the Deed Records at the McKean County Courthouse in Smethport: Vol. 117, December 20, 1901, p. 276, and Vol. 119, August 6, 1902, p. 355.

Details of family life and the anecdote about the lead mine in Missouri come from interviews with Mmes. Kelly and Pfohl.

Dresser's campaign and his election to Congress in 1902 and 1904 are described in the *Era,* October 9, 17, and 31, and November 4 and 6, 1902; and October 19, 25, and 26, and November 1 and 14, 1904. Brief items concerning his legislative activities are in the *Congressional Record,* November 9 and December 5, 1903; and March 21 and April 2, 1904. The family's life in Washington, D.C., is from family reminiscences described by Mmes. Pfohl and Kelly.

The Home of Solomon R. Dresser was privately printed in Bradford in 1903. The new office and warehouse for Dresser's company are described in the 1905 catalogue, as are the exhibits in St. Louis and London. The news story in the *Pittsburgh Dispatch* was reprinted in the *Era,* December 12, 1905. Incorporation of the S. R. Dresser Manufacturing Co. and financial details that follow are from the first volume of the company's minutes. Details about Ione Dresser Miller's company appear in an advertising brochure, "A True Story for Mothers," Pfohl papers. Mrs. Kelly related the details about life at the Dresser home as told to her by her father, Robert Dresser.

Dresser's bill for a new post office in Bradford was H.R. 22333, *Congressional Record,* Vol. 41. The new manufacturing facility at Fisher Avenue is described in the *Supplement to 1905 Catalogue,* Dresser Archives. The legal dispute is summarized in *Worcester County Gas Co.* v. *Dresser,* 153 Federal Reporter 903–905. Dresser's obituary appeared in the *Era,* January 23, 1911, p. 1.

Dresser Manufacturing Co.'s response to the Dayton Pipe Coupling advertisement appeared in the April 27, 1911, edition of *Oil and Gas Journal.* W. W. Strickler's advertisement appeared on May 25, 1911.

The 1918 catalogue describes the pipelines laid with Dresser couplings in the World War I period. Early employees of Dresser are pictured in a pamphlet entitled "Half Century of Progress, 1880–1930," published in 1930 to commemorate the company's fiftieth anniversary. This pamphlet also summarizes major pipelines laid during the 1920's with Dresser couplings.

Descriptions of the pipe-laying process come from Henry P. Westcott, *Handbook of Natural Gas,* 2nd ed. (Erie, Pa., 1915), pp. 185–213. Carl Dresser's role in the sale of the company was described in interviews with H. Neil Mallon and R. E. Reimer. L. L. Dresser of Tulsa, Okla., related details of Carl Dresser's activities in Tulsa.

CHAPTER 4

For the general outlines of this chapter I am especially indebted to the recollections of R. E. Reimer. Other interviews concerning the period were with H. Neil Mallon, George Pfefferle, Edward P. Torgler, and Clarence MacCormack.

Knight Woolley's *In Retrospect—A Very Personal Memoir* (privately printed, 1975) relates the anecdote on how Mallon became president of Dresser. Details about sales and profits come from annual reports and from the minutes of directors' meetings, which now begin to carry substantial summaries of all official meetings.

The *Oil and Gas Journal* issue containing a supplement on pipelines was published on August 29, 1929. The radial compressor project is described thoroughly in a file on that subject possessed by George Pfefferle. Directors' minutes, annual reports, and interviews with Reimer, Mallon, and Pfefferle also were helpful on the radial compressor.

CHAPTER 5

General historical background concerning this period is from Frederick Lewis Allen's *Since Yesterday: The Nineteen-Thirties in America, Sept. 3, 1929–Sept. 3, 1939* (New York, 1940) and his study of the American economic system, *Lords of Creation* (New York, 1935). Walter Lippmann's comment on Franklin Delano Roosevelt is from the *New York Herald Tribune*, April 28, 1932, as quoted by William Leuchtenberg in *Franklin D. Roosevelt and the New Deal, 1932–1940* (New York, 1963). Statistics concerning the impact of the depression come from Broadus Mitchell, *Depression Decade: From New Era through New Deal, 1929–1941* (New York, 1947), and Alex Groner, *The American Heritage History of American Business & Industry* (New York, 1972). Information concerning annual tonnage of Dresser's products and the price range of its shares are from editions of *Moody's Manual of Investments*. The acquisitions of Bryant Heater and Clark Bros. are related in the Dresser minutes and more particularly in pertinent company files. Mallon, Reimer, Pfefferle, Mrs. Beatrice Kilcoin, and John J. Murphy were helpful in personal reminiscences of the period. Press descriptions of the radial compressor project are in *Business Week*, May 23, 1936, p. 16, and the *New York Herald Tribune*, July 14, 1935, p. 35, as well as in the minutes and annual reports. A good overview of the company's objectives during the 1930's may be found in Dresser's *Report on Renegotiation, 1945*.

CHAPTER 6

The quotes from Broadus Mitchell and Leon Henderson at the beginning of the chapter are from Mitchell's *Depression Decade*. General information on business and the war came from Groner,

American Heritage History of American Business & Industry; John Morton Blum, *V Was for Victory: Politics and American Culture* (New York, 1976); and Dixon Wecter, *The Age of the Great Depression, 1929–1941* (New York, 1949).

Information concerning Dresser's participation in the war effort is gleaned from the company minutes, annual reports, and especially the 1942 and 1945 compilations entitled *Report on Renegotiation.* The portions concerning Dresser's involvement with the development of the atomic bomb were obtained from D. B. Harney of Pacific Pumps and F. M. McNall of Dresser-Clark; Lt. Col. Mark C. Fox, "Thermal Diffusion Plant Built Rapidly," *Engineering News-Record,* December 13, 1945, pp. 132–33; Richard G. Hewlett and Oscar E. Anderson, Jr., *The New World, 1935–1946,* which is the title for the first volume of *A History of the United States Atomic Energy Commission* (University Park, Pa., 1962); and the 1945 *Report on Renegotiation.*

Labor problems at Clark Bros. and Dresser Manufacturing are described in scrapbooks on those subjects compiled by the company and now in its archives. Information concerning Dresser's role in gas cycling comes from the minutes; an interview with Reimer; the "Petroleum Panorama," January 28, 1959, edition of *Oil and Gas Journal;* and the American Petroleum Institute's *History of Petroleum Engineering.*

The anecdote concerning O'Connor's flight to Africa is from an introduction of him by Dorris Kennedy for the Women's Transportation Club of Dallas, reprinted in *Big D Traffic Talk,* 1962. This, together with many O'Connor memorabilia, is in the files of Mrs. Beatrice Kilcoin of Dallas, his longtime secretary. Arthur M. Weis and Elmer Weis recalled the early days of Pacific Pumps in interviews. Mary Duggan of Pittsburgh, Pa., a former Dresser employee, recalled wartime working conditions at Bradford in a telephone conversation with the author. The histories of Payne Furnace and Day & Night are described briefly in *The Two Faces of Janus: The Story of Carrier Corporation* (Syracuse, 1977).

Thomas M. Foristall's column on Dresser appeared in the August 22, 1944, edition of *The Wall Street Journal.* The *Business Week* article cited near the end of the chapter is "E Pluribus Unum," March 31, 1945, pp. 44–45. Mallon's speech, "What Is Dresser Industries?" was reprinted by Dresser. A copy is in the company archives.

CHAPTER 7

A general summary of Dresser in the early postwar period is found in a 1946 company brochure entitled "Who We Are, What

We Make, How We Operate." Sales figures come especially from a company document entitled "Constructed Statement of Operations" covering the 1937–46 period. Analyses of Dresser by Reynolds & Co. were issued by that company in February 1945 and November 1955. Information concerning the liquefaction plant in the Soviet Union came from W. H. Reeder of Dallas and especially from his files, which include a series of articles appearing in the *Petroleum Times* entitled "Liquid Methane behind the Iron Curtain" on December 2, 1960; January 27, 1961; and February 23, 1962. News stories relating to the liquefaction plant are "U.S. Sifts Bid to Ship Goods to Soviet Union," *New York Times*, March 16, 1948, p. 8; and "Building an Empire on an Oil Supply Package," *Business Week*, April 5, 1958, p. 83. Mallon's comments concerning U.S. policy toward the Soviet Union are quoted by Thomas G. Paterson in *Soviet-American Confrontation: Postwar Reconstruction and Origins of the Cold War* (Baltimore, 1973).

Magnet Cove's early operations are described in a company booklet entitled *Magcobar: Two Decades of Dedication and Growth*, published in 1960. Willard Johnson provided personal details of the company's early years in an interview.

CHAPTER 8

The *Business Week* article, "Rolling Stone Gathers Moss," appeared on April 22, 1950. An item in *The New York Times* on November 23, 1949, related Cleveland's lament about the loss of revenue resulting from Dresser's move to Dallas. Details concerning the executive training program appear in a booklet entitled "First Executive Conference." Reimer's comments concerning profit goals appear in a booklet prepared for internal distribution entitled "The Importance of Profit Planning to Dresser Industries." The description of Dresser A. G. Vaduz comes primarily from a deposition given on April 2, 1964, to the U.S. Internal Revenue Service by Hans Berger, and also from interviews with J. Douglas Mayson and Reimer. The discussion on Lane and Wells and their development of gun perforating is from the *History of Petroleum Engineering*, pp. 590–91. Dr. Thomas P. Hubbard of Dresser Industries was especially helpful on the background of Lane-Wells. Mallon's comments concerning the organizational structure of Dresser were made in an April 4, 1955, memo to the presidents and executives of all Dresser companies and in an accompanying letter, "Functions and Responsibilities," both of which are in Mallon's files in Dresser archives. Information on Magnet Cove comes primarily from *Magcobar: Two Decades of Dedication and Growth*, and secondarily from "Answering Brief of Respondents," Federal Trade

Commission, Docket No. 7095 in the matter of Dresser Industries, Inc., and Magnet Cove Barium Corp., June 5, 1963, Dresser archives. Dresser-Ideco's tall television tower is described in "Man's Tallest Tower to Broadcast TV," *Popular Science,* February 1954, pp. 166–67, as well as in the 1955 annual report. The description of Mallon, O'Connor, and Reimer comes from the Reynolds & Co. analysis of Dresser issued in November 1955.

CHAPTER 9

The description of Dresser products as they pertained to American daily life came largely from the narrative in the 1953 annual report. The imaginary well is portrayed in the 1957 annual report. O'Connor's prediction that Dresser's foreign sales would double by 1959 appeared in "Heard on Wall Street," *Wall Street Journal,* April 3, 1957, p. 4.

Information on the turbodrill is found in several publications: "The West Is Still Wary," *Business Week,* May 19, 1956; "In Business Abroad," *Business Week,* June 16, 1956; "Oil, Eggheads, and American Destiny," *Saturday Review,* undated clipping from Kilcoin file; "U.S. Blocks Trade of Oil Drill Data," *New York Times,* May 17, 1956; "Pravda Bids U.S. End Trade Curbs," *New York Times,* May 23, 1956; "Trading with the Communists," *Business Week,* May 19, 1956; and "Turbodrills competing," July 28, 1958, "Turbodrills used at Herscher," July 7, 1958, and "Turbodrill gamble is paying off," August 18, 1958, *Oil and Gas Journal.* Of special assistance was a company file entitled "1957–58 Turbodrill Correspondence," Dresser archives.

O'Connor's promotion to president, his heart attack, and his recovery are in "Drilling for Size," *Time,* November 5, 1956, pp. 100, 102; various documents in the Kilcoin files, such as O'Connor's calendar; and a memorandum from Mallon to O'Connor, January 6, 1958, Dresser archives. O'Connor's speech at St. Bonaventure was reprinted in 1958 by that institution in a pamphlet entitled "The Battle of the World Market Place," Dresser archives. A draft of O'Connor's speech about the Soviet Union is in the Kilcoin files. A lengthy sketch of O'Connor appeared in the *Dallas Morning News,* March 15, 1959.

Newsweek's article on Mallon and the Dallas Council on World Affairs, "The World in Texas," appeared on April 29, 1957. Correspondence concerning the proposed acquisition of Gardner-Denver is accumulated in a notebook under that firm's name in the Dresser archives. A news article concerning that acquisition effort appeared in the "Heard on the Street" column in the August 14, 1957, issue of *Wall Street Journal*.

Mallon's observations about the mistakes in judgment he believed had been made in 1957 appeared in a memorandum to John O'Connor dated January 6, 1958; Mallon's comments in the fall of 1958 were made in an October 16, 1958, memo to O'Connor; Reimer's calculations about management expenses are in a February 13, 1958, memo; and Mallon's projections for the future are in a memo to O'Connor on July 28, 1958. All these documents are in Mallon's files, Dresser archives.

The final quotation in the chapter is from "Ready and Waiting," *Forbes*, February 15, 1959.

CHAPTER 10

Earnings and projected earnings of Dresser and individual operating units are detailed in internal profit plans for each year. Various documents concerning the Federal Trade Commission's action against Dresser and Magnet Cove are in the legal files of Dresser archives, as are papers pertaining to *WSI* v. *McCullough*.

Mallon's comment concerning Texas Instruments is in a memo to O'Connor, January 15, 1958, and his questions about long-range planning are in a memo to O'Connor, September 7, 1960, and in a memo to Reimer and others, July 15, 1960. A file entitled "Agenda of Planning Committee Meetings" lists subjects discussed.

The conclusion concerning tax savings resulting from Dresser A. G. Vaduz is reported in a letter from M. B. Newcomer of the law firm McAfee, Hanning, Newcomer & Hazlett to Mallon on April 15, 1960. Aside from routine sources, information concerning operations in Argentina was gathered from a speech by Mallon entitled "Problems and Opportunities of Doing Business in Argentina," Dresser archives, and "Oil Search Requires a Lot of Tools," *New York Times*, May 19, 1959.

CHAPTER 11

Details about John Lawrence's background were obtained in interviews with him and his wife, and from a sketch written of him by his wife. The *Forbes* article recalling the situation in 1962 appeared in "What's a Stockholder Really Interested In?" November 1, 1968.

The history of Manning, Maxwell & Moore and its operating units is in *Manning, Maxwell & Moore, Inc., 1880–1961.*

Directions on the format for profit-planning sessions appear in a memorandum from F. G. Fabian, Jr., to John Lawrence *et al.*, September 21, 1964. Correspondence concerning trade with Iron Curtain nations is in the "Iron Curtain Trade" file in Dresser archives. A brief notice of Fabian's resignation appeared in "Dresser Executive Resigns in Dispute," *New York Times,* January 22, 1965.

The description of the O'Connors' apartment appeared in "Treasures of Travels Made Elegant Apartment Haven," *Dallas Morning News,* February 2, 1964. An obituary that recounts O'Connor's life at some length is the *New York Times* notice which appeared on April 17, 1965.

Dresser's merger negotiations with Chicago Pneumatic, Link-Belt, Symington-Wayne, and Harbison-Walker received fairly extensive coverage on the financial pages of *The New York Times:* "Chicago Tool and Dresser Call Off Talks on Merger," July 5, 1966; "Link-Belt to Get Merger Offer," March 6, 1967; advertisement entitled "To the Shareholders of Link-Belt Company," March 7, 1967, p. 63; "Market Place," March 9, 1967; "Wayne Files Suit Against Dresser," July 12, 1967. *Forbes* summarized Dresser's progress in the 1960's in "What's a Stockholder Really Interested In?" on November 1, 1968. The proposed merger with Santa Fe is covered in *The New York Times* in "Santa Fe and Dresser to Merge," September 24, 1969, and "Companies Plan Merger Action," November 8, 1969.

The early history of Symington-Wayne was obtained largely from various newspaper articles, advertisements, and miscellaneous bits of information supplied by T. J. Krajci of Dresser's Transportation Equipment Division. Harbison-Walker's history up to the mid-twentieth century is from *History of Harbison-Walker Refractories Company.*

The awareness study concerning Dresser's image was made by Doremus & Co. in 1968. A copy of it is in the Dresser archives.

CHAPTER 12

A supplement to the 1970 annual report entitled "The Basic Philosophy of How We Manage for Growth" describes the uniform measurement and control procedures established by Dresser. The anecdote about the pelican on Mykonos is reported in "Pelican Progeny Assured," *Dallas Times Herald,* October 21, 1971. The visit of Dennis N. Chukwu to Houston is described in "Nigerian Chief Will Cheer Houston Astros," *Houston Chronicle,* August 17, 1973.

The founding of Boyles Bros. is related in "Boyles Bros.: A Historical Sketch," in that company's own publication, *The Core*

Box, IV (no date), and that of Ljungmans is in a company brochure entitled "Ljungmans 1924–1974."

Literature concerning the Dresserator is voluminous. Especially useful were "Ford Looks at Fuel Atomizing," *Automotive Industries*, May 1, 1974; and the August 1974 issue of *Environmental News*. The special truck designed by the Petroleum and Mineral Group is described in "Dresser Vehicle Views Environment," *Dallas Times Herald*, September 9, 1973. Lodge-Cottrell's interesting history is told in various company documents and early catalogues and in a typewritten summary entitled "The Earliest Days." These items were provided by R. W. James of Lodge-Cottrell in Birmingham, England, and Gary Tempest of Dresser Europe S.A., London. A *Dresser News* article, "Lodge-Cottrell Equipment Gets Performance Award," April 1975, tells of the company's status at the time of acquisition. Bay State's origin is described in the fifth anniversary issue of the *Bay State News*, November 1927.

Trade with the Soviet Union in the 1970's is related in several periodicals: "Russians seek to sell oil and gas to U.S. in return for help in developing resources," *Wall Street Journal*, August 22, 1973; "More U.S.-Soviet Cooperation on Trade," *Daily World*, October 30, 1973; and "Dresser Gets $27.5 Million in Soviet Contracts," *Washington Star News*, July 1, 1974.

The 1973 fire at Pacific Pumps was related in "Pacific Pumps Co. Hit by Fire," *Huntington Park Daily Signal*, September 4, 1973, and "Pacific Pumps Open House Attracts Employees, Families," *Dresser News*, January 1975.

Jeffrey Galion officials told of the reasoning behind the sale of their company in "Reason for Sale Explained," *Columbus* (Ohio) *Dispatch*, February 13, 1974. The background of the Jeffrey Co. is provocatively related in *A Short History of the Jeffrey Company*. The Galion Co.'s history comes from an undated company brochure entitled "A Pictorial History of the Galion Manufacturing Company." Information about the early days of Foote Bros., Whitney Chain, and Hewitt-Robins was obtained in a collection of early documents provided by Martin J. Horan and S. M. Sitta.

John V. James's comments in Houston about Jeffrey Galion and Dresser appeared in the *Houston Business Journal*, July 1, 1974. The *Forbes* article "From Stengel to Lawrence to James" appeared on August 1, 1974, and James's quote about making a decision anywhere in the world in half an hour appeared among other places in the *Dallas Times Herald* in "Dresser: On the 'road' to complexity," October 8, 1974. Ray P. Ward, director of operations, provided information about the company's flight activities.

Lawrence's prediction about Dresser sales reaching $4.5 billion appeared in the *Dresser News,* May 1976, in "Dresser sales to reach $4.5 billion in 1980." The *Business Week* article "Can James Win Signal?" appeared on May 24, 1976. A June 14, 1976, *New York Magazine* article by Dan Dorfman, "The Battle for Signal— Now an Unfriendly Tender?" offers another view.

Information about Marion Power Shovel Co. came from a press kit supplied by that company and from information compiled by Harold E. Boncutter, who currently is writing a history of that company. Mr. Boncutter provided me with a number of early documents.

The Tennessee politician's complaint about James's endorsement of Gerald R. Ford appeared in the *Dallas Morning News* on October 31, 1976, in "Dresser letter for Ford challenged." Corporate contributions to the 1976 presidential elections are given in "Labor Money Boosted Carter," *Milwaukee Journal,* February 1, 1977.

Index